PATTERN DESIGN

LEWIS F. DAY

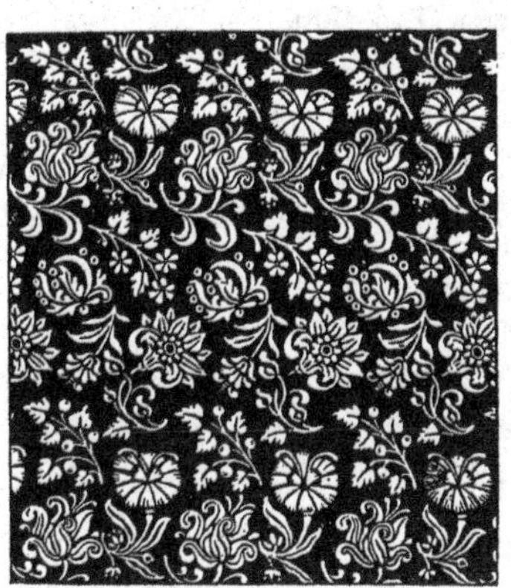

DOVER PUBLICATIONS, INC.
Mineola, New York

Bibliographical Note

This Dover edition, first published in 1999, is an unabridged and unaltered republication of the 2nd edition (1933; revised and enlarged by Amor Fenn) of the work originally published in 1903 by B. T. Batsford Ltd., London. It includes all 272 figures in black and white from the 1933 edition, as well as a color reproduction, on the inside front cover, of the frontispiece from that edition.

Library of Congress Cataloging-in-Publication Data

Day, Lewis Foreman, 1845–1910.
Pattern design / Lewis F. Day.
p. cm.
"An unabridged and unaltered republication of the 2nd edition (1933; revised and enlarged by Amor Fenn) of the work originally published in 1903 by B. T. Batsford Ltd, London."
Includes index.
ISBN-13: 978-0-486-40709-8
ISBN-10: 0-486-40709-8 (pbk.)
1. Repetitive patterns (Decorative arts) 2. Decoration and ornament–Themes, motives. I. Title.

NK1510 .D38 1999
745.4–dc21 99-045781

Manufactured in the United States by LSC Communications
40709809 2019
www.doverpublications.com

PREFACE TO THE SECOND EDITION.

THE exhaustion of a further edition of "Pattern Design" and the steady demand for the work are an indication of its continuing practical value as a textbook, but it seemed advisable that it should be thoroughly revised and brought up to date; and it was decided to entrust the work to Mr Amor Fenn, who, as a personal friend of Lewis F. Day, was conversant with his work and in sympathy with his aims and methods. Consequently, the book for the first time since its appearance has received a thorough overhaul; the order of the chapters has been rearranged, and that on Borders—a subject Mr Fenn has made particularly his own—has been transformed and re-illustrated. A number of illustrations have been redrawn or replaced, and others added, including two coloured plates, while the Editor has contributed a chapter summarising the course of the design of pattern during the past eighty years down to the present day, illustrated by the representative work of well-known English and Continental designers. It is the hope and desire of every one connected with the book that it may maintain its position as a standard work, and continue or enhance its usefulness to students and others connected with design and pattern, the importance of which in everyday life is being increasingly realised.

It is with deep grief and regret that we have to record that Mr Amor Fenn was suddenly taken from us while this book was passing through the press, and consequently did not survive to see the finished result of his work.

THE PUBLISHERS.

September 1933.

NOTE OF ACKNOWLEDGMENT.

I DESIRE to record my indebtedness to the following who have kindly supplied, or permitted of the reproduction of, material for new illustrations: Firma Julius Hoffmann, Stuttgart, Figs. 268 and 269 from "Der Moderne Stil," V., and frontispiece and Figs. 258, 272C and D from "The Art Worker's Studio"; Editions d'Art Albert Lévy, Paris, for Figs. 271, 272A and B from Georges Valmier, "Décors et Couleurs," Album No. 1; Charles Moreau, Editions d'Art, Paris, Fig. 270 from "Tapis et Tissus"; the Wallpaper Manufacturers Ltd., Manchester, for Figs. 261, 264B, 266A and B, and 267A and B. Fig. 165, drawn by the late Richard Glazier, is from his "Historic Textile Fabrics"; Figs. 23, 178, 183, 211, and 254 are from designs by Mr Harry Napper, and Fig. 268A and B by Mr C. F. A. Voysey. Figs. 265A and B are from the Publishers' "Modern Decorative Art in England," by W. G. Paulson Townsend, and Figs. 264A and 261B from B. J. Talbert's "Examples of Ancient and Modern Furniture."

AMOR FENN.

PREFACE TO THE FIRST EDITION.

A MAN has a right, I suppose, to pull down the building he once put up, and to raise another in its place. If he should see fit to use sometimes the very stones which belonged to it, he would only be stealing from himself. I have done something very much like that.

In the course of the last fifteen years the times have changed, and with them the standpoint of students and teachers of design; and, though my point of view has not altered, my outlook has widened with experience. When it came to the revision of "The Anatomy of Pattern" with a view to a fifth edition, it seemed to me I had done all I could do to it, that it was past mending, and that the simplest thing would be to start afresh.

The present volume, however, though it covers the ground of the former one, and answers much the same purpose, is not the same, but really a new book upon the foundations of the old one.

It contains, indeed, all that was in the other, but otherwise expressed. Here and there an explanation or description, which, by revision after revision, had been reduced to the fewest and plainest words I could find, has been allowed to stand. So with the illustrations, the greater number of them are new. Such of the old diagrams as were essential to the purpose of the book have been drawn again, not merely on the larger scale allowed by the page, but in a simpler and more self-explanatory way.

It will be seen from them and from the table of contents that "Pattern Design" covers much more ground than "The Anatomy of Pattern." But it does not go beyond its subject. The appearance, since the original publication of my little books, of a number of similar volumes each attempting to embrace more than the one before it, has firmly convinced me that the better plan is to confine oneself to a definite subject, and to treat it thoroughly. The last word, of course, is never said so long as there is life left in it.

I know very well that knowledge gained in practice can be only very partially conveyed in words; but something of the experience of five and thirty years and more in practical pattern design is surely communicable; and, for what it is worth, I give it here.

LEWIS F. DAY.

1st *September* 1903.

CONTENTS.

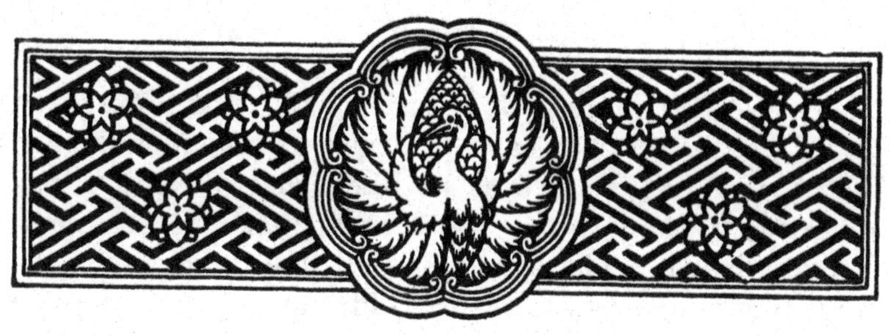

I. WHAT PATTERN IS.

Pattern not understood—The meaning of the word—Comes of repetition, and is closely connected with manufacture—Has always a geometric basis—Use and necessity of system in design—Lines inevitable, and must not be left to chance.

To readers of a book upon the subject, no apology for pattern is necessary. Modest as may be its pretensions to artistic consideration, it covers ground enough to command attention. It is here and there and everywhere about us. There is too much of it by more than half—and more than half of it is of such a kind as to make the discriminating wish they could do without it altogether. Still, there it is; and there is no escape from it.

If folk knew a little more about it, realised what was and what was not within the control of the designer, understood how pattern came to be, and something of its scope and purpose, as well as of the processes through which a design must pass before ever it comes (for their momentary delight or lasting annoyance) to be produced, they would be less at its mercy. For the difficulty of designing is by no means in proportion to the importance of the field of design; and in the case of repeated pattern, with which we have mostly to do—even those of us who are not concerned with trade or manufacture—the invention it requires is in inverse ratio to the free scope afforded. It is easier, as William Morris confessed, to design a big hand-made carpet, in which the artist is free to do very much as he likes, than to plan a small repeating pattern to the width of Wilton pile or common Kidderminster. The art of pattern design consists not in spreading yourself over a wide field, but in expressing yourself within given bounds.

The very strictness of such bounds is a challenge to invention. In the realm of applied design manufacture is autocrat, and the machine is taskmaster. Let who *can* rebel against their authority. For those who cannot—and they are the great majority—revolt is futile. We are all of us, artists no less than the rest of the world, dependent upon manufacture; and those of the title who stand aloof from it give ground for the accusation, commonly brought against artists, of being at best unpractical and wrong-headed. Their sense of fairness is at fault, too, in blaming manufacture because it falls short of art, while they stand by and refuse a helping hand to the makers of things which will be made, and must be made, and made by machinery too, whether they like it or whether they do not. It rests with those who have some faculty of design (their name is not legion) to come to the aid of manufacture, which, without help from art, is given over to the ugliness which they deplore.

Pattern, it seems plain, and repeated pattern, conforming to the conditions of manufacture and even to mechanical production, is a consideration of importance, not merely to manufacturers and others engaged in industries into which art may possibly enter, but to all whose comfort and well-being depends in any degree upon the beauty and fitness of their surroundings.

The word " pattern " is here used in a somewhat technical sense—not, as the dictionary has it, to mean " a specimen " nor yet " a shape or model for imitation," but ornament and especially ornament in repetition. Pattern is, in fact, the natural outgrowth of repetition; and in every case the lines of its construction may be traced; they pronounce themselves, indeed, with geometric precision. Geometric pattern grew, of course, out of primitive methods of workmanship. No mechanism so simple but it gives rise to it. To plait, to net, to weave, or in any way mechanically to make, is to produce pattern. The coarser the work, the more plainly is this apparent—as, for example, in the mesh of a coarse canvas; but, though refinement of workmanship may be carried to the point at which, as in the finest satin or the most sumptuous velvet, warp and weft are not perceptible to the naked eye, the web is always there, and forms always a pattern. The pride of the mechanist is to efface such evidence of structure. To the artist it adds an interest; and, far from desiring to obliterate it, he prefers frankly to confess it, and to make the best of the texture or pattern which a process may give. He regards it as a source of inspiration even, which to neglect would seem to him wasteful of artistic opportunity.

It is to his determination to make the best of whatever may naturally come of any way of working that we owe much of the simplest and most satisfactory, if not absolutely the most beautiful, patternwork.

So infallibly does the repetition of simple units, resulting no less from elementary processes of handwork than from mechanical production, end in pattern, that, wherever there is ordered repetition there it is. Take any form you please and repeat it at regular intervals, and, as surely as recurrent sounds give rhythm or cadence, whether you want it or not, you have pattern. It is so in nature, even in the case of forms neither identical nor yet recurring at set intervals. The daisies make a pattern on the lawn, the pebbles on the path, the dead leaves in the lane; the branches of the trees above, the naked twigs against the sky, the clouds that mottle the blue heavens by day, the stars that diaper their depths by night, all make perpetual pattern. The grain of wood, the veining of marble, the speckling of granite, fall so obviously into pattern that they have been accepted in place of intelligent design. The surface of the sea is rippled, as the sandy shore is ribbed, with wind-woven device, the rocks are covered with shellfish clustering into pattern. Your footprints, as you walk, make a pattern on the pattern of the dewy grass; your breath upon the window-pane crystallises into pattern.

Technically speaking, however, we understand by pattern

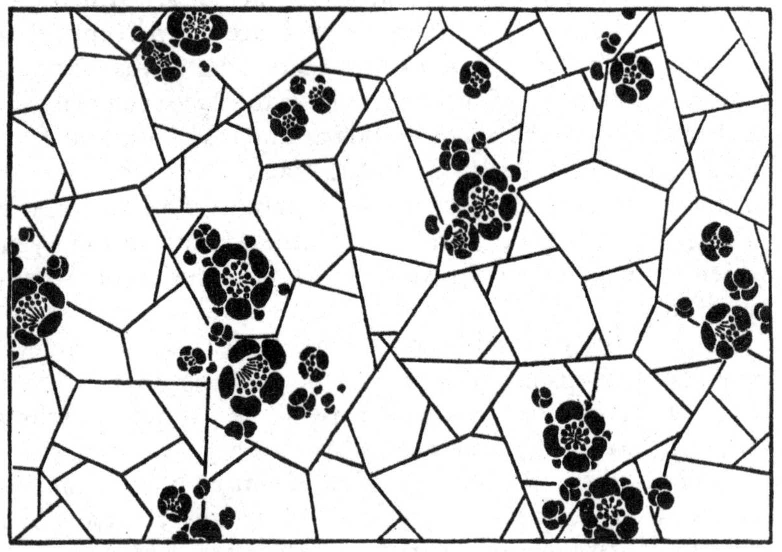

1. PEACH-BLOSSOMS ON THE ICE—JAPANESE.

not merely the recurrence of similar forms, but their recurrence at regular intervals. The Japanese rendering of peach-blossoms on the surface of thin ice is undeniably ornamental. It may be regarded as part of a pattern, but, to be complete, it should repeat, which here it does not.

It must not be inferred from the casual occurrence of what is called pattern that there is anything casual about design: the very name denies that it is so.

The artist's hand does not crawl aimlessly over the paper and trail behind it flowers of the imagination. There is scope in ornament for all the fancy of a fertile brain; but design is no mere overflow of a brimming imagination; it is cunningly built up on lines necessary to its consistency, laboriously, it might be said, were it not that to the artist such labour is delight. Whoever finds it irksome may be sure his bent is not in the direction of applied design.

The main lines on which repeated ornament is built are so few and simple that they can quite easily be traced. Just as the man of science divides the animal world into families and classes, so may the man of art classify pattern according to its structure. He is able, no less than the scientist, to show the affinity between groups of design to all first appearances dissimilar, and to lay bare the very skeletons upon which all possible pattern is framed.

The idea of setting out to design a pattern without regard to its logical construction is contrary to reason. It is all very well to protest that art is free of laws: they govern it none the less. And the pattern designer is bound to reckon with the dry bones of design. With regard to the unit of his design he is free; he may, if he will, throw taste to the winds; but when the pattern comes to be repeated, the very order of its repetition reveals the skeleton; it was in the cupboard all the while.

This insistence upon the geometric basis of design may seem like dogmatism; and all dogma cuts two ways, irritating the student into opposition where it does not convince him; but experience will prove to him that the way to avoid the appearance of formality is not to set to work at haphazard. Suppose one were to begin without any thought of formal distribution and to design, let us say, a scroll, in itself as graceful as might be. A series of such scrolls, side by side, would show lines not in the least contemplated by the draughtsman, and in all probability as inelegant as they were unexpected. Who has not suffered in his time from wallpaper or other patterns in which certain ill-defined but awkward stripes would thrust themselves upon his attention? And to the designer himself one of his strangest experiences is the trick a seemingly quite innocent pattern will play upon him in repetition. A design, for example, which appears to be quite evenly distributed will run, when hung, into lines which slant in such a way as to give the impression that the walls are not true, or that the paper has been hung askew.

In a pattern in which patches of the ground are left bare, the gaps are by no means accidental. They are most

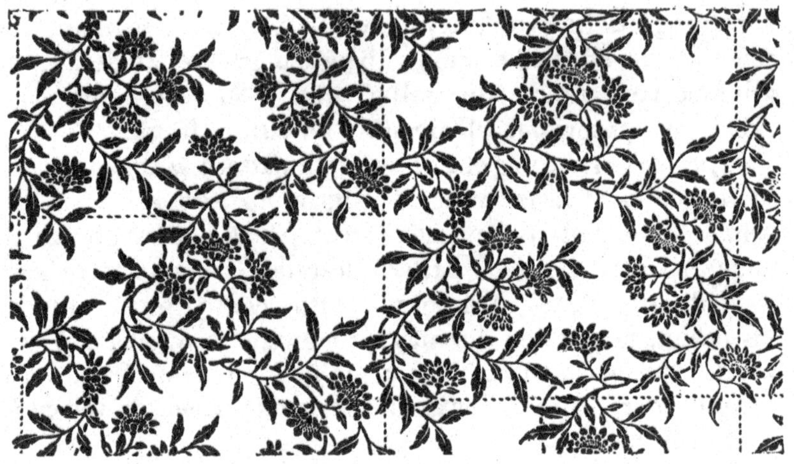

2. PREDETERMINED GAPS IN A PATTERN.

deliberately planned—and from the very beginning—or there is no knowing what havoc they might play in repetition.

Amateurs will tell you (and a painter is an amateur when first he tries his hand at pattern) that the lines which are so distressing in incompetent pattern are the result of mathematical planning. That is not merely false, but, as every practical designer knows, the very opposite of the truth. There is no more radical mistake than to suppose that the awkward stripes which come out for the first time when a pattern is repeated are the result of the designer's having worked upon the obtrusive lines: they are the natural

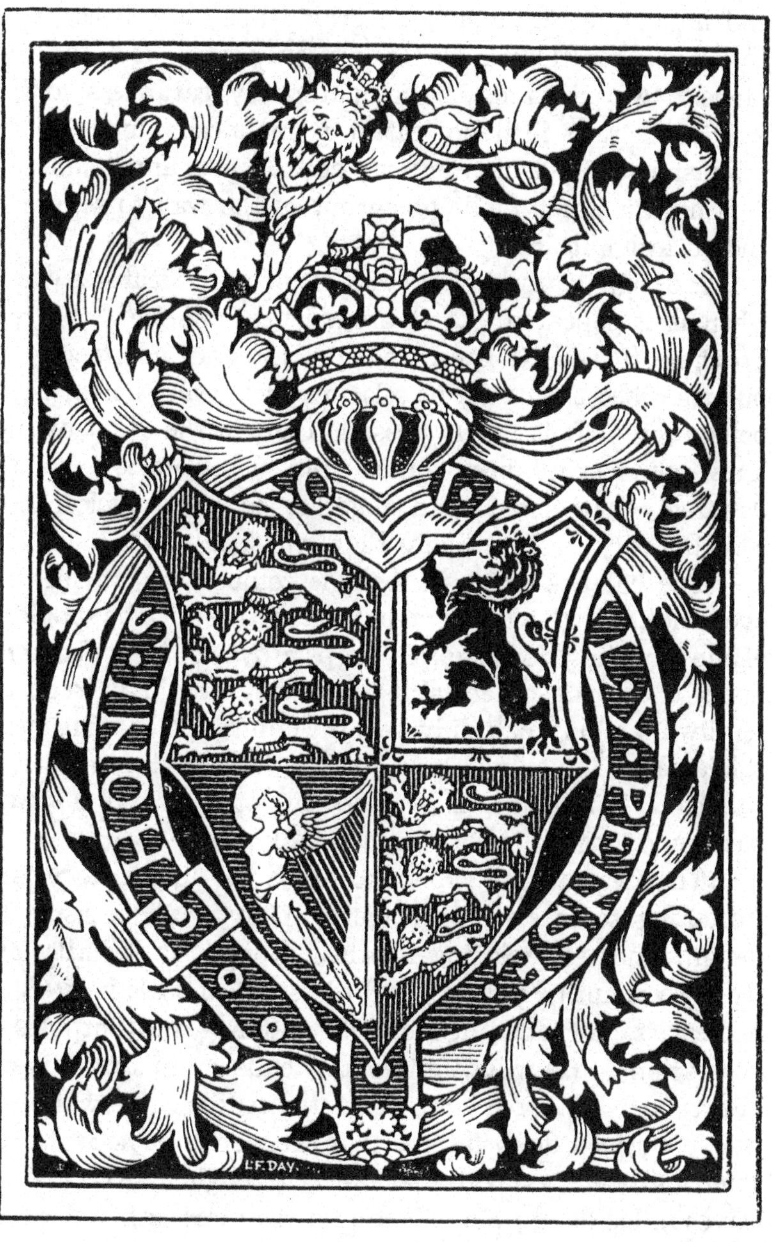

3. BALANCE OF ORNAMENT ENOUGH FOR A PANEL BUT NOT FOR A REPEATING PATTERN.

and inevitable result of not working upon any lines at all. If you work without a system the only safety is in insignificance. A pattern may be comparatively featureless; and, so long as there is in it no feature pronounced enough to distinguish itself, lack of order may perhaps pass unnoticed But it is hardly worth while going out of the way to secure an end so insignificant.

A design of any character has usually in it features which, when it is repeated, stand prominently out from the rest. To these the eye is irresistibly drawn; and, not merely so, but the lines they take in relation one to another insist on being seen. It is barely possible that, in the event of such lines not having been taken into consideration by the designer, they should fall together in the happiest conceivable way. More likely they will look awry.

The balance which in a single composition satisfies the eye is not enough when it comes to repetition. The shoulders of the mantling, for example, on page 7, one rising above the lion's back, the other falling below it, would in repeated scrollwork almost certainly give the impression of being out of the level. The only way to be sure that scrolls in repetition will balance is to begin by disposing them, as in the wall-pattern opposite, quite symmetrically.

The designer of experience runs no unnecessary risk. Accepting some sort of geometric plan as the basis of his design, and appreciating at their worth the severity and strength resulting from it, and the sense of scale it gives, he makes sure of lines deliberately fulfilling the purposes of decoration. He will counteract a tendency to stripes in one direction by features which direct attention otherwards; he will so clothe a doubtful line that there shall be no fear of its asserting itself, as in its nakedness it might. The lines he leaves in his design were chosen for their strength and steadiness. Such lines as reveal themselves are the lines upon which it was built, by no means unforeseen.

If lines left to chance reveal themselves, as they are apt to do, in sequence not to be endured, what else was to be expected ? Only by a miracle could they happen to fall precisely as art would have them. The best of players makes sometimes a happy fluke in design ; but he does not reckon upon such luck.

The point is this : it is, practically speaking, inevitable that lines shall in the end assert themselves in repeated pattern ; if the artist does not arrange for them in his design, they fall as may happen ; it is therefore the merest precaution of common-sense on his part to lay them down from the beginning, to make them the framework upon which his pattern is built, the skeleton of his design.

A practical designer has not, as a rule, much difficulty in tracing the bones of a design, amply as they may be wrapped in foliation or other disguising detail. To lay them bare enough, however, to demonstrate the anatomy of pattern, recourse must be had to dissection.

II. THE SQUARE.

Geometry the basis of all pattern—Breaks in the simple stripe give cross-lines—Hence the lattice and the chequer, on which a vast variety of pattern is built.

IT will be as well, before proceeding to dissect design apparently far removed from the geometric, to show the lines which of themselves make pattern. They prove to be the basis of all pattern.

The simplest of all patterns is the stripe—a series of parallel lines in one direction. But the limits of the mere stripe are soon reached; for any break in the repeated line or any deviation from the straight gives, by its regular recurrence, other lines in the cross direction. Gaps in a series of broken horizontal lines (4) give vertical lines; and in the same way the points of the zig-zags mark the upright (5). Any recurrent feature between the lines gives, again, lines

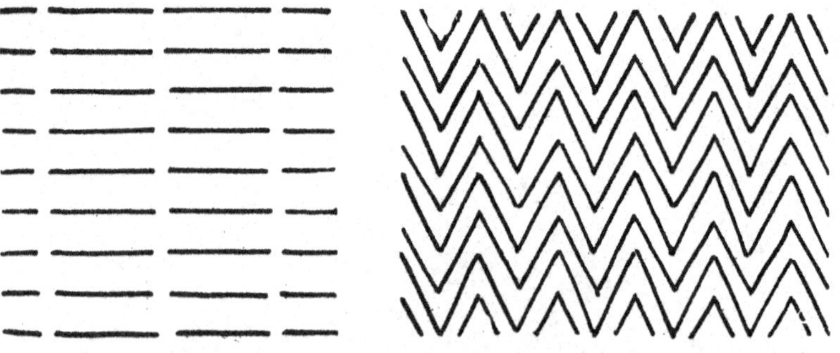

4. STRIPE—BREAKS GIVE CROSS-LINES.

5. ZIG-ZAG—POINTS GIVE CROSS-LINES.

6. STRIPES—ORNAMENT GIVES SLANTING LINES.

7. STRIPES—ORNAMENT GIVES UPRIGHT LINES.

across, slanting or at right angles to them, as the case may be (6 and 7). We arrive in effect, as the primitive basket weaver must have arrived in fact, at cross-lines; and upon these a vast amount of varied pattern is built up, the simplest forms of which are the lattice and the chequer (8). They must also have been the earliest evolved by the basket plaiter. Grasses all of one colour naturally showed the *lines* of interweaving, the lattice (9). Grasses alternately light and dark in colour asserted their chequered *masses* of colour, and gave the chess-board pattern. Strips of different colours led also to more intricate pattern (10); and the width of the coloured strips had only to be varied to give all manner of plaids and tartans.

Something of the variety of pattern resulting from the

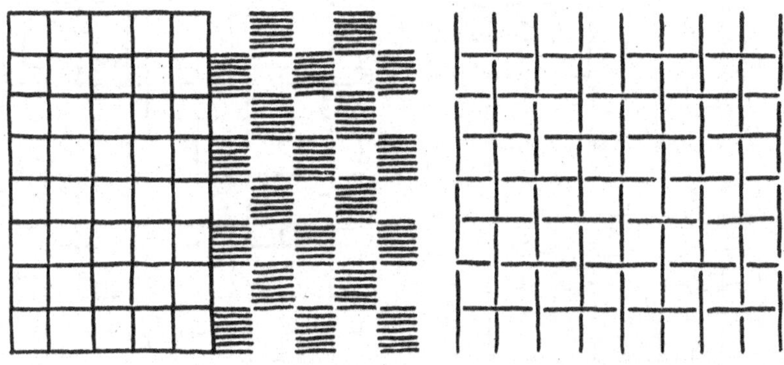

8. SQUARE LATTICE. CHEQUER.

9. INTERLACING.

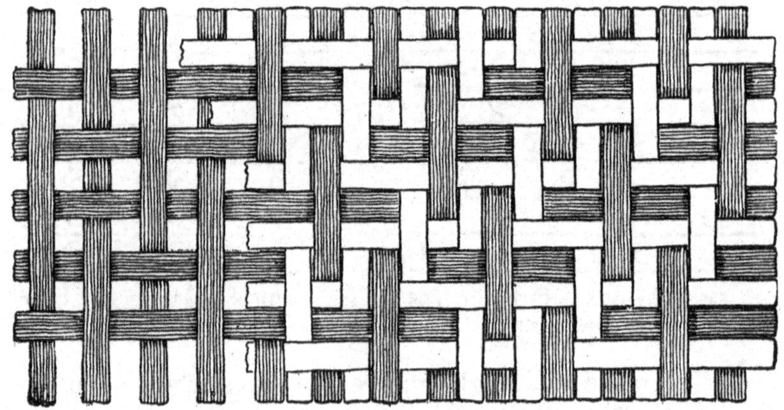

10. INTERLACING STRIPS OF DIFFERENT COLOUR.

closer or looser plaiting of equal strips is indicated below—as well as the further variety which comes of strips of unequal width (11 to 14).

On the regular network of cross-lines a vast number of patterns not necessarily regular may be built up, many of them suggestive of plaiting, if not actually suggested by it.

Taken singly, and filled in alternately light and dark, the squares give only the chess-board pattern; taken in groups of two, or alternately of two and one (15), they begin to show possibilities in the way of upright or diagonal patterns.

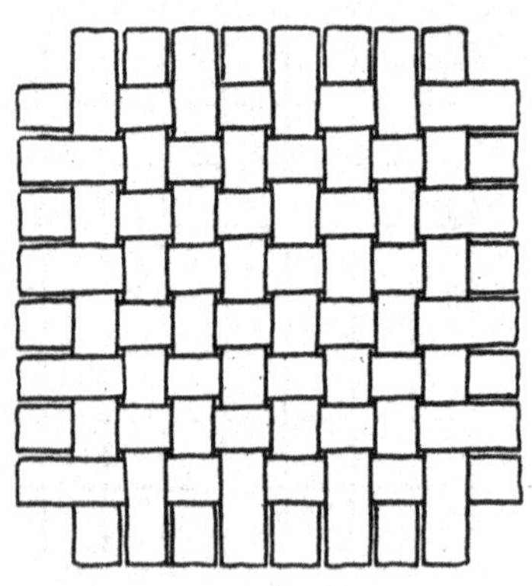

11. CLOSE PLAITING.

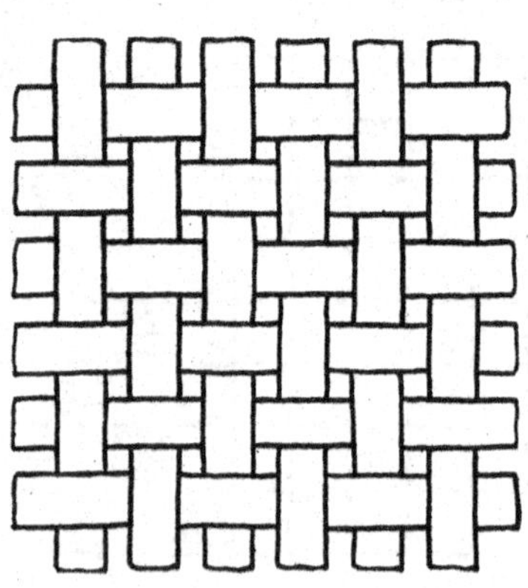

12. LOOSER PLAITING.

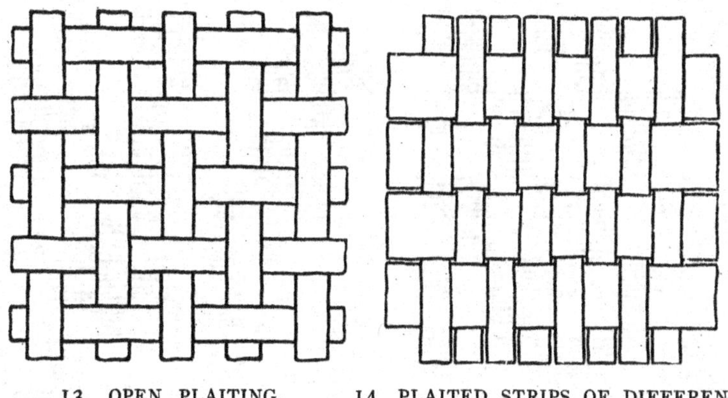

13. OPEN PLAITING. 14. PLAITED STRIPS OF DIFFERENT WIDTH.

Grouped in threes or fives (16) they give already independent units of design. The unit of the Arab diaper (17) is clearly a group of eight squares.

Working upon the *lines* of the lattice, we arrive, without in any way departing from them, but simply by intermitting some of them, at something in the nature of a key or fret pattern (18). The elaborate Japanese fret on page 16 is built upon that plan, upon which it will be seen (same page) all manner of interlacing and free diapers may be schemed.

There are two ways of setting about design of this sort, both of which amount practically to the same thing. The

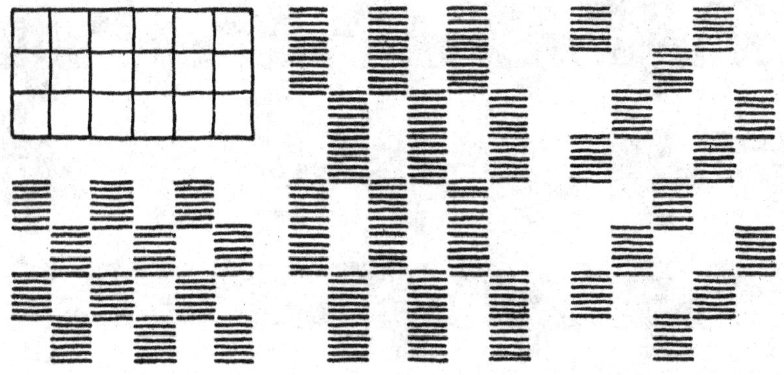

15. DIAPERS OF SQUARES AND GROUPS OF SQUARES.

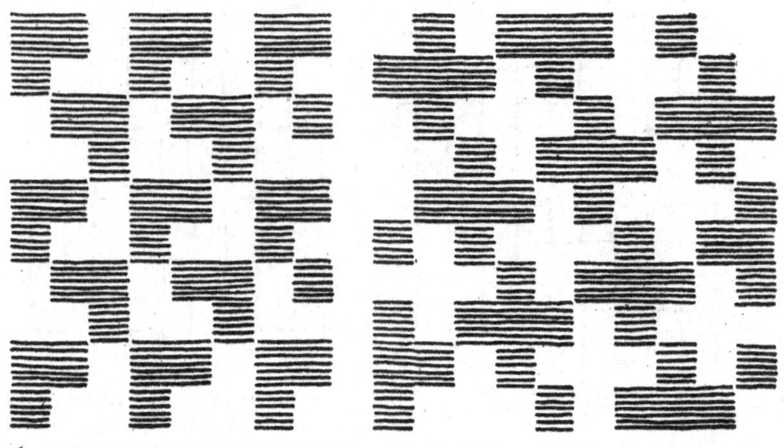

16. GROUPS OF THREE SQUARES GROUPS OF FIVE SQUARES.

one is to rule square lines and rub out parts of them, the other is to work with a pen or a brush upon faintly ruled paper—an exercise childish enough for the kindergarten, but by no means to be despised by the artist whose soul is not above pattern. It is wonderful what a vast and varied range of pattern is to be built upon the simple scaffolding of square lines.

The chess-board has only to be turned partly round to give us diamonds—but as they are still square, and it is only

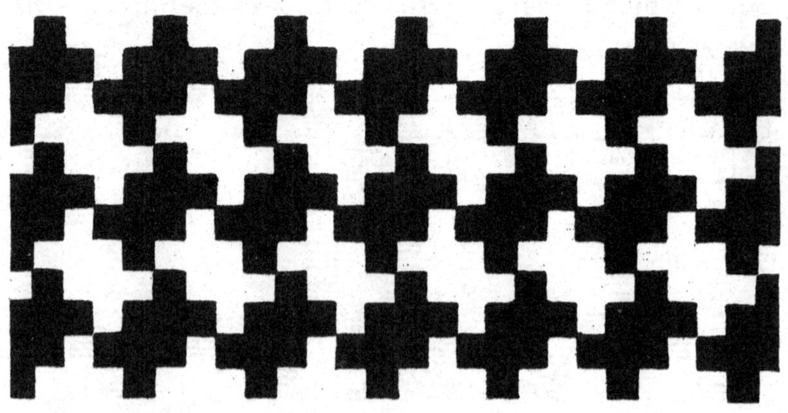

17. THE UNIT OF REPEAT A GROUP OF EIGHT SQUARES.

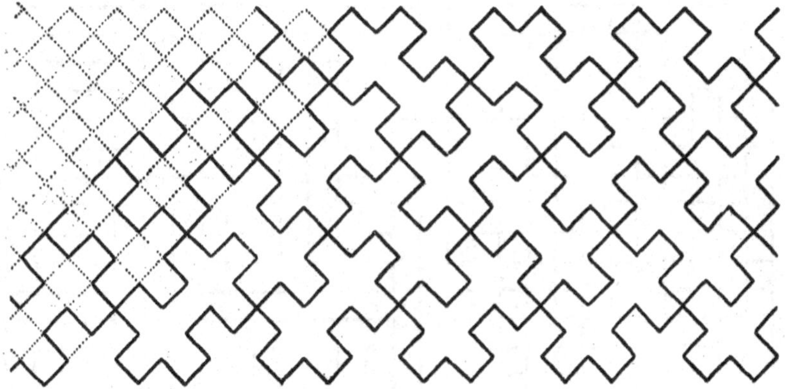

18. FRET PATTERN ON THE LINES OF SQUARE LATTICE.

the point of view that is altered, we have as yet (as in the case of a diagonal stripe, which is still only a stripe) no different plan, but only a difference of effect—so great, however, as to be worth noting, and of quite exceptional importance when it comes to the construction of freer pattern.

By altering the *angle* at which lines cross, we get at once not only a series of new shapes (19 to 21) but a variety of the diamond which for clearness' sake it will be convenient to distinguish as *the* diamond—not in itself so satisfactory a form as the square, but invaluable in connection with cross-lines in a third direction.

The plan of the rectangular lattice is, however, as a matter of fact, the basis of the great part of our pattern design.

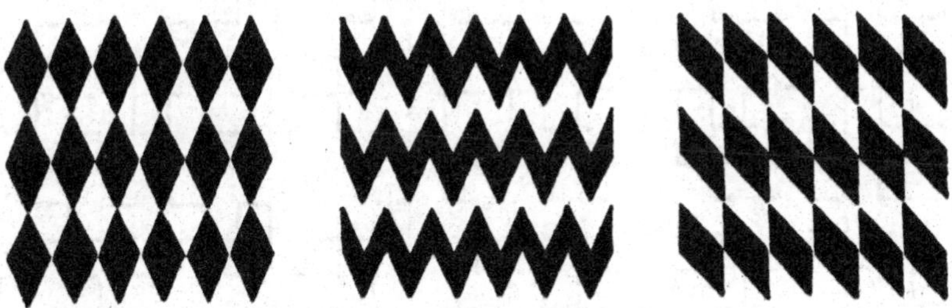

19. DIAMOND DIAPER. 20. ZIG-ZAG BUILT ON DIAMOND LINES. 21. DIAMOND DIAPER.

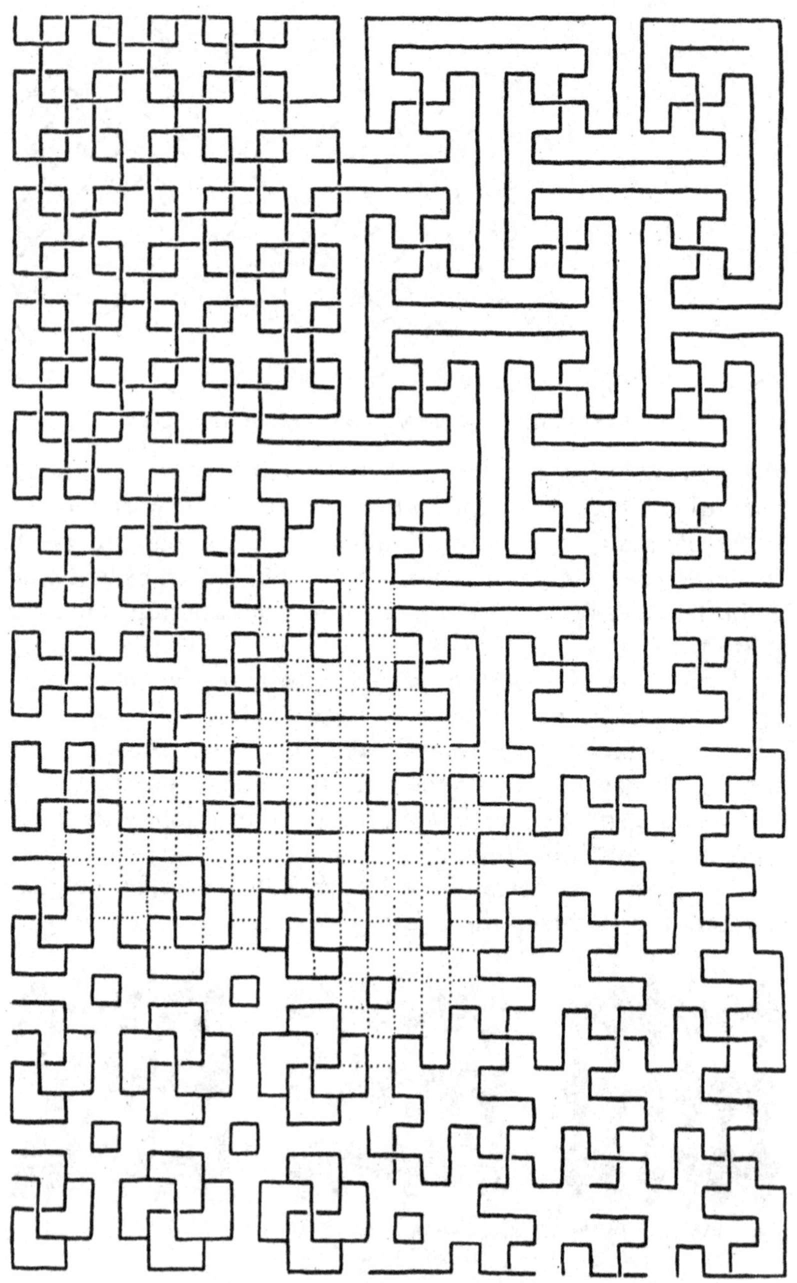

22. FRETS, ETC., ON LINES OF SQUARE LATTICE.

There are obvious advantages in the use, for example, of square tiles and right-sided blocks for printing and so forth; but, over and above convenience, it seems to come more naturally to us to think out a design on square lines than on any other.

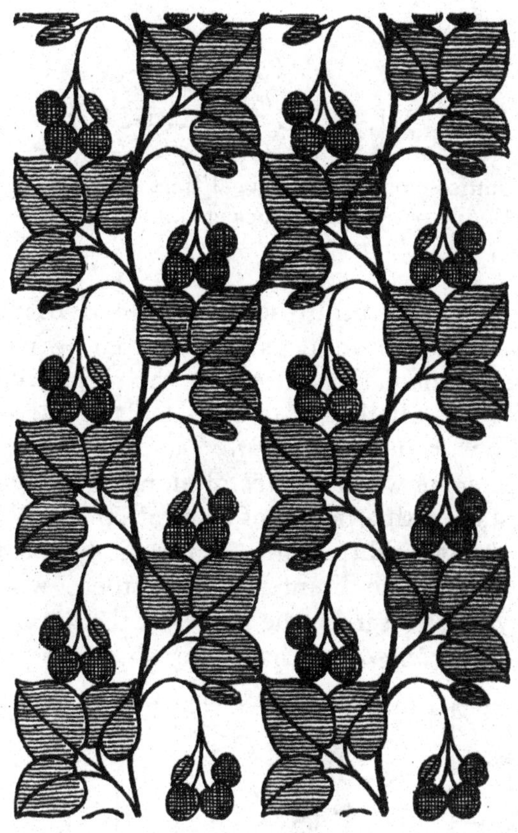

23. DESIGN FOR PRINTED COTTON BASED ON SQUARES.

III. THE TRIANGLE.

The square lattice crossed by diagonal lines gives the triangle—Hence the diamond—And out of that the hexagon, the star, and other geometric units familiar in Arab diaper.

THE introduction of a third series of cross-lines makes quite a new and most significant departure. Cross a square lattice by a series of diagonal lines bisecting the right angles, cutting the squares in half that is to say, and the halves give us a new form to work upon—the *triangle* (24). And so it is if we cross in the same way a lattice of elongated diamond shape. But if we start with a lattice of a certain proportion ; if, that is to say, the two sharp angles of the diamonds are together equal to one of the blunter angles, then, when they are bisected by a third series, the halves of the diamond prove to be *equilateral triangles*. That being so, or, to put it another

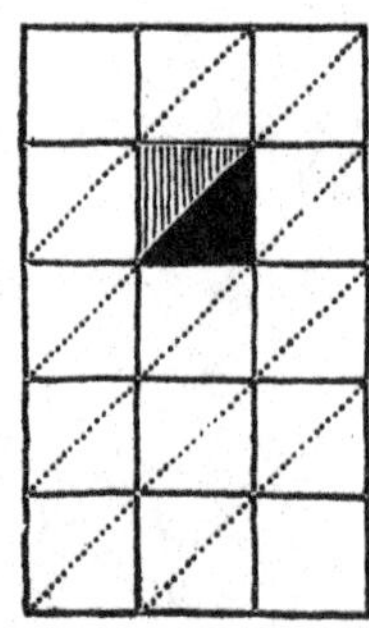

24. TRIANGLE.

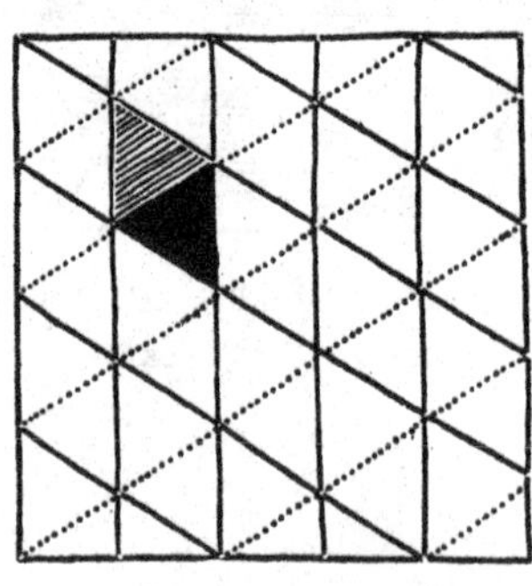

EQUILATERAL TRIANGLE.

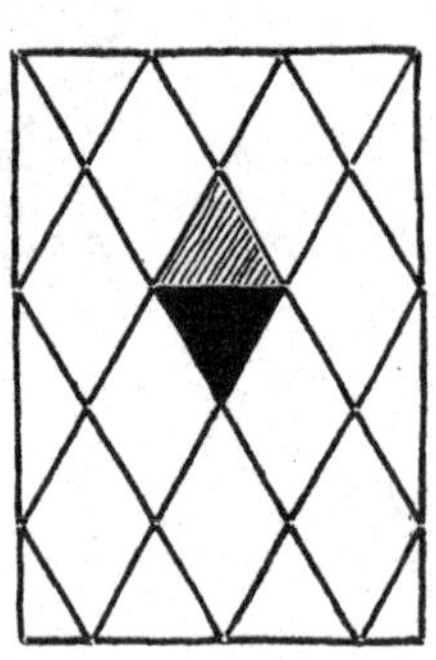

DIAMOND.

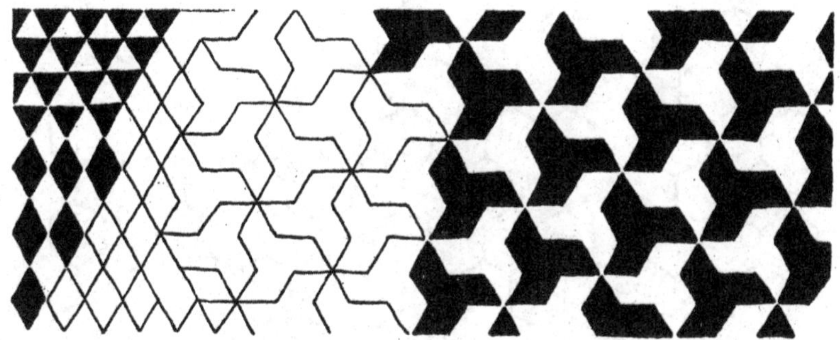

25. DIAPER BUILT ON TRIANGULAR PLAN.

way, our diamond being composed of equilateral triangles, new possibilities of design appear upon the horizon.

The equilateral triangle is the basis of an infinity of geometric pattern. The Arabs (or the Byzantine Greeks responsible for their art) made infinite use of it, building up their intricate patterns upon it (25) as Western nations built upon the square. From the triangle they derive not only the diamond, which is composed of two triangles, but other ingenious combinations, such as the unit of the diaper above which is composed of seven triangles or of a central triangle and three diamonds radiating from it. Six triangles form a hexagon (26), and six other triangles ranged round that result in a star.

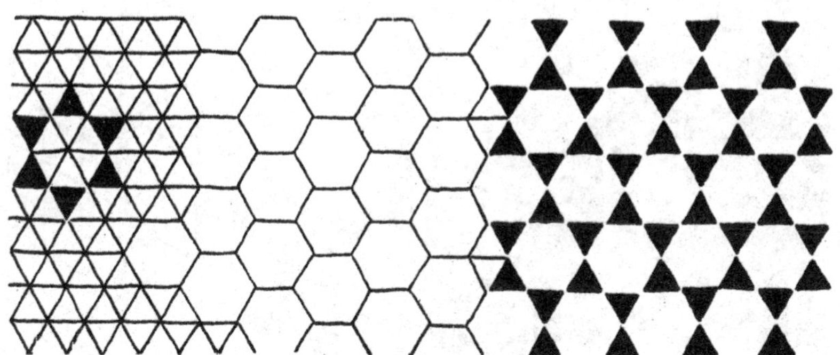

26. DIAPERS BUILT ON TRIANGLES. HEXAGON = SIX TRIANGLES. STAR = HEXAGON + SIX TRIANGLES.

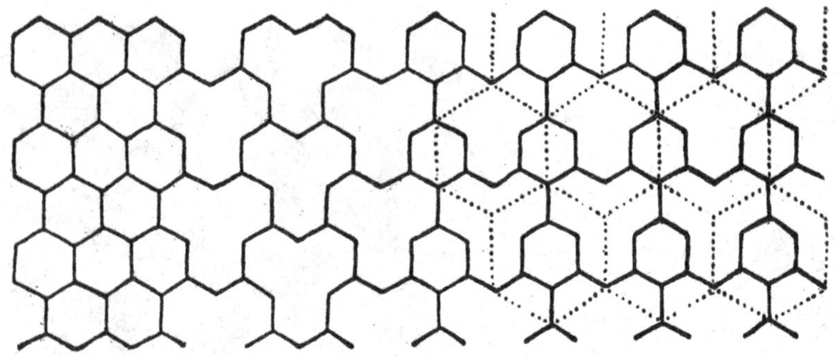

27. DIAPERS BUILT UP OF HEXAGONS.

The hexagon itself is a unit which makes a perfect repeat. The stars may be so arranged, point to point, as to leave only hexagonal intervals between. In the diaper on page 19 the central hexagons round which the stars are built range with the hexagonal intervals. The result is a

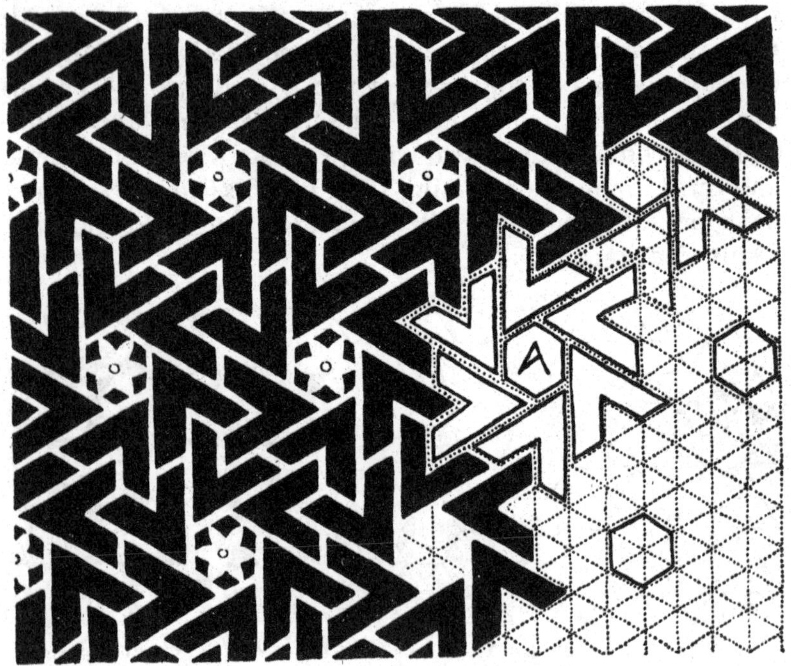

28. INDIAN LATTICE AND THE LINES ON WHICH IT IS BUILT.

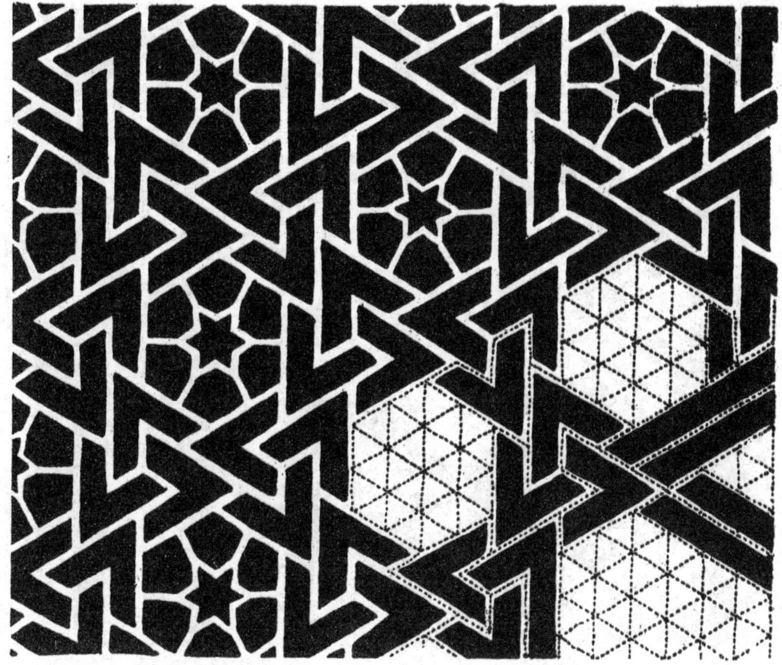

29. INDIAN LATTICE AND ITS TRIANGULAR BASIS.

starry pattern, composed of hexagons and triangles, in which the cross-lines in the three directions are very plainly marked.

Three hexagons together give a figure (27), commonly employed in Arab ornament, which repeats (it will be seen) either as a close-fitting diaper or with hexagonal intervals between. The figure itself is plainly related to the triangle—the side of which might easily be bent into zig-zags giving the other nine angles which go to make it.

The friendly way in which triangles, hexagons, stars, and other shapes compounded of the triangle unite to give complex and ingenious variety of pattern accounts for the persistent use of such units in Byzantine floor patterns and Moresque tile-work. It will be seen that the intricate Indian window lattices illustrated (28, 29, 30) resolve themselves

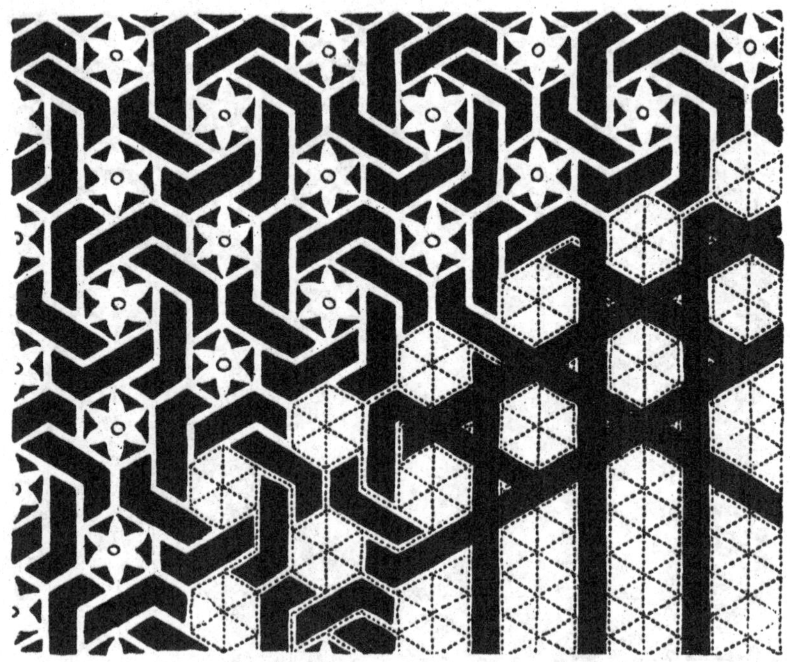

30. INDIAN LATTICE AND ITS TRIANGULAR BASIS.

(apart from the rosettes or stars inhabiting the central hexagons) into shapes either formed by lines crossing in the three directions or built up of equilateral triangles, in the ways already explained.

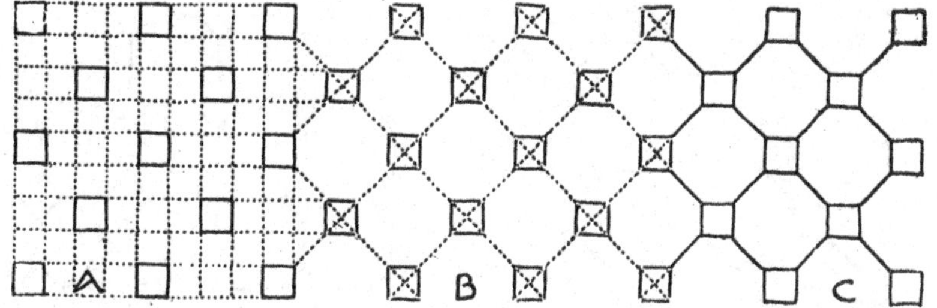

31. OCTAGON AND THE LINES ON WHICH IT IS BUILT.

IV. THE OCTAGON.

Four series of lines give the octagon—Not the unit of a complete pattern, but the basis of some radiating patterns—More complicated cross-lines, giving sixteen and eighteen sided figures, result in more elaborate pattern, but involve no new principle—Pentagon pattern really built on simple trellis lines.

A FOURTH series of cross-lines naturally gives new shapes, but no longer shapes which of themselves form a compact repeating pattern (31). The little squares at A are plainly formed on the trellis shown in dotted line. Cross that with a wider trellis, B, and you get the octagons, C. But, proportion them as you will, there remains always a series of square or oblong or diamond-shaped gaps between; and the two forms are together necessary to make a coherent pattern. The two octagon diapers (32) are of course identically the same, presented only from different points of view.

The lines of a double trellis, one crossing the other, cannot therefore be said to give a new geometric pattern unit; but they give new lines on which a vast number of radiating patterns are built, from the comparatively plain interlacing of a cane-bottomed chair (33) to the ornamental diapering on the lower walls of the Alhambra (34). It is upon lines

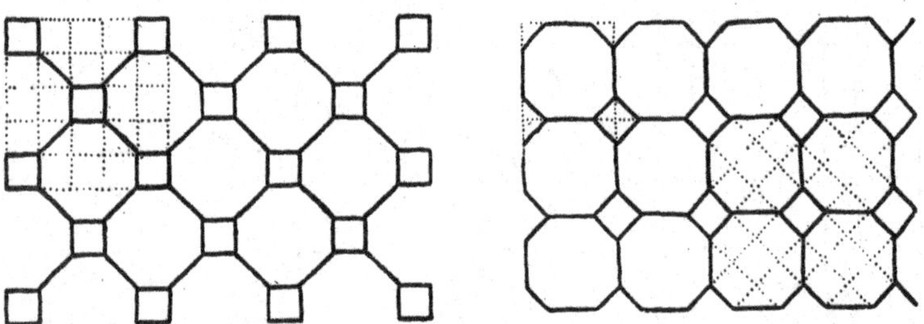

32. DIFFERENT VIEWS OF SAME PATTERN.

such as these that the bewildering patterns in which a race of mathematicians delighted are based. We are inclined to wonder sometimes how human ingenuity comes to grasp the thread of such intricate patternwork, much less invent it. Something of the wonder ceases when the tangled lines of its construction are unravelled.

The double lattice which gives the eight pointed figures in diagram 34 might be crossed by a similar lattice giving sixteen pointed figures, and that again by itself, giving figures of twice as many points, without the introduction of any new principle of design. The lines would merely be elaborated; they would resolve themselves into cross-lines

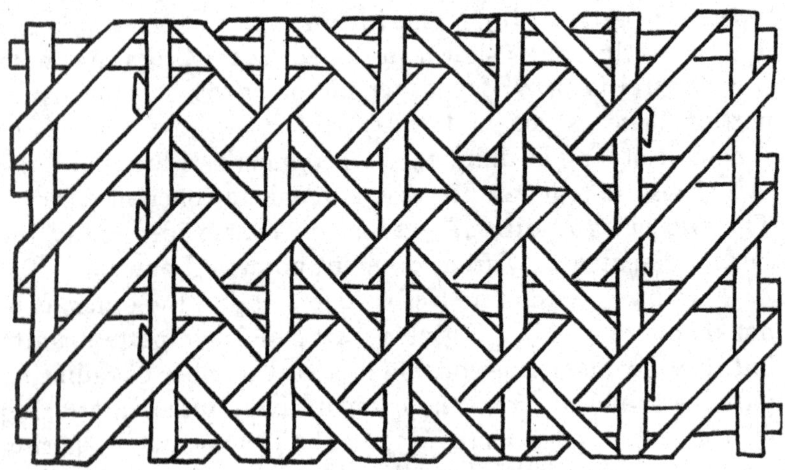

33. PATTERN FROM CANE-BOTTOMED CHAIR.

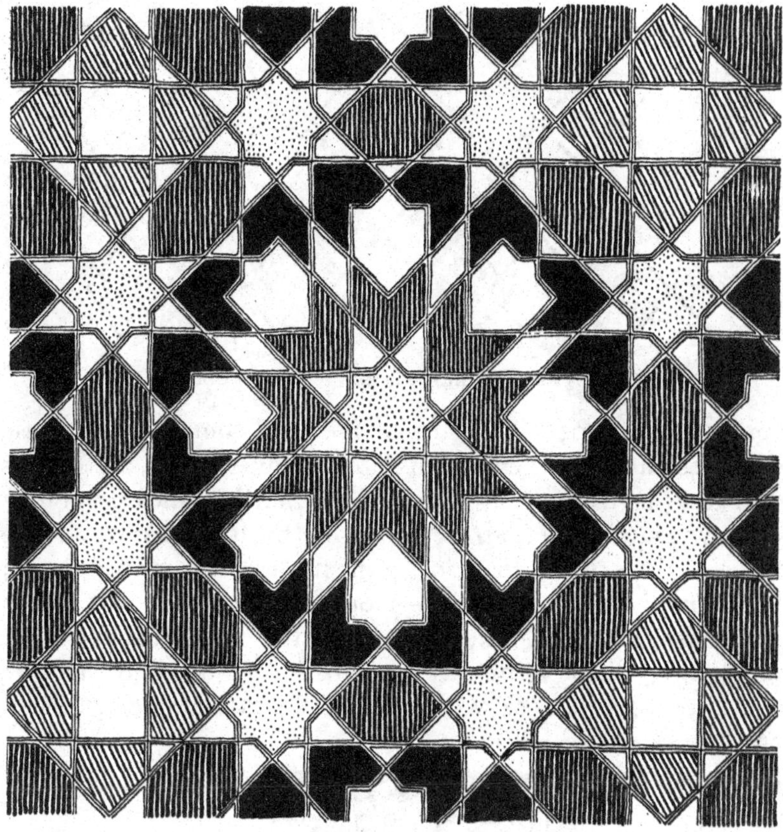

34. TILE WORK FROM THE ALHAMBRA.

not in four or eight, but in sixteen or thirty-two directions —that is all.

Practically, we have now exhausted the plans on which straight-lined patterns can be schemed. It is within the bounds of ingenuity to put together right-lined figures, such as the pentagon, in a way to mystify even the expert and to suggest a new discovery in pattern planning. Such a pattern is the cunningly counterchanged pentagon diaper (36). The star shapes within the larger pentagons and the smaller stars between, with their pentagonal centres suggesting other

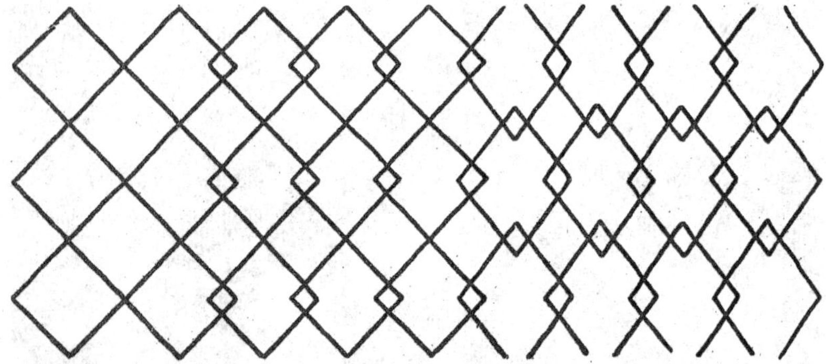

35. SIMPLE AND MORE COMPLICATED TRELLIS LINES.

pentagonal shapes (in point of fact not complete), confuse the lines on which the pattern is really built. But, artfully as they are disguised, they prove to be familiar lines involving no new plan. The pattern might be built indeed upon five series of lines in the direction of the five sides of the pentagon; but a network of such lines would be involved to a quite perplexing degree. The lines indicated on the diagram are more likely those on which the artist worked; and they are intimately related, as will be seen, to the simple trellis of cross-lines above.

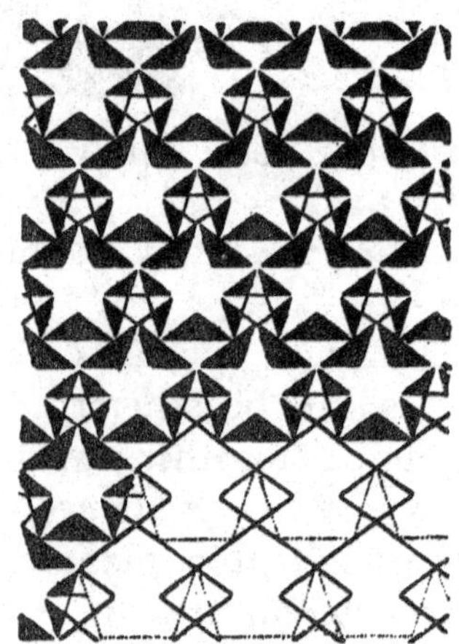

36. PENTAGON DIAPER AND ITS SKELETON.

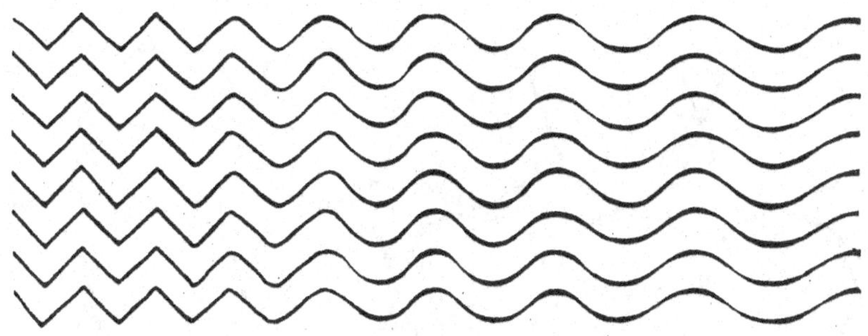

37. ZIG-ZAGS DEVELOPING INTO WAVE LINES.

V. THE CIRCLE.

The circle gives no new plan but only curvilinear versions of the foregoing—The wave a rounded zig-zag—The honeycomb compressed circles—Segments of circles give scale pattern, a curvilinear variation upon diamond—The ogee—The circle itself a scaffolding for design.

A MOST important element in geometric pattern is the circle: with it curvilinear design begins at once to flow more freely.

But (as in the case of the pentagon) the circle gives us no new plan to work on; it must itself be planned upon one or other of the systems already described; it must be struck, that is to say, from centres corresponding to the points of intersection given by a lattice of straight lines.

Curvilinear pattern is in its simplest form plainly only a suaver variety of rectilinear design. Flowing patterns can often be deduced from angular, and *vice versa*. The priority of either is open to dispute, but hardly worth disputing.

Long before geometric principles were formulated in the mind of man, he practised them intuitively. As to the use of the circle in ornament, we need not ascribe it to geometry, nor trace it back to the sun's disc and symbolism, nor yet to

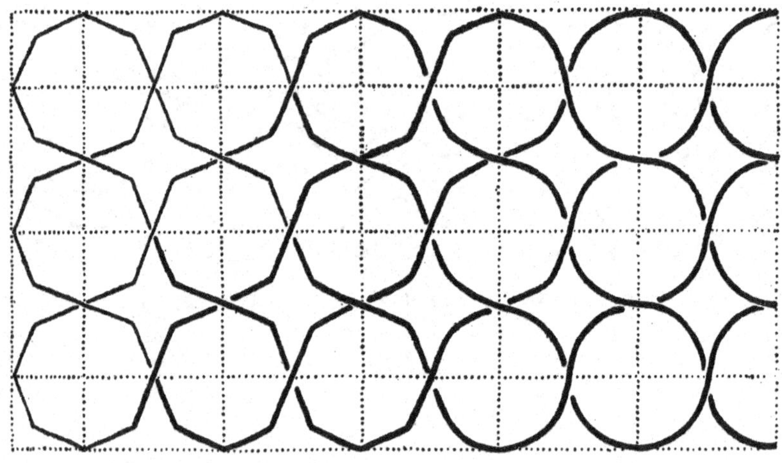

38. RELATION OF OCTAGON TO CIRCLE DIAPER.

conscious imitation. The primeval artist had but to pick up the nearest dry twig and indent the damp earth with it, and lo! a diaper of circular forms. Or, again, he might begin to scratch zig-zags, and, as his hand flowed on, they might develop into waved lines (37). Wave or zig-zag lines fall naturally into stripes: it is not the plan of the pattern, but only the detail that differs. The wave is in fact a zig-zag blunted at the points, the zig-zag an angular form of wave. A network of straight staves gives, as seen in slight

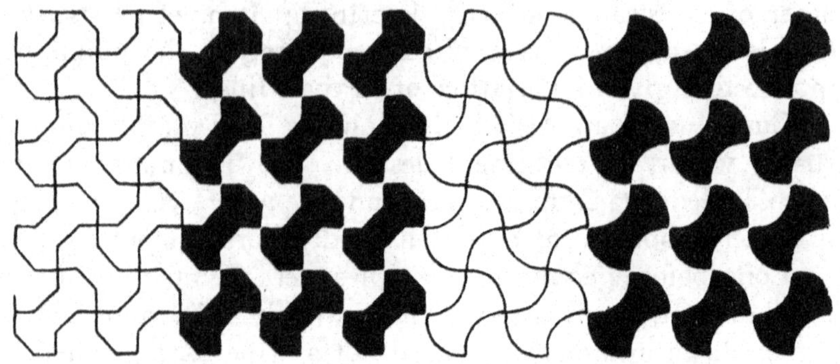

39. STRAIGHT-LINED AND CURVILINEAR VARIETIES OF THE SAME PATTERN.

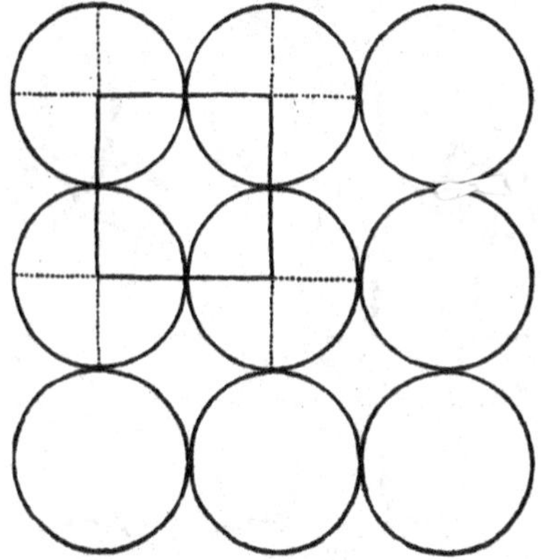

40. DIAPER OF CIRCLES PLANNED ON SQUARE LINES.

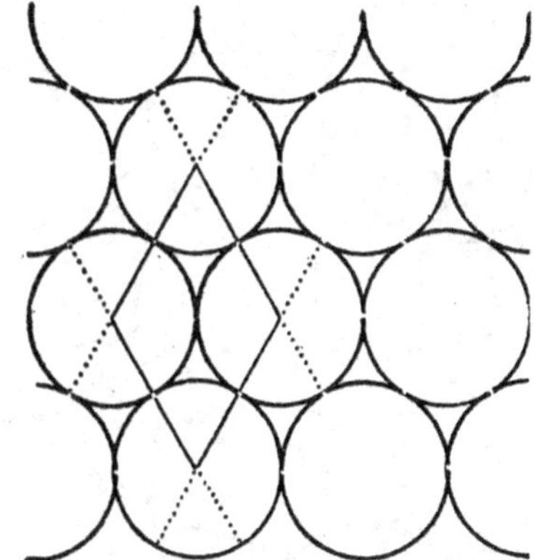

41. DIAPER OF CIRCLES PLANNED ON DIAMOND LINES.

perspective (look at any common hurdle), distinctly waving lines.

Again, round off the corners of the hexagon or octagon, and you have straightway a circle (38). Indeed, at a little distance, the lines of a sixteen-sided figure round themselves, to all appearance, and give the effect of a circle. The reduction of the circle to hexagonal shape is practically effected in the honeycomb. The busy bee, if one may so far throw

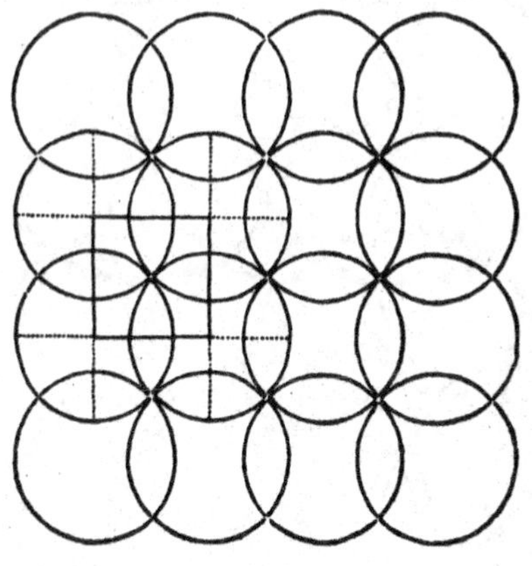

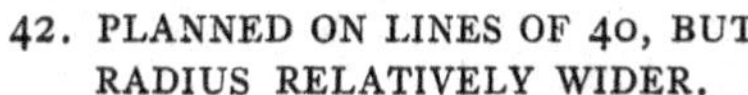

42. PLANNED ON LINES OF 40, BUT RADIUS RELATIVELY WIDER.

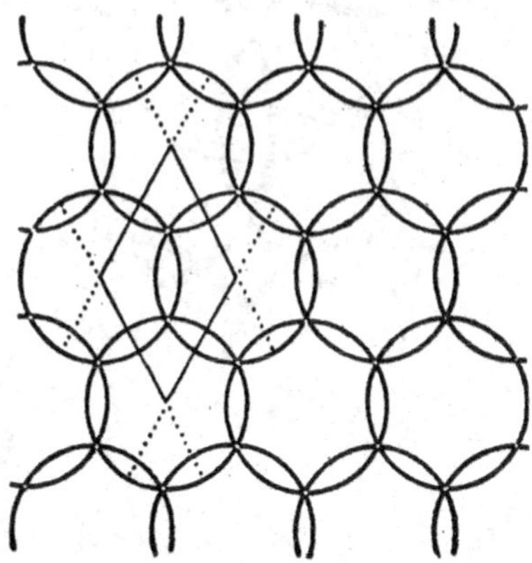

43. PLANNED ON LINES OF 41, BUT RADIUS RELATIVELY WIDER.

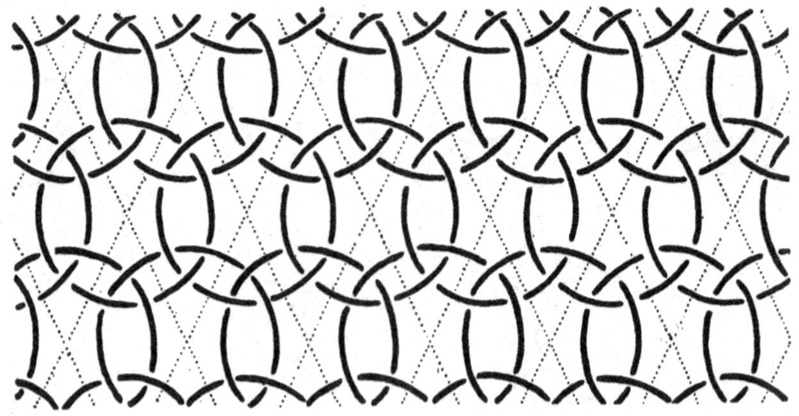

44. PLANNED ON LINES OF 41, BUT RADIUS RELATIVELY WIDER.

doubt upon his proverbial forethought, works blindly in a circle, and the shape of his cells is simply the result of gravitation. Cylinders crowded together crush themselves into hexagonal prisms. There is not a question of design: it is a matter of plasticity and weight.

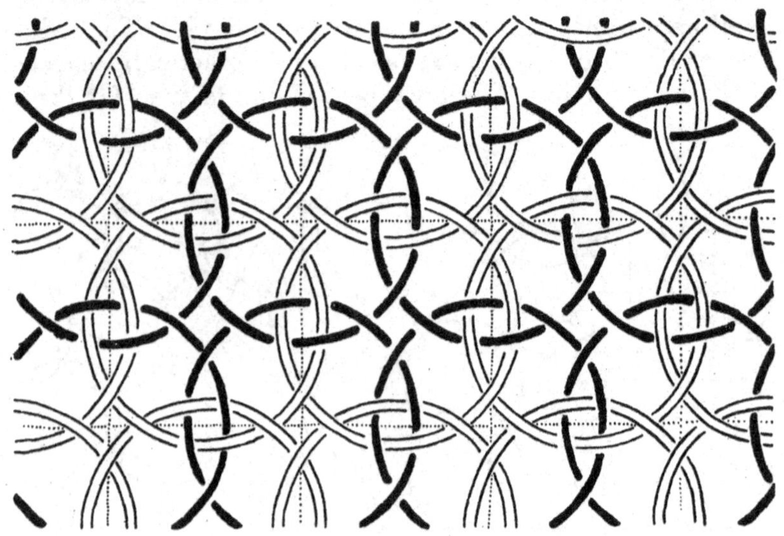

45. DOUBLE DIAPER OF CIRCLES PLANNED ON LINES OF 40, BUT RADIUS RELATIVELY WIDER STILL.

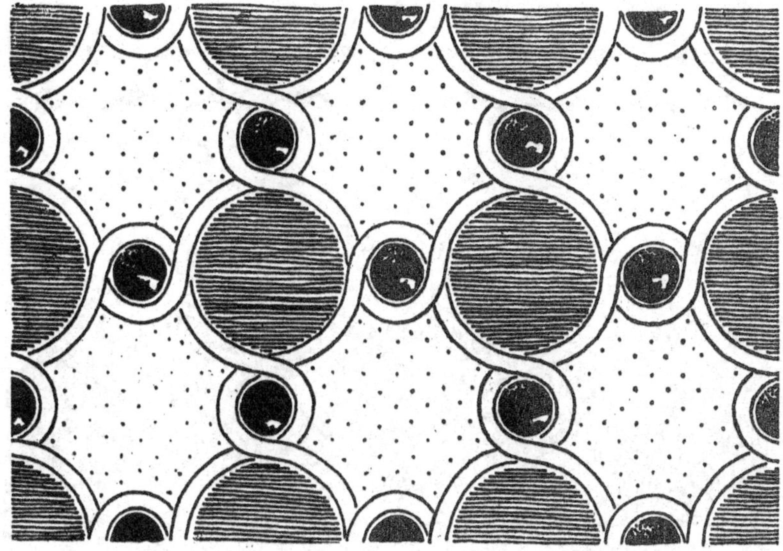

46. DIAPER OF INTERLACING CIRCLES.

It is clear on the face of it that we have in illustration (39) not so much two patterns as straight-lined and curved varieties of the same thing.

Circles closely packed to form a diaper show by the shape of the interspaces the plan on which they are put together.

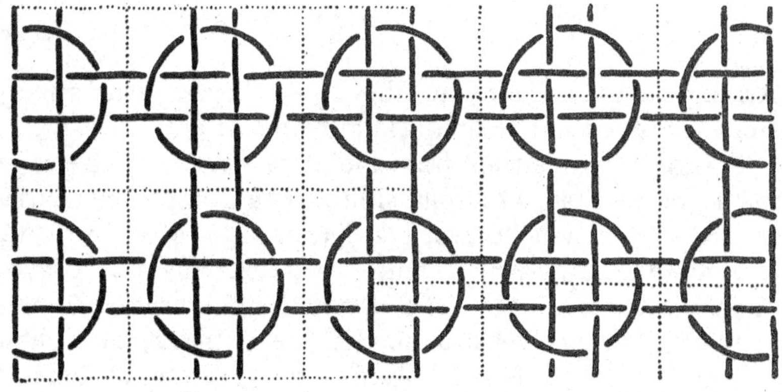

47. DIAPER OF CIRCLES INTERLACING WITH SQUARE TRELLIS.

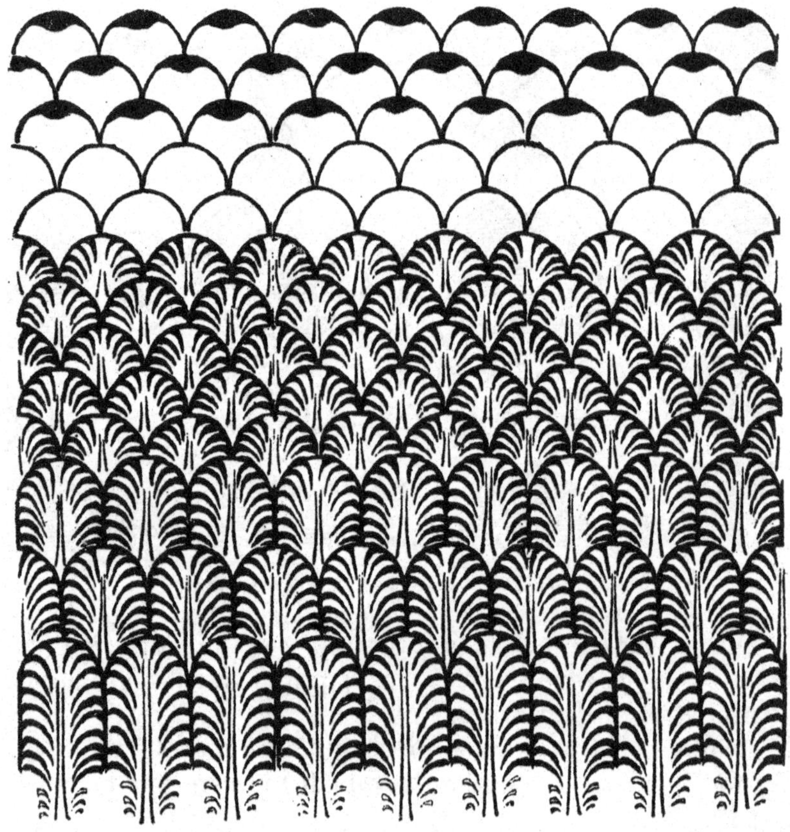

48. DIAPER OF SCALES AND DERIVATIVES FROM IT.

Arranged on the square (40) they show between them a four-sided space, on a diamond (41) a three-sided.

Larger circles struck from the same points, or circles of the same size struck from similarly arranged but closer points give, it will be seen (42, 43, 44, 45), more intricate-looking diapers. And infinite variations may be played upon the same tunes. The dotted lines in the diagrams fully explain the construction of the patterns, and show that no new principle is involved in the planning of them.

In the pattern (46) on page 31, the larger circles are

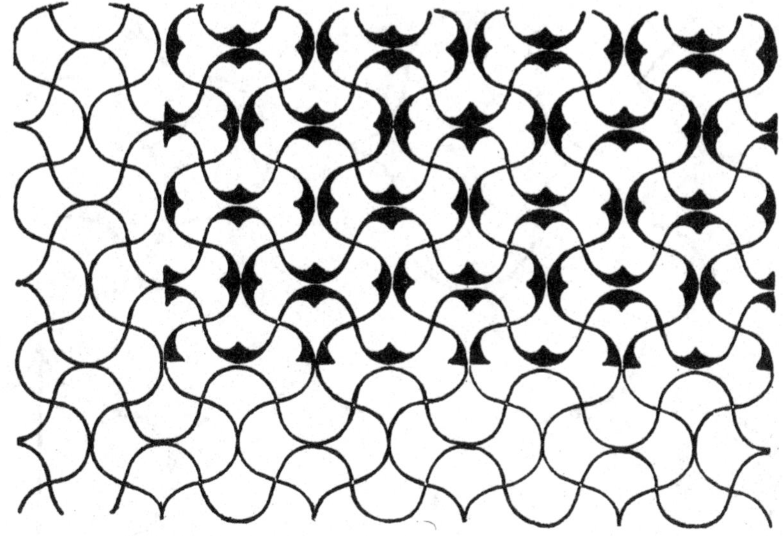

49. SCALES TURNED ABOUT TO MAKE FLOWING DIAPER.

struck from the points given by equi-distant lines crossing at right angles, and the smaller circles from points midway on the lines between these. The combination of straight with curved lines (47) helps only to show more plainly than ever the scaffolding on which the pattern was built. Other lines (square always) on which it might have been constructed are indicated by dotted lines.

As with the circle, so with its segments and its compounds (the trefoil, quatrefoil, and so forth); they give new forms, to be arranged always on the old plans—the quatrefoil naturally upon square lines, the trefoil or sexfoil upon the lines of the triangle. The segments of the circle give us the scale pattern (48), derived it might be from the scales of a fish or from the plumage of a bird's neck, but, practically speaking, only a translation of the diamond into curved lines.

Regarding the scales only as curvilinear diamonds, we are free to turn them about, as neither scales nor feathers would naturally grow, and to produce a flowing diaper (49) in which

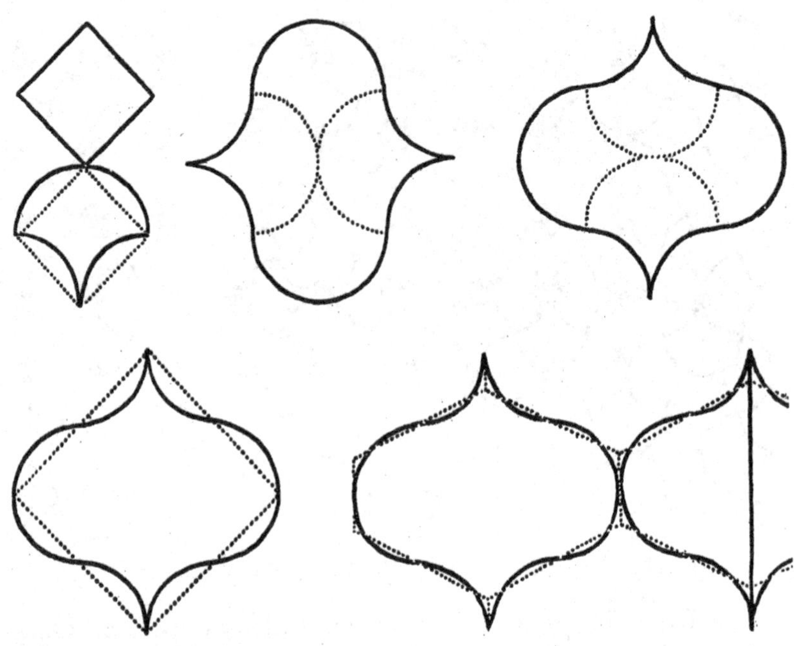

50. SHOWING RELATION OF SCALE TO DIAMOND AND OGEE, AND OF OGEE TO DIAMOND AND HEXAGON.

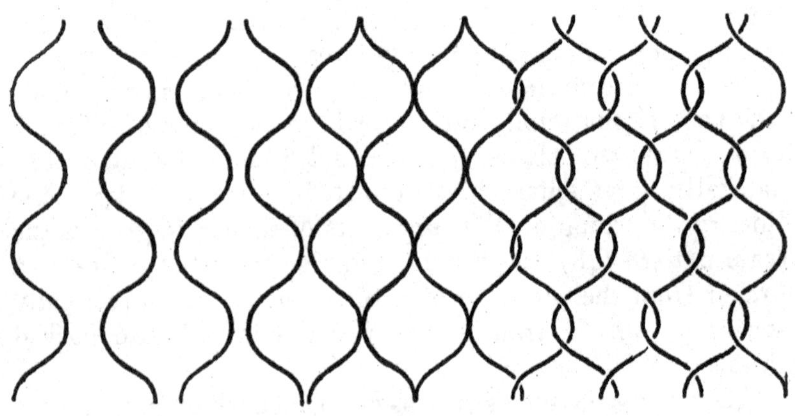

51. WAVE LINES, OGEE DIAPER, AND INTERLACING OGEES, GIVING HEXAGONAL SHAPES.

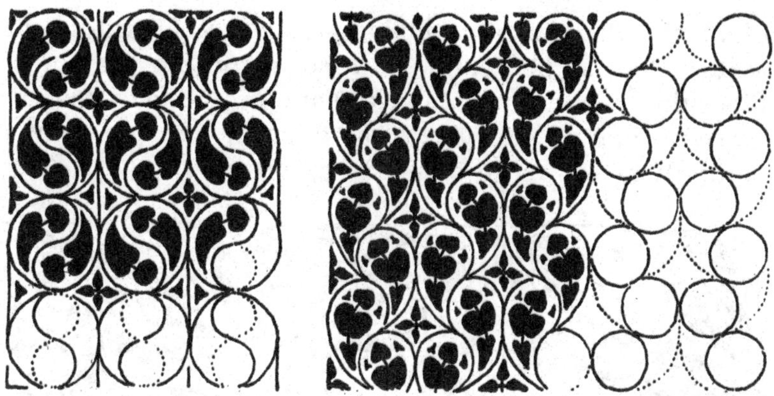

52. GOTHIC TRACERY DIAPERS CONSTRUCTED ON CIRCULAR LINES.

occurs a form, compounded of four scales, which itself may be regarded as a version either of the diamond or of the hexagon. All this is more plainly shown in diagram 50. The flowing shape occurs again in yet another diagram (51) together with the waved lines out of which it is composed. The interlacing of these waved lines gives a six-sided figure, the lines

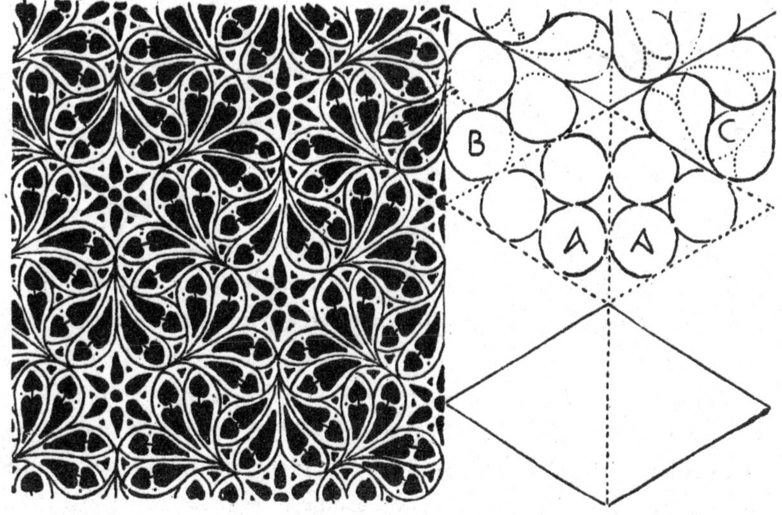

53. GOTHIC TRACERY DIAPER AND ITS CONSTRUCTIONAL LINES.

of which only want straightening to be recognised at once as the familiar hexagon. It is not surprising that in the fifteenth and sixteenth centuries pattern commonly took the graceful lines of the ogee. The designer fell into them as naturally as Mr Wegg dropped into poetry.

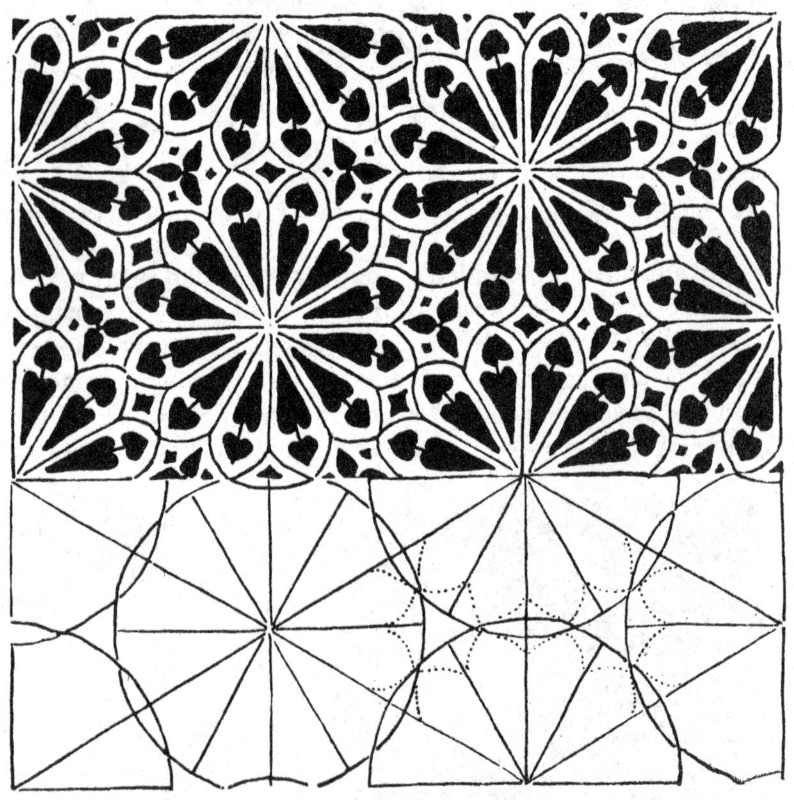

54. GOTHIC TRACERY AND ITS CONSTRUCTIONAL LINES.

The circle deserves further to be considered because it is itself the scaffolding, or at all events forms part of the scaffolding, upon which a great number of more or less geometric patterns have been devised.

The simple Gothic diaper (52) to the left on page 35

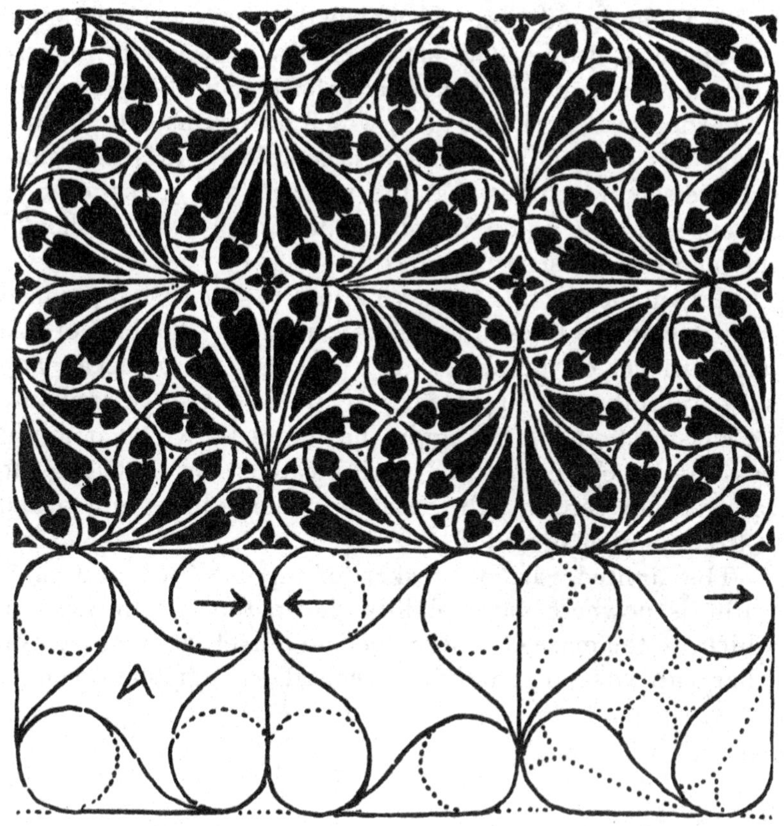

55. GOTHIC TRACERY DIAPER AND ITS CONSTRUCTIONAL LINES.

shows not only circles but forms into which the segments of smaller circles enter. One circle, it seems, begets others.

The tracery pattern next to it (52) is constructed by the help of small circles, themselves arranged on a circular (or hexagonal) plan, though what they give in the result is a sort of vertical wave pattern.

The rather more elaborate design at the bottom of the same page (53) repeats upon the lines of a hexagon, the points of which correspond with the centres of star-shapes. But the six of these enclose another star and the hexagon is seen to be a compound unit—of which the component diamond repeats as a drop. The small circles drawn within these diamonds at A, give by the mere effacement of a portion of them the twisting shapes at B, which only remain to be subdivided as at C, and the skeleton is complete. It is once more on intersecting circles that the pattern (54) on page 36 is set out; and the points of intersection give, as there shown, the points of the starry rosettes.

Yet another Gothic tracery pattern is given (55), planned this time on the lines of the double square. One half of this is a turnover of the other. It works as a drop repeat, and shows plainly that at an early stage the circle entered into its construction. Here again the stages by which it might possibly have been reached are indicated; but that is not to say with any certainty the designer may not have approached it from another direction.

The limited variety of skeleton upon which pattern is built, is nowhere more plainly shown than in the way in which, in the maze of design, we find ourselves, no matter on what path we set out, arriving over and over again at precisely the same point.

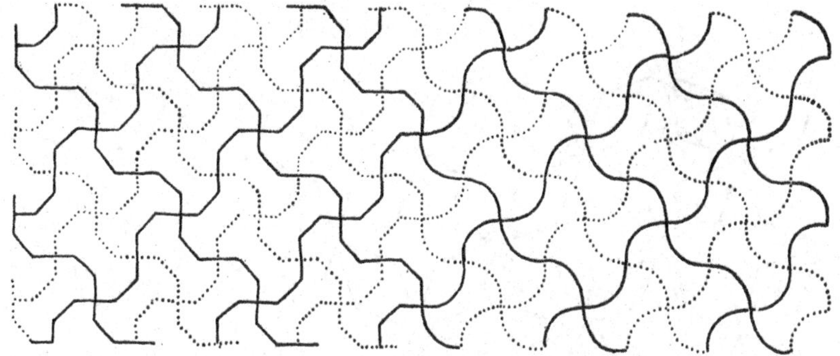

56. STRAIGHT-LINED AND CURVILINEAR VERSIONS OF DIAPER.

VI. THE EVOLUTION OF PATTERN.

Various starting points for the same pattern—Six ways in which it might have been evolved—The construction of sundry geometric diapers—Influence of material upon design—Some complex lattices.

IT is not safe to pretend to say with authority, the way in which a given pattern was evolved; there are usually several ways in which it might have come about. Close up the waved lines in diagram 51 and they give you an ogee diaper. Open out the ogee diaper and it gives you waved lines. The starting point of the interlacing pattern might equally well have been waved lines, the ogee, or the idea of a net.

In diagram 56 (straight and curved lined versions of the same thing) the dotted lines may be taken to indicate the way the larger unit was built up of four smaller units forming in themselves a repeat; but the smaller unit would result equally from, as it were, crossing the larger pattern by itself. The dotted diaper is the same as that in solid lines. Together they give a smaller diaper which may or may not have been its origin.

There are at least half-a-dozen ways in which a simple

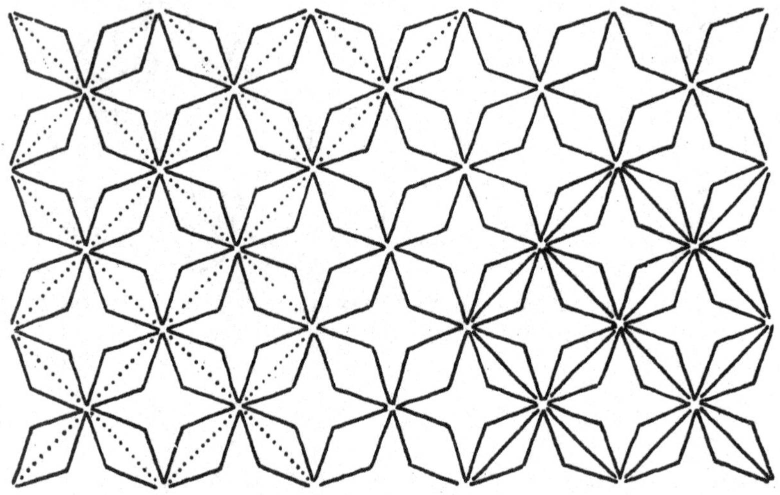

57. BEGINNING WITH RECTANGULAR TRELLIS.

star pattern such as that above might possibly have been arrived at:—

1. By beginning with a diamond lattice and occupying the spaces with four-pointed stars (57).

2. By arranging either star-shapes or diamonds point to

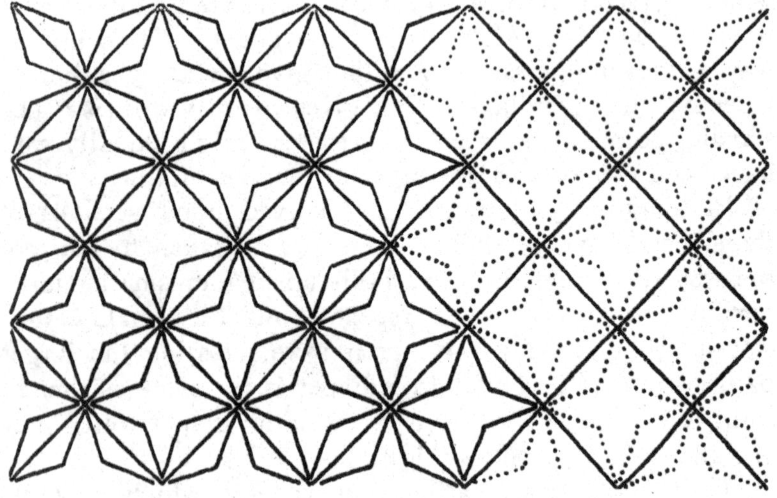

58. BEGINNING WITH FOUR-POINTED STARS.

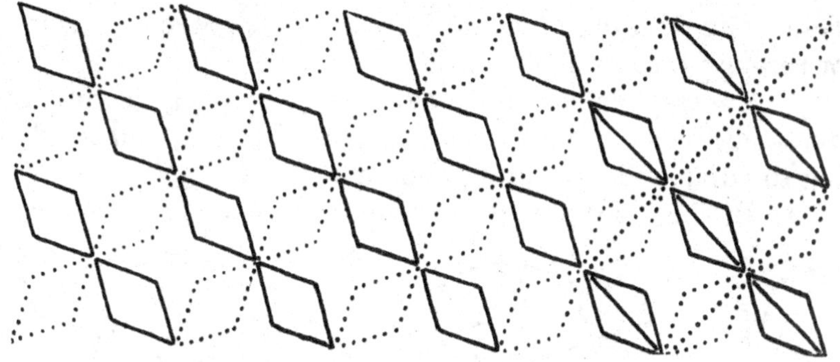

59. BEGINNING WITH CROSS BANDS OF DIAMONDS.

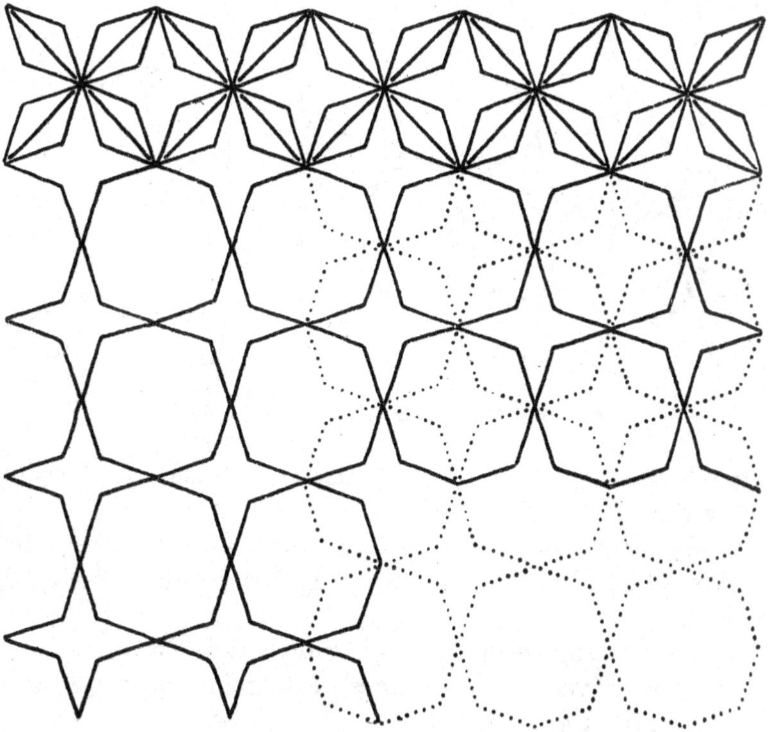

60. BEGINNING WITH OCTAGONS AND STARS.

point, and drawing diagonal lines across, between the stars, or through the diamonds (58).

3. By starting on diagonal lines, crossing a row of diamonds by a similar row in the cross direction, and steadying the diamonds by giving them a backbone (59).

4. By beginning with a diaper of octagons and four-

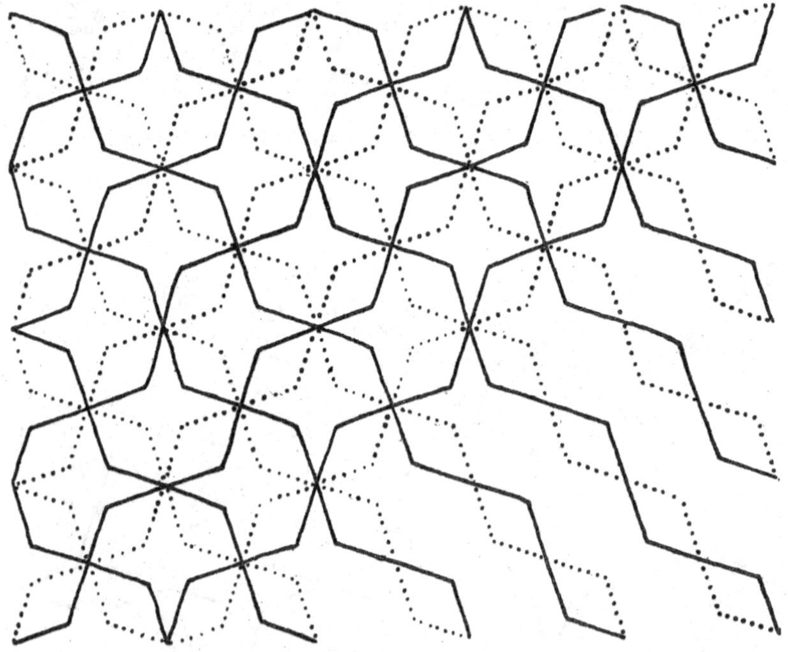

61. BEGINNING WITH ZIG-ZAG LINES.

pointed stars, crossing that by itself, and adding lines to steady the effect (60).

5. By beginning with zig-zag lines, crossing them by similar zig-zag lines, and crossing the pattern thus produced by itself (61).

6. By starting with the eight-sided unit—by no means necessarily arrived at on the lines of diagonal zig-zags—and crossing it by itself (62).

In the two last-mentioned diagrams the long diagonal

backbone lines are for the sake of clearness omitted, and the unit of a repeat common in Oriental diaper-work is emphatically expressed. A very similar unit occurs in the diaper (63), which may be built up, as will be seen, in the simplest possible way, on the basis of the square. The squares have only to be crossed by X lines alternately in transverse direction, and the framework of the design is there. Another

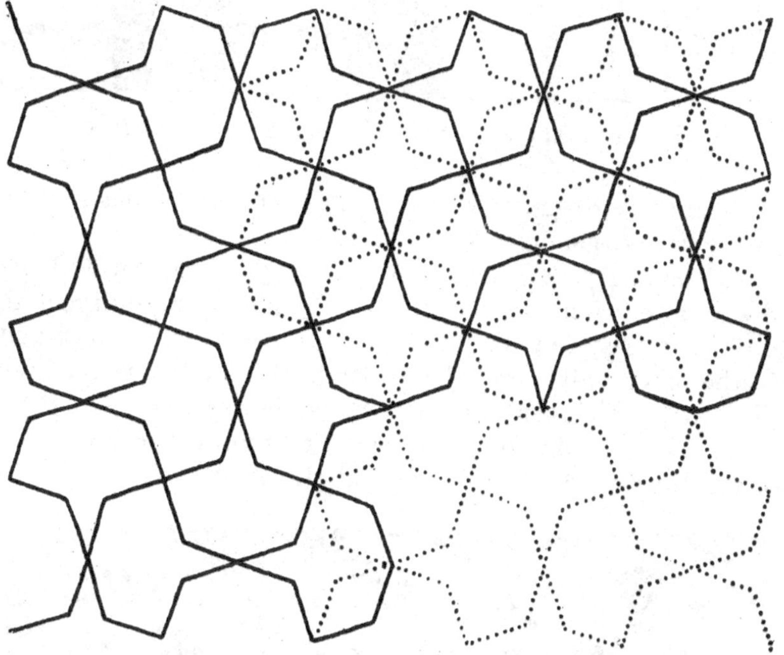

62. BEGINNING WITH EIGHT-SIDED UNIT.

simple way of producing a very complex result (64) is shown on page 45 (65), where the design is resolved into a comparatively simple square pattern crossed by itself. The construction of the Arab lattice pattern (64), shown in single line to the left of diagram 65, is better explained by diagram 66, from which it will be seen that the unit is merely a square enclosing a small diamond, the sides of which diamond are successively continued to the corners of the square.

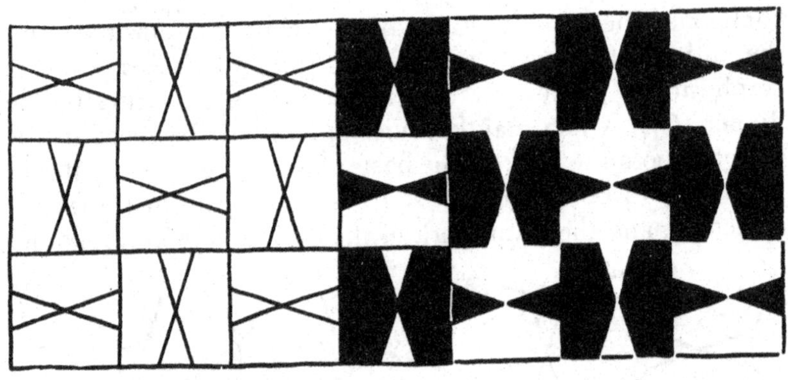

63. COUNTERCHANGE DIAPER AND ITS CONSTRUCTION.

The same diagram will help to explain the construction of the patterns shown at 67 and 70.

Given the base lines to the left of diagram 66, and the desire to counterchange the colour, what is the designer to do? It is easy to make the figures in one direction dark and in the other light; but there remain the small intermediate diamonds which can obviously be neither one nor the other. By effacing the diamond, however, and joining the loose ends of the lines to the left of the diagram in the way shown to

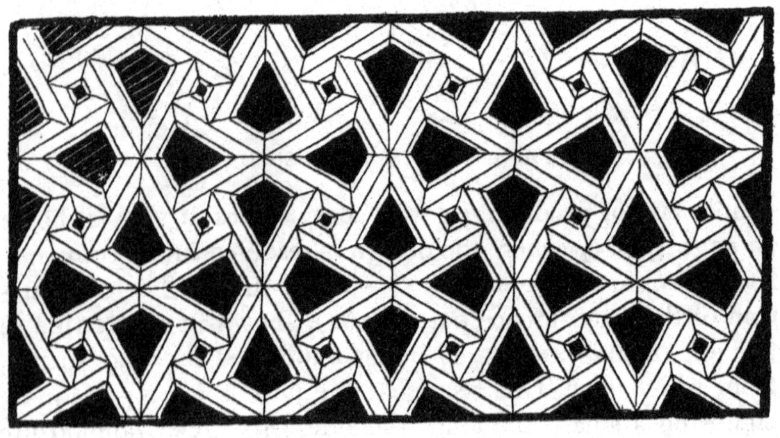

64. ARAB LATTICE PATTERN.

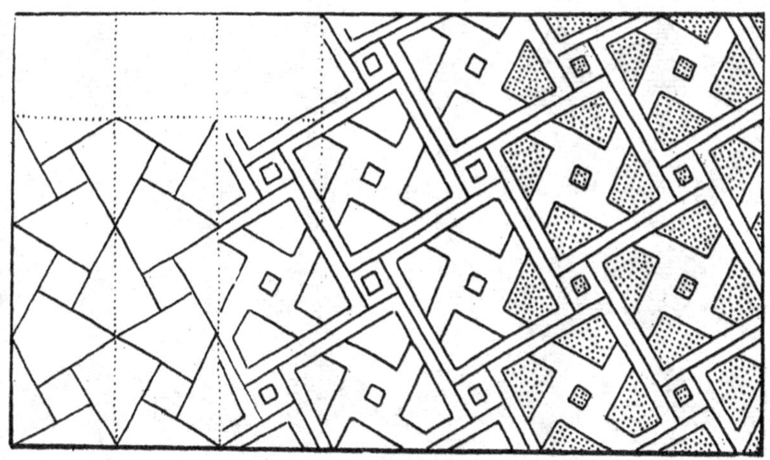

65. CONSTRUCTION OF ARAB LATTICE 64.

the right of it, the difficulty is at once overcome and we get the diapers (67) on page 46.

A similar difficulty is got over much in the same way in another Alhambresque tile pattern (70). The pointed projections at the sides of the oblong shapes corresponding absolutely to indentations at the ends of them, the parts fit together perfectly, except for the small square spaces between. By dividing these into four triangular parts, alternately light and dark, the patterns are made to counterchange. And the

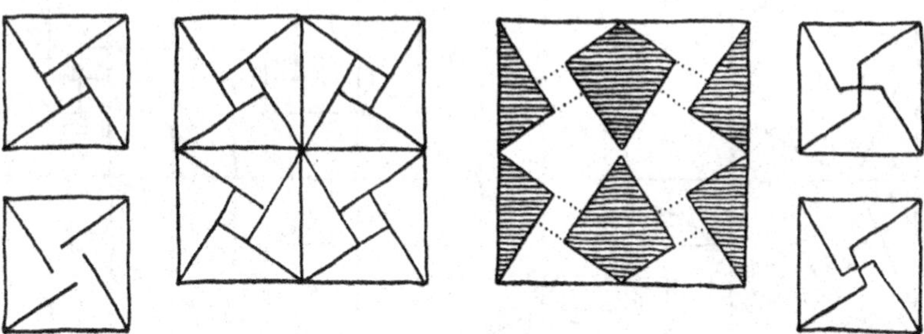

66. DIAGRAM EXPLAINING THE COMPOSITION OF THE UNIT IN PATTERNS 64 AND 65.

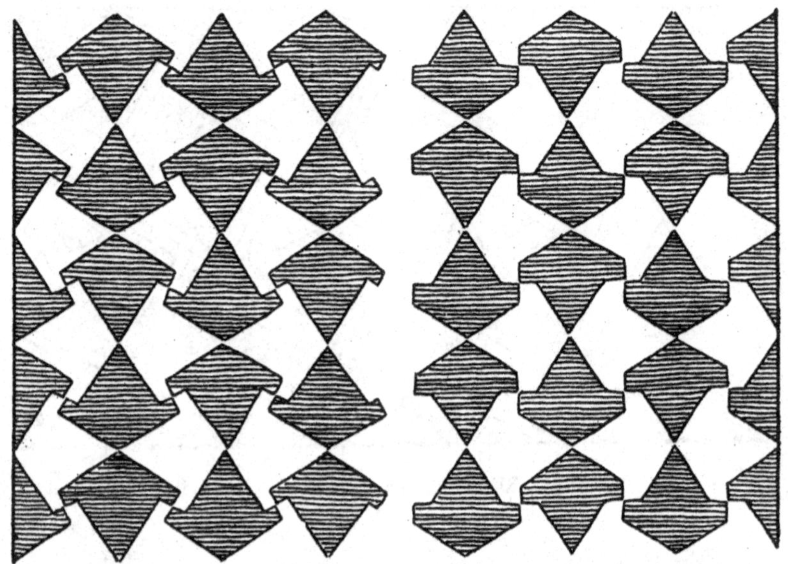

67. ARAB COUNTERCHANGE PATTERNS CONSTRUCTED AS 66.

expedient is just what would occur to an artist building up his pattern, as the Moors did, out of shaped pieces of tile.

The kind of key or swastika seen in diagram 66 occurs also in diagram 68 which is in some sort a key to the construction of the Roman pavement pattern 69. The most likely way of setting about such a design would be to divide

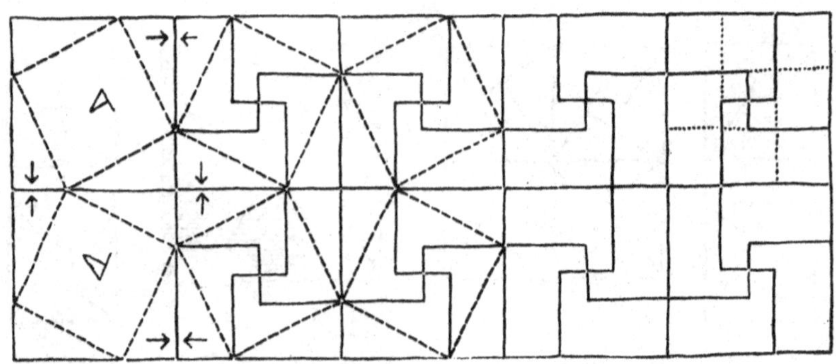

68. KEY TO CONSTRUCTION OF ROMAN PAVEMENT PATTERN 69.

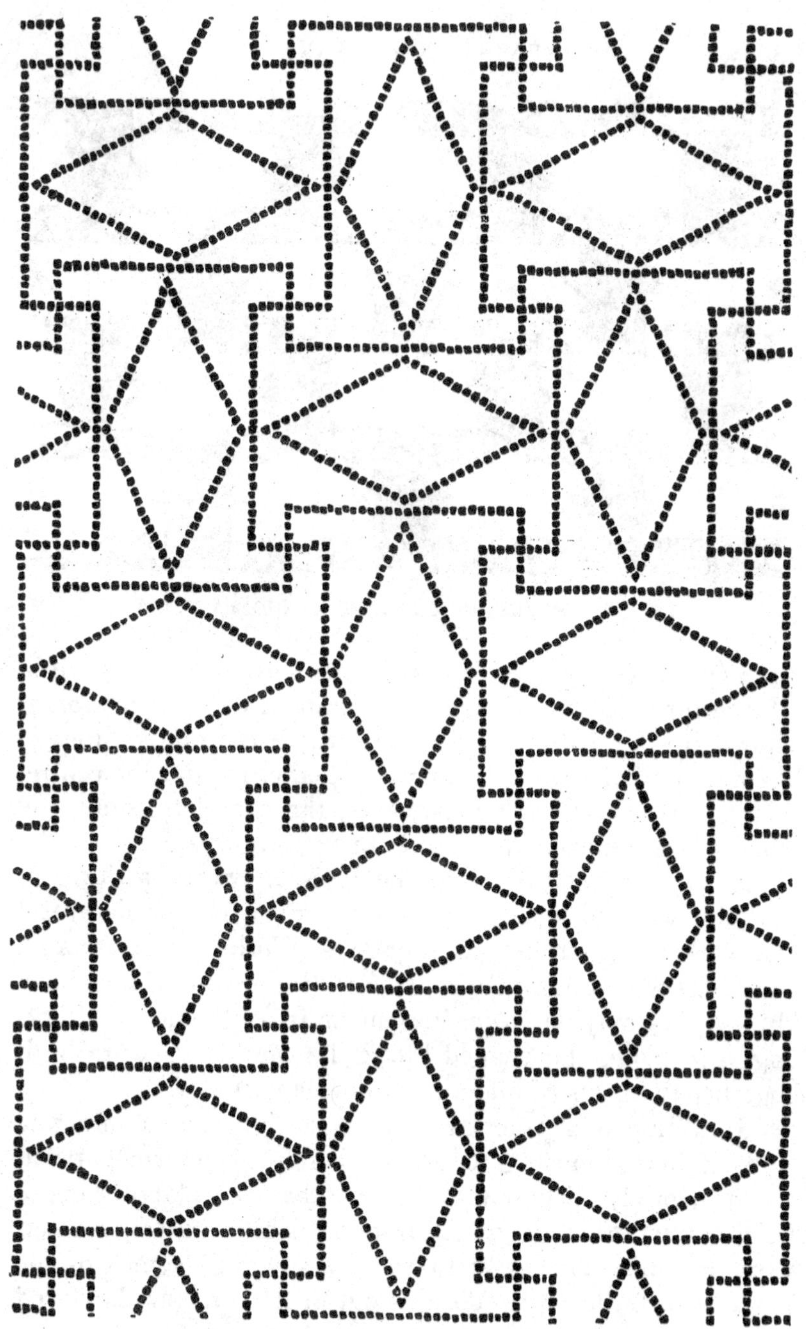

69. ROMAN MOSAIC PAVEMENT PATTERN.

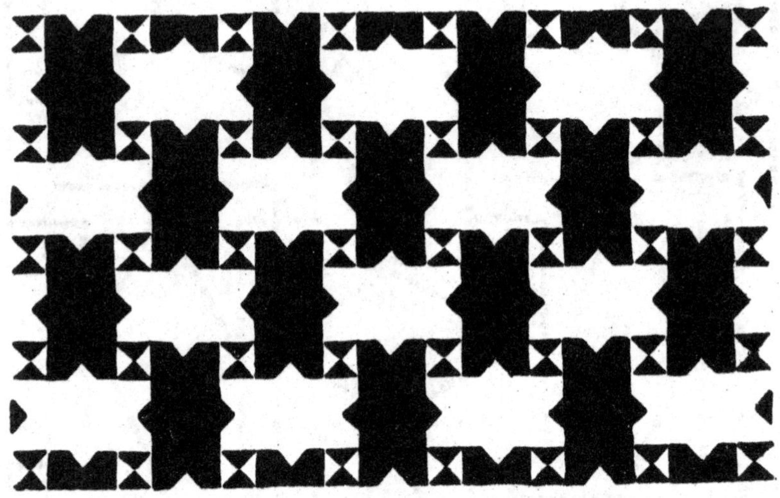

70. ALHAMBRESQUE COUNTERCHANGE PATTERN.

up a small square with swastika lines (as shown to the right of diagram 68) and to reverse the unit in either direction as shown by the arrows to the left—where the dotted lines of the diamond are given. The two together (nearer the centre) give, in the space of four squares, the complete compound unit, which repeats on the lines of the larger square.

A very broad hint as to the lines on which a designer actually went to work is sometimes given by the nature of the work on which he was engaged. Working in tesseræ, a mosaicist would naturally start with lines—which, somehow, thin as they may be, never look mean in a pavement. Working with triangular-shaped blocks he would as naturally fit together the parts of his pattern puzzle-wise.

Speaking as a practical pattern designer, and one who finds it most amusing to devise merely geometric pattern, I am strongly disposed to believe that the elaboration of Oriental patternwork (which resolves itself at last into a network of lines not easily to be disentangled) comes of the practice of building up designs out of little triangular-faced pieces of marble, glass, or tile.

The intricate lines develop themselves as the artist proceeds; and, having got them, he goes on to emphasise them. Carvers and others translate the tile pattern into line, as in the natural course of their craft they must, and in that way we get the cunningly intersecting line work of pierced lattices and so forth (71). Designing upon the lines themselves he would get caught in the meshes of his own pattern, and lose the sequence of line so difficult to keep in view.

It dazzles one to think of the plan of no more elaborate

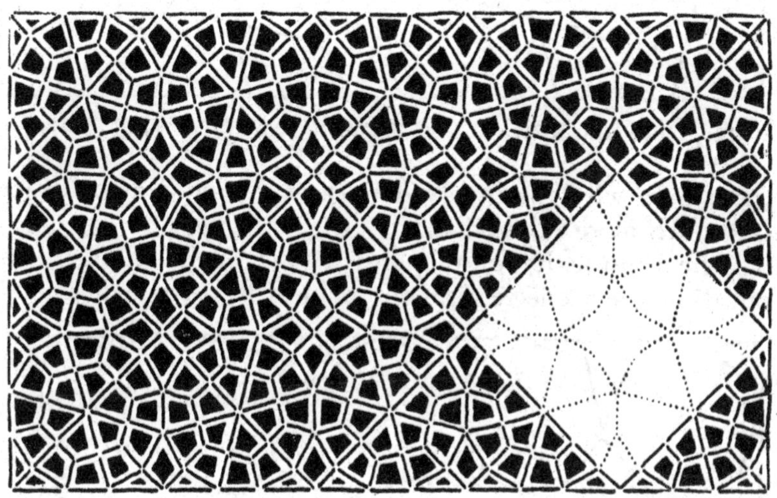

71. LATTICE PATTERN, POSSIBLY DERIVED FROM TESSELATED WORK

a lattice than that above. The simplified unit of the design is shown in dotted lines. It might equally have been built up upon the lines of either of the diagrams (72-73), octagons point to point, with four-pointed star-shapes between. And in this particular case it is not clear that any great advantage would have been gained by building up the pattern; but where the component shapes are triangles or compounds of triangles, it is not only easier to play with

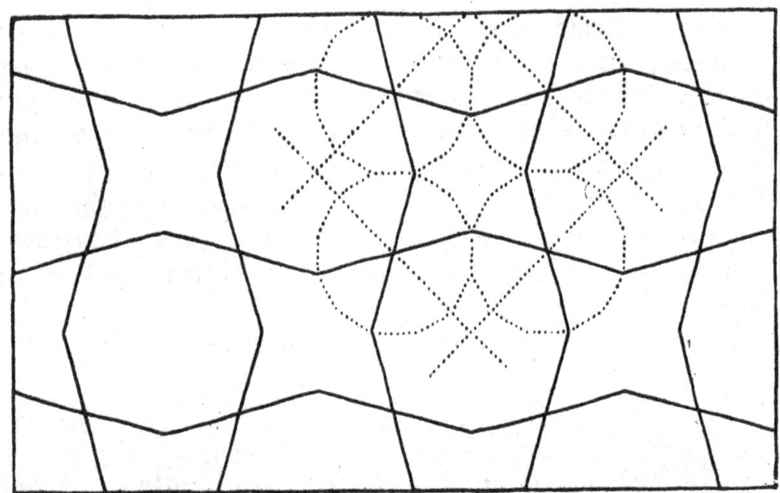

72. LINES ON WHICH LATTICE 71 MIGHT HAVE BEEN BUILT.

them than with the involved lines of a complicated lattice, but much more fun to do so.

The complexity of the lattice (74) on page 51 is less puzzling when one realises the plan of it, a squat diamond,

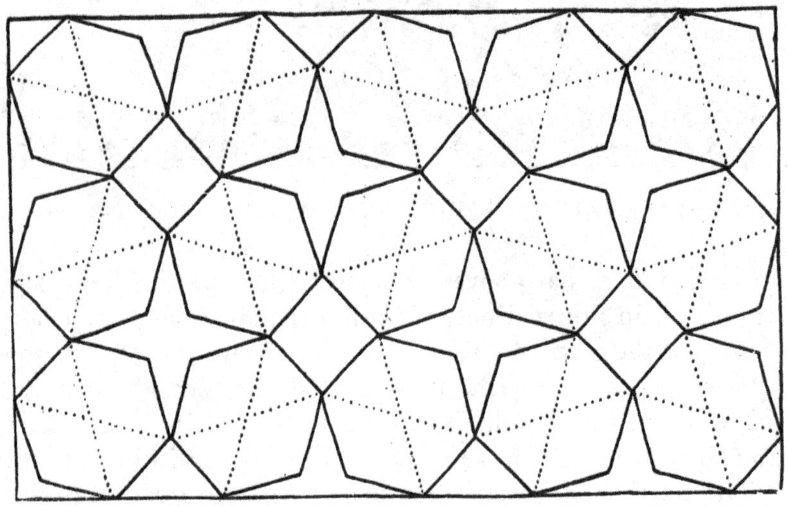

73. LINES ON WHICH LATTICE 71 MIGHT HAVE BEEN BUILT.

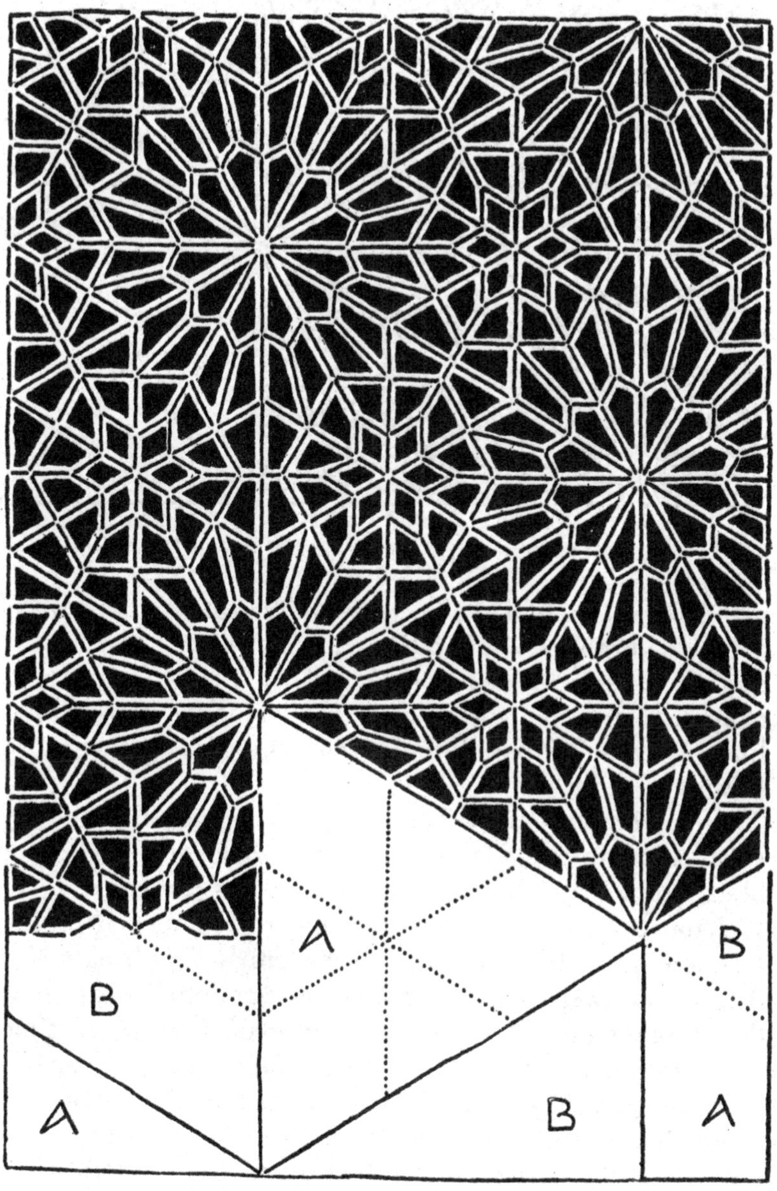

74. ARAB LATTICE AND THE LINES OF ITS CONSTRUCTION.

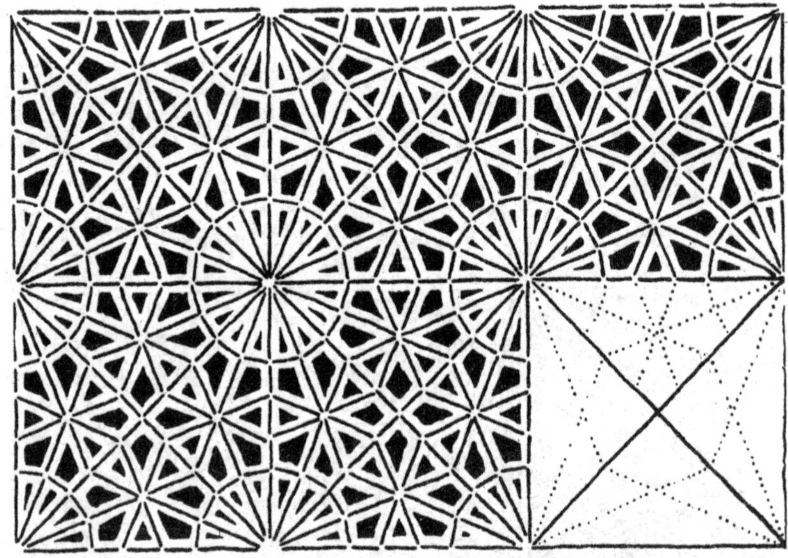

75. ARAB LATTICE AND ITS CONSTRUCTION.

which may be divided into two equilateral triangles A and B (one a turnover of the other) either of which may be subdivided, as the dotted lines show, into equal equilateral triangles and the corresponding diamonds. Given those lines it is a comparatively simple thing to build up the lattice.

One more instance. The repeat of the pattern above (75) (equivalent to the tile which would go to make it, or the block from which it could be printed) is indicated in the skeleton to the right, a square; but the component unit is all there in the triangle which forms only a fourth part of it. And of the twelve parts of which (as the dotted lines show) that is made up, all but one are repeated three or four times over, so that it takes figures of only four different shapes to make it—presumptive evidence at least that that is the way in which the design came about, not perhaps in this particular instance of the lattice, but in the case of some pattern which was its prototype.

VII. BORDERS.

What a border is—Includes frieze, pilaster, frame, &c.—Simplicity—Short interval of repeat—Flowing and broken borders—Mere lines—"Stop" borders—Frets—Evolute—Zig-zag—Chevron—Undulate—Guilloche—Interlacing—Chain—Strap—Branching lines—Spiral scroll—Counterchange—Intermittent borders—Block border—Panel border—The S scroll—Natural growth—Enclosed borders—Fringes, &c.—Strong and weak side of border—Direction of border—Corners and their influence upon design—Circular and concentric borders.

A BORDER may be described as confined always within fixed marginal (usually parallel) lines which, whether expressed or understood, determine its depth or breadth. The pattern of it is repeated lengthwise only.

This would seem to simplify the problem of design by just one half. But it is not so. There are considerations, such as the necessity of turning a corner, which make the task by no means so straightforward. And, then, the comparative narrowness within which borders are confined, and the very simplicity of the lines into which they naturally fall, make it difficult to invent anything new. It seems almost as if everything that was worth doing had been done already and nothing remained to us but to echo it.

These very circumstances, however, enable me to give something more than the geometric ground plans of border design, and, in fact, to survey the various steps of border which have been built upon them.

The term border is fairly comprehensive. It may be taken to include frieze, pilaster, and framing patterns

76. DIAGRAMS OF FLOWING AND BROKEN BORDERS.

generally. Some of these are of individual importance, and may rightly claim prominence in a scheme of decoration; they are, if not precisely the picture, interesting incidents in it. A border in the narrower sense is, however, as a rule, at best a frame, and steps out of its place when it attracts much notice to itself. The simpler it is the better. It is just the simplest borders which are most difficult to design. The mere adjustment of parallel lines to the framing of a drawing wants tact and taste. "You can always tell a designer by his borders," said an artist to me once, himself distinguished in design.

With regard to the actual planning or setting out of border patterns there is not much to be added to what has already been explained in reference to the construction of repeated pattern generally. In so far as merely geometric recurrence is concerned the problem is simplified—reduced, as before said, to a pattern which repeats lengthwise only. Borders, therefore, simple or elaborate, are built on lines already described; and here again the tendency of those lines will be to reveal themselves in the recurring pattern.

The direction of a border—horizontal or upright, whether it frames a panel or runs round a circle—is a question rather of detail than of planning. Still, to some extent it affects the plan of the design; for, though potentially the same lines will serve in any case, practically they will not; for the position of the border will determine always which of the possible lines are appropriate.

Conditions applying to borders generally are: that they should be simple, that they should repeat at no very long interval, that they should lend themselves to satisfactory management in turning a corner. A short interval of repeat has, over and above the economy obviously effected by its means, two clear advantages: it steadies the effect, and it facilitates the adaptation of the unit of repeat to two or more lengths—a necessity, continually occurring, which in itself complicates the scheming of border design.

There are, broadly speaking, two descriptions of borders, those in which the lines run *with* the margins, and those in which they *cross* from one to the other (76). These two systems may be, and often are, combined. The flowing border may be bridged at intervals; the lines between the steady features in a broken pattern may run on; but, practically, it is usually the business of a border either to flow smoothly or to stand steady; and the first thing the designer has to do is to make up his mind which of these it shall do.

If any classification of borders is possible, it is into flowing, growing, waving, "fret," spiral and other *continuous* borders, and into "stop," "block," "turnover," panel and other crossways or *broken* borders, upgrowing as it were from the margin. It is no use attempting to group them as leaf, rosette, "honeysuckle" borders and so forth, according to

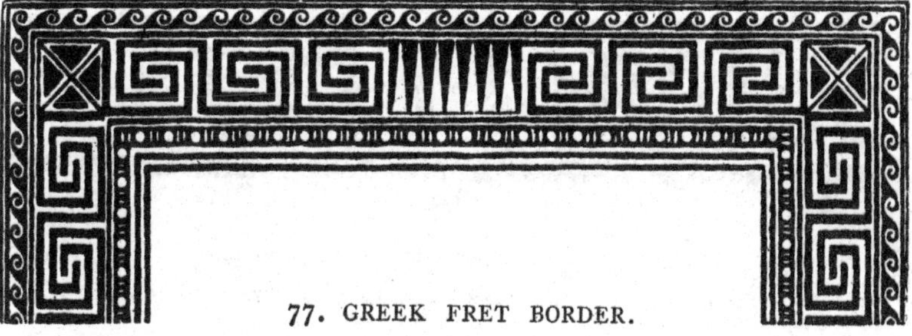

77. GREEK FRET BORDER.

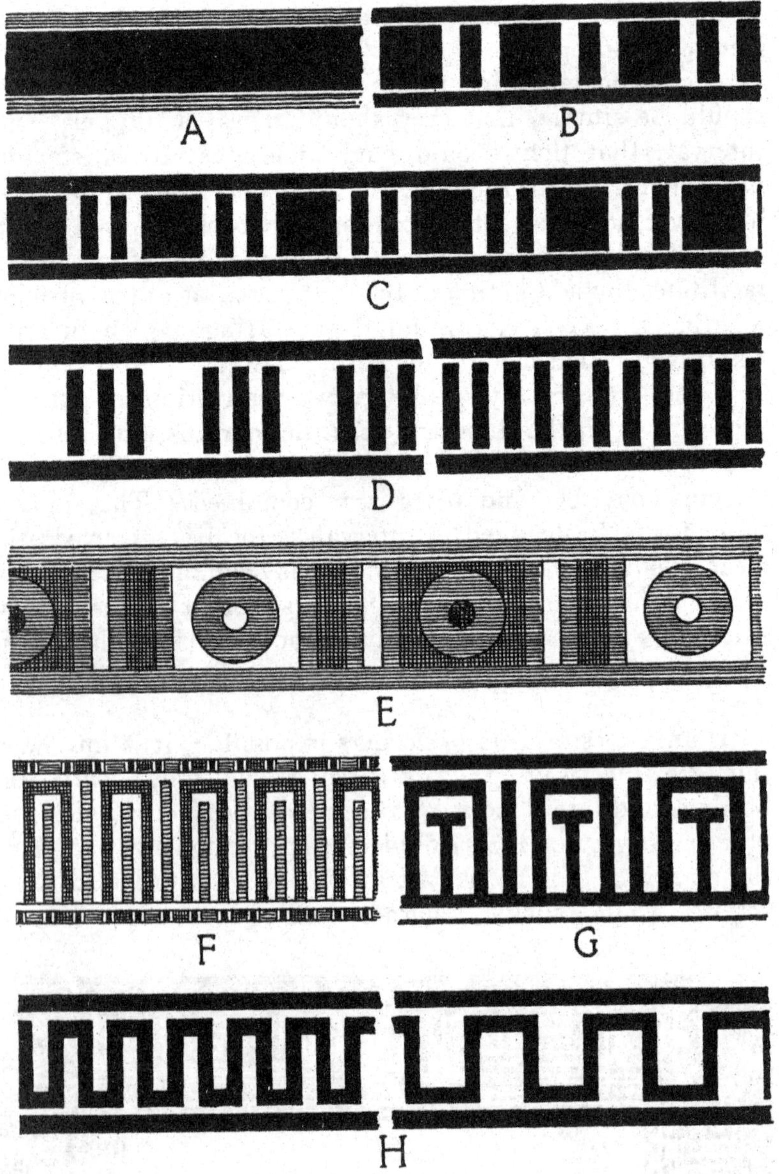

78. A, PLAIN BAND. B, C, D, BAND BROKEN BY CROSS LINES.
E, PAINTED DETAIL ON MUMMY CASE, EGYPTIAN.
F, G, PAINTED DETAIL ON MUMMY CASE, EGYPTIAN: EARLY EXAMPLES OF FRET PATTERNS.
H, SIMPLEST FORM OF CONTINUOUS FRET BORDERS.

their detail: there is no logical end to such description. Besides, detail affects construction only in so far as there must naturally be consistency between the two. And here perhaps a word of warning may not be amiss. Though certain forms of detail happen commonly to have been found in association with certain lines of construction, that fact, while it may serve as a sign-post or a danger-signal to designers new to the road, should not be regarded as in any way a barrier against possible new departures in invention.

Of all conceivable borders the simplest is a line or band (78 A). Next to that comes a series of lines; and here begins design—if it did not begin, before that, with the determination of the thickness of the single line. To apportion the width of parallel lines and their distance apart is already an effort of artistic judgment, as will be at once admitted if we take those lines to represent the light and shadow given by a series of mouldings.

The elementary form of broken border is where cross lines occur at intervals (upright in a horizontal border) as in 78 B, C, and D, in which varied spacings are shown.

Groups of cross lines or any simple spot, patera or other pattern at regular intervals give what is conveniently described as a "stop" border. The Egyptian border (78 E) is an example.

From the equally spaced straight line pattern (78 D) it is but the shortest of steps to the running border (78 H) which brings us to the *continuous* group, of which the fret, simple or elaborate, may be regarded as the full development. The fret is too important a form of border to be passed over. Whether it is to be regarded as an angular and rectilinear form of the symbolic wave, or as a pattern begotten of the mechanism of basket plaiting, and how it happens to be found among Chinese and Mexicans, among Greeks and Fiji islanders—it is not here the place to inquire. But the degree of refinement to which it was carried by the Greeks makes it impossible to overlook it.

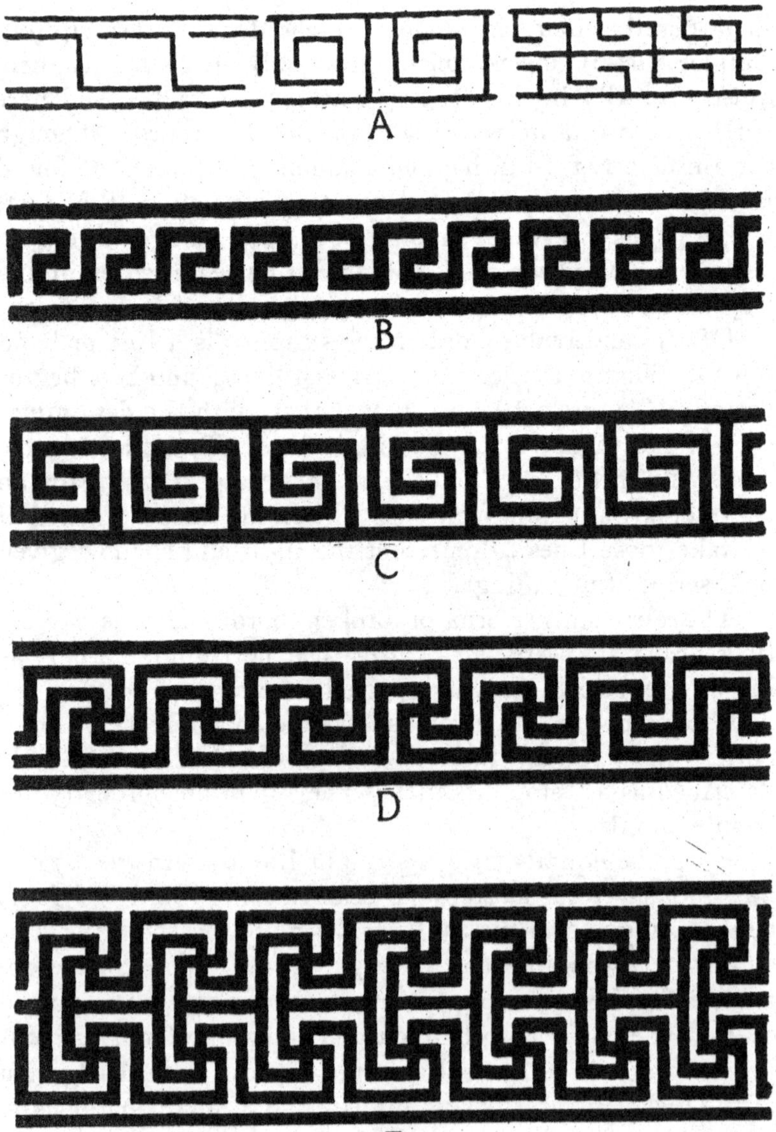

A

B

C

D

E

79. A, FRET BORDERS, EARLY GREEK VASE PAINTINGS.
B, C, FRET BORDERS, GREEK VASE PAINTINGS.
D, FRET BORDER GREEK VASE PAINTINGS, RESULT OF TWO INTERSECTING BANDS.
E, FRET BORDER, GREEK VASE PAINTINGS, DOUBLE VERSION OF D.

The earlier frets consisted of a continuous line or band, but later became more involved. Two bands are employed in 79 D which cross, resulting in the Swastika form; the following design (79 E) is further complicated in being a double version of 79 D. Another example is 80 G.

It is mere futility, of course, to copy the Greek fret and think you are designing, but it remains a "motif" which the ornamentist cannot afford to leave out of account. The fret has qualities of balance, flatness and simplicity, of monotonous rhythm, of reticent yet sufficient strength, which make for many purposes a quite perfect border. It says something for it that the Greeks thought it worthy of so much attention, and, having perfected it, were content to go no further.

It is seen to most advantage in its comparatively simple forms, and when it flows in one direction. It is less happy when it faces both ways (80 A and B), or is broken or disjointed (79 A). It is unhappier still when oblique (81 E and F). The masonry patterns (81 C and D) from Mitla, in Mexico, are very interesting, but have no claim to Greek perfection.

Should the fret include a "stop" of any kind, it is better that this feature should take the square lines uniform with the fret (80 C, D, E, F, G). Elaborate frets in two or three tiers or stories, such as the one framing the central patch or panel in the Roman mosaic on page 247 (250) have their place, perhaps, but it is quite an exceptional one.

A form of broken fret is shown (80 D). It will be seen that the black lines, which are painted, are not continuous; but in effect the fret is not broken, as the white ground gives the united lines of the pattern. This was often done by the Greek vase painters, who deliberately at times painted in the ground spaces, leaving the ornament the colour of the vase.

Oriental frets differ from the Greek in that they are not, as a rule, continuous: see Chinese example (81 G).

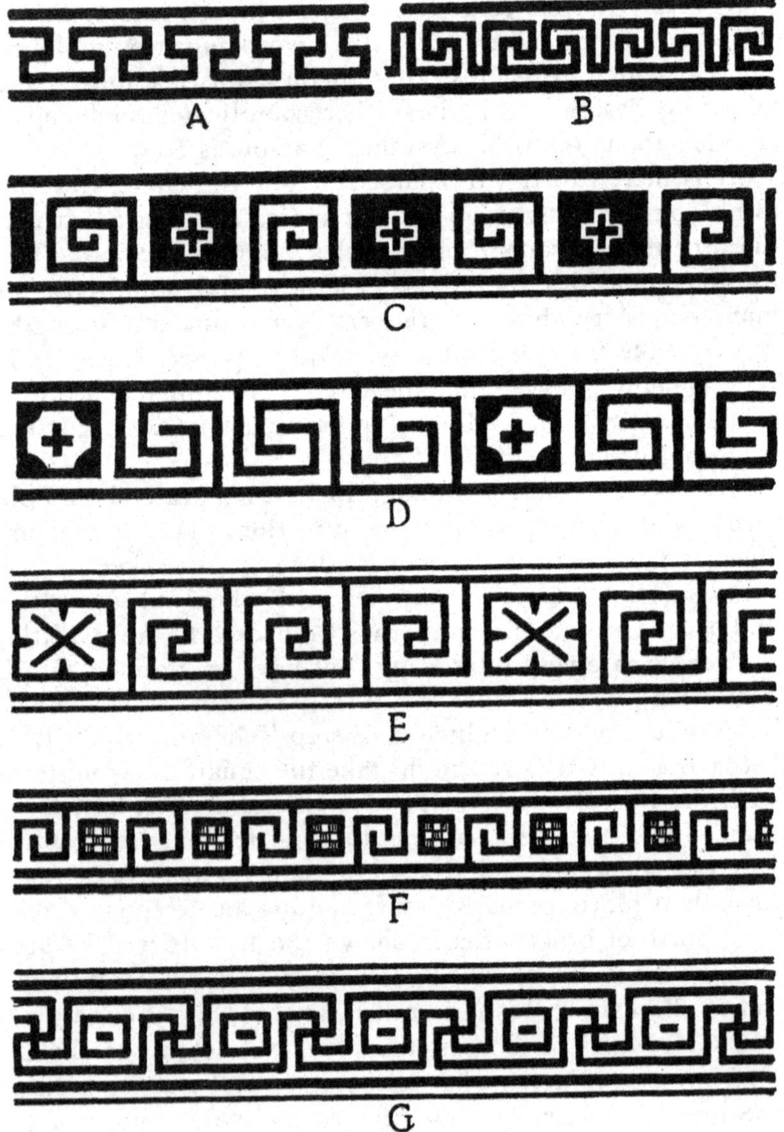

80. PAINTED FRETS FROM GREEK VASES.

A, B, CONTINUOUS FRETS FACING BOTH WAYS.
C, FRET WITH STOPS, RECIPROCAL ARRANGEMENT.
E, F, G, FRETS WITH STOPS, CONTINUOUS IN DIRECTION.

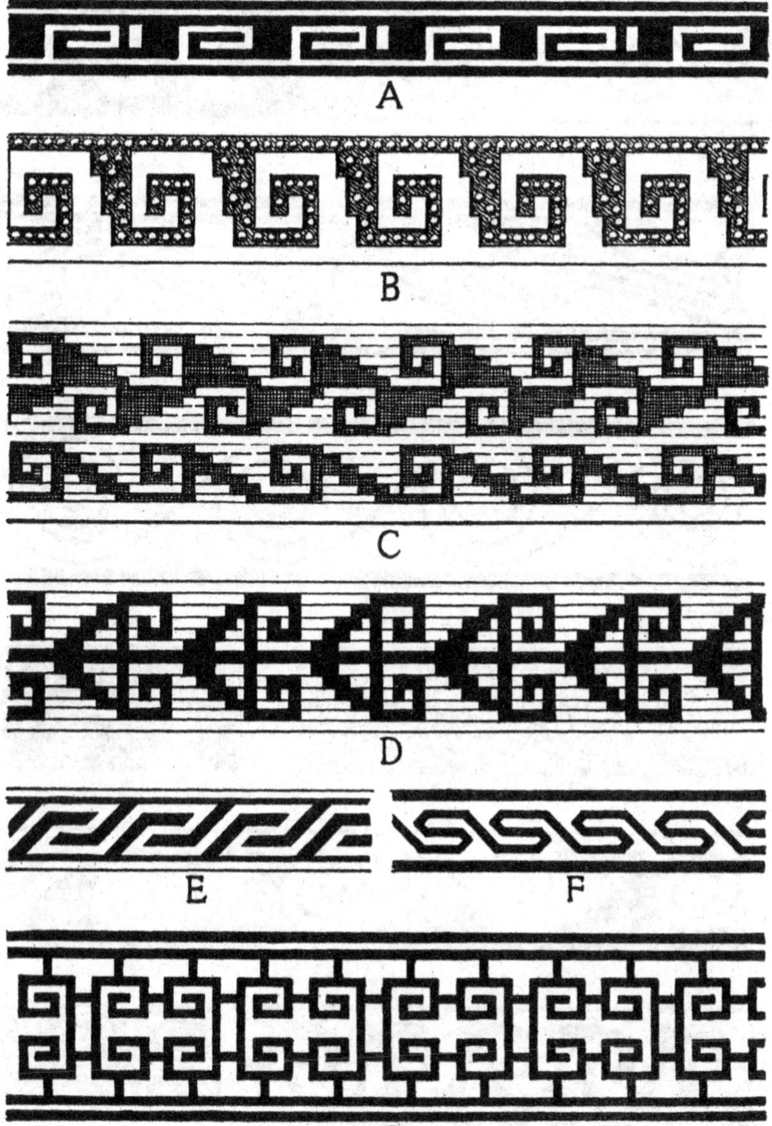

81. A, PAINTED FRET, ANCIENT MEXICO.
B, SCULPTURED FRET, ANCIENT MEXICO.
C, D, FRETS FORMED BY MASONRY, ANCIENT MEXICO.
E, F, PAINTED FRETS, ARABIAN.
G, CHINESE FRET.

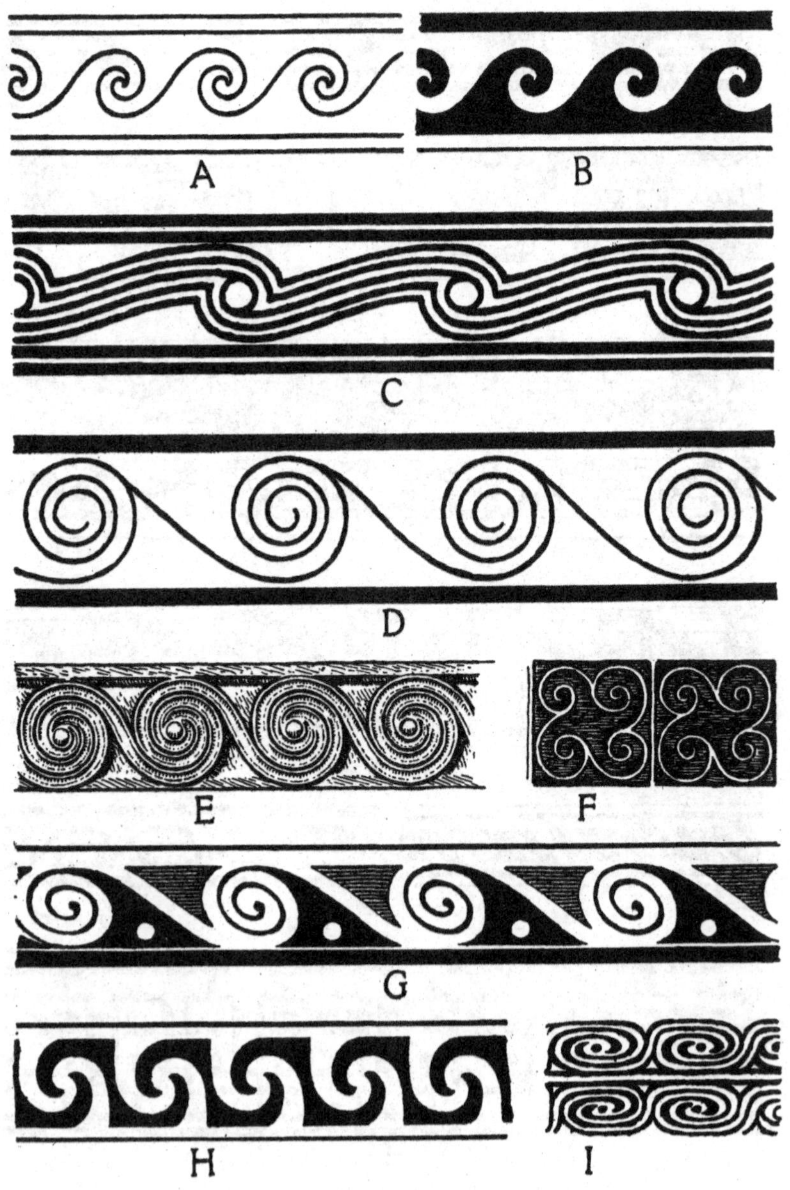

82. THE WAVE OR EVOLUTE SPIRAL.

A, B, GREEK. C, ARCHAIC GREEK, PAINTED.
D, CYPRUS, 800 B.C.
E, STONE CARVING, TREASURY OF ATREUS, MYCENÆ.
F, METAL INLAY, ANGLO-SAXON.
G, PAINTED DETAIL, ANCIENT MEXICO.
H, CARVED DETAIL, ANCIENT MEXICO.
I, SAVAGE ART, NEW GUINEA.

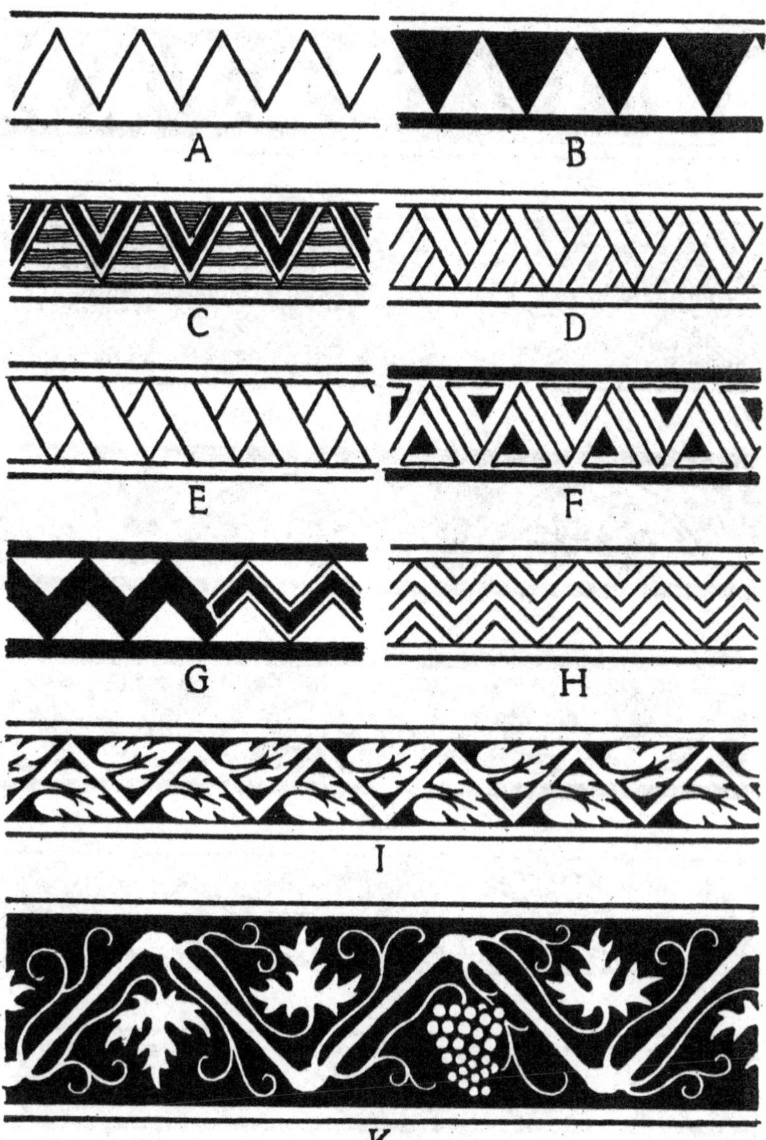

83. THE ZIG-ZAG OR CHEVRON.

A, B, C, D, H, EGYPTIAN MUMMY CASES.
E, CONTINUOUS FOLDING RIBBON.
F, PAINTED DETAIL, SAVAGE ART.
G, CONTINUOUS BORDER.
I, ZIG-ZAG FOLIATED STEM.
K, ZIG-ZAG FOLIATED STEM, GREEK.

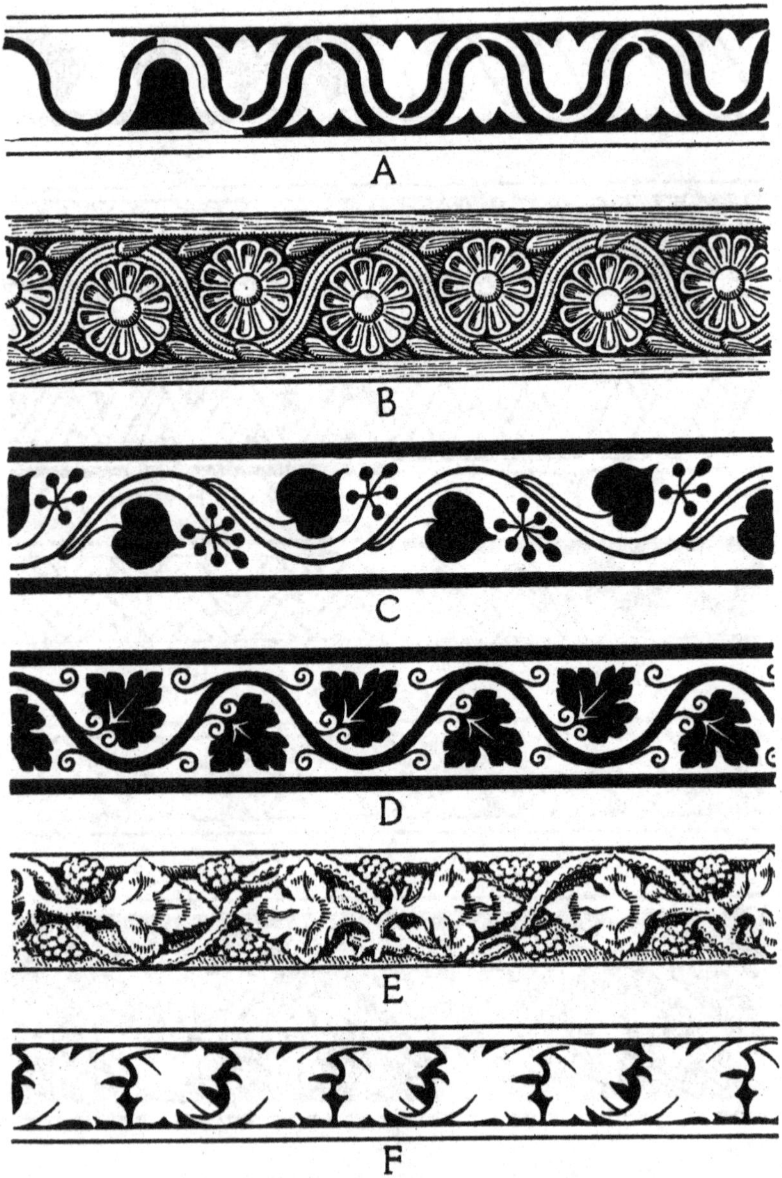

A

B

C

D

E

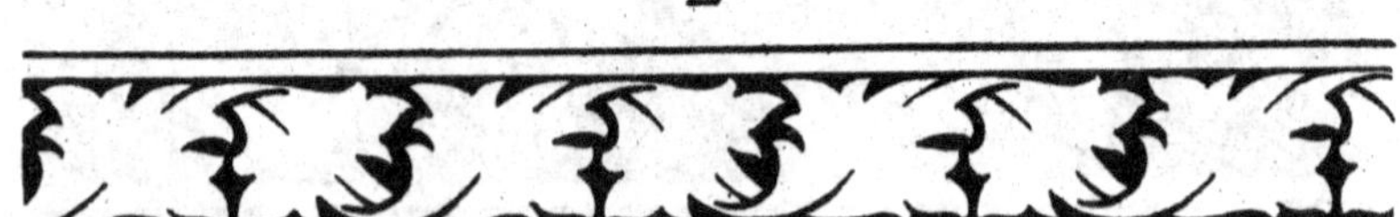

F

84. THE UNDULATE OR WAVED LINE.

A, PAINTED DETAIL.
B, INDIAN STONE CARVING.
C, PAINTED DETAIL, GREEK.
D, WOVEN MATERIAL, COPTIC.
E, GOTHIC CARVING.
F, GOTHIC PAINTING.

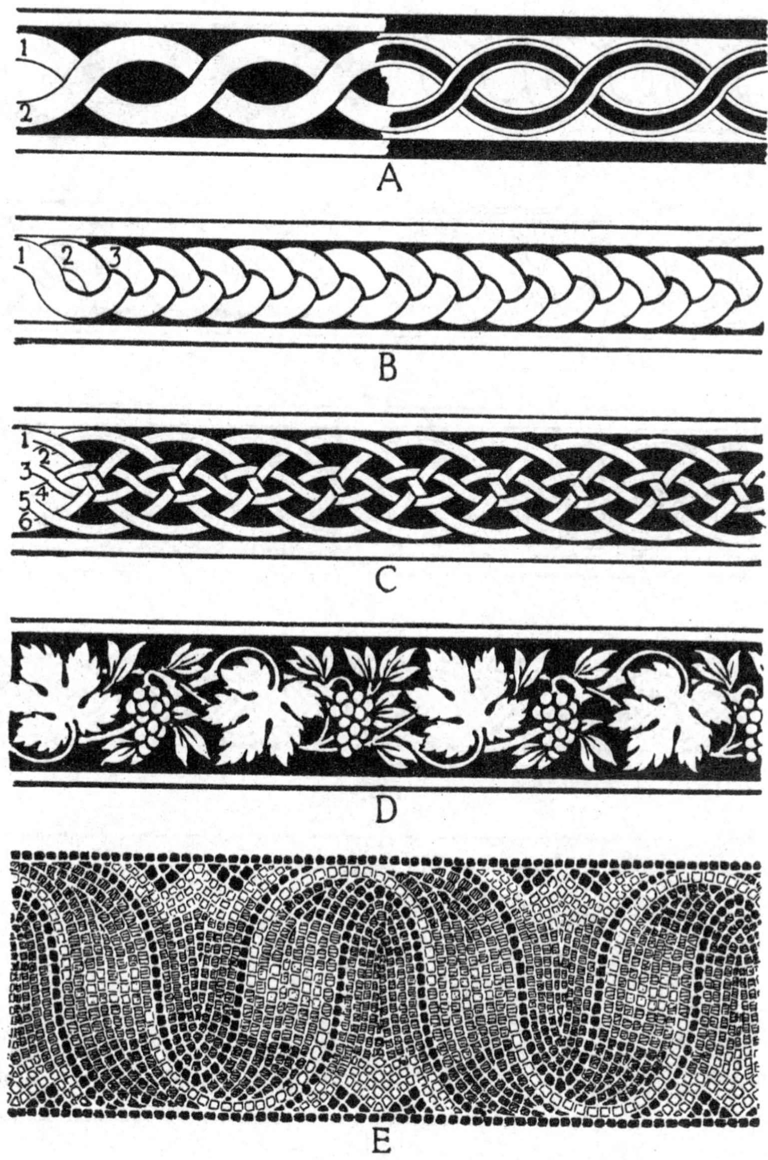

85. INTERLACING OR PLAITED UNDULATES.

A, TWO BANDS OR PLAITS. B, THREE BANDS OR PLAITS.
C, SIX BANDS OR PLAITS. D, FOLIATED INTERLACEMENT, TWO STEMS.
E, RIBBON FORMED OF TWO UNDULATES, ROMAN MOSAIC.

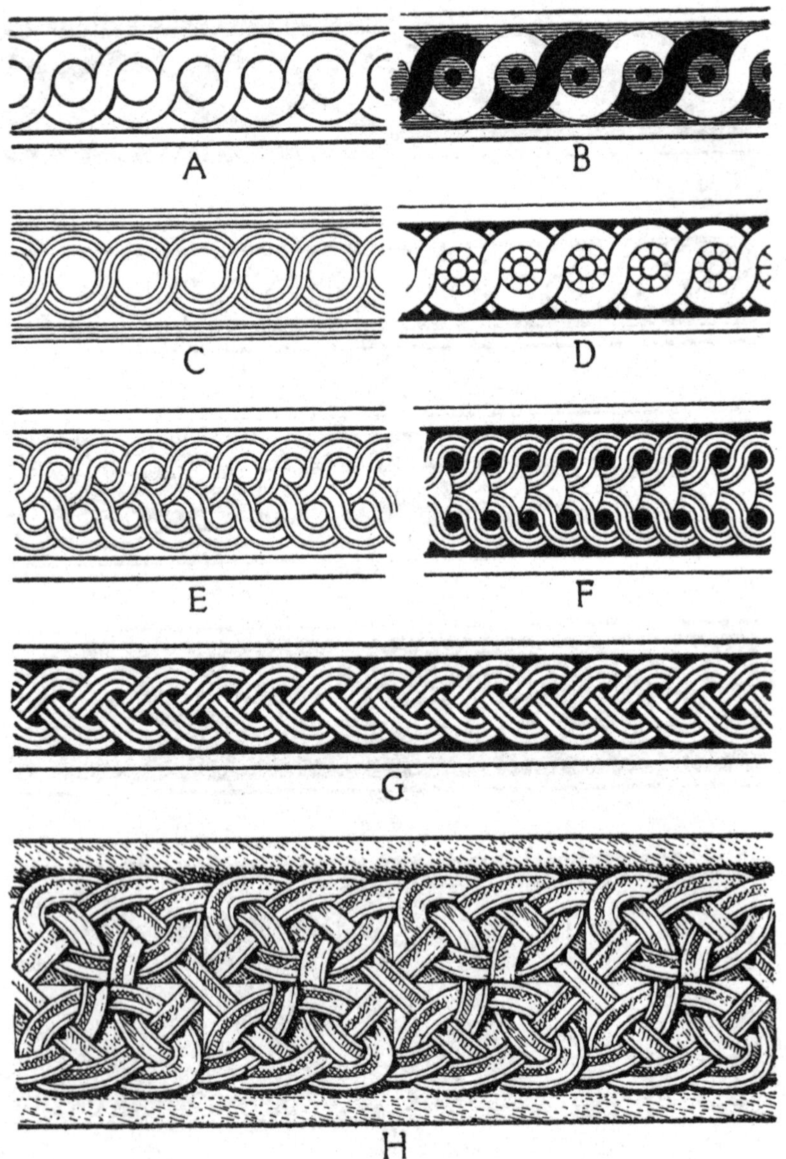

86. THE GUILLOCHE.

A, C, SINGLE GUILLOCHES. B, ASSYRIAN. D, RENAISSANCE.
E, F, DOUBLE GUILLOCHES, GREEK. G, BYZANTINE STONE CARVING.
H, BYZANTINE INTERLACED BORDER, STONE CARVING.

It is as a painted pattern that the fret is most satisfactory. In carving, one set of lines, the vertical or the horizontal as the light may determine, are emphasised by strong shadows in such a way as to distort the design.

Some artistic prejudice against these right lined borders is due to the mechanical way in which they have been drawn —but never by the Greeks. They sketched them always with a delightfully free hand—a very different thing from a careless or incompetent one.

A fret pattern is most easily planned on a trellis of vertical and horizontal lines, which really form the square basis of its construction.

The fret may be regarded as the rectangular form of the overturn wave pattern, or evolute spiral (94 A). The evolute is also known as the "Vitruvian scroll," and, as in the case of the fret, appears in many phases of classic and savage art, as illustrated on page (62).

The zig-zag, or chevron, is the straight line form of the simple wave-line, or undulate. Illustrations on page 63 (83) show examples from various sources.

The waved or undulate line, which forms the basis of most scroll ornament, is obviously a softened form of the zig-zag, and, like the fret and the evolute, its employment has been universal. For various renderings see 84. The undulate is usually reinforced by other detail and seldom appears by itself, the effect being somewhat thin and open. Where two or more lines or bands are employed, they are more satisfactory. Reference to Byzantine and Celtic examples will show how interesting interlacement can be (85 and 86).

The interlaced form known as the guilloche is generally based on circles, and appears in Chaldæan and Greek art. It is essentially geometric in construction (86).

Instances of less obvious geometric interlacing occur in Celtic ornament (87), delightfully intricate at times, but, however mysterious, coherent always, to be traced by any-

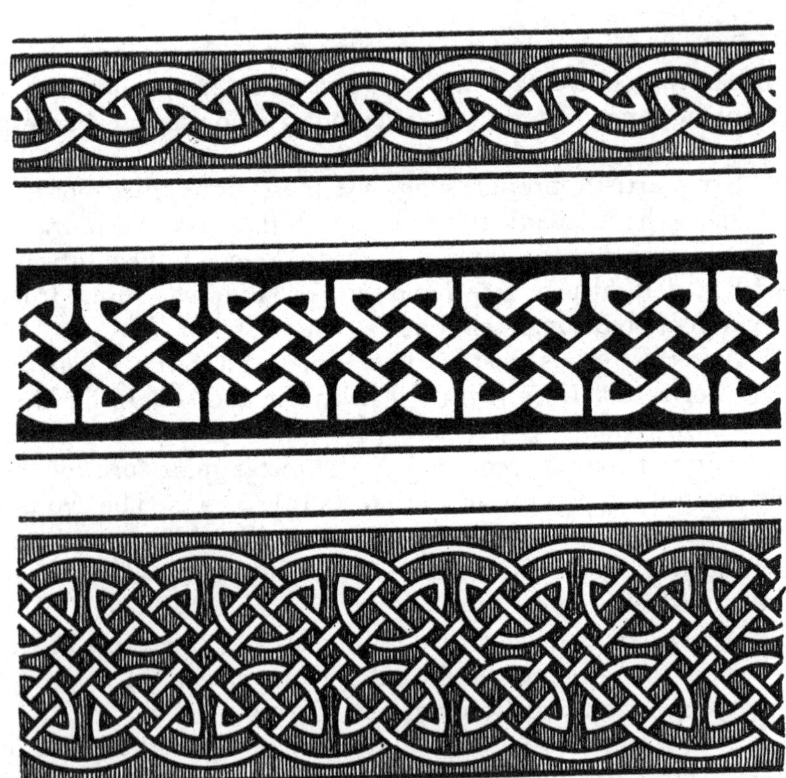

87. INTERLACED BORDERS—CELTIC.

one who has the patience, throughout their convolutions. In Anglo-Saxon or Celtic ornament, and its Byzantine original, are to be found a variety of interlacing borders, in which there are not merely continuous bands that are interlaced, but, as it were, independent links, forming chains of ornament rather than plaits (86-87).

A simple chain pattern makes rather a poor border: it is weak at the edges—just where it should be strong. Ornamental links, however, can be made to keep in a line with the margins; and they are—if not so interesting as the more flowing interlacings—steadier, which is sometimes an

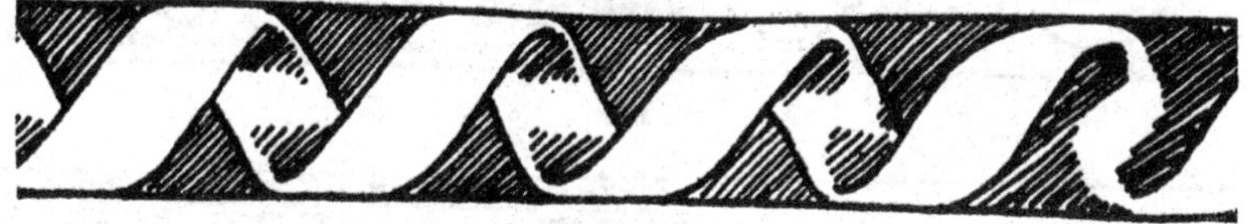

88. FROM CHEVRON TO WAVE.

advantage. Generally speaking, the most pleasing interlacing patterns are those in which the lines are rounded; but straight-lined and angular straps may be quite happily associated.

Merely angular and straight-lined interlacings compare disadvantageously with the fret.

The waving strap (88) may be evolved from the zig-zag or from the wave.

A strap bent alternately in the vertical and horizontal direction (89) brings us, by the softening of the lines of the turnover, at all events in the direction of the wave.

There soon comes a point in the design of the wave-pattern at which further development can only take place in one direction, namely, in the way of branching. That is how the spiral scroll occurs. The spirals may be regarded as so many branches from the parent wave stem. In 90 B is indicated how the undulate line that forms the main stem is determined by adjacent circles. In fact this really happens. The Indian metal-worker has no drawn design to follow—he works on a local tradition—and in this instance the method was to strike or scribe a series of circles, and then to go direct to work with his tools, forming flowers or other

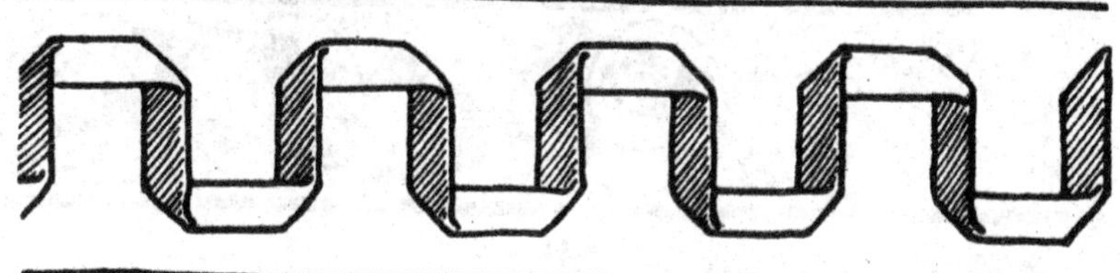

89. BENT STRAP—TRANSITION FROM RECTANGULAR TO WAVE FORMS.

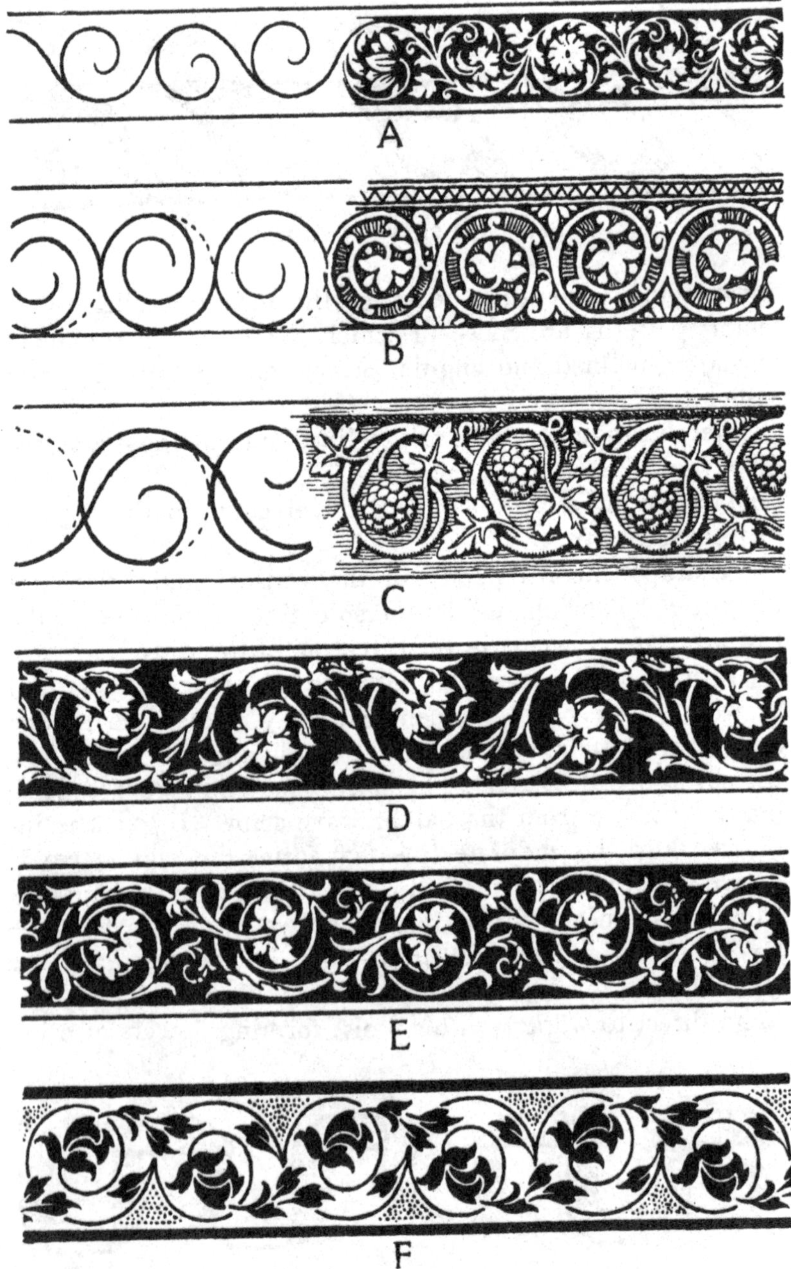

90. THE SCROLL BORDER.

A, THE UNDULATE LINE WITH SPIRAL BRANCHING. ITALIAN RENAISSANCE.
B, SCROLL PATTERN BASED ON ADJACENT CIRCLES. ENGRAVING ON METAL, INDIAN.
C, CONSTRUCTION AS B, WOOD CARVING. ENGLISH, EARLY SEVENTEENTH CENTURY.
D, RENAISSANCE SCROLL BORDER, UNITY IMPARTED BY DETAIL BREAKING ACROSS STEMS.
E, CONTINUOUS SCROLL PATTERN, THE RUNNING LINE EMERGING FROM SCROLL CENTRES.
F, SCROLL BORDER WITH SPANDRELS OCCUPIED BY DIFFERENT COLOUR TO GENERAL BACKGROUND.

91. LEAVES DESIGNED TO FIT SPACES.

details in the centres of the circles and in the spandrels, and connecting them, when desirable, with the stems. This simple method ensures equal distribution of detail. Possibly the native worker does not trouble to use geometric instruments, and draws the circles freehand, but evidently adherence to exact geometric form is not a consideration.

A similar method is apparent in the work of the English

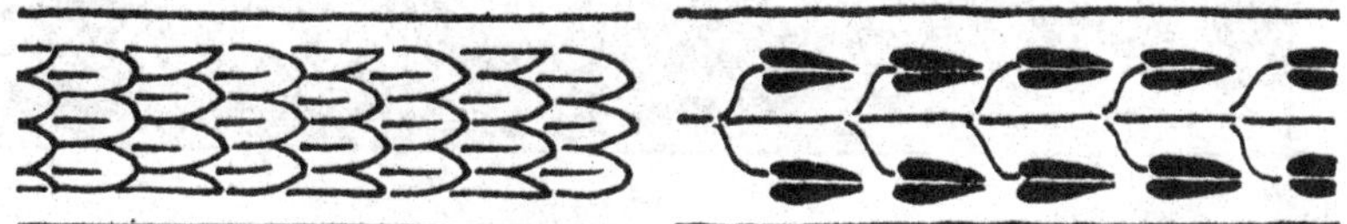

92. PARALLELISM IN BORDER DESIGN.

carver (90 C), who also was probably working from tradition and not from a special design. It will be observed that the scroll branches cross the main stem, imparting strength and unity to the design. Unity is also achieved (90 D) by carrying the pistil-extensions from the flowers across the stem lines.

A departure from the usual principle of the undulate line with branching scrolls is shown (90 E), where the continuous stem is taken through the scroll branches, a characteristic of Salembier, a French designer of the eighteenth century.

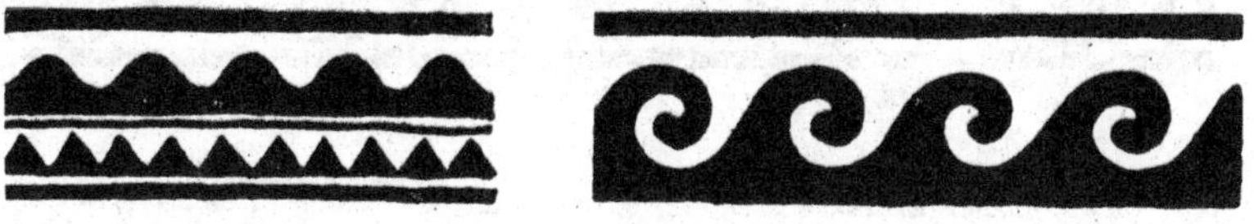

93. BORDERS WITH STRONG AND WEAK SIDE.

A B

C

D

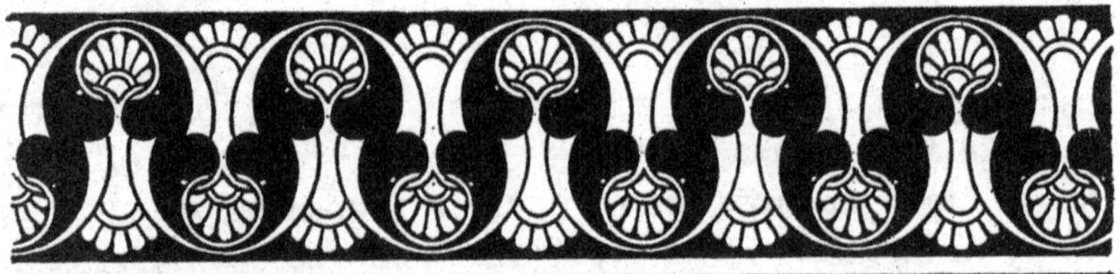

E

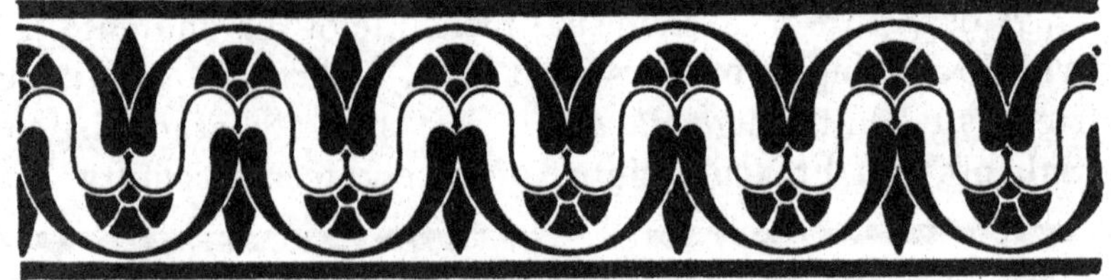

F

94. A, B, THE CONTINUOUS FRET AND EQUIVALENT IN CURVED LINES.
C, D, BORDER PATTERNS BASED ON B, WOOD CARVING. ENGLISH, EARLY 17TH CENT.
E, F, BORDER PATTERNS BASED ON B, GREEK PAINTED ORNAMENT.

With the development of the branches from the main wave-stem into leaves and flowers occurs a danger—not always avoided even by the Greeks—of the leafage looking too natural for the stem which bears it, or of the line of growth appearing too arbitrary for the leafage upon it (84 C). The great mistake is to halt, or to seem to halt, between two opinions. The difficulty is happily solved in Gothic work by deliberately designing leaves to fit the spaces between stem and margins (91).

A wave line accentuates, of course, the parallelism of the marginal lines—and this is further emphasised by details running parallel with it and with them as in the arrangement of leaves in borders 84 C, D, and E. Parallelism can also be achieved by filling the spandrel-shaped ground spaces with a different colour (90 F). But parallelism is as much a matter of detail as of construction—sometimes even more so (92).

A division in the parallel direction, such as results from a wave or zig-zag line (93), gives an opportunity of strengthening one side of the border by means of stronger colour. The more fully developed wave in the same diagram gives a perfect counterchange pattern.

Another system upon which the unit of a design repeats on both sides of the border, but not opposite, may be compared with the "drop repeat." The lower part of 94 B is an exact turnover of the upper, shifted along half the width of the repeat. Examples of this form of arrangement are given on the same illustration.

The counterchange pattern (95) is clearly devised upon the diagonal lines of the zig-zag, though it repeats also upon the dotted upright lines. The upright tendency gives it the effect, no longer of a flowing, but of a steady pattern; and we arrive at length at a form of pattern which turns over undisguisedly on lines at right angles to the margins. From this to the interrupted or broken borders, which form, as I said, a class distinct from the flowing, is only a step.

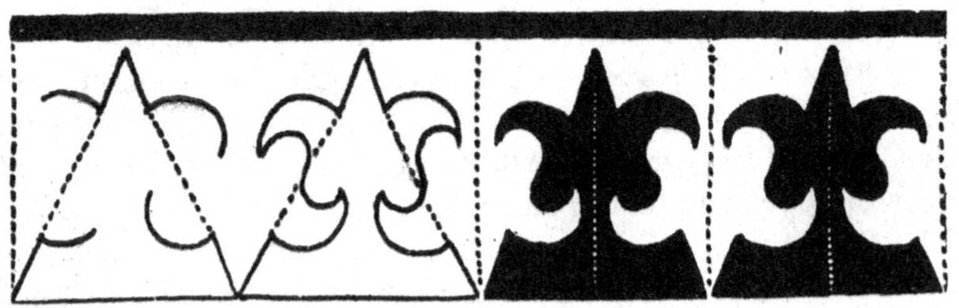

95. THE COUNTERCHANGE BORDER ON ZIG-ZAG LINES.

There is first the intermittent border (96), which makes not even a pretence of continuity, the unit of design recurring at set intervals with plain space between. It is among

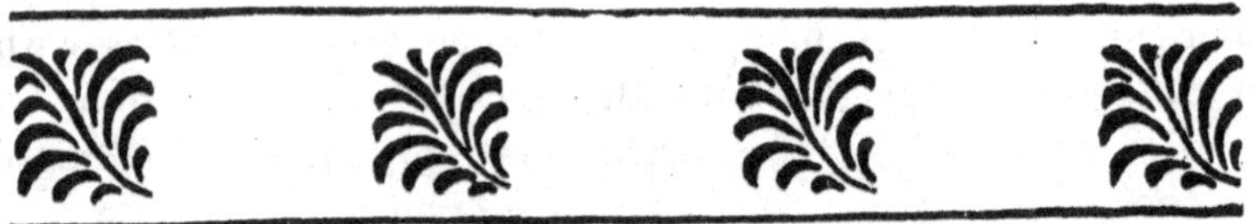

96. INTERMITTENT BORDER PATTERN.

borders what a sprig pattern is among diapers. A yet simpler form of broken border is that in which the space is broken up into equal areas alternately light and dark (97), equivalent to the chequer in allover patterns.

97. EQUIVALENT TO CHEQUER IN ALLOVER PATTERN.

98. ALTERNATING FEATURES.

Barely one move further, and we get alternate spaces filled each in a different way (98), the contrast being no longer between the masses of light and dark, or ornament and plain ground, but between simpler and more elaborate features. Geometric borders of the kind illustrated in diagram 99, counterchanging as it happens (cf. 97), are exceedingly useful, both because of their steadiness and their modesty.

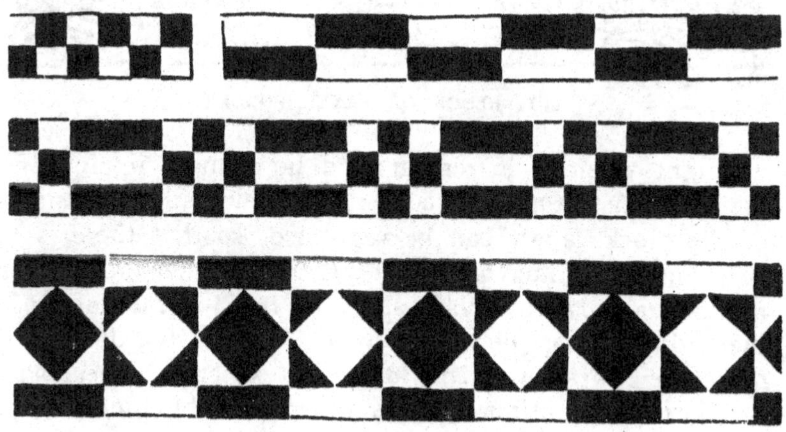

99. COUNTERCHANGING GEOMETRIC BORDERS.

Some of the borders last illustrated are, as it were, cut up into blocks. One very useful device in border design is simply to break the plain band with blocks of ornament (rosettes and what not) at regular intervals. Or it may be the parallel lines of mouldings, etc., of which the flow is interrupted (100). This occurs commonly in Gothic architecture. It is a plan frank to the point sometimes of brutality, but not necessarily brutal—witness the border of cherubs so dear to Andrea della Robbia.

The " block " in its severest form is a sort of panel in miniature (101), and the panels sometimes included in a frieze design may be regarded as magnified blocks. In either case the idea is to provide stopping points and so to steady the effect. The use of something of the kind is very

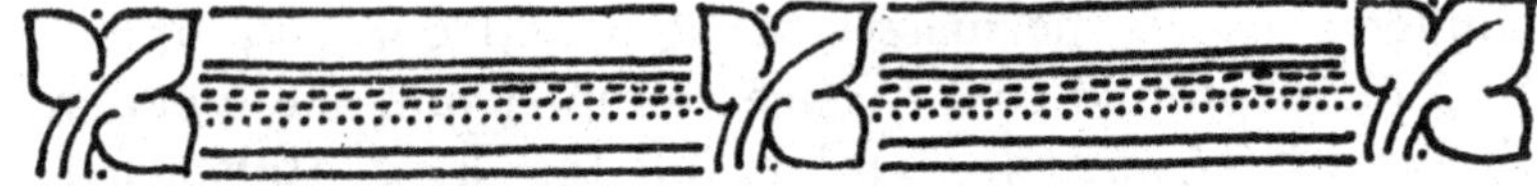

100. BLOCK BORDER.

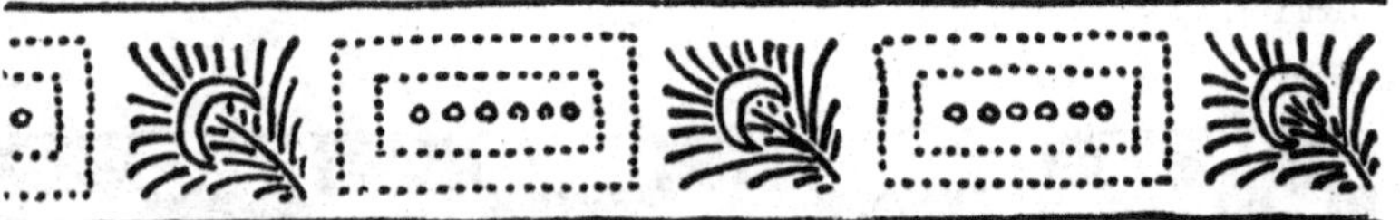

101. BLOCK OR PANEL BORDER.

apparent when it is remembered how much it simplifies the difficulty of turning a corner, and how easily the distance of the blocks apart can be regulated, so that there is no occasion to contract or spread out the ornament to make it fit unequal spaces. Plain space or lines of mouldings or mere diaper may be ruthlessly cut short; but it is only quite the lowest organisms of design which will bear such mutilation. Continuous lines interrupted by blocks often have the appearance of running behind them (100 and 102). In the case of a fully developed pattern like the fret (77), it would be cruel to mutilate it; the stopping places must be accommodated to the running design.

When a border is made up of alternating blocks (101), say of freer and more formal design, it is not easy to say which may have been the starting point. In the diagram (103) inset opposite, mere diaper assumes exceptional importance, and the panel, stop, or block takes almost the aspect of background.

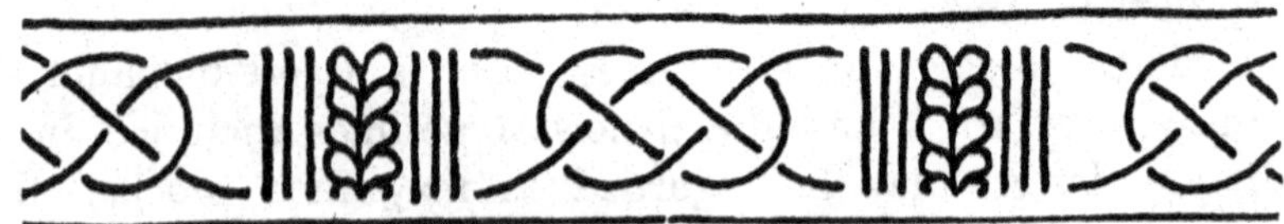

102. CONTINUOUS LINES, AS IT WERE, DISAPPEARING BEHIND UPRIGHT FEATURES.

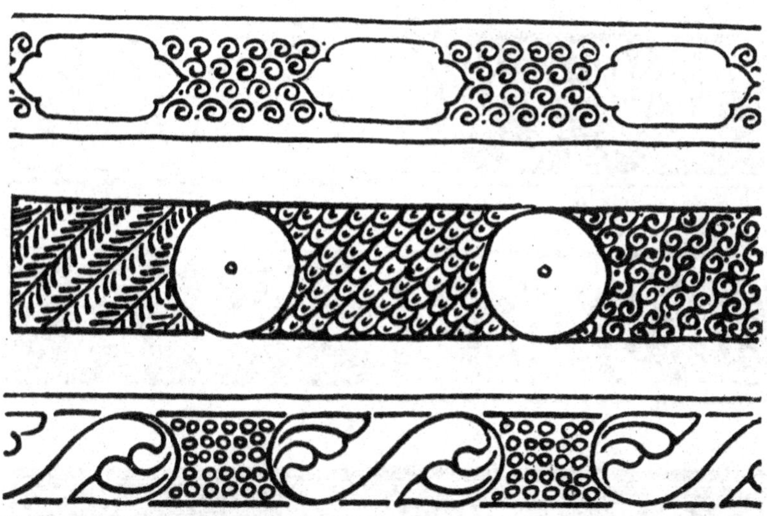

103. ORIENTAL USE OF DIAPERED INTERSPACES.

A sure way of stopping the flow of a border is, not merely to introduce lines crossing it, but to make the pattern *turn-over* on those lines as in 104 A and B, where the wave becomes a scalloped stem bursting into bud. In 104 C and D the ∽-shaped scroll, itself made up of two inverted parts, turns over on itself, and forms the base line from which upsprings a bi-symmetrical growth. We have here a typical form of construction especially useful where the repeat is necessarily short. But the ∽-shaped scroll does not lend itself readily to foliation, unless we abandon the principle of growth—a departure from nature unpardonable in proportion as the detail of the foliage approaches the natural.

The ∽-scrolls have only to be planned on the zig-zag (104 E and F) to give a border of which each margin is equally pronounced. That is even more plainly the case when the zig-zagging ∽-lines are, as it were, crossed by themselves (104 G). If the depth of the border allows, the design can, of course, be turned over on a line midway between the margins (104 H).

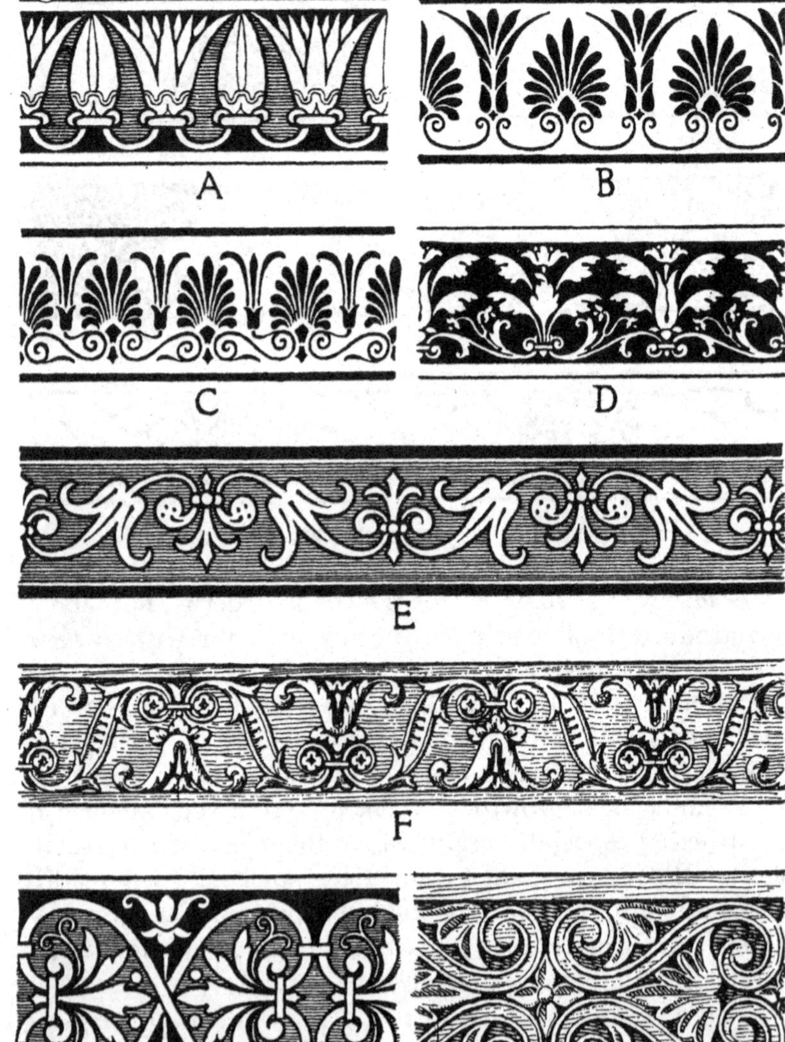

104. CRESTING PATTERNS.

A, ASSYRIAN. B, C, GREEK. D, ITALIAN RENAISSANCE.
E, BORDER PATTERN OF OPPOSING ∽-SCROLLS.
F, WOOD CARVING, EARLY FRENCH RENAISSANCE.
G, BORDER PATTERN OF CROSSING ∽-SCROLLS.
H, VERTICAL AND HORIZONTAL OPPOSITION OF ∽-SCROLLS, WOODCARVING. ENGLISH, EARLY SEVENTEENTH CENTURY.

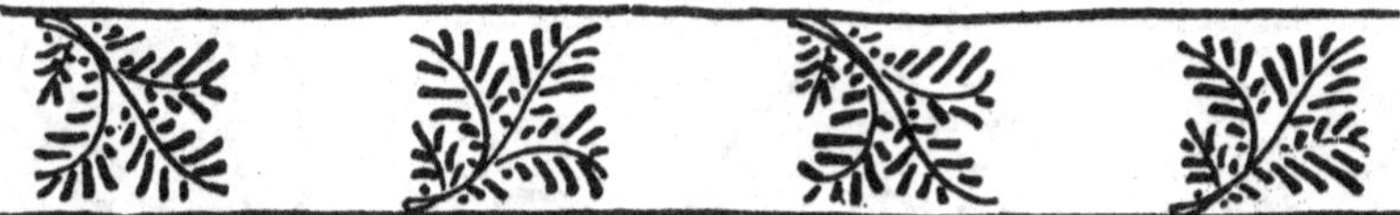

105. BORDER GROWING ALTERNATELY FROM EITHER SIDE.

Yet another plan is, as it were, to turn over (but not opposite) a design which grows from one of the marginal lines. This amounts to the same thing as a pattern growing alternately from either margin (105).

It has been assumed, thus far, that a border is enclosed within marginal lines. That is sometimes not the case; but enclosing lines are understood, if not expressed; the design acknowledges its confines; otherwise it would hardly fulfil the function of a border or a frame. A frame is of course a border, the inner line of which is often more strongly marked than the outer. Another form of border which emphatically acknowledges one margin or boundary line is a cresting. Fringes again, valances, and scalloped edgings depend on one margin for their rigidity. All such borders are strong on the side from which they grow or hang, weak on the outer edge, though such weakness may be to some extent counteracted by weight of detail on that side and by acknowledgment of

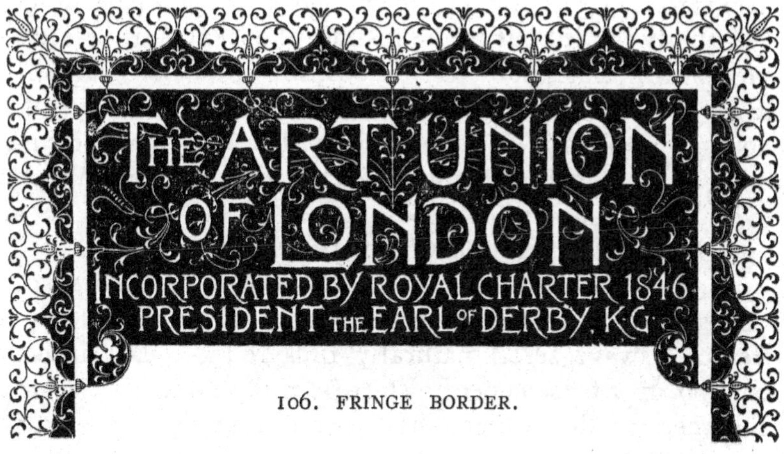

106. FRINGE BORDER.

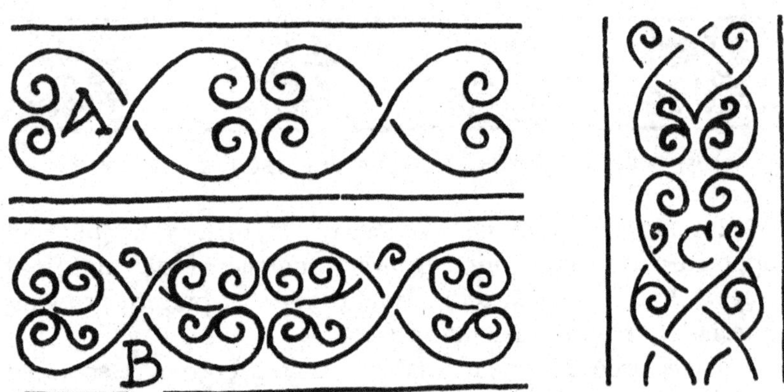

107. THE PLAN OF THE BORDER IN RELATION TO ITS DIRECTION.

the straight line (106). The softening and weakening of effect of a fringed outline needs no pointing out. Even in the case of a border within double marginal lines the strong side is naturally (but not inevitably) that from which the pattern grows.

It is not so much the construction as the detail of a border which is affected by its position—upright like a pilaster, or horizontal like a frieze; but the lines of growth naturally depend to some extent upon its direction. Here again the lines possible may be quite inappropriate to the situation. The scrolls, for example, shown at A in diagram 107 might eventually launch out in the manner shown at B or C according to the horizontal or vertical position of the border. Still, there are very clear reasons for the choice, let us say, of a flowing scroll for a horizontal border, and for a central upright for a perpendicular one. In fact, the central stem in a horizontal border needs almost to be waved; in an upright one it often needs to be straight or nearly so.

It stands to reason that borders which have to turn a corner must be designed to turn. A flowing pattern such as a fret or a wave scroll naturally runs round. But it need not. It may be schemed to start from the centre of the strip and meet at the corners—or to start from the corners and

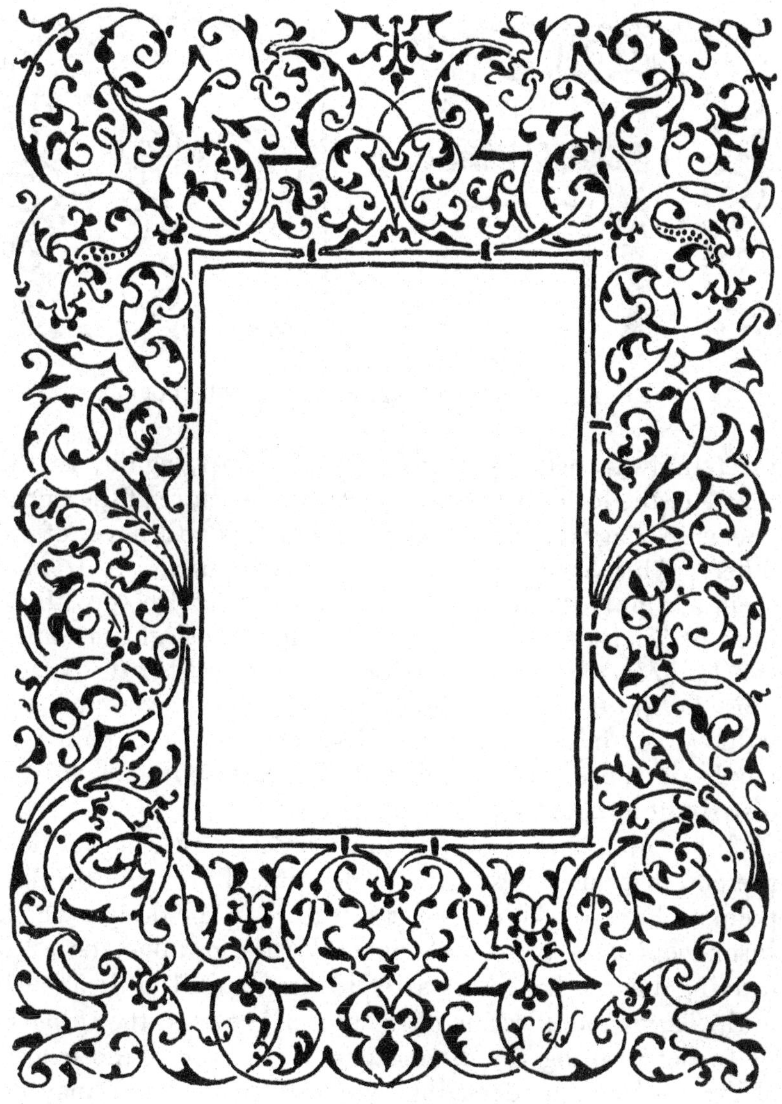

108. FRAME DESIGN, THE PATTERN TURNED OVER, BUT OTHERWISE NOT REPEATING.

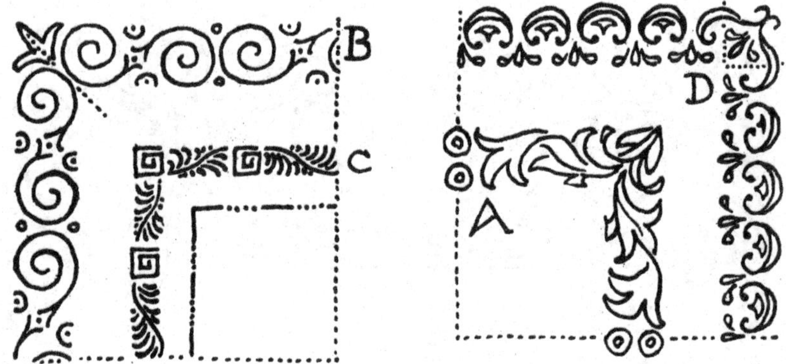

109. THE BORDER IN RELATION TO THE CORNER.

meet midway between them. It may start, again, in the centre of the lower border and meet in the centre of the upper one as in diagram 108, one-half of which is a turnover of the other. This hardly amounts to repeated pattern. It may seem a simple thing thus to sketch a pattern freely without heed or hindrance of repetition, but it is no slight tax upon the designer's faculty of distribution. For, either the design must be quite equally spread, so as to give very much the value of a tint, or else some leading lines and points of emphasis must be determined, and this, without orderly distribution, is not an easy thing to do.

It has been shown already that borders which do not flow present in some cases little or no difficulty at the turning points. Except where there is a feature in the design which just occupies the corner (a " block " for example—109, C) a framing border has necessarily to be planned with a view to the happy modification of the unit of repeat at the corners.

In determining the dimensions of the repeat, the length of the border or borders, into which it must divide, may be reckoned, either from the line which marks the mitre at the corner (109, B) or from the cross line where one border would intersect the other (109, D). The design may turn over at the corner on the diagonal or on square lines.

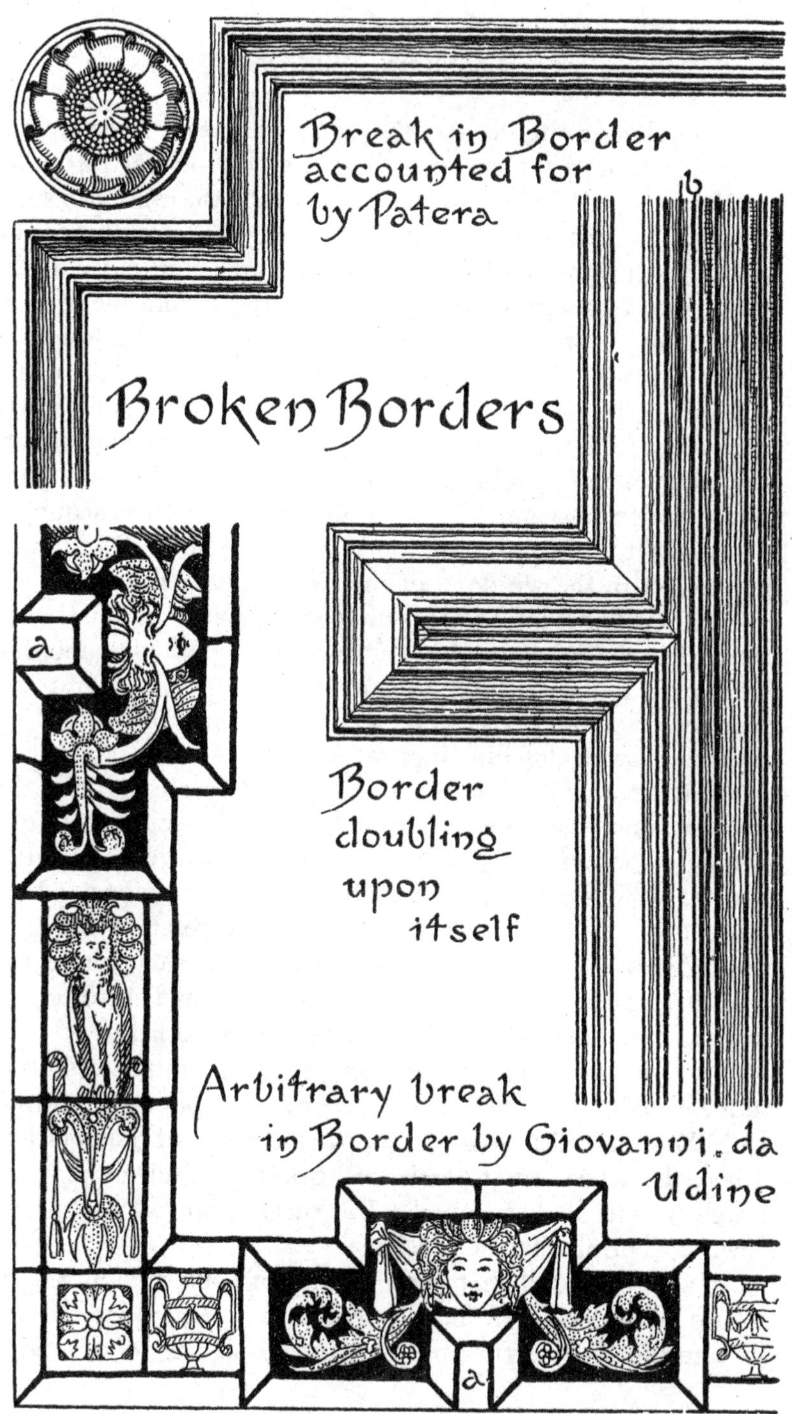

110. BREAKS IN THE BORDER.

The shorter the border, the more important becomes the consideration of the corner. That may be the starting point of the design. Indeed, it may constitute the whole design, which then turns over both upon the diagonal mitre lines and upon the upright and horizontal lines which would divide the panel into four equal parts (109, A). Apart from the corner, there may be breaks in the border (110) which (unless it is of the simplest lines merely) have naturally to be taken into account in its design. A break in the border is sufficiently accounted for by a patera or some such device. The deliberate snipping out of spaces, as at *a a* (110), so as to form gaps round which to bend the border and thus break the sequence of straight lines, needs some justification. Da Udine adopted it in the windows of the Certosa near Florence.

A circular border presents no more difficulty than a simple strip of given length: the length of the repeat is at the discretion of the designer: he may divide the space into any number of equal parts. The design may be constructed on radiating or on flowing lines or on both.

In the common case of a series of concentric borders, the two systems may conveniently be used to counteract one another—the radiating lines are of course steadier. Flowing borders may flow, if need be, in opposite directions. As a rule, it is well that there should be some relation between the repeats of concentric borders—at all events where the repeat is apparent. They need not by any means be of equal length; but they should divide one into the other.

The plan of a pattern (border or filling) influences or is influenced by the detail of its design. The one is bound up with the other. In settling a plan, one thinks of the detail to come; in determining detail, one bears in mind the plan on which it is to be distributed. But there is no rule to be laid down excepting that of consistency.

It will be found that certain lines of construction are in accord with certain forms of ornament. Rigid detail goes with formal geometric lines, relatively natural foliage with free growth; and between those two extremes there are infinite gradations from severe to formal treatment, determining, or determined by, the lines of distribution.

But neither Arab on the one hand nor Japanese on the other, neither Greek nor Goth nor artist of the Renaissance, has settled anything for us beyond the necessity of correspondence between detail and its distribution.

How to do it is our affair: we have the experience of the past to guide us; but to adopt just what has been found to answer well enough is the last shift of laziness—if it is not mere dullness. The happy conjunction of this detail with that construction is evidence of *their conformity* only, not of the incongruity of other combinations personal to the artist. It is possible to fry without bread crumbs.

VIII. PRACTICAL PATTERN PLANNING.

Possible and practicable lines of pattern construction—Lines often fixed for the designer—Conditions of production affect plan—Triangular plan, oriental—Rectangular plan, western—Relation of one plan to the other —of triangular and octagonal repeat to rectangular—Possibilities of the diamond—Design regulated by proportions of repeat.

THE lines of the square or of the parallelogram, of the diamond or of the triangle, are naturally, as a glance at our illustrations will show, conspicuous in geometric design; and, even where they do not make up the pattern altogether, they constantly make part of it. The design opposite (111) is, for example, in its main lines only a translation into waving lines of the simple hexagon and star pattern on page 19. But these same square, diamond, and triangular lines underlie also repeated pattern of the freest kind. And it is because they are the basis of all repeated pattern that it behoves the designer to acquaint himself with certain simple geometric principles, as indispensable to him as a knowledge of superficial anatomy to the figure-draughtsman.

The fact is that to many arts, or to proficiency in them, and certainly to proficiency in pattern design, there goes a modicum of science—without which the merely practical conditions imposed by the necessity of repetition, and especially of repetition within a given area, are hardly to be overcome.

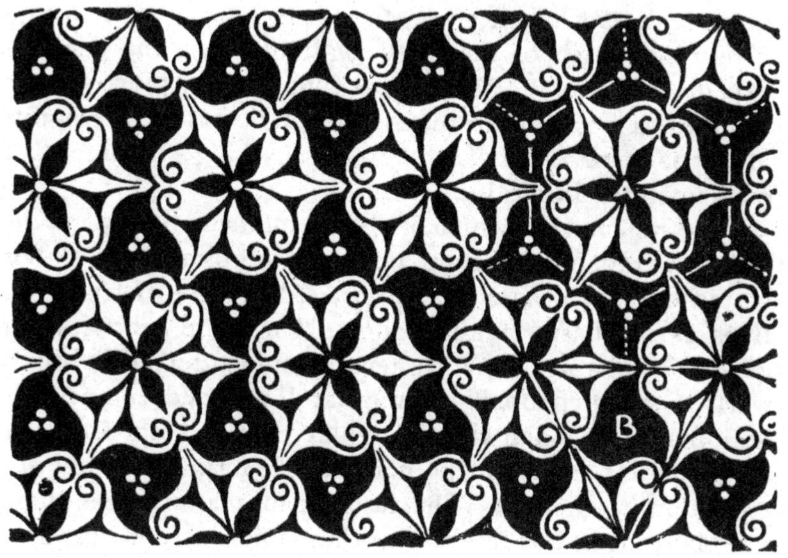

III. CURVILINEAR DEVELOPMENT OF DIAGRAM 26.

The art of the pattern designer is, not merely in devising pretty combinations of form, but in scheming them upon lines not of his choice at all, mapped out for him, on the contrary, by the conditions of his work, by no means always those which he would have chosen for himself as the most promising. His task is to get beautiful results out of no matter what unpromising conditions. Then indeed he may claim to be an artist.

I have been at some pains to lay down the lines on which pattern may *possibly* be constructed, but the possible lines are not in all cases practicable. Conditions of production have to be taken into account, and they affect not merely the character of design, but its plan also.

A necessary preliminary to design is the determining of the lines on which it shall be distributed—to plan it, that is to say. The possible lines are few, and the more clearly the artist realises what they are, the easier it will be for him to determine which of them are available, and the one it is expedient to adopt. Mechanical conditions or practical considerations may so limit his choice that he has no alternative, and it is mere waste of time to do anything but proceed at once upon the inevitable course.

The system upon which of old the mathematically-minded Oriental craftsman built up, out of the simplest units, elaborate schemes of ornament, encouraged the use of triangular lines as the basis of his design. The more practical and expeditious habit of the Western manufacturer leads him to work more often upon rectangular lines, and compels the designer to abandon the triangular basis, except in so far as triangular units can be made to conform to rectangular repetition (see below). The designer for manufacture, therefore, is restricted as the handworker is not. He works, however, on the old lines still—manufacture following constantly in the footsteps of handicraft.

We put down early methods of design to tradition. But traditions grew out of ways of working; and we find ourselves to-day using expedients of design which, if they had not

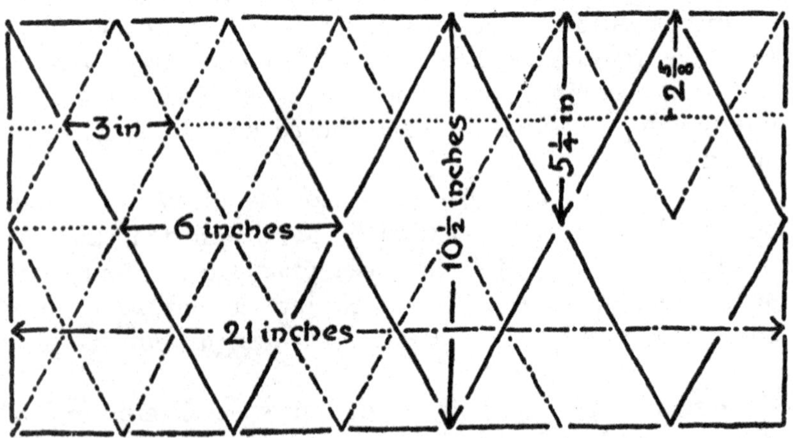

112. DIAGRAM SHOWING RELATION OF EQUILATERAL TRIANGLES AND HEXAGONS TO SQUARE REPEAT.

resulted from the simple contrivances of elementary handicraft, would most certainly have been evolved out of the more complex conditions of modern manufacture. The square lines, for example, given us by the most rudimentary form of tapestry are equally imposed by the power loom.

It is on square lines that we have mainly to work, and our design has to be considered in relation to the rectangular repeat which the conditions of to-day determine.

The possibilities of working upon other plans are limited. To adapt, for example, the equilateral triangle or octagon to a square repeat measuring let us say 21 inches either way, is possible only on a scale which makes it not often worth doing.

Take 21 inches as the base of an equilateral triangle. It will be found to measure from base to apex 18 inches. The difference between 21 and 18 is 3, the greatest common measure of both. This gives us an equilateral triangle of 3 inches from point to point as the largest which will repeat precisely within an area of 21 inches by 21.

The accompanying diagram (112), though it represents only half that area (21 inches by $10\frac{1}{2}$), explains the situation and proves the point. It shows also the possibilities of adapting a diamond equal to two equilateral triangles to the rectangular space.

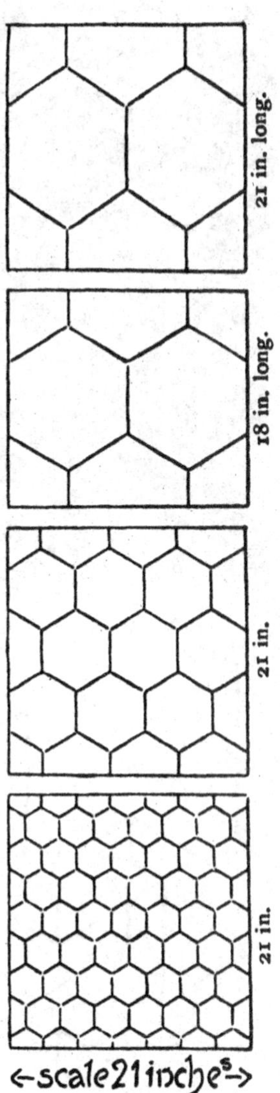

113. DIAGRAM SHOWING HOW HEXAGONAL DIAPERS WILL REPEAT ON RECTANGULAR LINES.

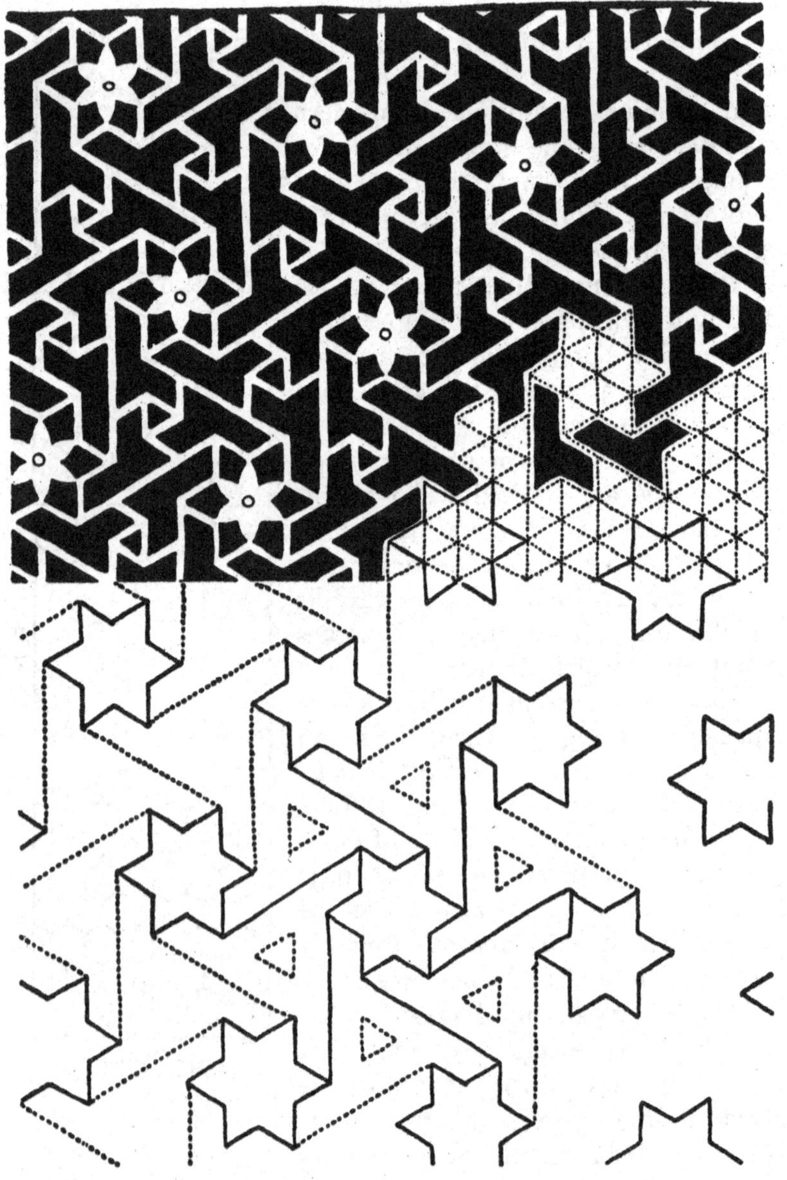

114. INDIAN LATTICE PATTERN BUILT ON TRIANGULAR LINES.

A diamond measuring 10½ inches by 6 inches repeats in the width 3½ times (which would work out only as a "drop" pattern—presently to be discussed, page 100). To repeat on the square, or as a straight-running pattern, these diamonds must needs be quartered and reduced to 5¼ by 3 inches.

The hexagon, which is a multiple of the equilateral triangle, adapts itself no more readily to the square (113). Hexagons half the width of the square, though they would repeat lengthwise in it, would not be equal-sided, but of the elongated form shown at the top of the diagram. True hexagons would not fill the square, but only a space of 21 by 18 inches.

Equilateral hexagons of 6 inches from side to side would repeat 3½ times in the width (and work therefore only as a "drop"). Like the triangles, they would need to be reduced to 3 inches wide before they would repeat in horizontal order.

The designer is frequently asked by inexperienced people to adapt designs to proportions which put them quite out of the question. If he is not well aware of the possibilities, and especially the impossibilities, of so doing, he is likely to waste valuable time over a task which was from the first hopeless. Few persons would realise, until failure had taught them, how proportionately small a triangle or hexagon it is which lends itself to a square repeat.

Let any one try and make the lattice pattern on page 90 repeat on rectangular lines of given dimensions, and he will realise, as no verbal explanation can possibly prove to him, how difficult it is to think of it, even, as built up on anything but the triangular lines which are in great measure responsible for it.

IX. THE TURNOVER.

A weaver's device—Doubles width of pattern—Exact turnover not desirable where conditions do not make it necessary—Balance must be preserved—Use of doubling over in border design—Suited to stencilling and pouncing.

To the practice of folding or doubling over in the vertical direction, may be traced a large class of bi-symmetrical designs. Mere doubling makes a sort of pattern; and some of the steadiest and most satisfactory designs rely to a large extent for their symmetry and steadiness upon the reversing of their lines.

To the weaver the "turnover" (115) is a veritable god-send, enabling him, without increase of cost or trouble, to double the width of his pattern. It does not even involve the cutting of more cards; it is simply a question of the gear of the loom.

So obvious is the advantage of the "turnover" to the weaver that the device might well have originated with him. But that is a point upon which it is useless to speculate. A man has only to double a sheet of paper and he can with one action of the knife cut out the two halves of what when it is opened out is a bi-symmetrical pattern.

Once invented, the "turnover" proves the easiest and simplest means of doubling without more ado the width of a pattern.

Apart from the fresh facilities afforded by it for broader pattern planning, and the much larger scale of design which it makes possible (observe how very narrow is the strip turned over in what is in effect a bold Gothic tapestry (116)), designers generally, even though they may have no technical grounds for so doing, will "turn over" the lines of a design, partly perhaps with the idea of economising draughtsmanship, but chiefly with a view to the value of the steadiness of effect to be obtained by that means. They permit themselves, however, in that case (or they lay themselves open to the charge of rather niggardly invention), considerable variety of detail within those steady lines. When rigidly exact repetition is no part of the conditions imposed by manufacture, it is almost incumbent upon the designer to assert his freedom, and not, for example, to suggest that his printed pattern is woven. He does well to avoid making one side of his design a mere reflection, as it were, of the other; and in particular its too mechanical turnover at the axis (117).

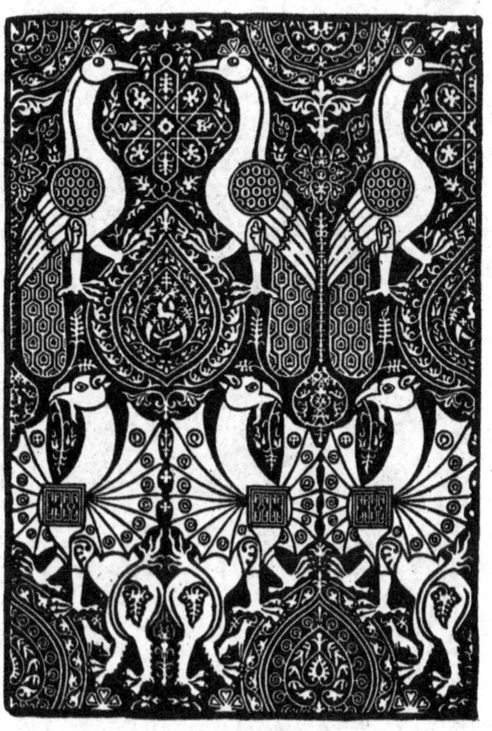

115. BYZANTINE "TURNOVER" PATTERN.

The absolutely strict turnover of any but the most rigid pattern, especially when the main stem is its axis, is so unsatisfactory that weavers often arrange their looms so that there is a central space of some inches (S) in which there is no turning over (118).

There is no occasion or excuse for the objectionable

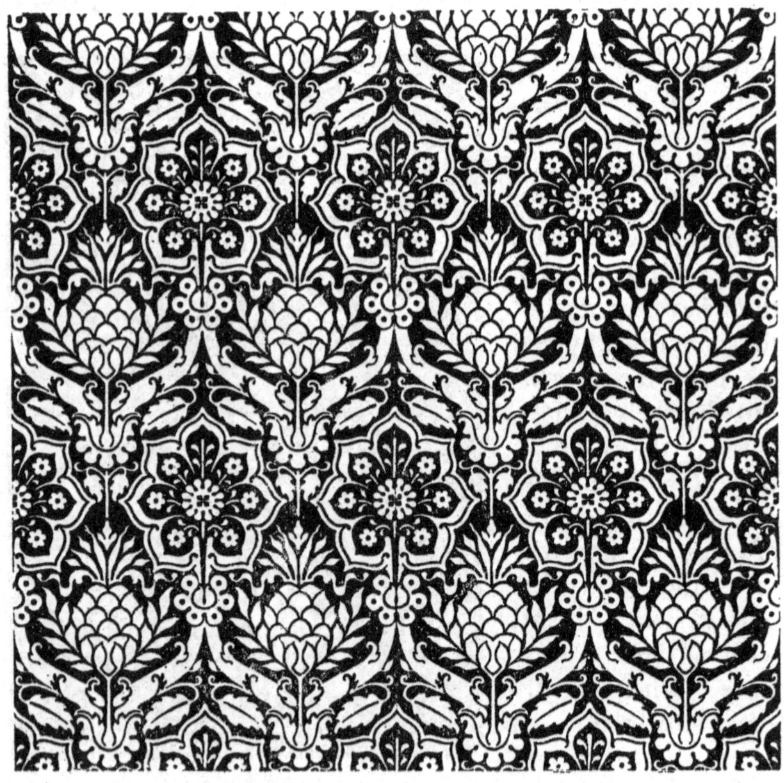

116. GOTHIC "TURNOVER" PATTERN.

mechanism when, as in printing, the conditions do not compel it.

Although it adds greatly to the interest of a pattern in which the main lines are reversed to introduce, if the conditions allow it, variety of detail, it is not safe to take liberties with the lines themselves or with the proportions of the opposite masses, else the balance of the design, which it is

117. QUASI-"TURNOVER" PATTERN.

most important to preserve, may be lost. It is essential, too, that, for example, any two opposite features should be precisely opposite, and that their branches, curving from the central stem or towards it, should turn, like the spirals on page 98 (119), on precisely the same level. Inaccuracy in either of these respects, though it may pass in a drawing for artistic freedom, is almost sure, in repetition on the wall, to give the impression that it is out of the straight. The eye expects a level; and it is strange how slight a deviation from it will produce an unfortunate effect. And so with any

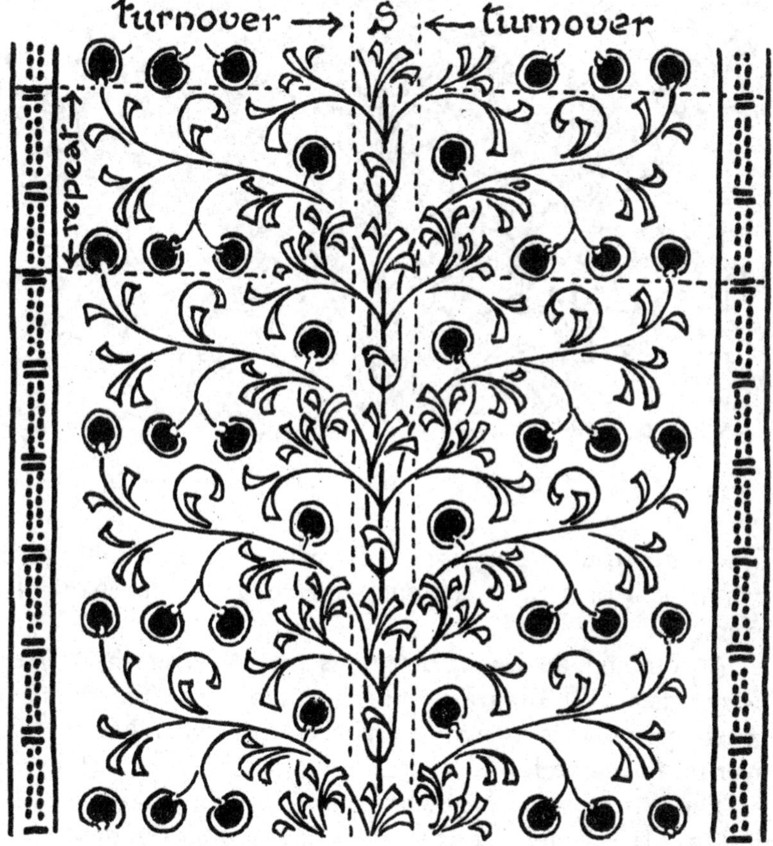

118. TURNOVER DESIGN WITH CENTRAL STRIP NOT TURNED OVER.

119. "TURNOVER" AND "DROP" PATTERN.

departure from the upright. In what concerns the equilibrium of a pattern it is impossible to be too mechanically exact.

A common device in design is to turn over the *unit of design* as in the diagram opposite (120), but that does not constitute what is known as a *turnover repeat* unless it turns over on the same level.

The "turnover" is nowhere more valuable than in border design. It is a most useful means of stopping the flow of the pattern, and of giving the lines *across*, which go so far towards

120. NOT A TURNOVER REPEAT.

the stability continually demanded in a border. Such lines may be expressed or understood: the counterpoise of parts suggests the axial line even when it is not put down.

A sprig or other pattern for wall decoration may just as easily be turned over as not. A stencil or a pounce has only to be turned face to the wall to give the design in reverse.

X. THE "DROP" REPEAT.

Scope given by drop repeat—Designed on diamond lines—And on the square—Geometrically same result—Practically different patterns—Opportunity of carrying pattern beyond width of stuff—Brick or masonry plan—Octagonal plan—Step pattern—False drop.

THE mystery of the drop repeat is more easily explained than how it came to be a mystery at all. The root of the trouble in designing it is perhaps in the fact that the inexperienced will not take the trouble to set out repeats enough of their pattern to show how the lines of it will come. Designers of experience do that as a matter of course—because of their experience.

The pattern of a woven or printed stuff must naturally follow on throughout the length and across the breadth of the piece—the top edge of the design must, that is to say, join on to the bottom edge, and the one side on to the other. But, whilst it is obvious that the pattern must follow in a continuous line throughout the length of the stuff, it is not a matter of necessity that it should be designed to take the same level when the strips come to be sewn together or hung upon the wall. They have to tally—that is all. The pattern may just as well be schemed to "drop" in the making up or hanging.

It is quite possible to design a pattern which shall repeat both on level lines and as a drop. The diagram opposite (121) shows that very plainly. It was drawn by Professor Beresford Pite to explain how some wall-papers of his design could be hung either way.

The planning of a drop repeat is in reality a very simple

matter, how simple may be seen in the diagram overleaf (122), in which the upright lines mark the width of the stuff, and the squares the limits of the repeat. It will be seen that the central feature in stripe A does not in stripe B range with it, but falls midway between two repeats: it "drops," in fact, one-half the depth of the repeat. In the third stripe, which drops again in the same way, the feature finds once more its level; in the fourth it drops again, rights itself once more in

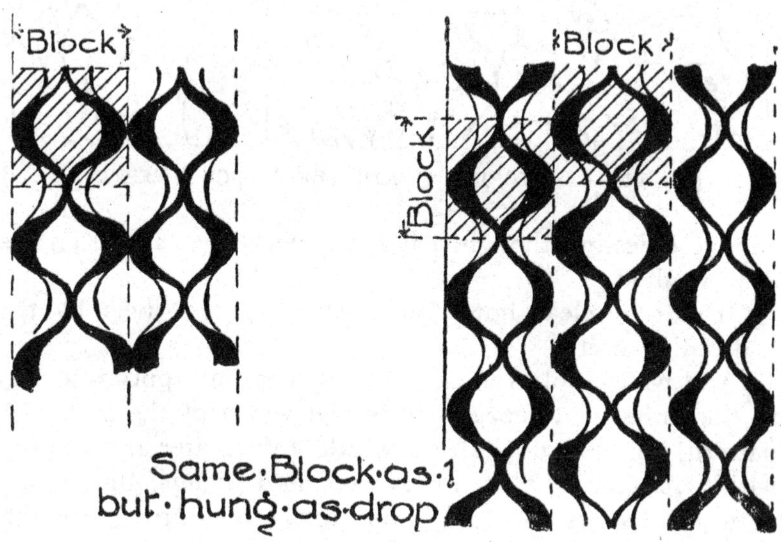

121. DIAGRAMS SHOWING HOW A PATTERN MAY BE DESIGNED TO HANG IN TWO WAYS.

the fifth, and so on to the end. A further effect of the drop is seen in the direction of the stem; the wave, instead of repeating itself, seems to take the opposite line, and not to follow but to be turned over or reversed.

The modern animal and fish patterns (258, Nos. 1 and 3) are schemed on the usual lines of a drop repeat, but the units are joined up into a continuous whole that gives a diaper effect, and also conveys the impression of flight or movement. This kind of diaper founded on living forms is typical of

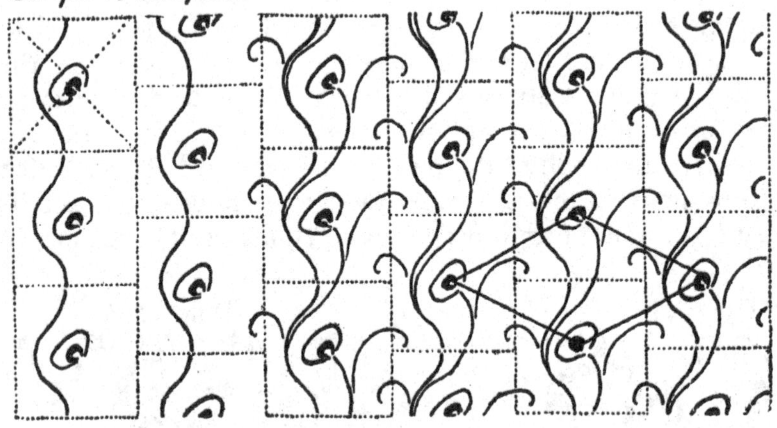

122. DIAGRAM TO ILLUSTRATE THE "DROP" REPEAT.

Japanese design, though it is not generally designed on the drop method.

It will be clear how much new scope is given by the "drop" pattern.

And what applies to the strip of material applies no less to the units of a repeat within the width of the stuff. A pattern, for example, half the width of the material may drop within its area so that, in the stuff as it hangs, the double pattern does not drop. A drop pattern one-third the width of the stuff would hang as a drop again.

Referring once more to diagram 122, it will be seen that, though the pattern is built upon the square, lines drawn from

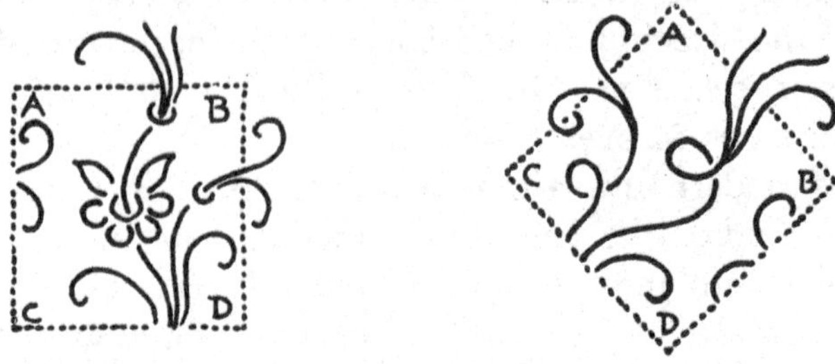

123. DIAGRAM TO ILLUSTRATE THE WAY REPEATS MUST FIT.

centre to centre of a given feature in it form a diamond; and this diamond, equally with the square, contains all the parts of the pattern, and may, just as well as the square, be regarded as the unit of repeat.

The difficulty which the inexperienced have in scheming a drop pattern would be considerably diminished if they would only accustom themselves to think of it as a question

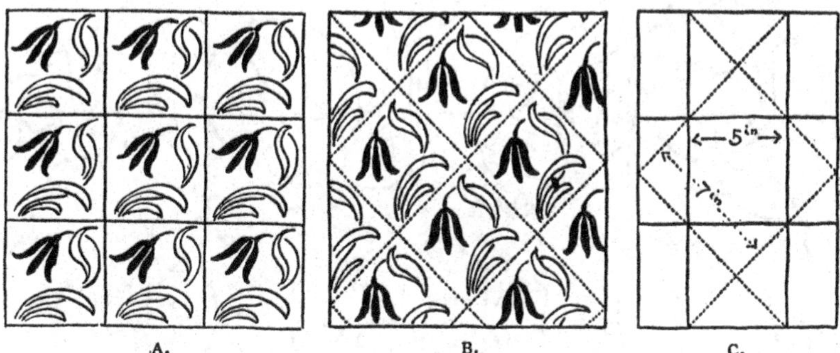

124. DIAGRAM TO ILLUSTRATE DIFFERENCE OF MEASURE WHEN A SQUARE REPEAT IS TURNED ROUND TO WORK AS A DROP.

of filling a diamond instead of a square. That is all it is —designing, in fact, within a trellis of diagonal, instead of vertical and horizontal, lines.

The diamond is merely a square or parallelogram turned part way round. In designing upon the one plan an artist would probably proceed to do differently from what he would have done upon the other; but the problem is the same. The opposite sides of either pattern have to tally. The lines ending at A B (in diagram 123) must be taken up at C D, or *vice versa*. In the same way whatever portion of the design extends *beyond* the margin B D or A C must recur again *within* the margin on the opposite side, no matter whether of square or diamond. The pattern has only to join on and fit.

It should be observed, however, that if a pattern designed upon square lines is turned part way round, though it repeats

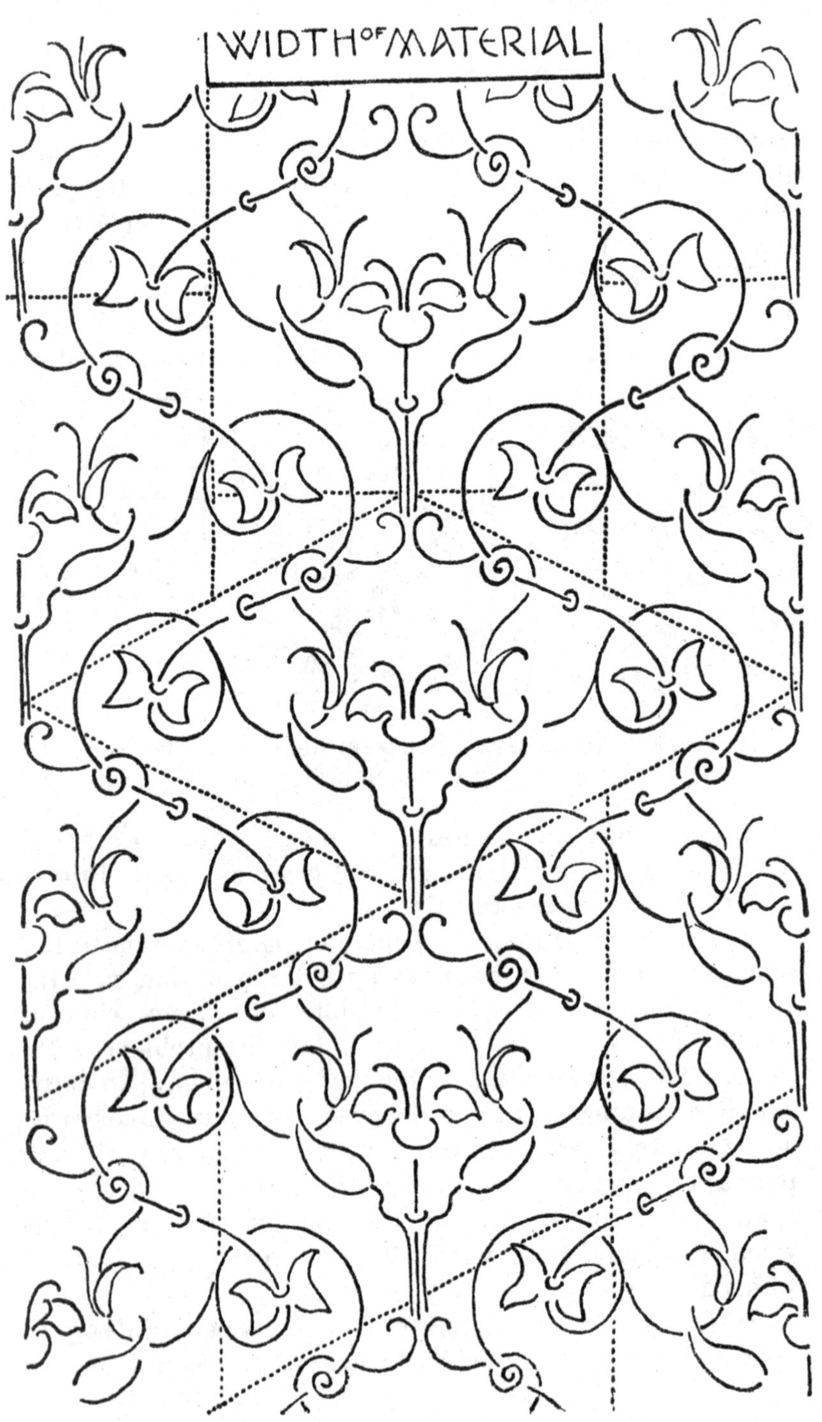

125. DIAGRAM TO SHOW A PATTERN MAY BE CONTAINED EQUALLY WITHIN SQUARE AND VARIOUS DIAMOND LINES.

as a drop upon the lines of the diamond, the *measure* of the repeat (as manufacturers reckon it, from top to bottom and from side to side) is no longer the same. If, that is to say, the squares in A of diagram 124 measure 5 inches each way, the diamonds in B (though it is the same pattern drawn to the same scale) measure 7 inches from point to point; and that is the trade way of reckoning, with which it is advisable to fall in.

It is sometimes quite worth while, bearing this danger always in mind, to *start* a design (124, C), not the full width of the stuff, but on a diamond seven-fifths of its width. This would work out as a drop pattern of the right width twice as long as it is wide; but the start would suggest a pattern which could never have occurred to any one working within the narrower strip. The expedient is useful especially in designing floor or ceiling patterns in which the *direction* of the design is not meant to be obvious.

It would be difficult to overestimate the value of the drop repeat, or of the diamond plan upon which it is commonly but not invariably devised.

Mechanically speaking, there is no reason why the design should drop just half its depth. It might drop any distance; and there are occasions when a pattern which drops a third is extremely useful. But if the drop were very slight, say only one-sixth of its depth, it would take six repeats before the design righted itself; and, moreover, the recurrence of any pronounced feature in it would be apt to mark a diagonal line. A stepped pattern has naturally a tendency that way. One great use, indeed, of the diamond plan is, that it minimises the danger of *horizontal* stripes, likely always to occur in a pattern repeating on the same level. In the case of a drop of one-half, the stripes go, as it were, alternately up and down, and give zig-zag lines, if any, or perhaps the lines of a trellis, to which there is little or no objection.

Another condition materially affecting design is the area

126. TWO PLANS UPON WHICH THE SAME DESIGN MIGHT HAVE BEEN BUILT.

of the repeat, the proportions of which are determined often by conditions quite beyond the control of the artist.

It was shown in diagram 122 that a drop pattern designed upon square lines was contained also within the lines of a diamond. In the same way a pattern designed within the lines of a diamond is contained within the lines of a rectangular figure working as a drop. Many drop patterns are designed upon the lines of the diamond. They may be designed equally within the lines of a diamond two sides of which run parallel with the width of the fabric. It will be seen in diagram 125 how the pattern there given in skeleton is contained equally within the square, the squat diamond, and the diamond formed by upright and slanting lines. It will repeat, that is to say, as a square pattern occupying the width of the material, as a diamond, and as a pattern of the width of the material cut, as it were, upon the slant.

In theory the design might have been started upon any one of these plans. In practice such a pattern would have been more likely to have resulted from working upon the lines of the diamond: as a point of fact it did result from it.

The design opposite (126), actually planned upon the diamond, might possibly have come about upon rectangular lines; it would certainly not have resulted from working upon the diagonal lines shown in diagram 125.

Such a pattern, on the other hand, as Walter Crane's (130) was clearly built upon the upright lines given by the width of the repeat (shown in dots) and lines across (from left to right) meeting them at the points emphasised by the puff balls of the dandelion. The sweep of marguerites, plainly the leading feature of the design and perhaps the start of it, falls very comfortably within the slanting shape, which seems almost to have suggested the composition of the flowers, evidently planned to take their graceful line, and afterwards provided with stalks.*

* Having made this assertion, I thought it as well to ask Walter Crane's authority for making it, and he tells me I am quite right.

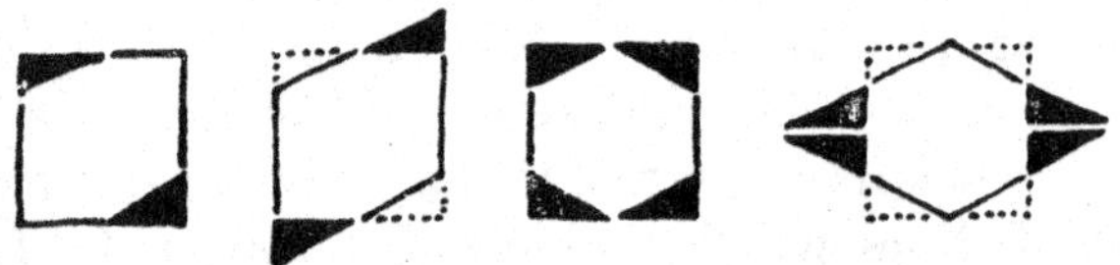

127. DIAGRAM SHOWING MECHANICAL RELATION OF VARIOUS PLANS.

Mechanically it all amounts to precisely the same thing. You have but to snip off the two opposite corners of the square to the left of diagram 127, and shift them to a position beyond the lines of the square, and they give you the oblique shape. You have but to snip off the four corners and arrange the pieces on either side of the remaining hexagon, as shown to the right of the diagram, and they give you the squat diamond. Artistically it makes all the difference in the world to the designer upon which plan he sets to work. Either one of them would encourage him to do something which the others would not. His design is materially influenced by the shape he sets himself to fill. It would never occur to him, for instance, to stretch a wreath of flowers across a width of space which he did not see before him. And the idea of extending a design far beyond the width of the material in which it is to be executed, may be set down as directly due to working on the lines of the diamond. A designer does not, except in certain deliberately formal patterns, keep his design within the lines upon which it repeats. But he has them always in view; and he does not stray from them so far that it ceases to make a difference what lines he works on. The advantage

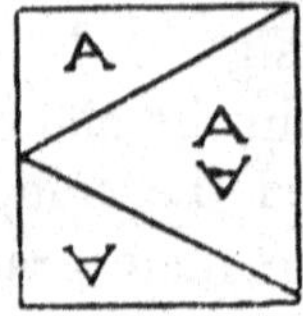

128. DIAGRAM SHOWING DIVISION OF SQUARE REPEAT INTO THREE PARTS.

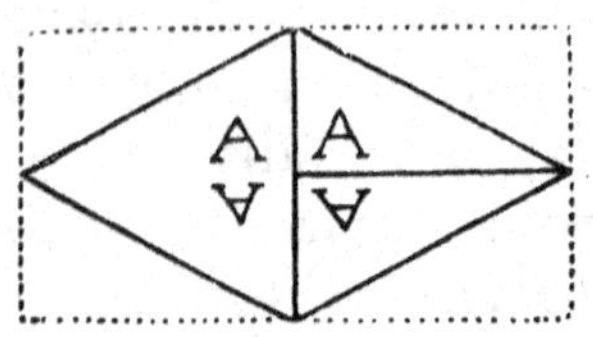

129. DIAGRAM SHOWING TRANSPOSITION OF PARTS OF SQUARE TO FORM WIDE DIAMOND.

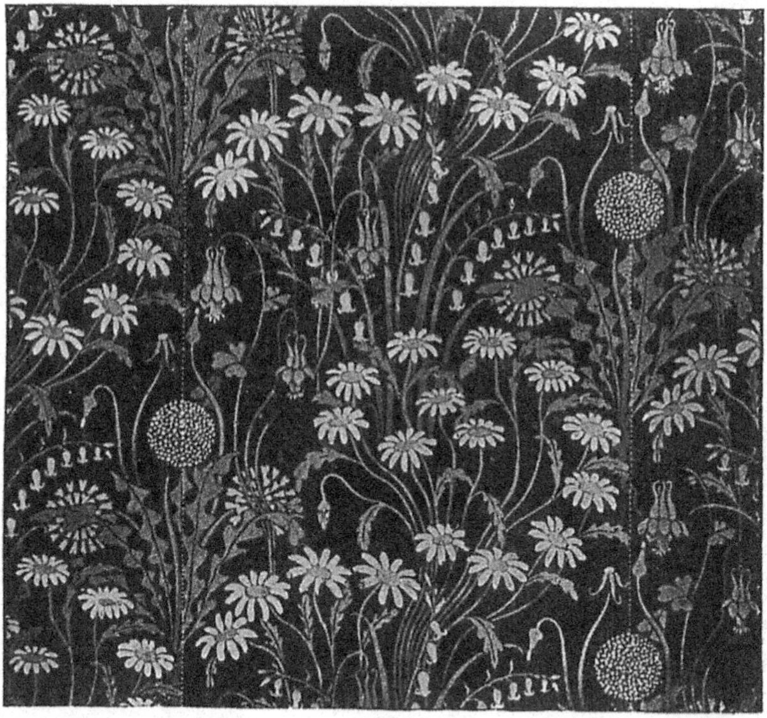

130. WALL-PAPER DESIGN BY WALTER CRANE.

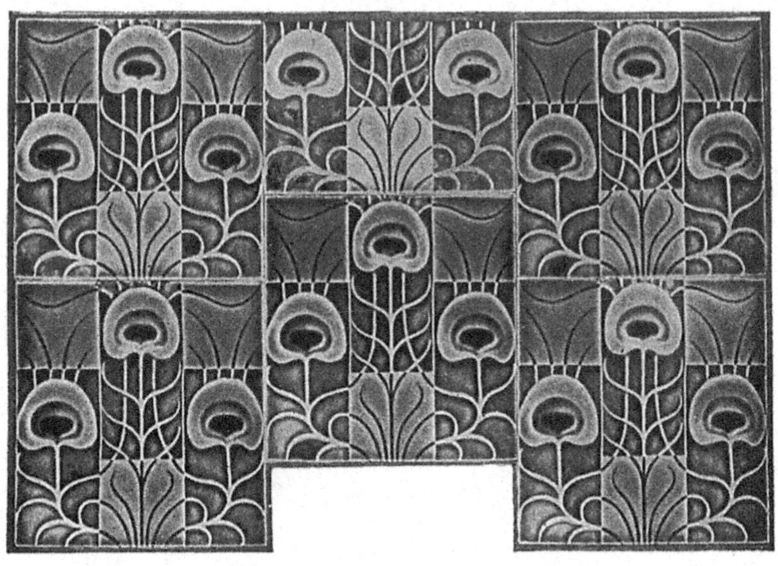

131. STEP PATTERN WHICH IS NOT A DROP REPEAT.

of setting out a drop design upon the plan of the diamond is, that the simplicity of the four straight lines enables him to keep more clearly in view than the other lines upon which the drop is worked, the ultimate relation of the parts of his design, and the order in which they will recur. Perhaps the most conspicuous advantage of the drop repeat is that it enables one to perform the apparently impossible feat of designing a pattern twice the width of given material, which yet works out perfectly as a repeat within its limits.

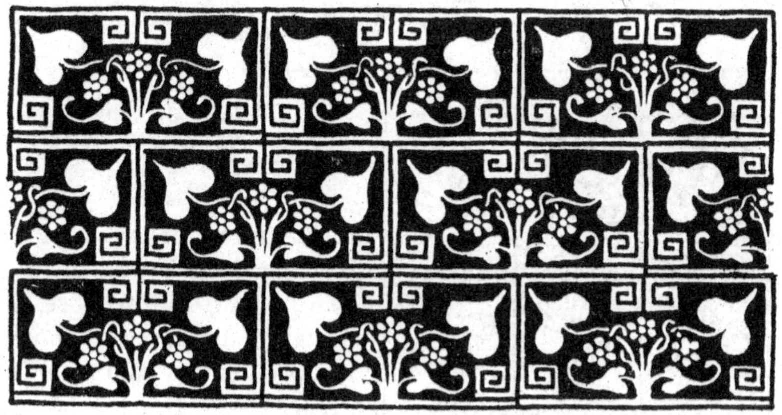

132. BRICK OR MASONRY PATTERN.

Working on the lines of the diamond, it is easy to do this. You have only to subdivide the area of your square repeat as here shown (128), (it might just as well have been a parallelogram as a square) so that two smaller divisions A and V together equal the larger $\frac{A}{V}$. Then if you transpose the smaller parts A and V so that together with $\frac{A}{V}$ they form a squat diamond twice the width of the original square, you have the repeat of a design which amounts to, mechanically, the same thing as a square repeat of half that width. In the case of materials which can be dropped one-half their depth in hanging or in making up this is clearly a great gain.

The advantage, it may be argued, is only apparent: what

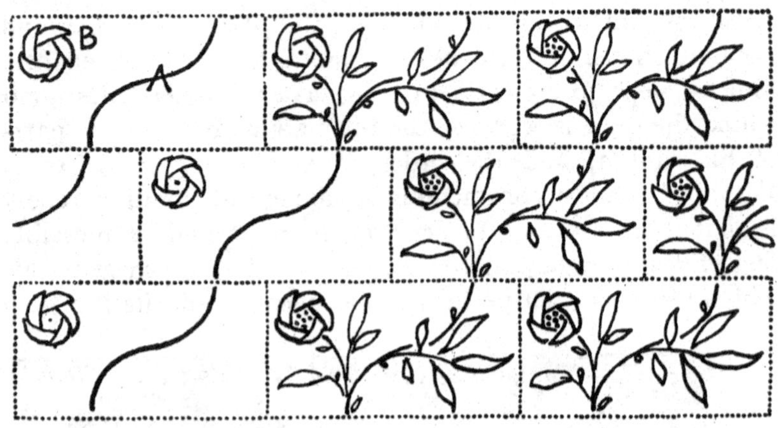

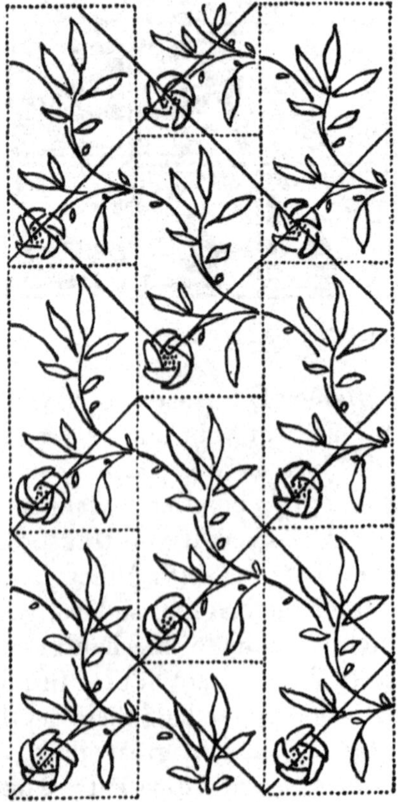

133. DIAGRAMS OF BRICK PLAN AND ITS RELATION TO DROP REPEAT.

is put into one strip is, as it were, taken out of the other; but in the case of pattern appearance must be allowed to count for a great deal. It is for want of knowing things like this, the common property of trade designers, that, genius notwithstanding, artists inexperienced in practical work fall short even of the trade standard of efficiency.

The skeleton given by the upright marginal lines of the fabric and parallel lines in a diagonal direction across it, is plainly helpful in the design of a diagonal stripe. The angle of inclination determines the depth of the drop.

An all-over pattern may also be designed within those lines; and they encourage greater freedom than rectangular or diamond lines; but it is not easy on such a scaffolding to balance the parts of a design; and if there are emphatic features in it they are liable to come out awkwardly in repetition.

Another very useful stepped plan on which to scheme especially patterns which take diagonal lines is the brick or masonry basis—which also works out as a drop.

In the tile pattern (132) the masonry lines form part of the design, and materially influence the lines of its growth.

It will be seen from the diagrams opposite (133) that a pattern designed upon brick lines and one upon the lines of the ordinary drop may amount to precisely the same thing, though either plan would naturally affect to some extent the growth of the pattern. (The diamond lines in

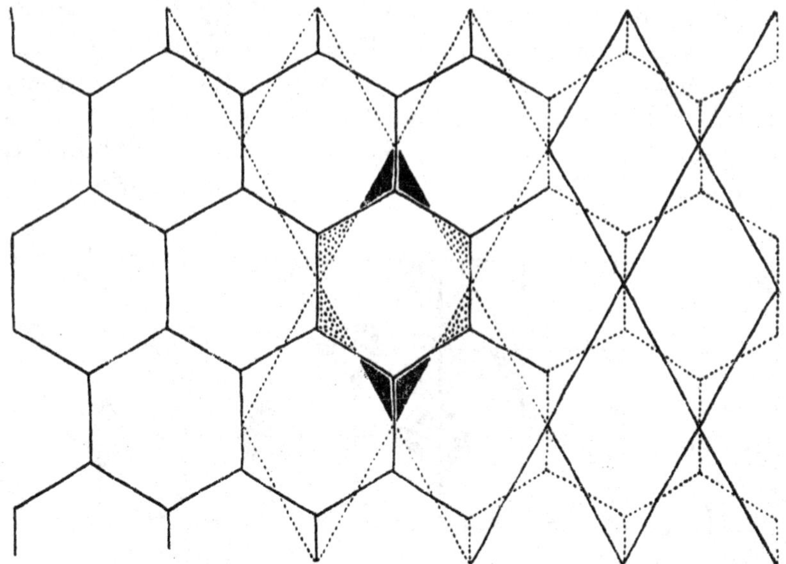

134. HEXAGON PLAN—ITS RELATION TO DIAMOND.

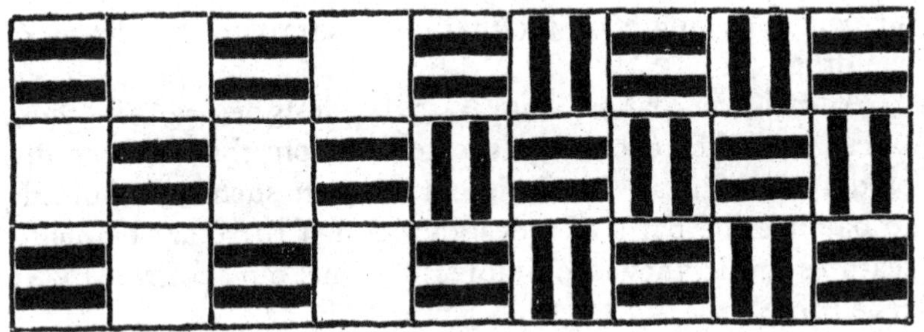

135. COUNTERACTING LINES OF DESIGN—REPEAT A DOUBLE SQUARE.

the lower of the two diagrams show plans upon which theoretically it might have been, but practically would not have been, constructed.) The diagonal lines may wave as freely as you please within the four sides of the brick, at the same time that the rigid skeleton of brickwork enables you to distribute your flowers or other free-growing features in strict order.

The adoption of the brick plan leads sometimes to confusion as to the *dimensions* of the repeat. The brick pattern above would not answer to the description of " a drop repeat twice as wide as it is deep." As a unit of those dimensions, it does not drop in the technical sense. It drops, in fact, as a repeat twice as deep as it is wide, or as a right-angled diamond. If, therefore, a drop repeat *of given dimensions*

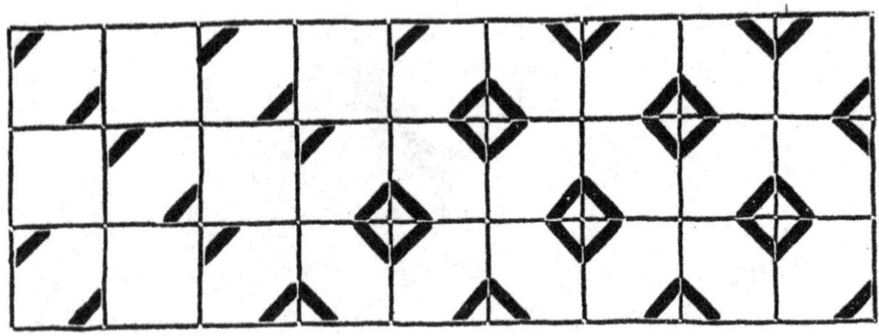

136. DIAMOND FORMS RESULTING FROM COUNTERACTING LINES—REPEAT A DOUBLE SQUARE.

were specified, and the artist were to send in a design planned on a brick of those proportions, he might have it thrown back upon his hands, as not being to size.

The hexagon, again, does not drop in the orthodox manner, though it amounts to the same thing as a diamond which does drop. Diagram 134 will show how, if the dotted portions of the hexagon were cut off, and attached again in the position of the solid black triangles, the result would be a diamond.

But it is not convenient to design upon the hexagon. It gives you no scope which the diamond does not; and it

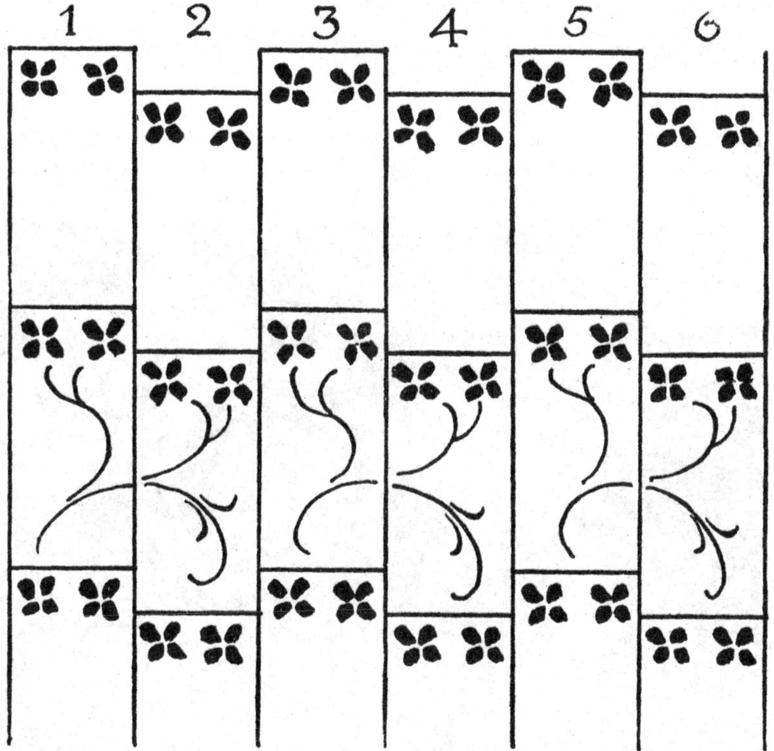

137. DIAGRAM OF STEP PLAN WHICH DOES NOT GIVE A "DROP" REPEAT.

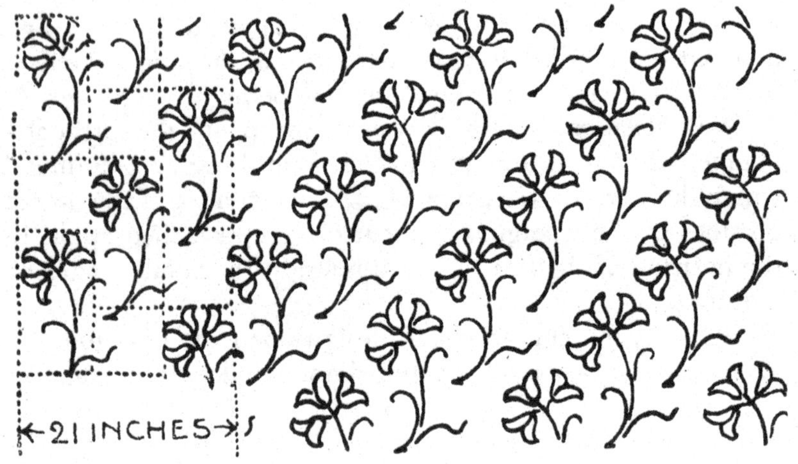

138. DIAGRAM OF PATTERN WHICH DROPS ONE-THIRD OF ITS DEPTH.

does not help you to avoid a too horizontal arrangement of features, as the diamond does. It may be at times

139. PATTERN WHICH DROPS ONE-QUARTER OF THE DEPTH OF REPEAT.

convenient to *prove* a design planned upon the diamond on the lines of the hexagon.

A drop design upon vertical and horizontal lines, say upon the square or other rectangular *step*, does not afford the opportunities given by the diamond plan; but it has compensating advantages of its own, especially where it is desirable to give an upright tendency to the pattern, and more especially still when the depth of the repeat happens to measure (as in some manufactures—tiles for example—it is convenient it should) precisely twice its width. The unit of repeat being in this case a double square, gives us the trellis on which the chessboard pattern is built. A chequer pattern (illustration 135) works as a drop repeat one square wide and two squares deep.

The unit of a double square planned to step half-way is most convenient in the case where it is desired to preserve square lines of construction in the design and yet to avoid any tendency it might have in one direction or the other. This is effectually done by counteracting the vertical tendency of the lines in one division of the repeat by horizontal lines in the other (135). Counteracting *diagonal* lines give, in the same way, diamonds (136).*

Further uses of the step, in lieu of the diamond, will be apparent when it comes to the discussion of freer patterns designed on its lines.

There is one form of step pattern which does not really constitute what is understood by a drop repeat. The second strip in diagram 137 drops slightly; but the third reverts again to the level of the first (or, if it can be said to drop, it takes a step out of all proportion to the last). As a consequence any such features as the flowers at the top of the repeat would, in recurrence, give a sort of zig-zag line.

True, a drop pattern may recover itself in the third

* Another variety of the drop pattern in which the unit is not merely of the proportions of a double square, but is built deliberately upon the two squares counterchanged, is shown on page 142.

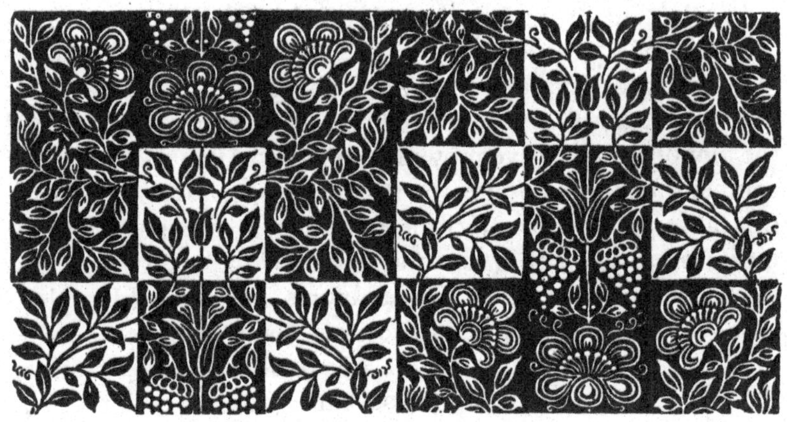

140. PATTERN WHICH DROPS ONE-THIRD OR TWO-THIRDS OF ITS DEPTH—UNIT OF REPEAT SUBDIVIDED AS IN 131.

repeat; but only on the condition that it drops just half its depth. A drop of one-third its depth recovers itself only in the fourth strip (138); a drop of one-fourth its depth, only in the fifth (139), and so on. In a drop repeat, properly so-called, each successive strip drops, and drops always the same distance. It does not jump up and down. The repeat in diagram 137 is really two strips wide; it does not drop; and there is no mechanical reason why the two flowers, any more than the stems (indicated in the lower part of it), should be repeated.

The peacock feather tile (131) is not a regular drop pattern; it drops in the second row two-thirds of its depth; but in the third it starts afresh on a level with the first.

The tile pattern above (140) is designed to drop regularly two-thirds of its depth, and would recover its level naturally in the fourth row, as would a pattern designed to drop only one-third of its depth. As a matter of fact, though it drops two-thirds if we work from left to right, from right to left it drops only one-third. That may read as if it were impossible, but if you work it out on paper you will find it is so.

141. "FALSE DROP" PATTERN.

Patterns of which diamonds, or equivalent ogee shapes, are the basis (141), have always an air of being drop patterns;

142. "FALSE DROP" PATTERN.

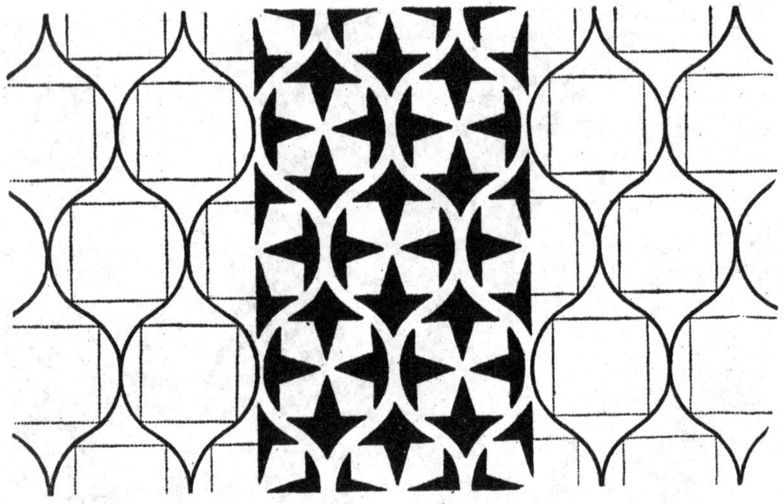

143. FRET DESIGNED ON OGEE AND SQUARE LINES.

but they do not really work on that plan unless the pattern in the diamonds or ogees also drops. But this sort of " false drop " plan is useful. The framework of severe lines steadies the ornament, which yet may be varied ; and there is perhaps a charm of unexpectedness in the result. One starts sometimes with the idea of a drop pattern (142) which develops, nevertheless, into a pattern which works only on square lines. There is no harm in this, so long as it is not necessary that the pattern should step in the working—which it may be.

It has been shown how no new principle is involved in designing on waved lines. They are but another version of the straight-lined skeleton, and amount to the same thing, except that their curves give the designer a lead which he is often wise to take.

Working upon the lines of the diamond, of which the ogee shape is the curvilinear equivalent, he would not so easily have arrived at the fret pattern (143) above. Starting with opposite wave lines, filling each ogee with a square, and just making pointed encroachments upon this, he arrived almost inevitably at what he did.

Another very useful form of "false drop" is where the unit of design occupying, let us say, a diamond or ogee, is turned over in the dropping. A sprig pattern, for example, in which the sprigs are alternately reversed—one row of flowers turning from left to right, the other from right to left—may with advantage be planned on the diamond; but the fact that the sprig in the diamond which drops is not a repeat of the first, but the reverse of it, removes it from the category of drop patterns proper. The unit is now the *double* diamond; and that no longer drops in repetition.

This may appear to the reader a mere verbal quibble not worth discussing; but it has a very practical bearing upon design. If, for example, the unit of design occupying diamond B in diagram 145 (see page 123) were reversed in diamond C, it would naturally be reversed also in the two quarters at a a, and would not join on to the half unit at A facing the same way as at B, and the pattern would not work.

Every fresh skeleton plan is a boon to the designer; for, working upon any fixed proportions (such as the conditions of any manufacture are sure to lay down for us), we fall inevitably into certain grooves of design; and all opportunity of varying them is to the good. It is because they offer each its own particular lines of construction (by which design cannot but be influenced) that it is worth the designer's while to puzzle over the various plans upon which pattern may possibly be built.

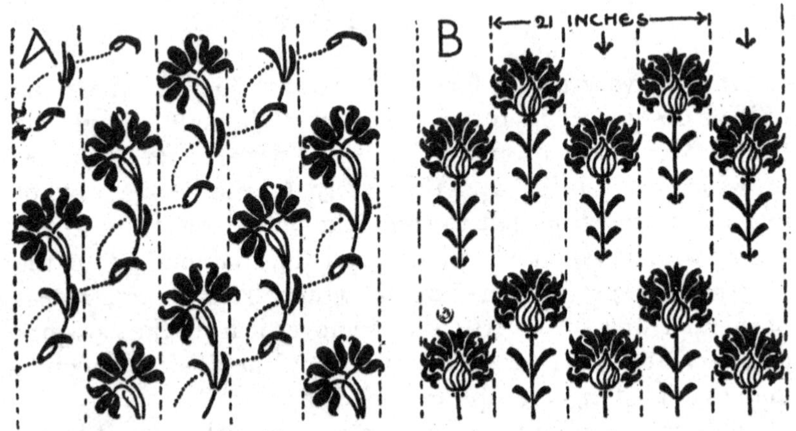

144. DIAGRAMS SHOWING DROP AND STEP REPEATS WITHIN THE WIDTH OF MATERIAL.

XI. SMALLER REPEATS.

Width of repeat divisible into width of material—Repeat two-thirds or two-fifths of width of material—Full width repeat seeming smaller—Variety in apparent uniformity—Weavers' ways of doing it—Same principle applied to larger design—Method and haphazard—More complicated system—Other plans for disguising precise order of small repeats.

As a rule, the designer is anxious to get the most out of the space he has to deal with. The use of the drop, it has been explained, enables him to go even beyond the width of his material. But it is not always that he wants the whole width allowed. There are reasons of economy and use (economy of design no less than of manufacture) which make it necessary at times, and especially in certain classes of design, that several repeats of the design should occur in the width of the stuff. If the repeat is on horizontal lines it must clearly be contained exactly twice, or three, or four, or more times, in the width; otherwise, when the material comes to be joined

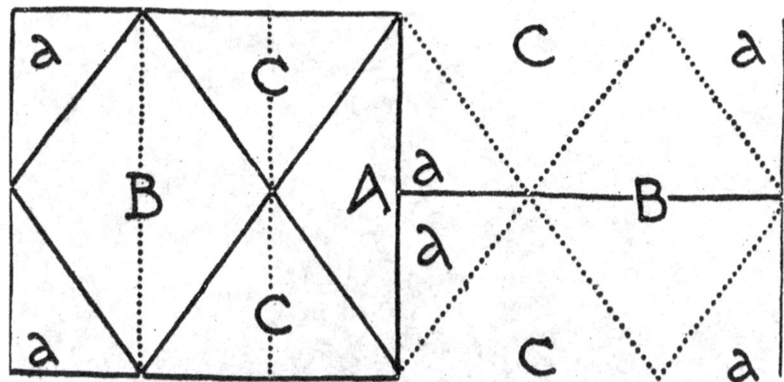

145. DIAGRAM SHOWING PLAN OF DROP REPEAT TWO-THIRDS OF THE WIDTH OF MATERIAL.

up, the design will not match, without cutting the stuff to waste.

A drop-repeat within the width of the material does not, it should be mentioned, entail a corresponding drop in joining or hanging. Suppose the material in diagram A (144) to be wallpaper 21 inches wide, and the repeat to be only 7 inches wide, and drop just a third or two-thirds of its length. In that case the paper will hang not as a drop

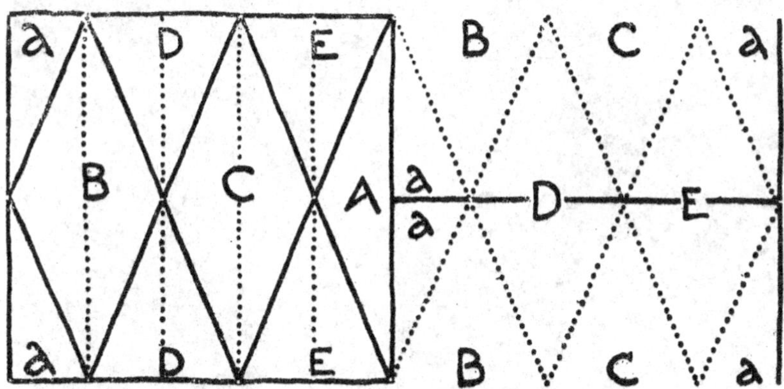

146. DIAGRAM SHOWING PLAN OF DROP REPEAT TWO-FIFTHS OF THE WIDTH OF THE MATERIAL.

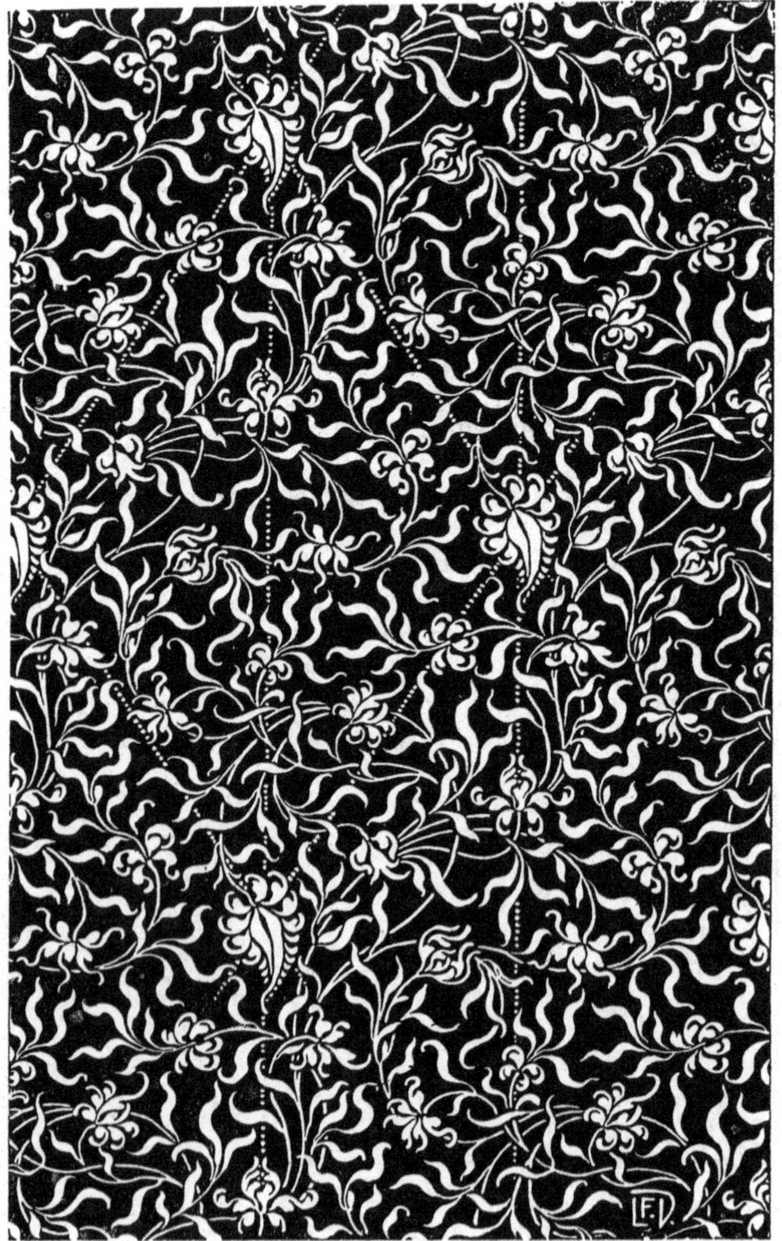

147. DROP DESIGN SCHEMED ON A DIAMOND TWO-THIRDS OF THE WIDTH OF THE MATERIAL.

but on level lines. The step pattern B, on the other hand, which recovers itself after the first repeat, will hang in corresponding fashion, dropping in one strip 7 inches, and in the next recovering itself again.

The "drop" offers yet further possibilities in design, and makes possible a repeat measuring, not merely a half, a third, a quarter, but two-thirds of the width of the material, or two-fifths of it, or two-sevenths, and so forth.

If, as in diagrams 145 and 146, you divide the area of possible repeat vertically into three, or into five, a pattern designed on a diamond the width of two divisions will work as a drop. All that is necessary is that the half diamond A on the one side and the two quarter diamonds a a on the other should join on. They form, in fact, together the unit of the repeating pattern—supposing, that is to say, diamonds A, B, C in the one case (145), and A, B, C, D, E in the other (146), to be filled in the same way.

The design (147) on page 124 shows a 21-inch material of which the design is schemed on a diamond 14 inches by 21 inches.

Ceiling pattern 148 works on a similar plan; but, as it happens to turn over within the diamond, it works also as a drop repeat 7 inches wide by 14 inches long. The block from which it is printed measures 21 inches by 14 inches.

The repeat, however, in such patterns is not dependent upon the filling of the diamonds all alike. So long as in diagram 145 the half diamond A and the two quarter diamonds a a make one complete diamond, and the two half diamonds C C another, the three diamonds (A, B, and C) may be occupied each with a separate figure. The design (149) on page 127 is planned upon the system of diamond divisions measuring two-thirds the width of the material. The diamonds (A), of which only half would occur in the width of the stuff, are occupied by sprays of foliage, and through the zig-zag space (B) between (equivalent to the other two diamonds) winds a separate growth.

There are many occasions on which it is advisable to reduce pattern to a scale far less than the mechanical con-

148. DROP REPEAT 7 INCHES BY 14 INCHES PRINTED FROM A BLOCK 21 INCHES BY 14 INCHES.

ditions would allow. In that case it may nevertheless be well to take advantage of those conditions in order to get variety, which, though not perhaps immediately apparent, is always pleasing when it is discovered. What is in effect quite a small repeat may, in point of fact, occupy the full width of a wide material.

An expedient that is often useful is to set out the lines of your pattern as if for a small repeat, and within those lines allow yourself all possible liberty. For example, you may devise a small sprig pattern, and then amuse yourself by playing variations upon it, so as to suggest perhaps, even in mechanically produced pattern, something of the freedom of handiwork—at all events avoiding the mechanical effect of too obvious repetition. In the Byzantine piercing (150) on page 128 a pattern of interlacing bands is diversified by filling the geometric spaces with sprigs as it were accidentally

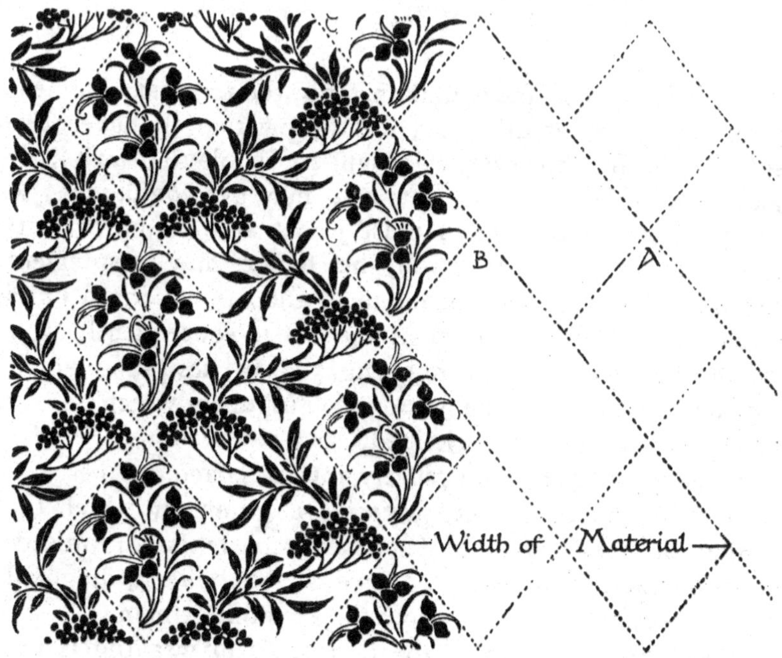

149. DIAGRAM OF DROP REPEAT ON DIAMOND LINES, THE DIAMONDS NOT FILLED ALL IN THE SAME WAY.

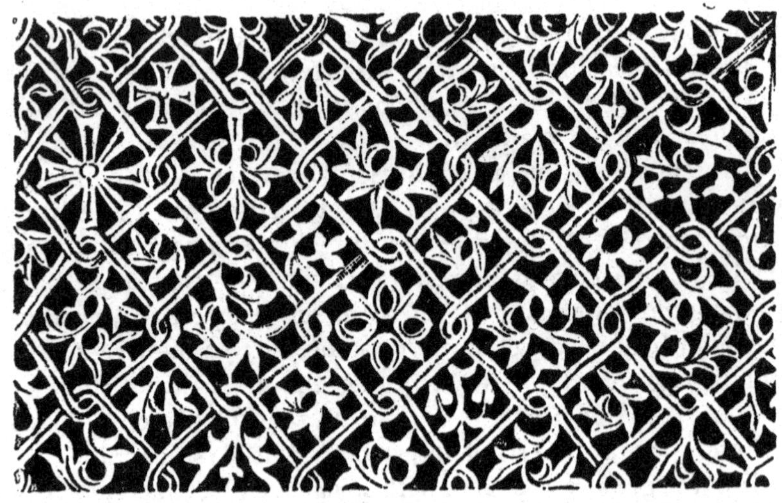

150. BYZANTINE PIERCED WORK WITH GEOMETRIC DIVISIONS ENCLOSING ORNAMENT WHICH DOES NOT REPEAT.

dispersed. In this particular instance the foliated ornament does not repeat at all. But it might very well have done so. There are, however, two dangers in playing any little game like this; the one, that you may get confused as to the particular units which must join; and the other that, failing system in the variation, the changes may be sufficient to throw the design out of balance, and allow certain units to assert themselves detrimentally. It is consequently well worth the pains of any one engaged in designing small repeats to work out the various plans upon which sprays and so forth may be schemed, so as not to recur quite obviously, and yet to fall surely into satisfactory lines.

Weavers have, in fact, perfected a system by which the danger of apparent lines in small repeats is minimised. Some of these arrangements * give, it will be seen, diagonal lines, others afford a ready means of avoiding them.

How they arose out of the necessities of weaving is not

* "Sateens" they are technically called.

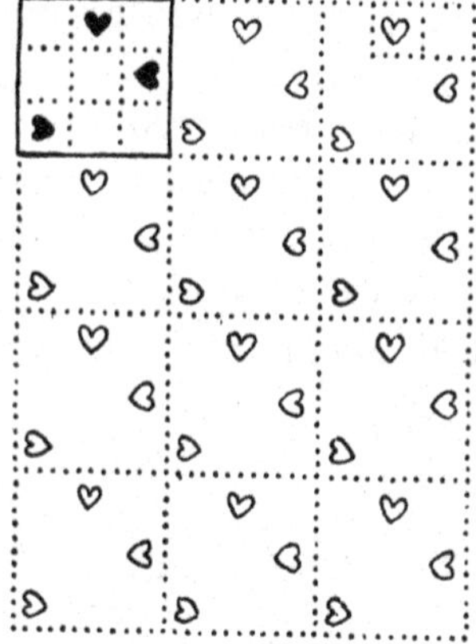

151. DIAGRAM OF THREE-SPOT REPEAT.

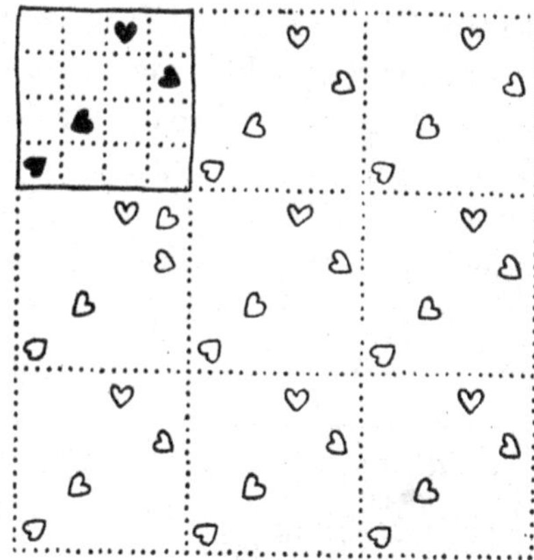

152. DIAGRAM OF FOUR-SPOT REPEAT.

here the question. Nor is it necessary to go into the matter of "ends," "counts," "picks," "treads," and other technicalities familiar enough to the expert in weaving, and to those who are not, more puzzling than explanatory. But, as they may be helpful to designers of no matter what

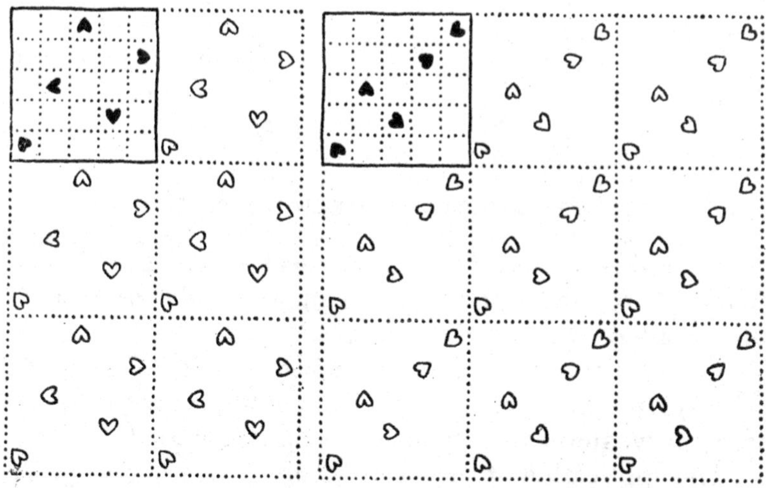

153. DIAGRAMS OF FIVE-SPOT REPEAT.

kind of pattern so long as it repeats, it is worth while giving them for what they may be worth.

The designer begins by dividing his repeat into squares 3, 4, 5, 6, 7, or 8 each way, as shown in the corner of each diagram. He has then to occupy 3, 4, 5, 6, 7, or 8 of these squares in such a way that in any row of squares, from top to bottom or from side to side, one of them, and one only, is inhabited.

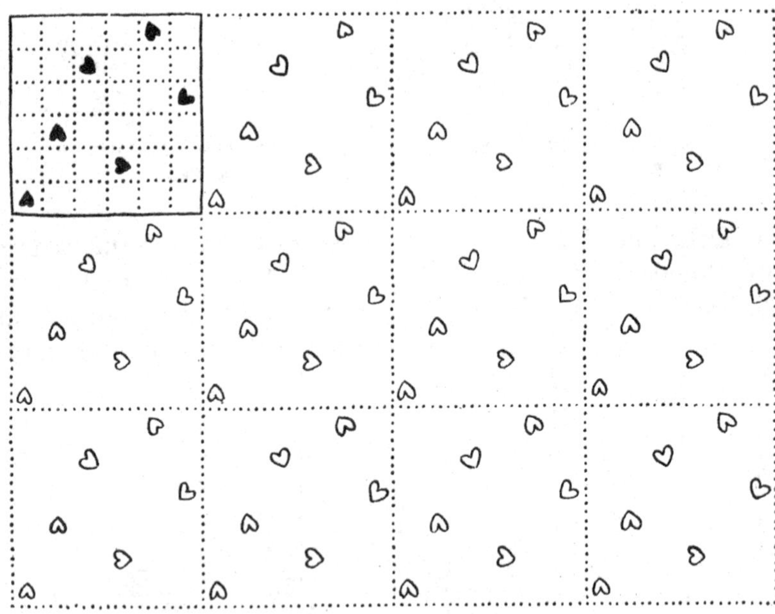

154. DIAGRAM OF SIX-SPOT REPEAT.

How this works out in the repeat—whether it takes a stripe or not, and what stripe, is shown by the repetition of this group of squares in outline.

In the diagrams, the heart-shapes, it will be seen, face all ways about, to show how, at the option of the artist, the spray or whatever it happens to be may be varied.

The application of such a principle as this to design on a comparatively large scale as in the ceiling paper on page 133

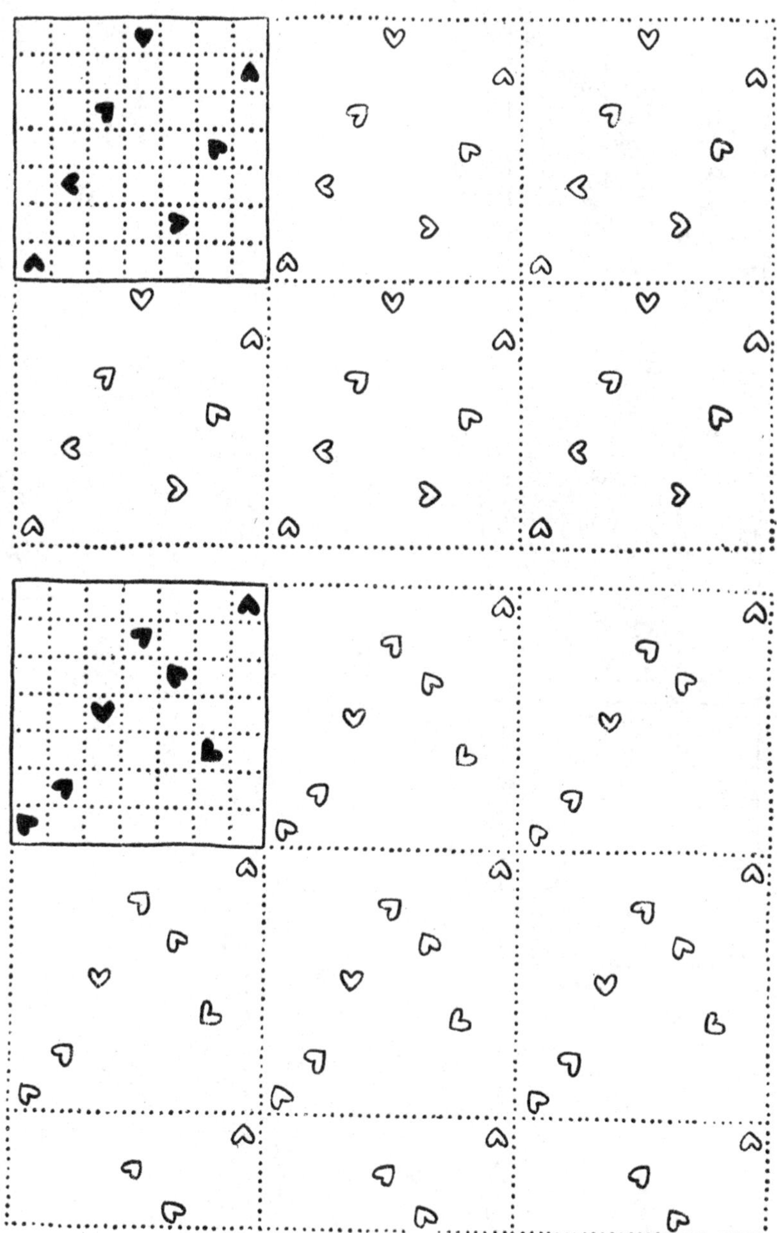

155, 156. DIAGRAMS OF SEVEN-SPOT REPEAT.

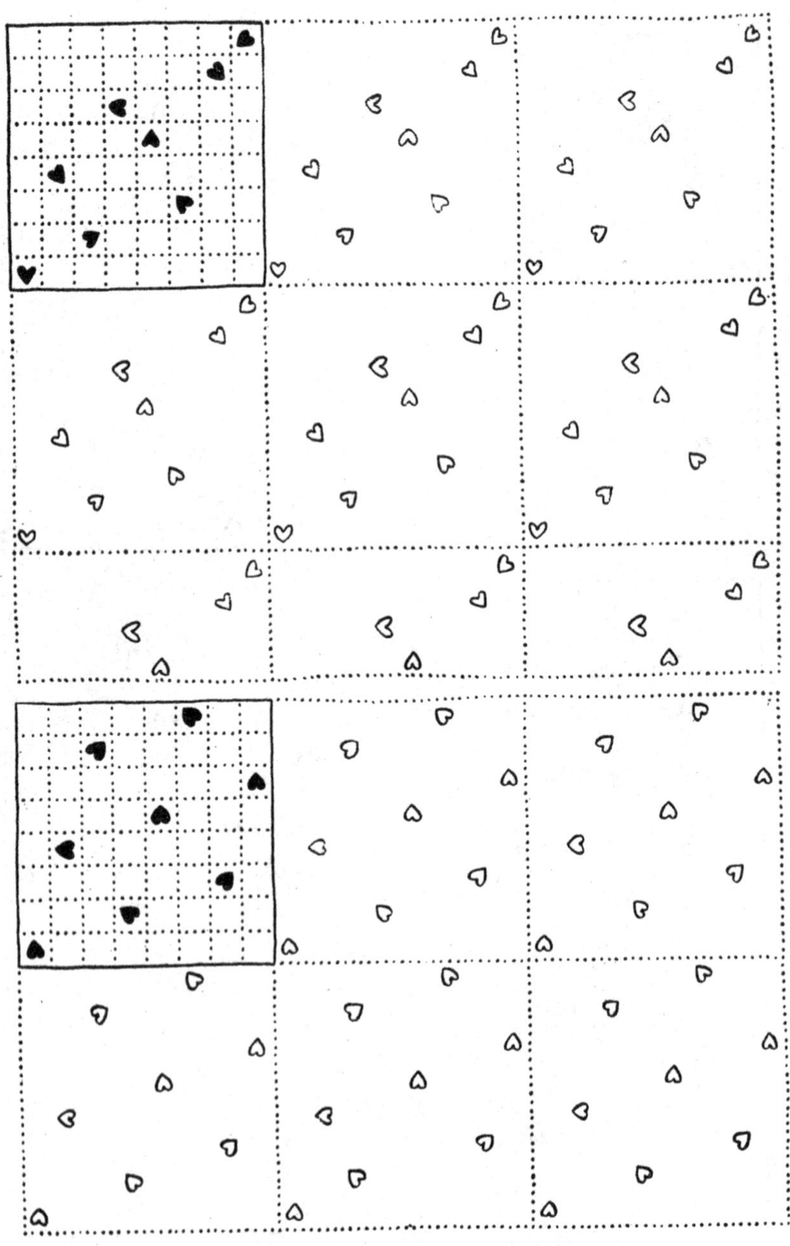

157, 158. DIAGRAMS OF EIGHT-SPOT REPEAT.

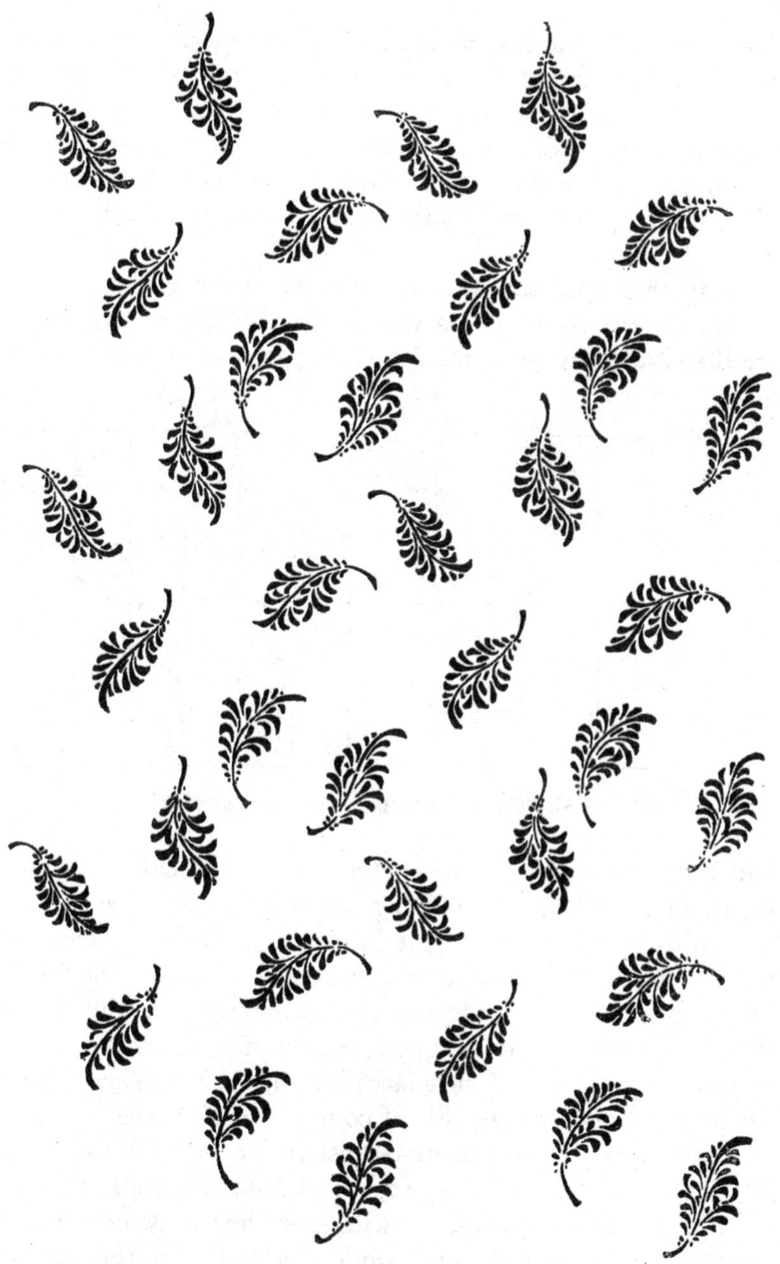

159. CEILING PATTERN DESIGNED ON THE PLAN OF SIX-SPOT REPEAT.

is explained by the diagrams which follow (160). In the first is shown the occupation of six squares by forms not yet carefully considered. In the second these begin to take leaf shape extending somewhat beyond the boundary lines. With the more careful drawing of these leaves and the breaking of them up into feathery composite foliage, the design takes its final shape.

A further application of the idea is shown in yet another diagram (161) in which only the main features of the design are distributed systematically. The position of such heavier

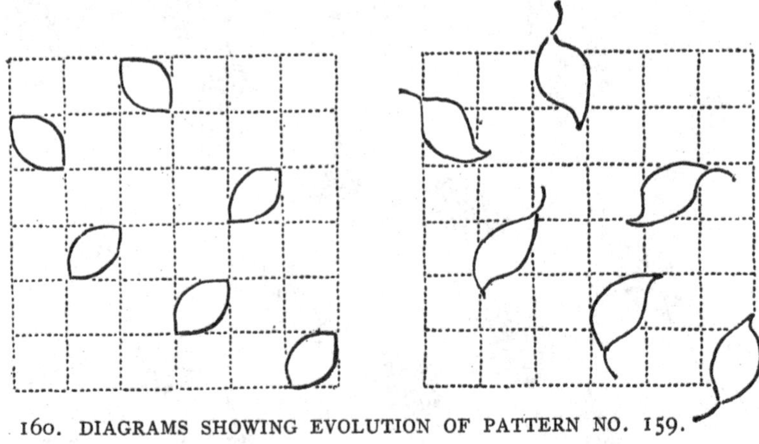

160. DIAGRAMS SHOWING EVOLUTION OF PATTERN NO. 159.

and more emphatic masses determined, it is safe to sketch in the more delicate connecting scrollwork quite freely.

Similarly the squares (one in each row) may be reserved, not for the pattern, but as spaces free from ornament (162), places of rest, where the eye can appreciate the quality of plain material. The diagram insists, for emphasis' sake, upon the squareness of the spaces left, but in a finished design the scaffolding lines would, of course, not be there.

An alternative to the more systematic manner—and one which appeals to the ungovernable frame of artistic mind—is to begin with sprays, or whatever they may be, on the margin of the repeat, and work gradually to the centre,

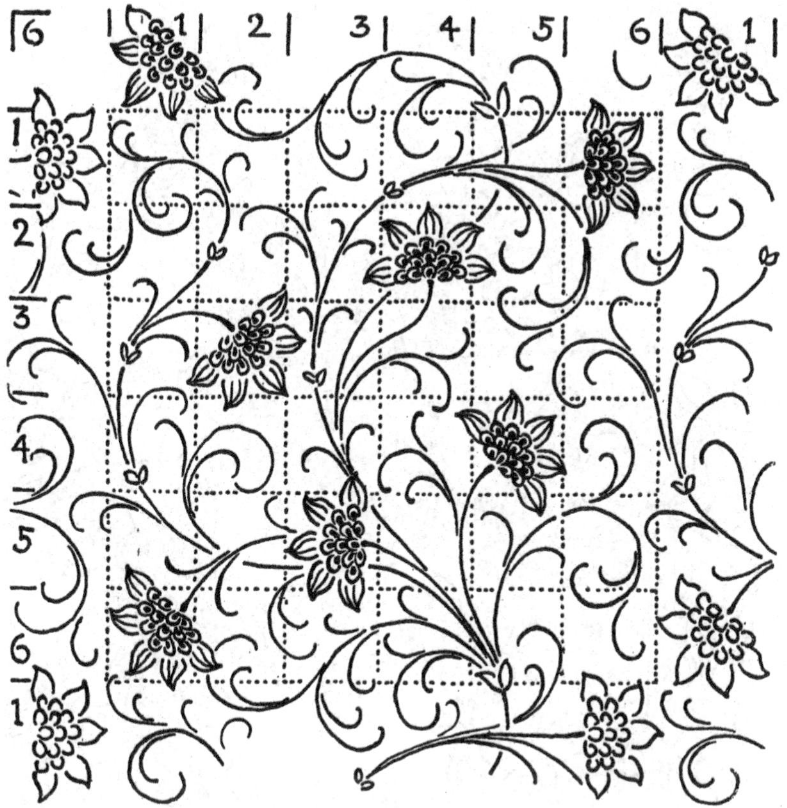

161. DIAGRAM SHOWING DISTRIBUTION OF FLOWERS ONLY ON THE PLAN OF A SIX-SPOT REPEAT.

trusting to the guidance of artistic instinct. That seems, perhaps, the readiest way; but it is in the end the longest—if ever it leads to anything but disappointment.

The full possibilities of the systematic principle are indicated in the last of this series of diagrams (163), designed to show the successive stages by which, first, six of the squares are occupied with leaf forms; then, in a similar way, six other squares with spirals; then others in succession with flowers, stars and butterflies. The result is not a pleasing pattern—that was not aimed at—but an unmistakable chart

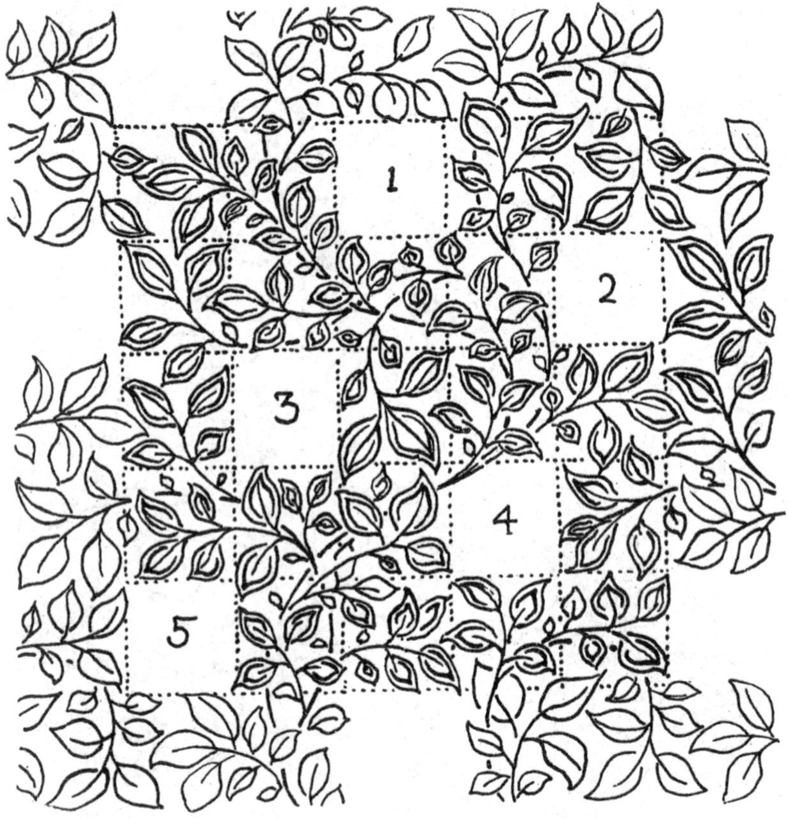

162. DIAGRAM SHOWING DISTRIBUTION OF OPEN SPACES IN THE GROUND ON THE PLAN OF A FIVE-SPOT REPEAT.

of the steps by which the designer may proceed to fill out his design. It should be useful also as an indication of the way in which, employing always the same or similar sprays or whatever they may be throughout his design, he may vary their colour. Let the five features represent five tones of colour, and the monotony of a single spray of ornament would be vastly relieved. Let the sprays be further slightly (more or less accidentally) varied in design, and an element of mystery would be introduced which seldom fails to add to the charm of pattern.

Two other plans upon which sprays, &c., may conveniently be distributed are worth showing (diagram 164).

Mark on the sides of a square central points, and from these to the corners draw parallel lines obliquely across. That will give you a centre square and eight parts of corresponding squares. Complete the four squares which want least to make them perfect, and you will have a cruciform unit of five divisions, no one of which is in a vertical or horizontal line with another.

Or, again, mark on the sides of a square two points *a* and *b*, dividing them into three equal parts, and from *a* draw oblique lines to the corners, and from *b* to *b* lines parallel with them. That will give you four complete squares and twelve portions of corresponding squares. Complete as in the last case, the four of these which are most nearly perfect, and two of the half squares not opposite one to the other, and you will have a unit of ten divisions no one of which is in a

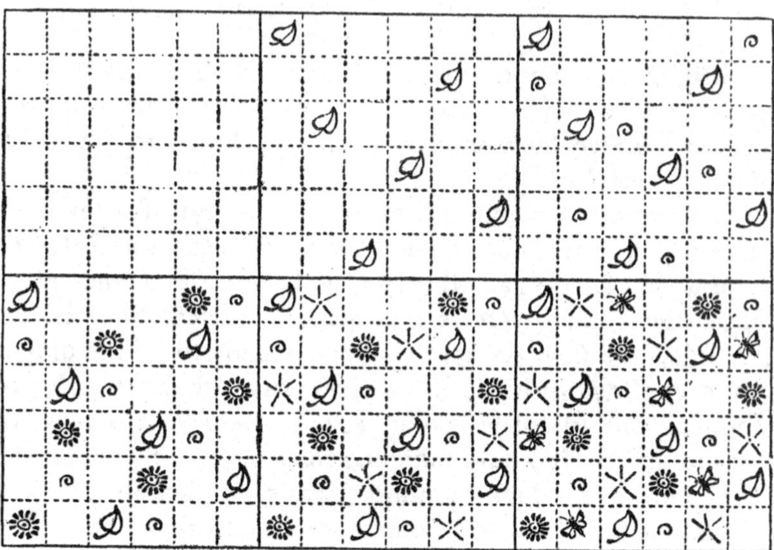

163. DIAGRAM SHOWING FURTHER DEVELOPMENT OF THE PRINCIPLE OF DISTRIBUTION ALREADY EXPLAINED.

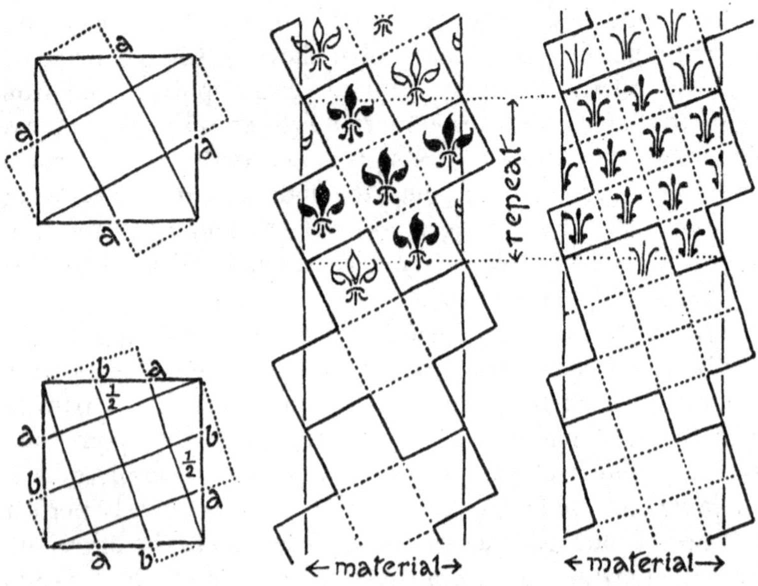

164. DIAGRAMS ILLUSTRATING ANOTHER PRINCIPLE ON WHICH SPOTS MAY BE DISTRIBUTED.

vertical or horizontal line with another. The result is in either case a square lattice askew. It is shown in the diagrams above both in repeat and in relation to the width of the material.

Any pattern occupying these squares would, if it followed the slope of the lattice, take slanting lines, and little or nothing would be gained. But in an upright spray, more especially if there were in it a marked vertical line, as, for example, in a fleur de lis, the upright tendency of the diaper would contrast with the lines of the plan, and the order of repetition would not be too apparent. Remove the trellis of scaffolding and it would take one some time to make out the precise order in which the diaper was sprinkled about.

The value of systems like these is just that. It makes the order of an obvious repeat less obvious.

XII. SUNDRY SCAFFOLDINGS.

Importance of variety of plan—Area of pattern not confined to area of repeat—Excursions compensated by incursions—Lines thus disguised—Wave-lines, turned over, result in ogee—Wave-lines result from working within narrow upright lines—Uprightness of narrow repeats counteracted by lines across—Diagonal wave-lines to connect features forming horizontal band—Designs obviously based upon slanting and horizontal lines—Wave-line from side to side of broad repeat—Scaffolding of an old Louis XVI. pattern.

INEVITABLY as repeated patterns fall into the lines of the square, the diamond, or perhaps the triangle, those were not by any means invariably the lines on which the designer set to work. Reference has been already made to some possible scaffoldings; others remain for consideration; and, in view of the vital way the lines on which a man works influence his design (one plan suggesting what another does not so much as allow), it is important that he should have the widest possible base of operations.

Beginners, by the way, seem always to be unnecessarily bothered by the *shape* of their repeat—square, oblong, diamond, or whatever it may be. I have seen it somewhere stated, for their guidance, that they need not confine the lines of their design to it. Indeed they need not. It would be safe to say that, except in mere diaper, they must on no account do so. If they do, the line of the repeat, not crossed by ornament at all, will assert itself, very probably in a way that is anything but desirable.

A marked vertical line results from keeping the pattern

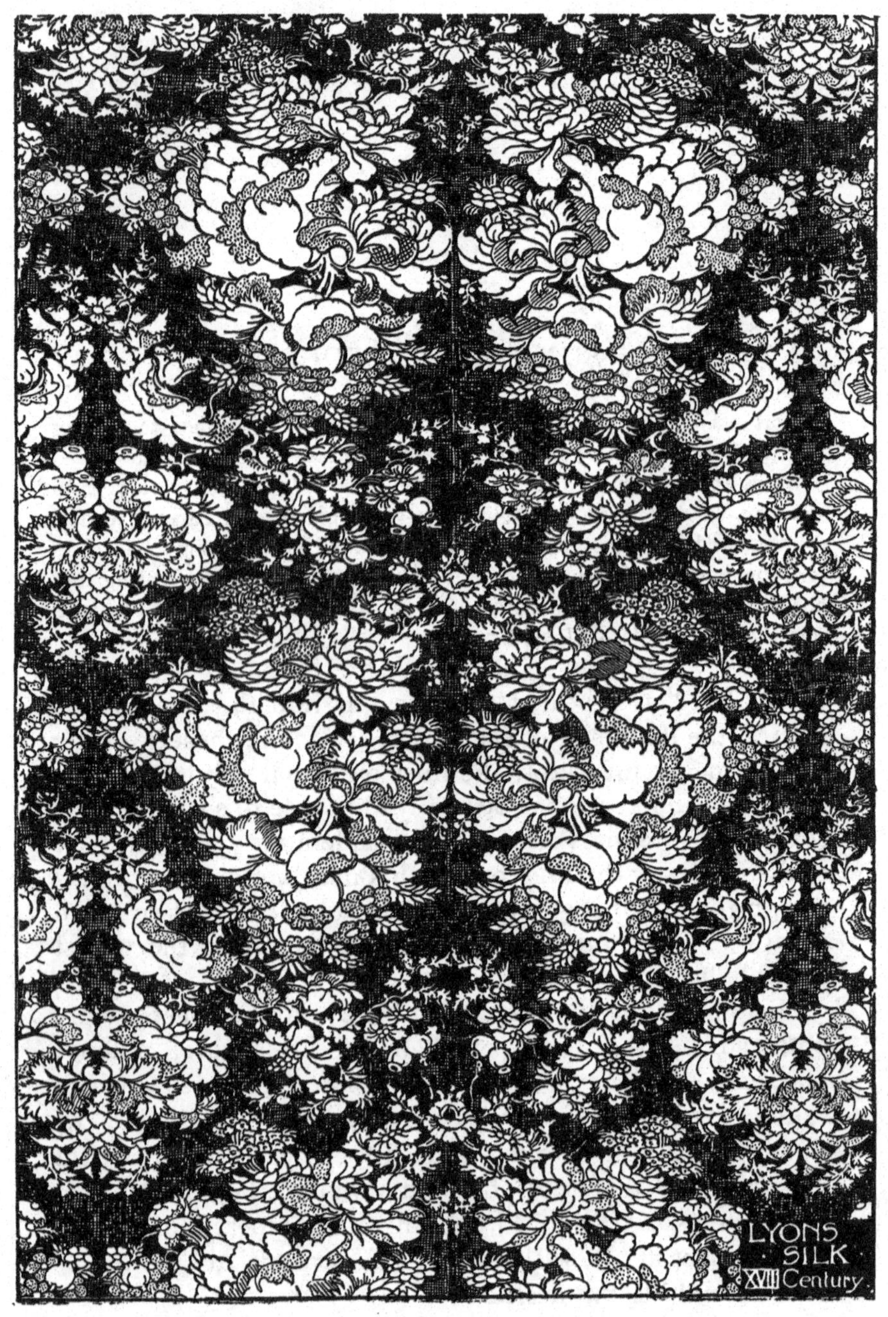

165. TURNOVER PATTERN, REVEALING THE VERTICAL LINE ON WHICH IT IS REVERSED.

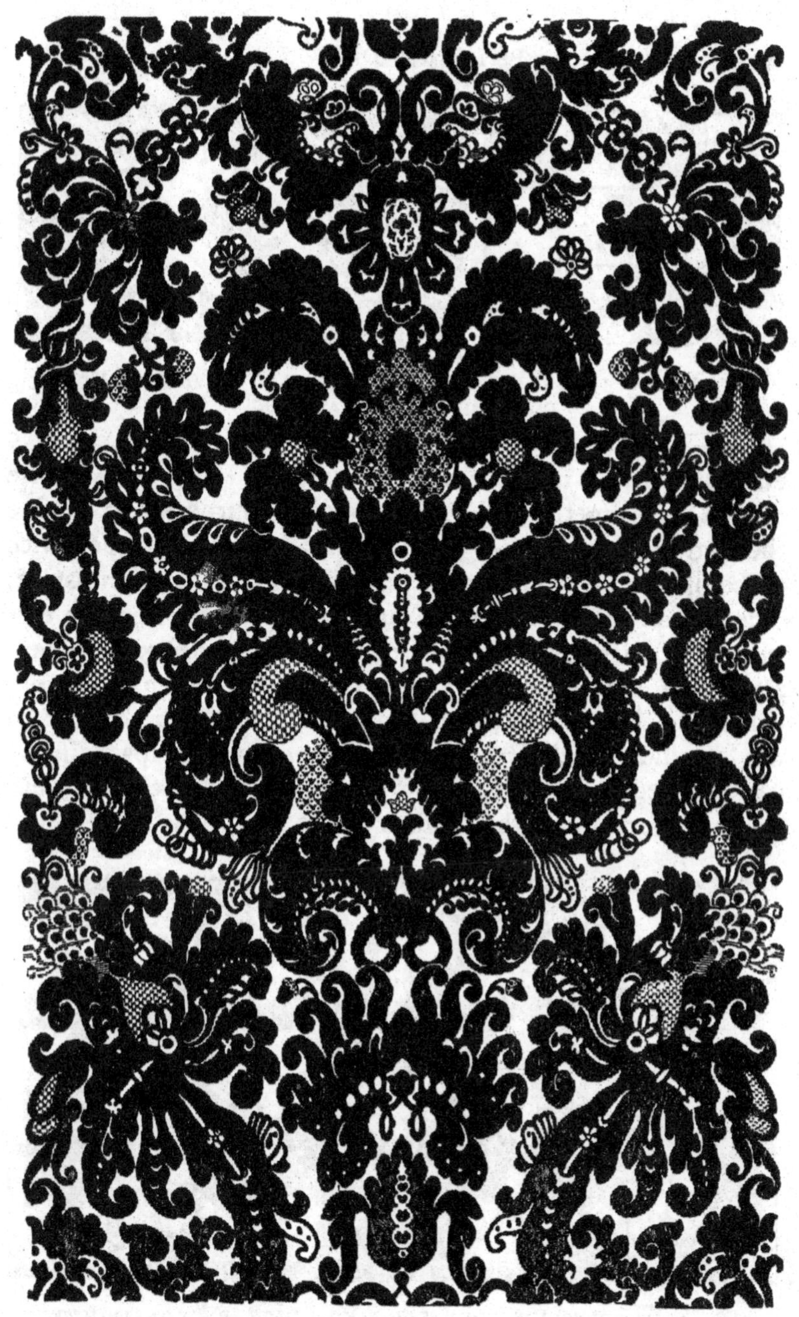

166. DESIGN ALMOST BUT NOT QUITE SELF-CONTAINED WITHIN THE WIDTH OF THE STUFF.

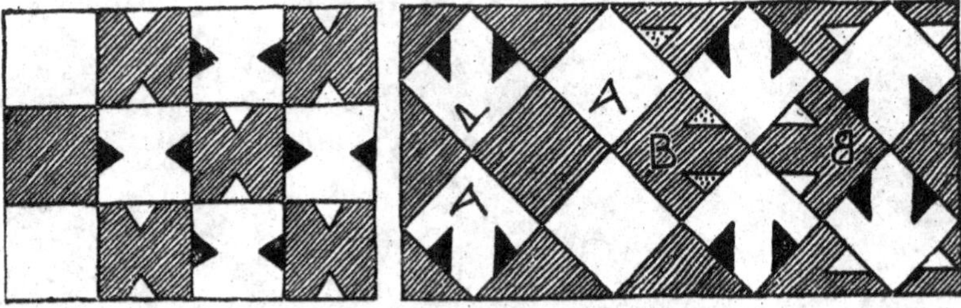

167. DIAGRAM SHOWING CONSTRUCTION AND DEVELOPMENT OF COUNTERCHANGE PATTERNS.

entirely within the width of the repeat (165). In textile design it is sometimes thought advisable purposely to confine the pattern in this way, so that it may have the appearance of completeness when made up in furniture or upholstery. The tapestry design (166) is arranged so that, when so employed, it will have the effect of a purposely designed panel. As a rule it is expedient, even where the design is mainly contained within the width of the stuff, to block the gap in the ground which would occur where two strips join by carrying comparatively insignificant, but sufficiently substantial, portions of the pattern across it.

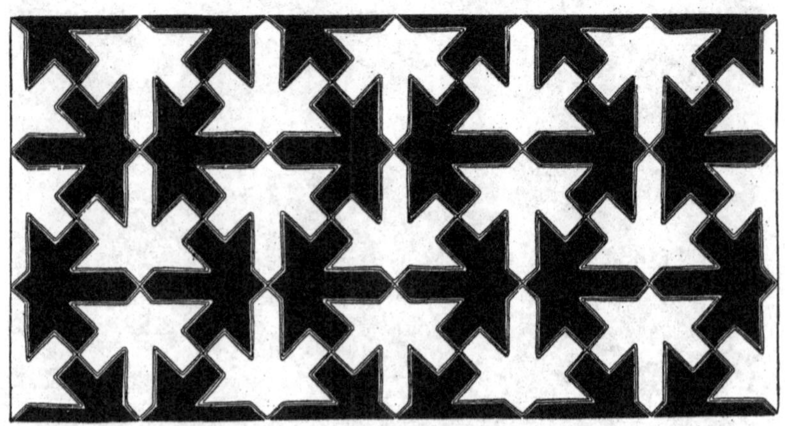

168. ALHAMBRESQUE COUNTERCHANGE PATTERN CONSTRUCTED ON THE LINES OF DIAGRAM 167.

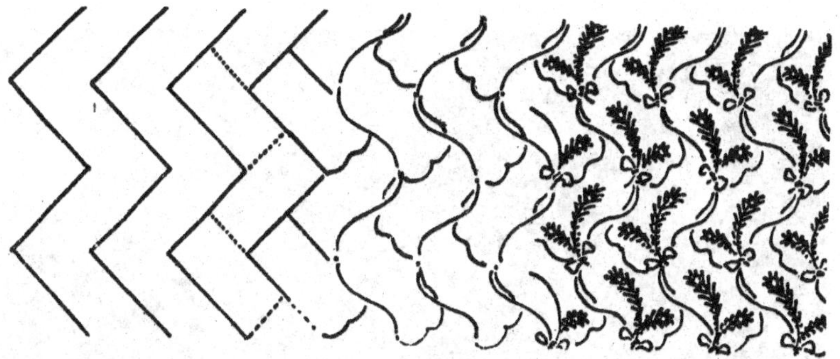

169. DIAGRAM SHOWING CONSTRUCTION AND DEVELOPMENT OF RIBBON AND FEATHER PATTERN, DIAGRAM 170.

A test by which to judge the competence of a pattern-designer is the way he manages to give you in his designs features extending far beyond the limits of his repeat,

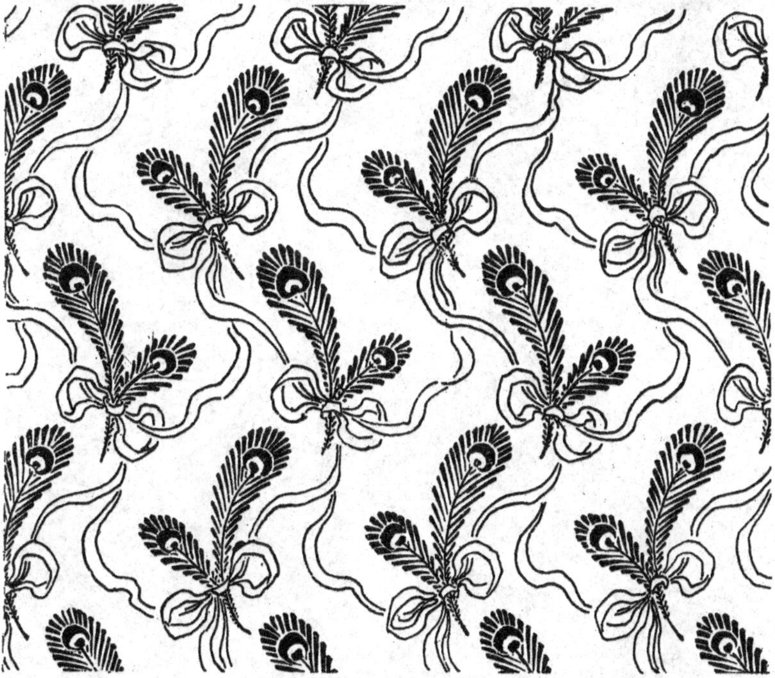

170. RIBBON AND FEATHER PATTERN CONSTRUCTED ON LINES OF DIAGRAM 169.

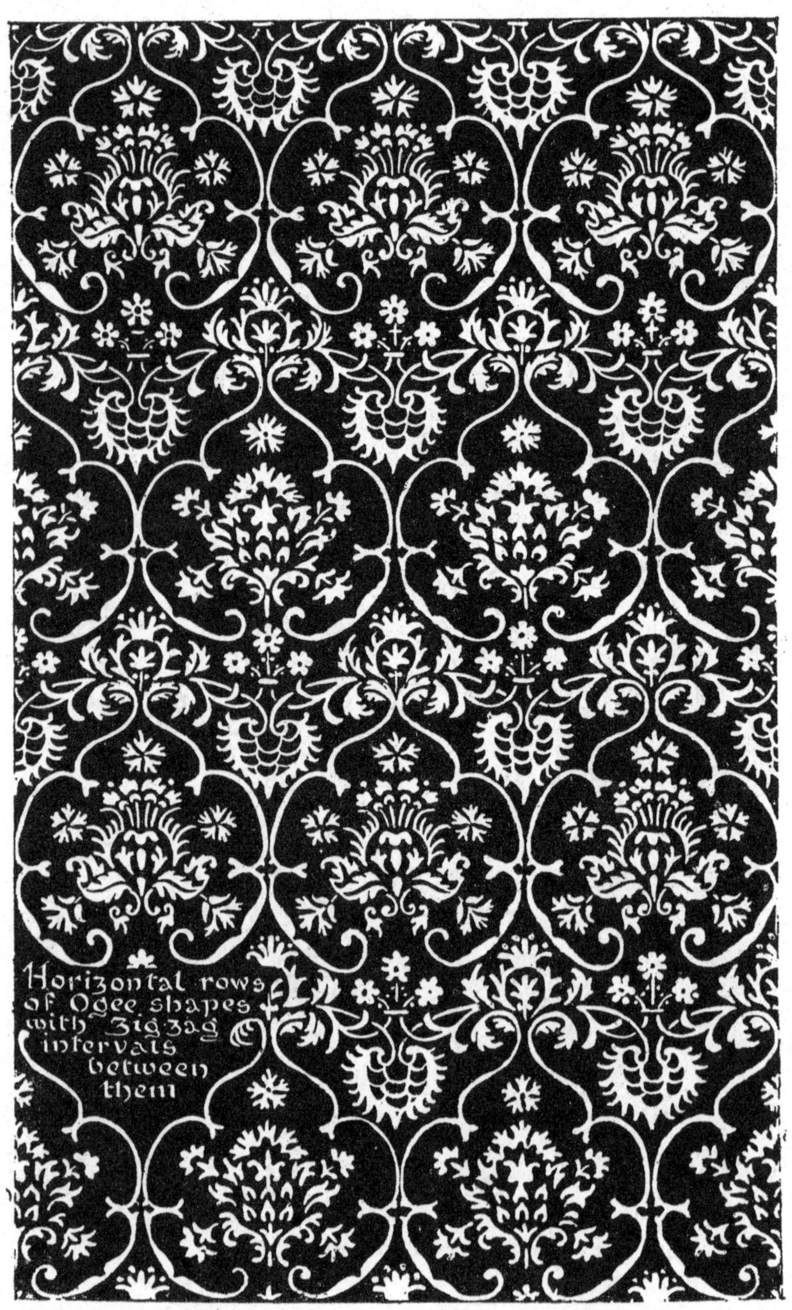

171. LATE GOTHIC VELVET PATTERN.

172. PATTERN IN WHICH WAVE-LINES DIVERT THE EYE FROM VERTICAL.

obtaining by that means a bolder scale and a freer line than are otherwise to be got. There is no great art in thus exceeding the limits of the repeat. One has only to remember that excess on one side of it must be compensated on the other. It is a question of addition and subtraction.

This is very plainly shown in those geometric patterns of which the scaffolding forms part of the design.

Given a chequer of black and white, any inroad of the black into the white has only to be followed by a

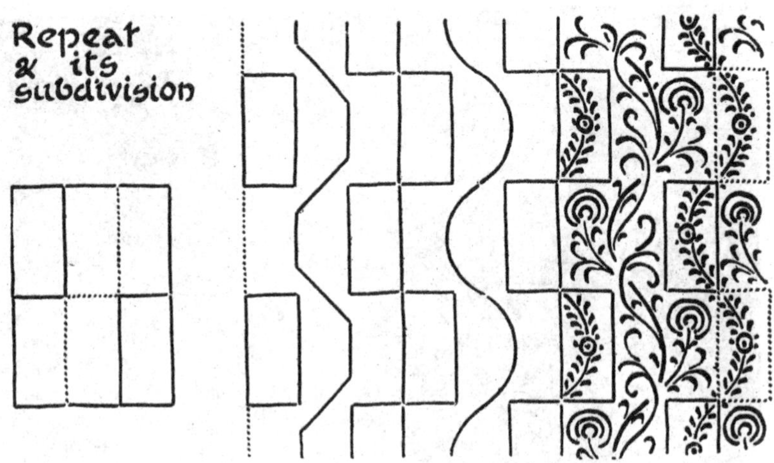

173. DIAGRAM OF SCAFFOLDING AND THE LINES OF A PATTERN RESULTING FROM IT.

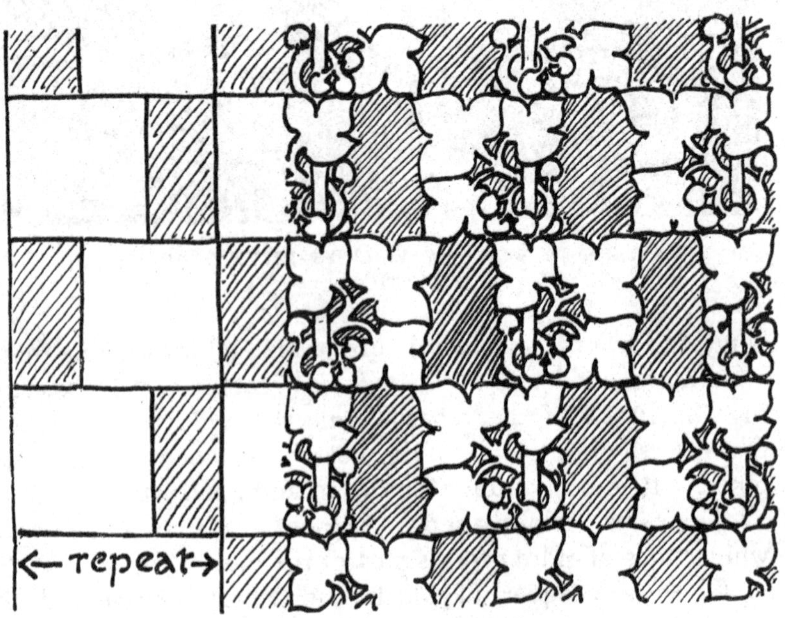

174. ANOTHER PATTERN BUILT ON THE SAME LINES AS 173.

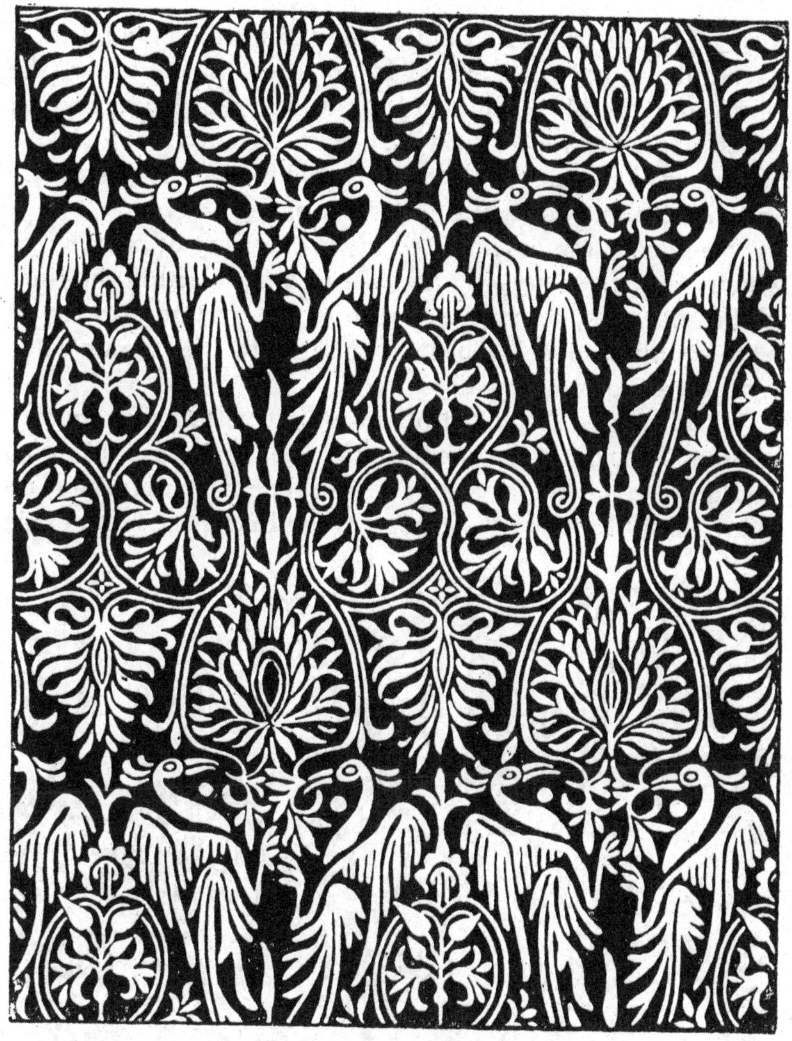

175. OLD DUTCH PRINT.

corresponding inroad of the white into the black, and you have a well-balanced pattern.

That explains itself at a glance in diagram 167. But more intricate-looking patterns come about in precisely the same way. The inroads of the black into the white diamonds at A have only to be compensated by identical incursions of the white into the black diamonds at B, and you have the unit which gives the very satisfactory counterchange (168) at the bottom of page 142. The two (black) bites out of one square are paid for by two (white) bites out of the other.

Practically the only way to avoid the lines of open space which result from keeping the unit of design within the lines of the repeat is, to cover so little of the ground with it, to leave so much space about it, that it resolves itself into some sort of a sprig or spot pattern.

They may be disguised by designing within, not squares or diamonds, but some such broken geometric scaffolding as would be given by, say, four of the shapes in diagram 168 (which would themselves repeat on the lines of the diamond)

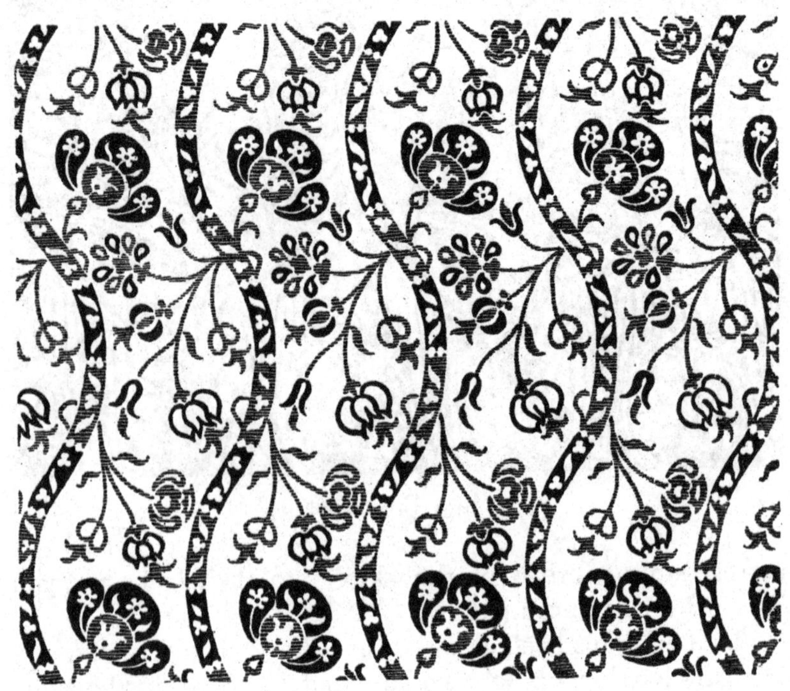

176. CRETAN WOVEN PATTERN.

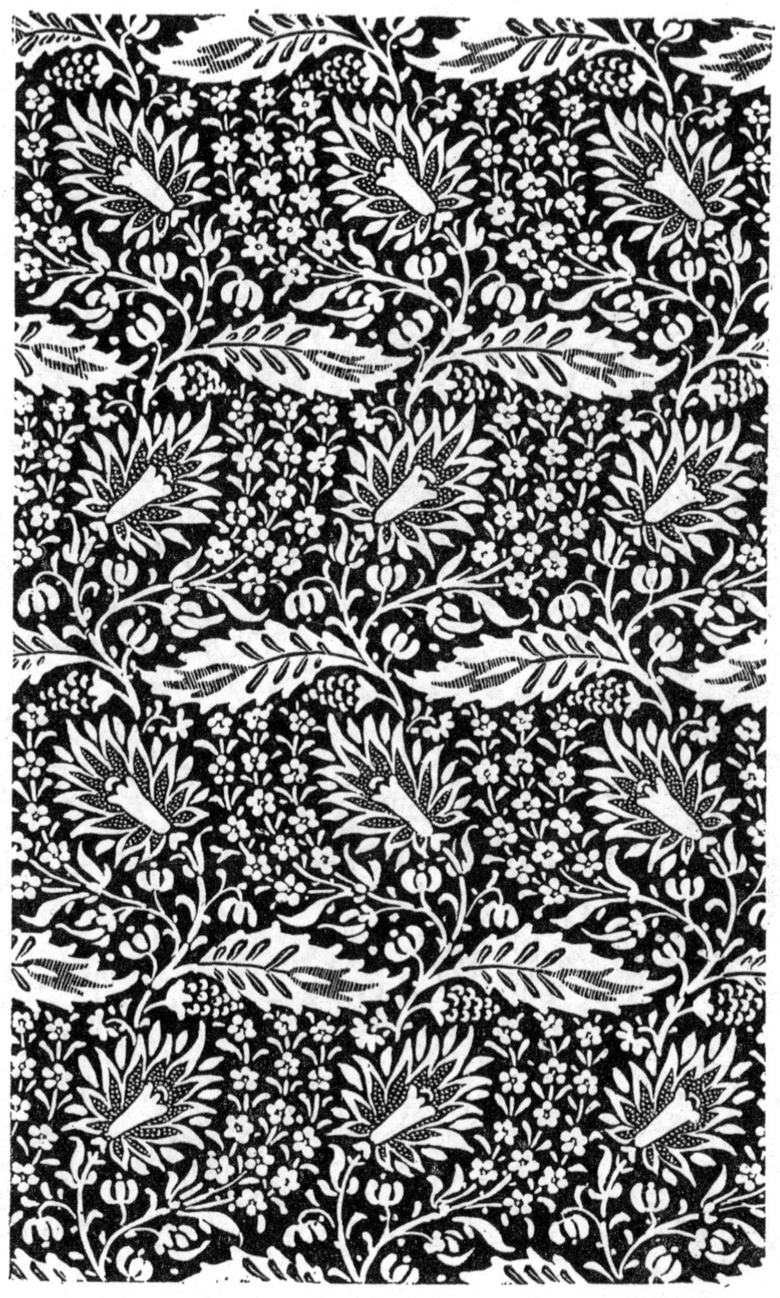

177. PATTERN IN WHICH THE HORIZONTAL LINE IS DELIBERATELY MARKED.

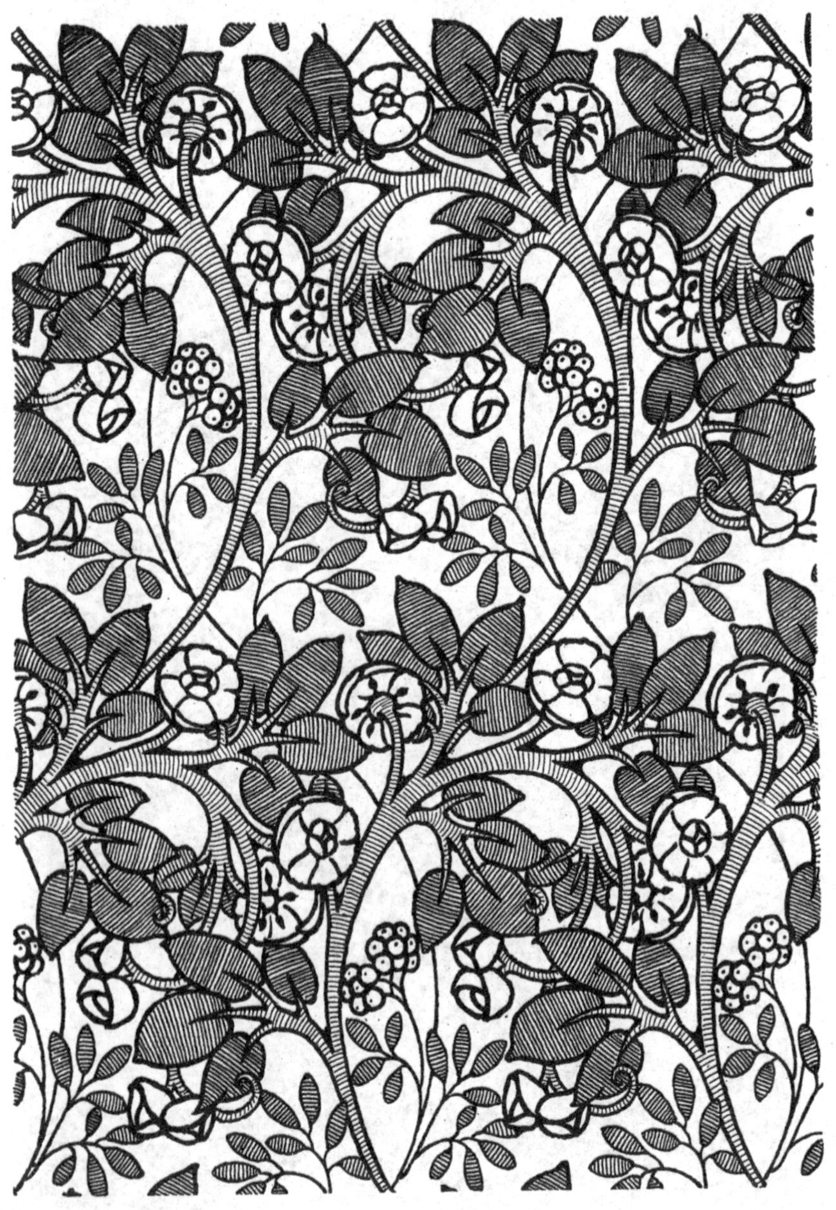

178. PATTERN FOUNDED ON OGEE.

or within some equally broken but less regular shape. For my own part, I have never thought that worth doing. It might, however, be worth while to design a narrow flowing pattern, in which it was desired to avoid anything like a vertical direction within the lines of a zig-zag (169) or of the slanting "herringbone" (169) which results from continuing the diagonal lines until they meet at right angles. It is long unbroken lines in one direction which are so apt to assert themselves.

In an old Italian velvet (170) the above-mentioned diagonal brick lines have been adopted as the plan of a peacock's feather pattern tied together by ribbons, which mark, not precisely the brick, but a flowing-lined variant upon it.

A vast number of excellent patterns have been frankly built upon the ogee, which curved variety of the diamond seems, wherever it is employed, to command acknowledgment. Pattern 178 is an instance. The foundation of the design is an interlacing ogee net, the lines of which determine the stems. The procedure was to arrange the balance of the leaves and flowers of the dominant growth; the detail of the subsidiary growth was an after consideration, and occupies the spaces left in the earlier arrangement.

The late Gothic patterns of which that on page 144 is a type, seem to be the result of simply opening out an ogee

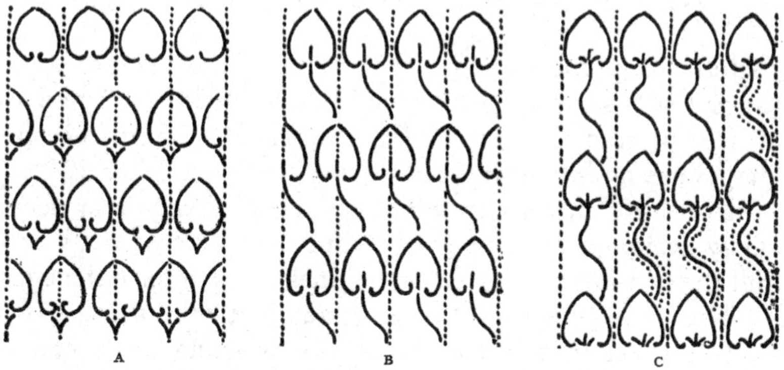

179. DIAGRAMS OF SCAFFOLDINGS.

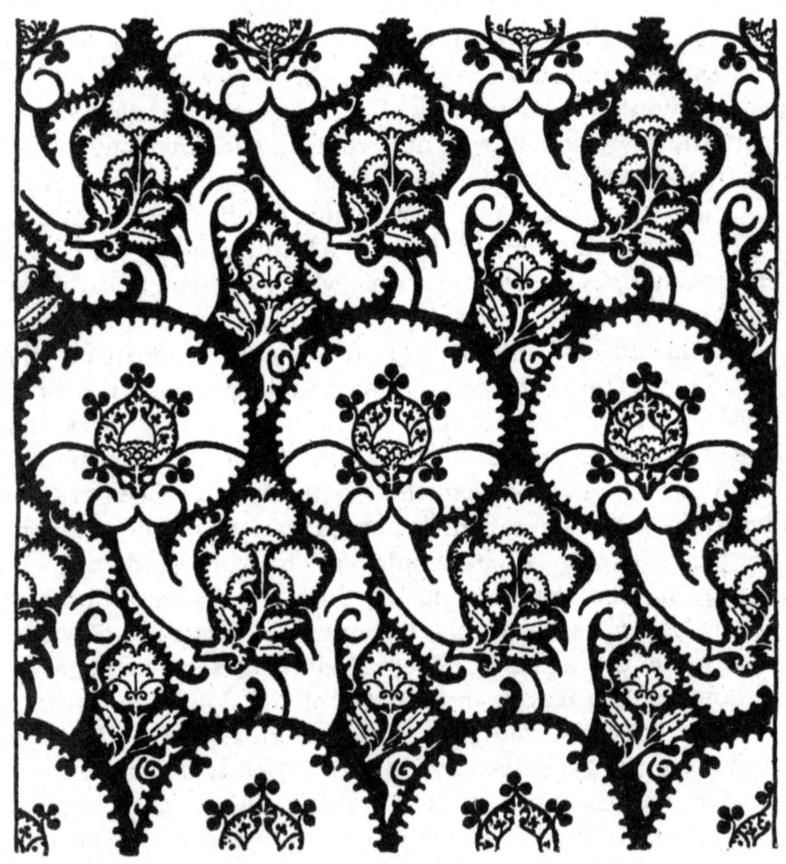

180. SILK BROCADE ON THE LINES OF DIAGRAM 179B.

pattern, dropping the ogee shapes, that is to say, some distance apart, so as to give zig-zag bands between. These are still to be traced in the design illustrated, though the ogee shapes are no longer intact.

Not every pattern in which the ogee occurs, was necessarily designed upon its lines. One may start with a scroll, and the turning over of the wave-lines gives at once the ogee.

The wave-line itself comes (though it may seem like a contradiction in terms to say so) of working upon narrow upright lines, or between them. There is no readier means

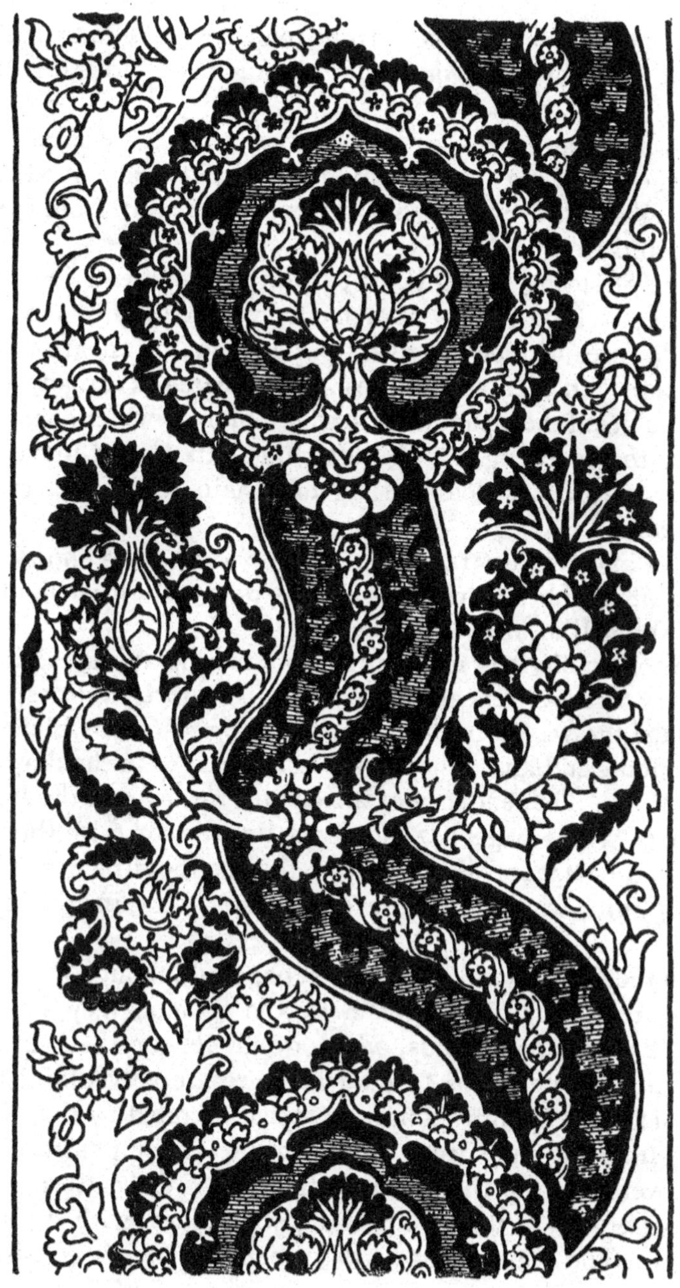

181. SIXTEENTH-CENTURY VELVET ON THE LINES OF DIAGRAM C.

of counteracting the too upright tendency of a long narrow repeat than by lines or bands waving from side to side of the confined space.

Even when the space is not narrow, as in the design (172) on page 145, it may be convenient to anticipate any possibility of vertical lines by carrying the eye alternately from left to right and from right to left.

A scaffolding which leads to new developments in design is to be got by means of a trellis which divides the rectangular area of repeat into six parts, grouping them as (173) on page 146. If these lines are repeated a broad space reveals itself between the smaller oblongs which, when it comes to occupying it with pattern, results almost inevitably in a wave-line as does the zig-zag chain of parallelograms between.

Yet another diagram (174) on the same lines shows that even when the square lines of the plan are insisted upon, something like wave-lines result.

Another obvious means of counteracting the uprightness of very narrow repeats is to cross the upright lines, and perhaps the waved lines within them, by features which give a pronounced band either in the horizontal or in the diagonal direction. The tendency of the narrow turnover in the Dutch print (175) on page 147 is effectually overcome by the pronounced horizontal line of birds, though the direction of the stalks into which they develop helps also in the same way.

In the Cretan weaving (176) on page 148, though the wave-lines are not actually broken by the flowers, they form in repetition compact bands, which go far to stop their upward tendency. One seems to read in that case very plainly the genesis of the design—a narrow repeat dictated by the loom; wave-lines, to take from its straightness; emphatic bands of flowers, to stop the upward direction of the pattern; and further breaks in the colour of the wave-lines, with the same object. The plan might be described as a trellis consisting of upright wave-lines and straight lines crossing them horizontally.

It is true that horizontal lines of the kind here shown result, whether the designer will or no, from the repetition of any feature which nearly takes up the full width of the repeat. It was very likely that which gave the hint to weavers; but they were not slow to take it, and to turn it to very deliberate and constant use.

No designer will doubt for a moment that the long leaves in the pattern (177) on page 149 are an artifice by which to stop the flow of blossom and sprays, and to steady the effect.

A natural thing to do in a narrow turnover pattern (with a view to interrupting its straight-up direction) is to plant,

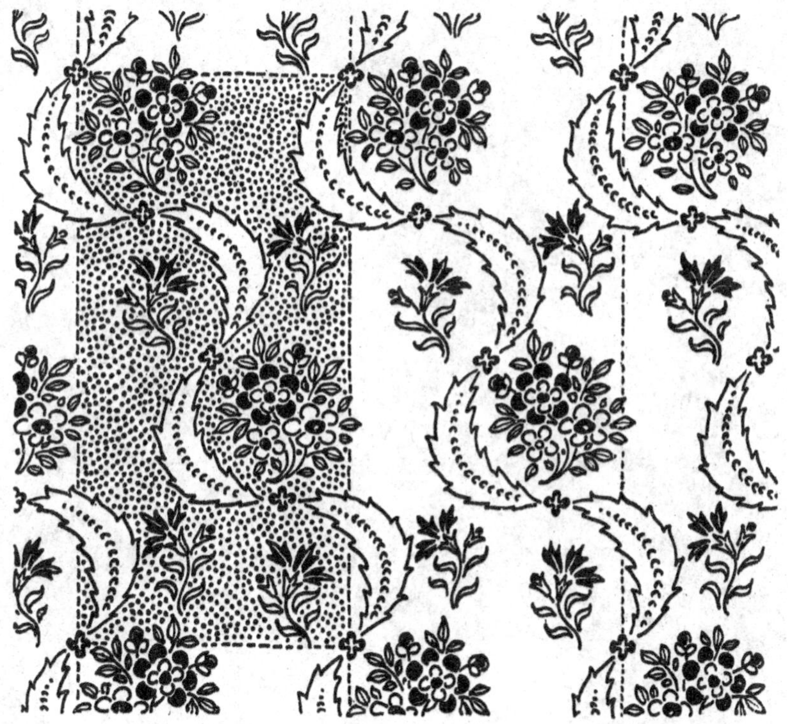

182. PATTERN IN WHICH THE STARTING-POINT WAS A DIAGONAL WAVE.

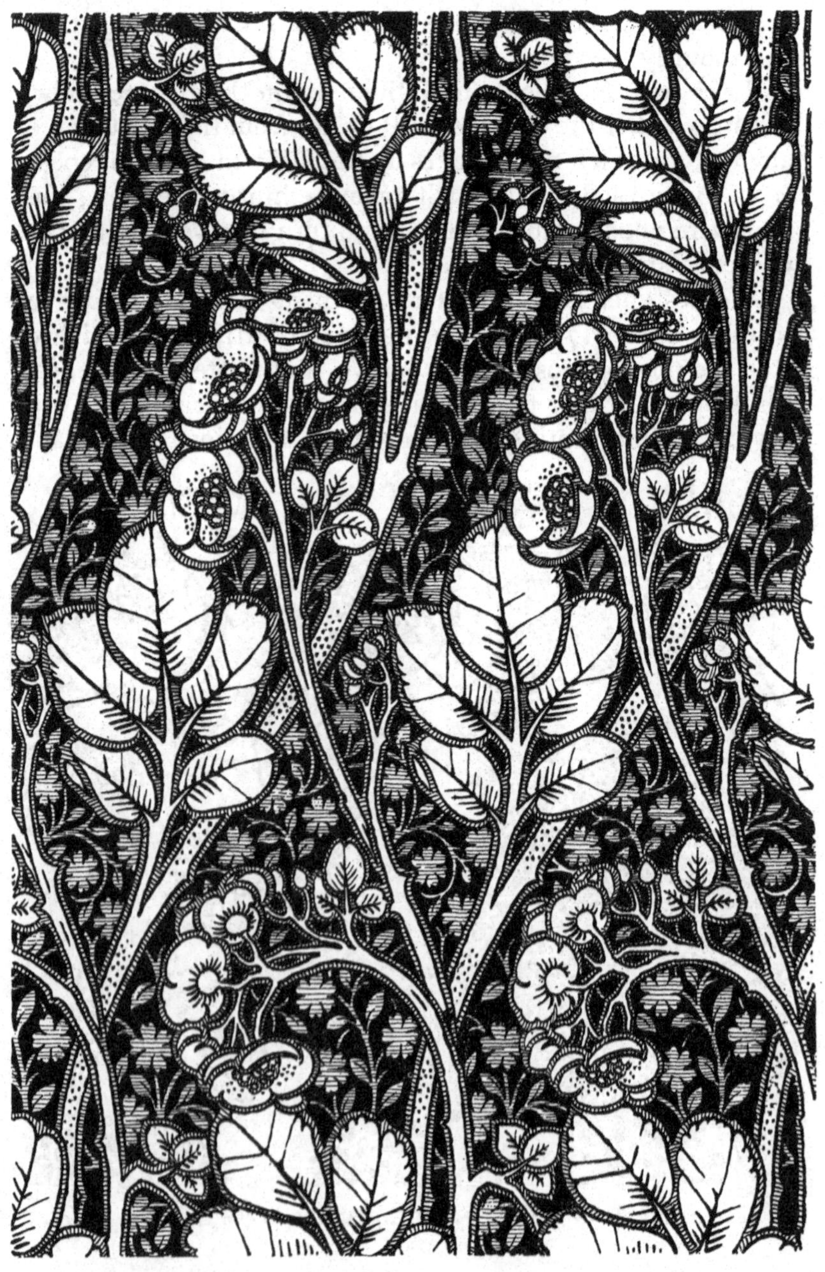

183. MODERN DESIGN FOR CRETONNE, PLANNED ON DIAGRAM 179B, IN WHICH THE LENGTH OF STEMS IS MODIFIED BY CROSSING

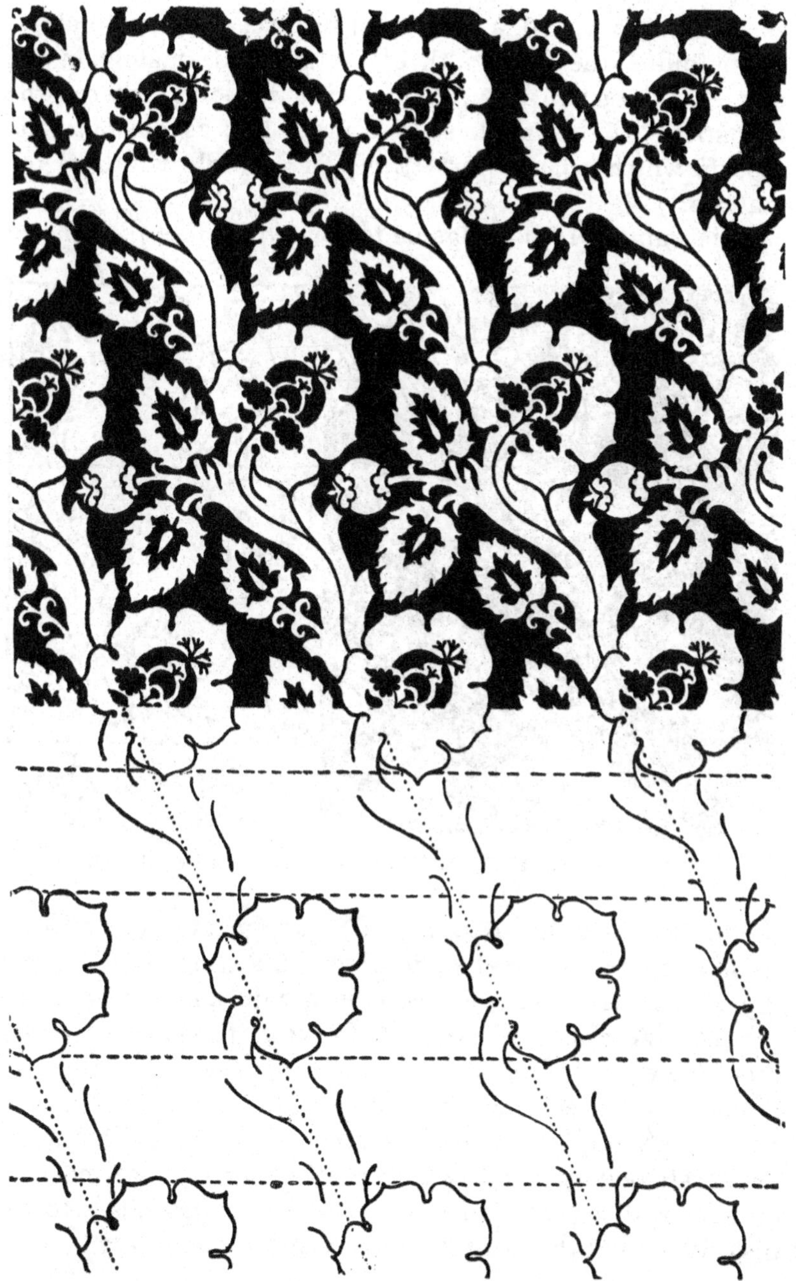

184. FIFTEENTH-CENTURY PATTERN AND ITS SCAFFOLDING.

as in diagram A, 179, a prominent feature, occupying nearly, if not quite, the full width of the stuff, alternately in the centre of the strip and centring with the joint between the two strips. (This applies, of course, just as much to the repeats which recur several times in a single width of the material.)

Diagram B (179) brings us to something like the plan of

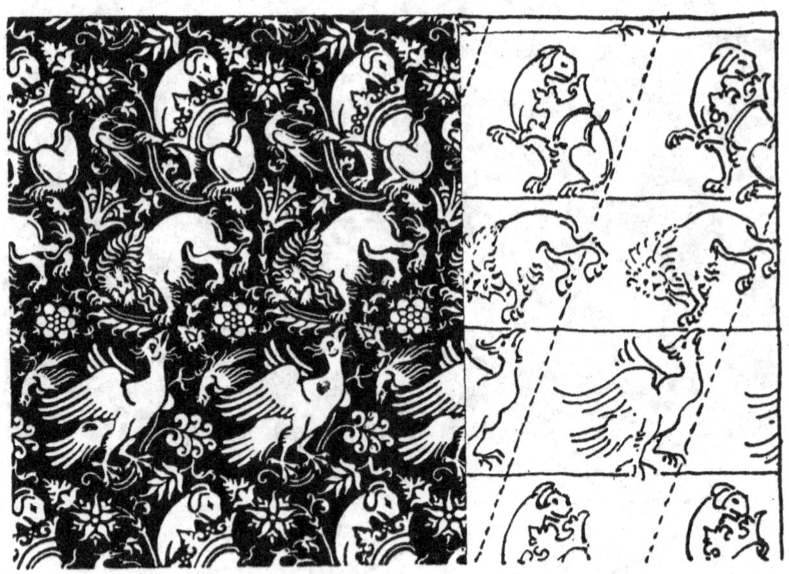

185. SICILIAN SILK PATTERN AND ITS SCAFFOLDING.

the fifteenth-century pattern (180) on page 152, and may be resolved into a diamond scaffolding. But, if the strips or the repeats are narrow, and there is a fair amount of space between the alternate bands of features, flowers let us call them, any lattice of stalks connecting them, whether on diamond or ogee lines, would be too long-drawn-out for beauty. A single line from flower to flower would be much more satisfactory—from which results (whether we mean it or not) a diagonal stripe—more or less ingeniously to be disguised as in the fifteenth-century silk on page 152.

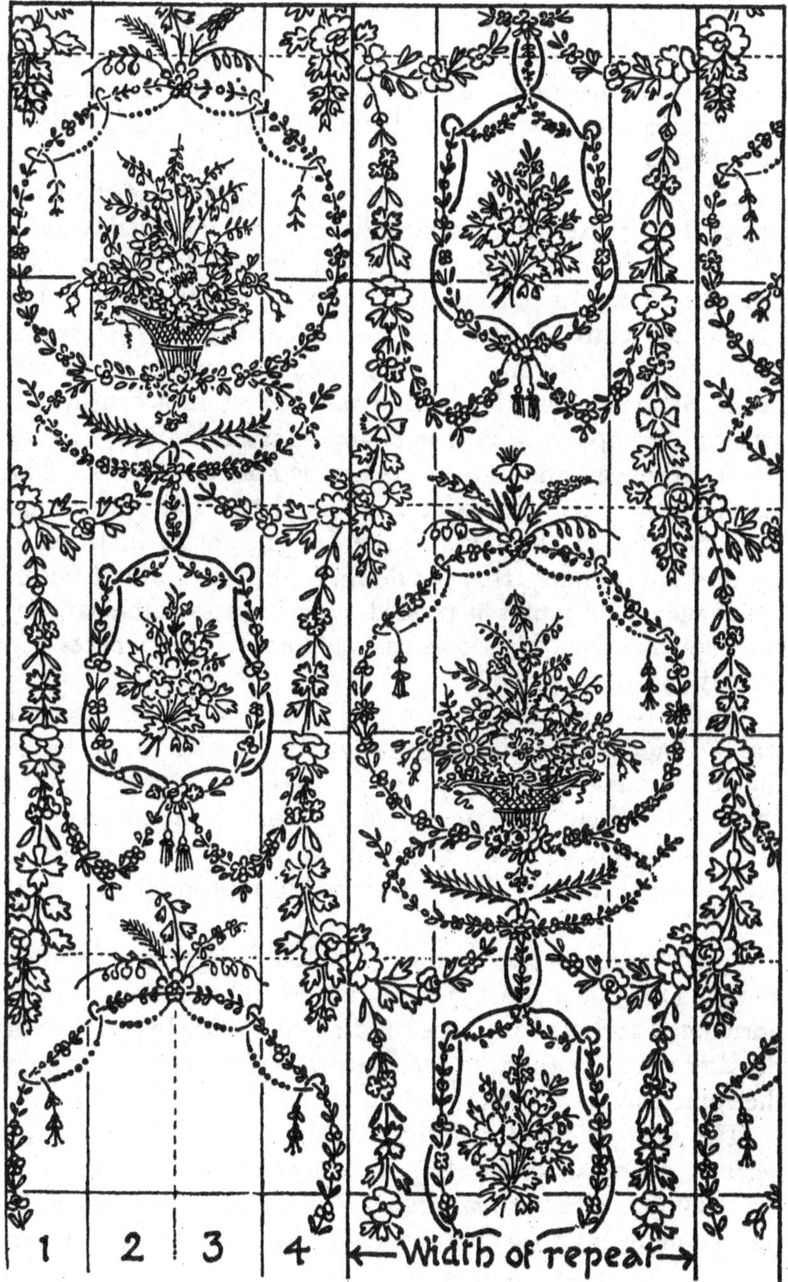

186. PLAN OF A FRENCH DESIGN OF THE LOUIS SEIZE PERIOD.

In the design for cretonne (183), the diagonal direction is not so marked, the balance being preserved by branches in the opposite direction. This is a modern design, planned on 179, diagram B, in which the length of the stems is modified by crossing.

Diagram C (179) explains the genesis of some of the most sumptuous patterns of sixteenth-century brocaded velvets (181). Their starting-point seems to have been a huge conventional flower or pine-apple, occupying nearly, if not quite, the entire width of the material, recurring, of course, at intervals, with one broad waving stem from flower to flower, not, it is clear, running behind the flowers in a continuous sweep, but appearing rather to stop against the flower below it; at all events the flow of the line is not continuous. The puzzling thing at first about these handsome patterns is that you don't follow the logic of the design. I am inclined to think there is none; that the designer did not bother himself about the repeat; that he trusted to the bigness of the pattern, the sequence of which one can seldom see, and takes too readily for granted.

In the pattern (182) on page 155, it is clear that the start was a diagonal line waving gaily from corner to corner of the repeat, and that the sprays of flowers were put there to steady the effect. For the diagonal stripe came at an early date not merely to be accepted but to be insisted upon as an acceptable feature in design—which to unprejudiced eyes it still is.

There seems to me no room for doubt that patterns such as that (184) on page 157 were deliberately planned on the horizontal and slanting lines indicated in the lower part of the diagram; or that the Sicilian silk (185) was built up on the same sort of scaffolding.

The scaffolding of a design by a French designer of the period of Louis Seize (186) is interesting and instructive. The heavier of the vertical lines give the width of the material (rather more than two widths are shown), the finer of them stand for the pencil marks which the artist ruled for his guidance. The horizontal help-lines mark the length of the repeat and its subdivision into four parts, two of which give the drop. It will be seen that he has divided the width of the material also into four parts, two of which (2 and 3) are reserved for the central features of the design, whilst the other two (1 and 4) confine the hanging wreaths (which frame the central features) within easily manageable areas. It is plain that the scaffolding lines assist him in carrying these wreaths from one width of the material to the other. You feel, in fact, that without this scaffolding he would not easily have arrived at a composition which even those who have no sympathy with the style of it must admit to be exceptionally graceful.

It is well worth while working out for oneself plans of this kind, as a means of compelling the invention out of the ruts sure to be worn by continually working on the same lines.

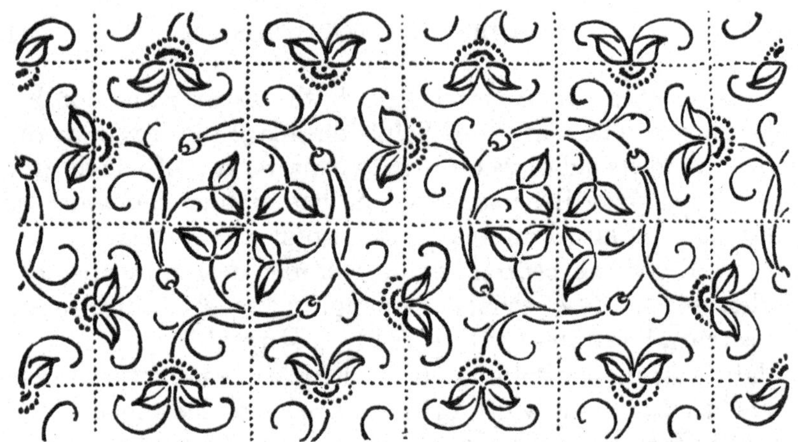

187. DIAGRAM SHOWING SQUARE REPEAT WHICH TURNS ROUND.

XIII. THE TURN-ROUND.

Unit of design may be turned part way round—Unit of 6 by 6 inches results in repeat of 12 by 12 inches—Works either on the straight or as a drop—For radiating pattern a triangle half the size of smaller square suffices for unit—Fold and fold again—Arab lattice pattern dissected.

IN designing for tiles and such like, the condition of continuity obvious in the case of woven pattern no longer exists, and possibilities occur which are denied to the weaver. The repeat of a 6-inch tile, or of the two or more 6-inch tiles which go to make the complete pattern, need no longer be always in the one direction. The designer is free to devise a unit which has to be turned completely round in repetition, or half-way round, or three-quarters of the way; he can, consequently, out of a 6-inch unit get a design which will not repeat on a straightforward trellis in less than four times its area.

In this way the repeats above (187), supposing them to be 12 inches square, could be got out of a unit only 6 inches

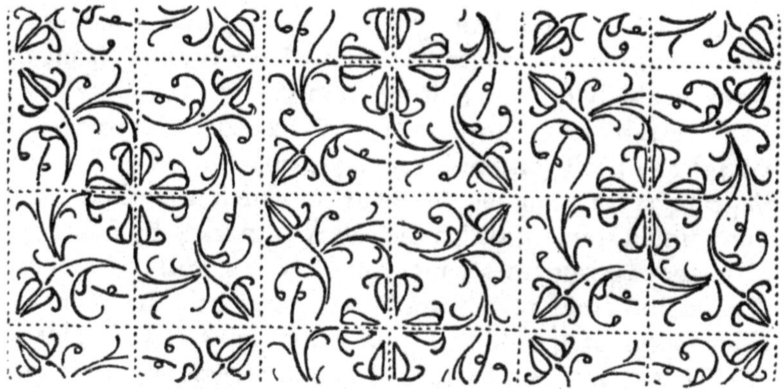

188. DIAGRAM SHOWING SQUARE REPEAT WHICH TURNS ROUND AND DROPS.

square, provided it could be turned round (as a tile could be) in the way above described.

In the case of a pattern repeating on horizontal lines, the design might extend (187) beyond the lines of the repeat. In the case of one that stepped (188), it would be necessary to keep within the four square lines.

If that were so, the pattern could without difficulty be schemed to work, not only as a drop, but on the straight also; and, as a matter of practice, many tile patterns are so designed.

In a tile pattern such as that (189) overleaf, which radiates instead of following round, assuming the squares to measure 6 inches, and the pattern 12 inches across, the unit of repeat (except for the interlacing of the lines, which is no part of its construction) reduces itself to a triangle half the size of the square—or rather, that being itself a "turnover" again, to one a quarter of its size.

The building up of such a repeat on diamond lines is on the face of it apparent.

It is an Eastern practice (I have been told by Sir Caspar Purdon Clarke) to design on the lines of a sheet of paper folded in parallel lines, and folded again in lines at right angles to those, and then again in the diagonal direction—a practice which one ought almost to have divined from the nature of the patterns resulting from it.

The Arab lattice opposite (190) is just such a pattern. Or it might be built (on the lines very similar to those shown in diagram 38) of octagons, the centre of which is marked C, and four pointed stars, of which the centre is marked by four dots; or on the zig-zag lines which give those shapes. It repeats also on the lines of a rectangular diamond, the points of which occur at C; or of a parallelogram A B which drops half its length; and as A is only the reverse of B it works

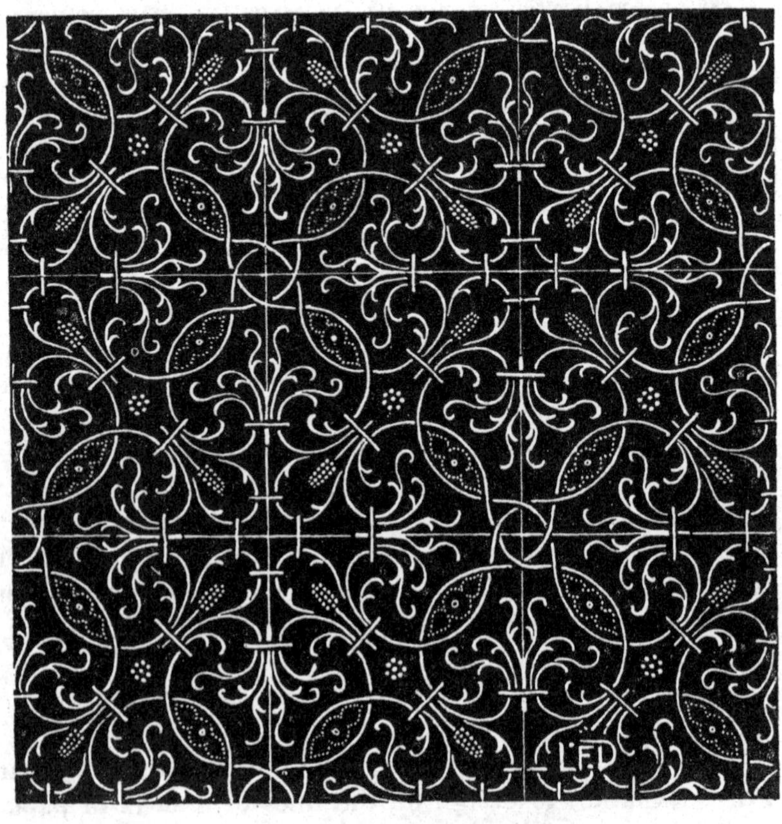

189. TURN-ROUND PATTERN.

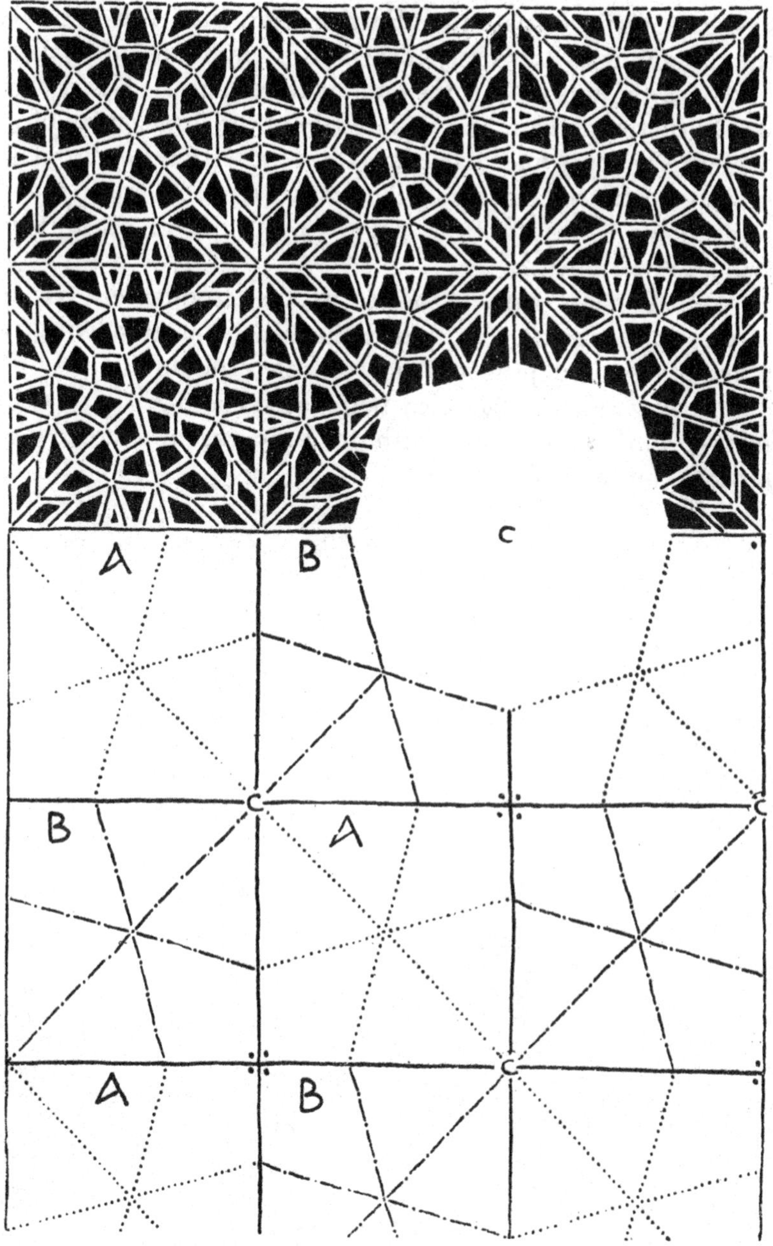

190. ARAB LATTICE AND THE LINES INTO WHICH IT MAY BE RESOLVED.

also as a turnover pattern. Further than that, B is actually the same unit as A, merely turned part way round until what in A was the top is in B the side of the square. The design would therefore work as a square tile of the dimensions of A.

Patterns of somewhat similar construction, even more plainly to be set out upon the lines given by folding and folding again, are shown on pages 49, 51, and 52, all of them typical Arab lattices.

The Persian carpet shown in the frontispiece is an interesting example, in which the centre portion with its pairs of opposed peacocks has complete double symmetry. The filling outside has also both lateral and vertical symmetry, while the border with its peacocks and crocodiles repeats continuously.

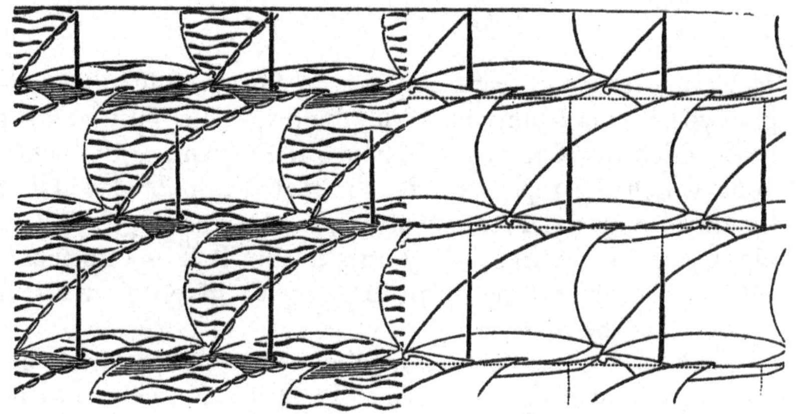

191. WOULD-BE FREE PATTERN FALLING INTO THE LINES OF THE BRICK REPEAT.

XIV. HOW TO SET ABOUT DESIGN.

Free patterns planned on formal lines—Features recur at intervals determined by unit of repeat—Planning the only way to avoid unforeseen effects—Means of disguising formal lines—Necessity for system—Genesis of counterchange border—of geometric diaper—How not to do it—Detail not to be determined too soon—Genesis of conventional floral pattern starting with the masses—of a drop pattern—of a pattern starting with line—of a floral pattern starting with distribution of flowers—of a velvet pattern starting with severe lines—" Inhabited " pattern—Evolution of Italian arabesque pilaster—Animal form in pattern —Starting at a venture—and from an idea—Afterthoughts.

GEOMETRIC patterns have, as a rule, much less reticence in exposing the lines of their construction than others. You see more plainly in them the various plans of construction upon which such stress has been laid. The freest and loosest of patterns will be found, however, to repeat as geometrically as the severest, and on precisely the same lines: it is for that reason so much stress has been laid upon geometry. A flowing pattern does not flow so freely as might be supposed.

Mark any recurrent feature in it—and four such features will give you points from which may be drawn the four straight lines which mark the square, or parallelogram, or diamond, upon which the repeat works. It may be doubted whether the quasi-pictorial French wall-paper (191) on page 167 was planned upon the lines of the brick,* but it falls into them, and the masts of the ships practically give the vertical divisions of the plan.

Each and every feature in a design recurs at intervals determined by the proportions of its unit. Let your unit be a square, for example (192), and, in a cluster of four squares, any given detail will mark by its recurrence the proportion

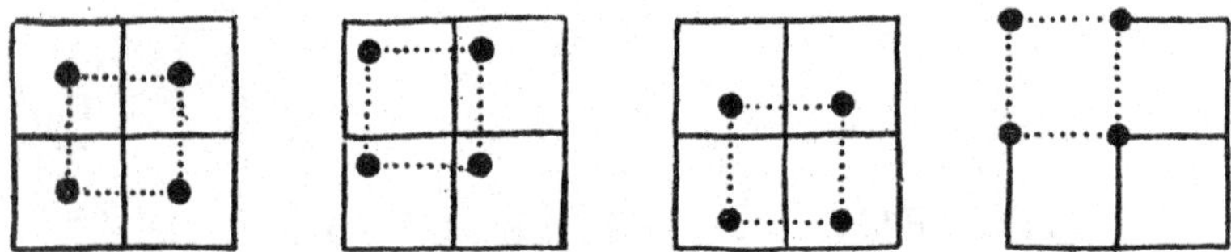

192. DIAGRAM SHOWING HOW RECURRING FEATURE MARKS THE PLAN OF A PATTERN.

of the square, no matter whereabouts in the square it may occur. The diagrams above show this.

The recurrence of the details of the pattern is a certainty. It is as well to make certain of the sequence in which they shall recur. Any reliance upon haphazard at the beginning is sure to give trouble in the end. Happy-go-lucky arrangements seldom work out happily; there is no reason why they should.

A painter may, and often does, go jauntily about his work and put in a diaper upon a screen behind his figures without taking the pains to plan it; but the further he goes the wider he gets of accuracy, and the more plainly his carelessness is revealed. In the diaper opposite (193), for example, the "repeat" does not repeat. This matters nothing in a painting. It even gives the painter an opportunity of

* See page 112.

adapting the pattern to his pictorial needs. In a design for practical purposes it would matter everything. It would be, in fact, not a design but only a suggestion for one.

A designer, like other artists, trusts largely to his instinct; and rightly relies upon it for artistic prompting throughout his work; but it will not supply the place of order, to which in the nature of things he is pledged. He is free *only within the limits of his repeat*—practically a right-angled space, or a diamond of given dimensions.

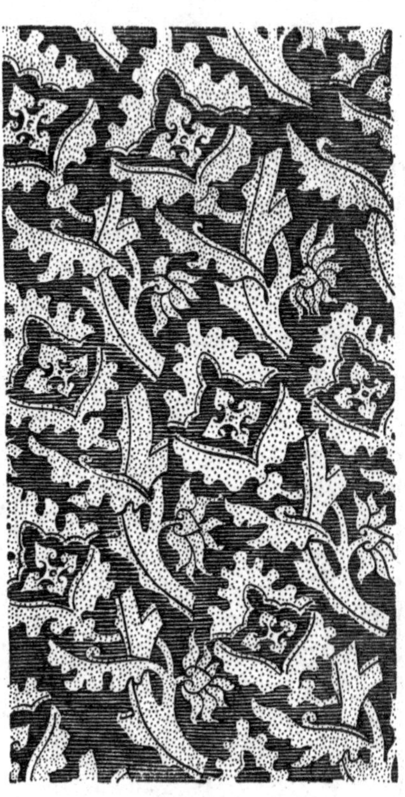

193. PAINTED GOTHIC DIAPER IN WHICH THE "REPEAT" DOES NOT WORK.

Suppose it to be a square. Within the four sides of that he may do as he likes. He may sprinkle sprigs about in the most admired disorder. There may be no more geometric relation between them than between the six black spots in the central square overleaf (194); but, where there is no geometric relation between the members of the group, it is not easy to anticipate, as a designer should, what will be the effect of the group itself when it comes to be repeated. It will be seen that in repetition the spots fall into irregular lines with awkward gaps between—just the kind of line which comes by accident, and might easily have been avoided by careful contrivance (see page 5).

For want of more systematic planning the pretty damask pattern opposite (195) falls into stripes which, it seems to me, the artist did not foresee. They are comparatively harmless there—and would be equally so in a table damask—but in a wall pattern, for example, they might assume distressing prominence.

A stripe is by no means necessarily to be avoided in design—and it is in obedience rather to the prejudices of a timid public than to their own artistic instinct that designers avoid frank lines. Artists know how useful they are. But they should be the lines that play their part in the pattern; and, to do that, they must be well considered; not left to chance: the chances are all against a happy fluke. One way out of the difficulty is boldly to insist upon the stripe and make a feature of it. Another is to cover the ground with uniform pattern in which is no break and no feature more

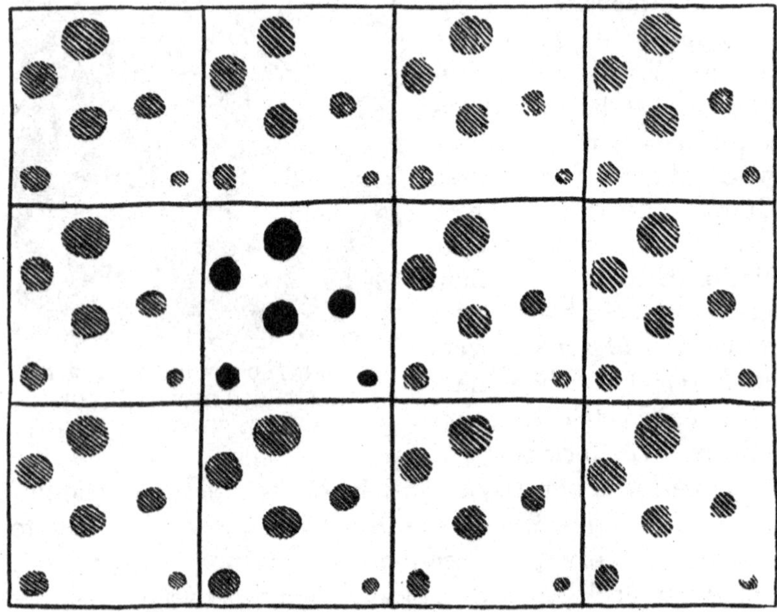

194. DIAGRAM SHOWING GEOMETRIC RECURRENCE OF FEATURES NOT GEOMETRICALLY DISTRIBUTED.

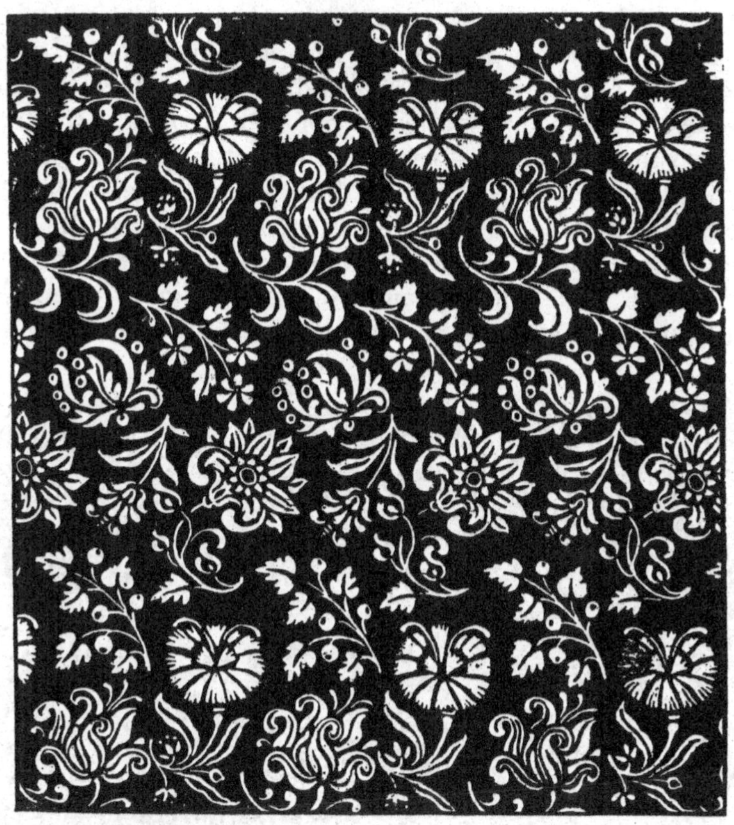

195. OLD LINEN DAMASK PATTERN FALLING INTO STRIPES.

prominent than another—in the manner of the daisy pattern overleaf (196)—and that is an exceedingly difficult thing to do. But the way to do it is, not gaily to scatter daisies about upon the paper, but to plan them (see page 130 *et seq.*), and, even then, the uniform covering of the ground involves an amount of experiment and reconsideration, which is in itself enough to explain the comparative rarity of such patterns. Unpretending they may be; but there are occasions when what is wanted is simplicity verging even upon insignificance, and where yet obvious geometric forms would not do. Hence the need for all-overish ornament—pattern which is meant to break a surface or a colour and not much more. Even then it is not a bad plan to introduce into it features such as the circular groups of flowers opposite (197), and the little flowers in upright pairs between, which, though in a measure lost in the even distribution of detail, may be relied upon to assert themselves, if anything catches the eye at all; and these are planned, of course, with a view to their effect in repetition. The difficulty and danger of design is lessened in a pattern in which there are such points of emphasis (however

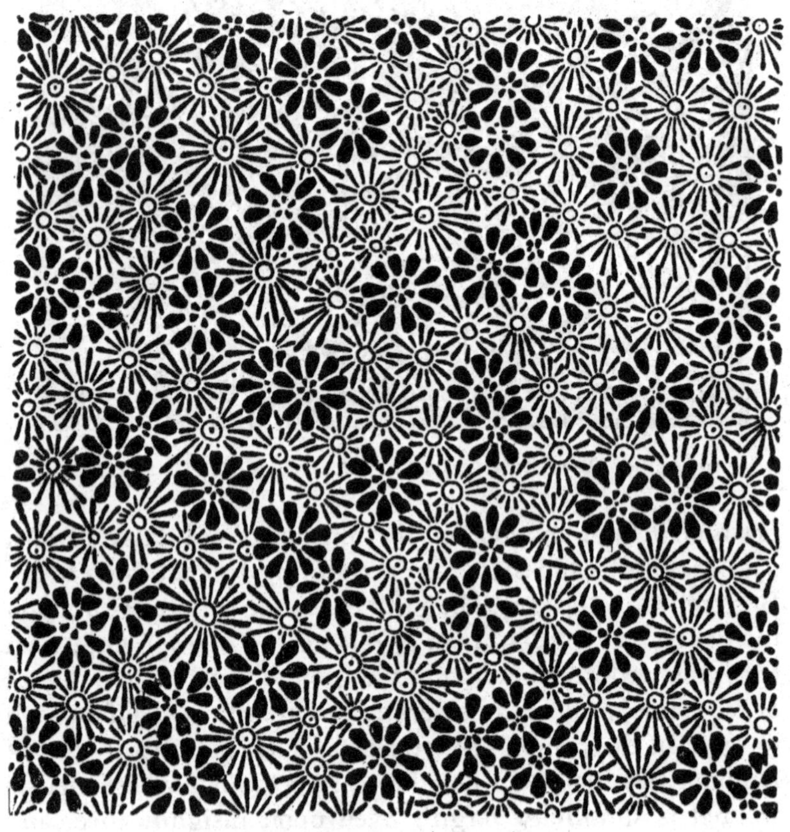

196. FEATURELESS "ALLOVER" PATTERN.

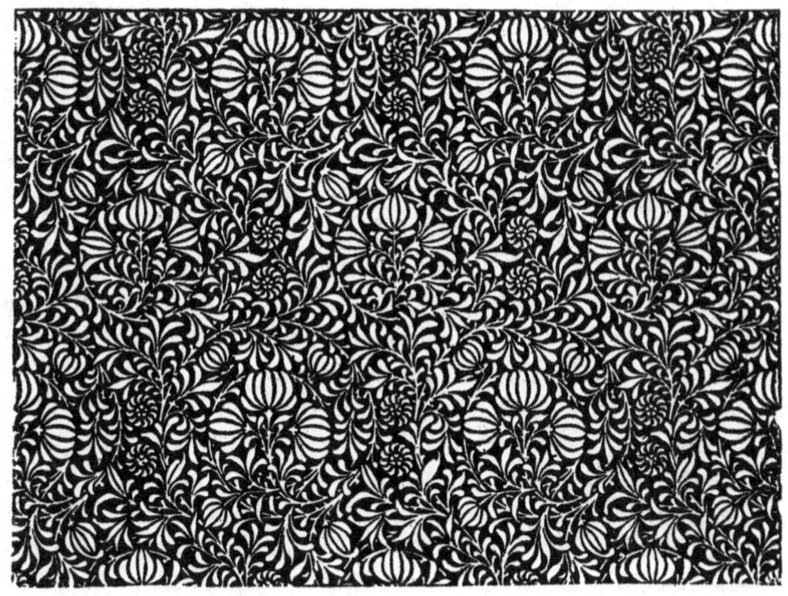

197. FEATURES DISGUISED BUT NOT QUITE LOST IN "ALLOVER" EFFECT.

slight), features balanced one against the other, supporting it may be or counteracting one another, and yet producing an effect of even weight; or in a pattern in which there are marked governing lines, whether symmetric and plainly revealed, as in illustration 198, or flowing as it were freely, and partly lost in scrollwork or leafage. To lose the lines of recurrence altogether, as in illustration 199, is not easy.

Insistence upon the necessity of governing lines in pattern must not be taken to imply that they must always be insisted upon or that they may not assert themselves too strongly. There is a point at which they are an annoyance.

It may be expedient to subdue them—even to efface them at times. The necessary subjection may be effected in various ways. They may be arbitrarily interrupted. They may be overpowered by detail, not perhaps very significant in itself. Two or more schemes of design may be interwoven, the one asserting itself here, the other there, and each calling attention from the other. The lines themselves may be so ingeniously interlaced that it is hard to disentangle them. Some of them may be traced merely in outline, hardly strong enough to hold its own against more substantial features, or in a colour having more affinity with the ground than with the ornament generally.

But the most usual way of disguising the skeleton is, taking the hint from nature, to clothe it with something in the way of foliation—by which the bare constructional lines are as effectually hidden as the branches of a tree by its leaves. By this means the spirals of a scroll can be made to assert themselves as much or as little as occasion may demand. Only if the curves are not well considered it is hopeless to try and make up for that by foliation, to disguise bad lines by leafage. A broken-backed scroll betrays itself beneath it all. There is no disguising its native infirmity. Pattern is vertebrate; and in a scroll the spinal cord is very plainly pronounced.

As to whether it is better to reveal or to disguise the construction of a pattern, to insist upon it or to call attention away from it, that is a question to be answered partly according to the temperament of the designer, partly by the circumstances of the particular case. Either plan is best upon occasion. But it is a point upon which the artist should in every case make up his mind at once. He should know what he is going to do, and do it deliberately.

Referring to the popular prejudice against anything like formality in design and especially against anything which "you can count," as they say, the public has a right to call the tune it pays for, and will no doubt get what it wants. If it will have nothing of severity or restraint in pattern, so much the worse for design. If, however, any student of ornament should feel that way, so much the worse for him, or for his chances of success in this direction. His wiser course would be to turn his attention to some branch of art

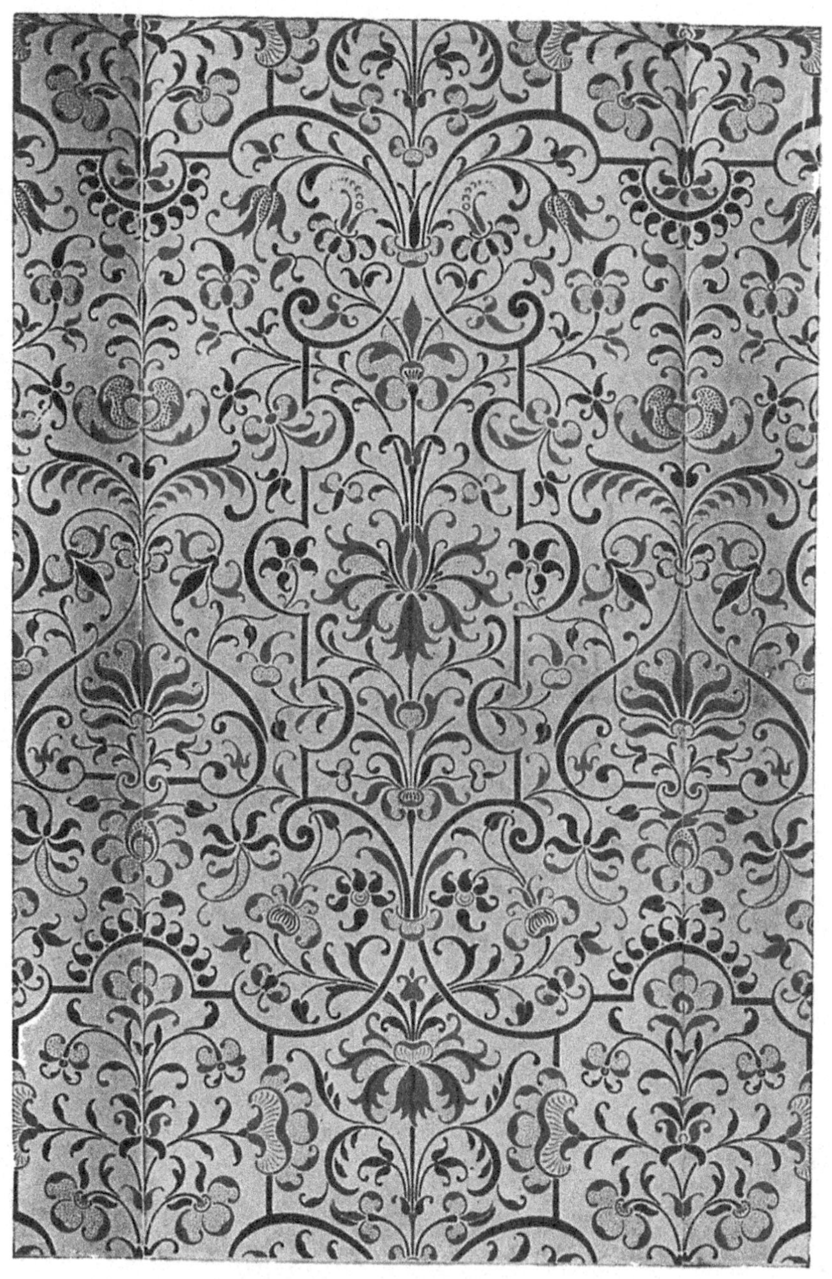

198. DESIGN IN WHICH MARKED GOVERNING LINES STEADY THE EFFECT.

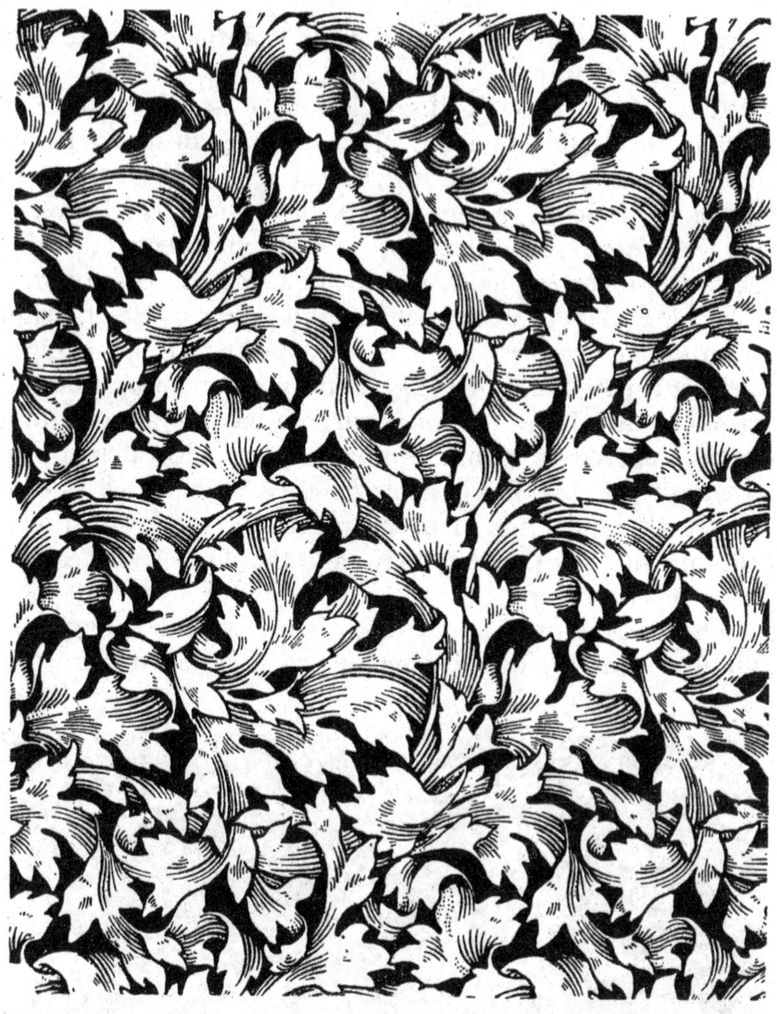

199. WALL-PAPER PATTERN IN WHICH THE LINES OF RECURRENCE ARE PURPOSELY LOST.

for which he has more aptitude: he lacks the instinct of pattern design. A wilful world will have its way. An artist should know that, in sacrificing everything in the nature of formality, we renounce much of the dignity which belongs to the best in whatever form of art. The finest of old pattern work is invariably formal and owes to formality something of its noble character.

Apart from that, it simplifies, as was said above, the problem of design, to accept the recurrence in it of a feature more or less plainly marked. And it is not altogether a matter of choice. In any design not absolutely all-overish one feature, or some features, must be more emphatic than the rest. Over-emphasis is provided against by points of lesser emphasis, to balance them, and points of lesser weight again to balance these perhaps. By the careful balancing of parts, it is possible, if not easy, to draw off attention from any formal plan. Indeed to such purpose has the art of hiding art been exercised in this respect, that the advocates of "go as you please," seeing in some good patterns no evidence of construction, are not to be persuaded that they were ever built upon a plan. They may take the word of a designer for it that they were.

The dress pattern below (200) is of the class called free. But it was as deliberately set out as if the geometric con-

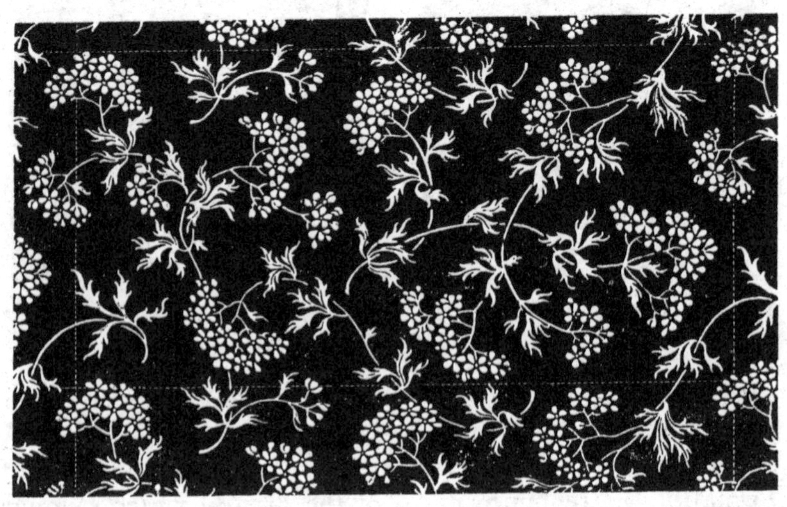

200. "FREE" DRESS PATTERN DELIBERATELY PLANNED.

struction were conspicuous in it. If you detect no formal lines in it, it is not because the plant was allowed to trail as accident would have it—there was nothing free and easy about its disposition—but because the lines of growth were from the first schemed with a view to seeming freedom, and the details were so plotted as to divert attention from the system upon which they are distributed. The system is there.

If you would avoid the unforeseen in your completed work—and the unforeseen reveals itself often in the most unsatisfactory manner—system is essential.

A practical designer does not idly let the pencil in his hand meander about upon a sheet of paper, in the vague hope that something may come of it. He starts with a definite notion of some sort—a happy thought, an image in his mind perhaps, or, if not that, the idea at least of the sort of thing he wants, the thought of certain lines or masses, or the combination of the two, which promise when repeated to make pattern.

The lines upon which a design is planned need not, it

201. DIAGRAMS SHOWING DEVELOPMENT OF A "COUNTERCHANGE" BORDER PATTERN.

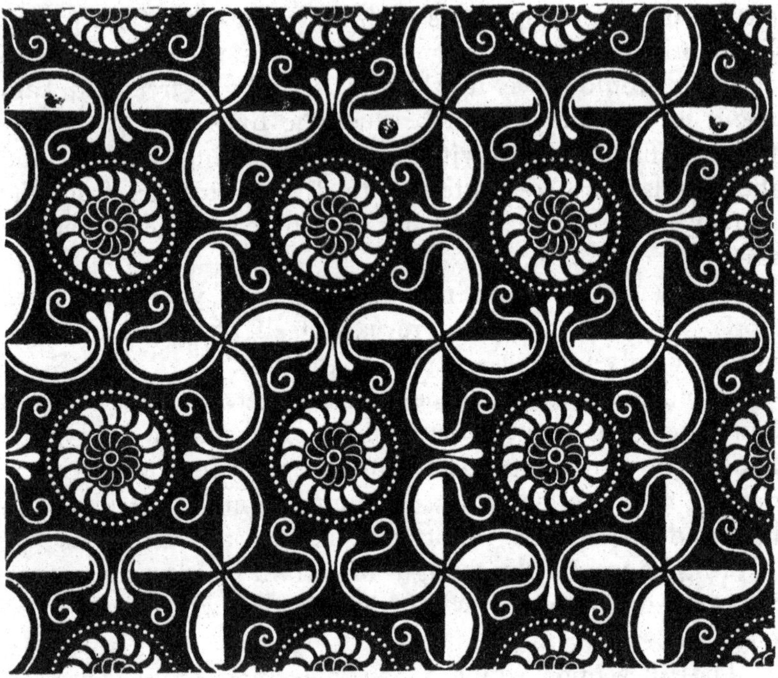

202. GEOMETRIC DIAPER PLANNED AS IN DIAGRAMS BELOW.

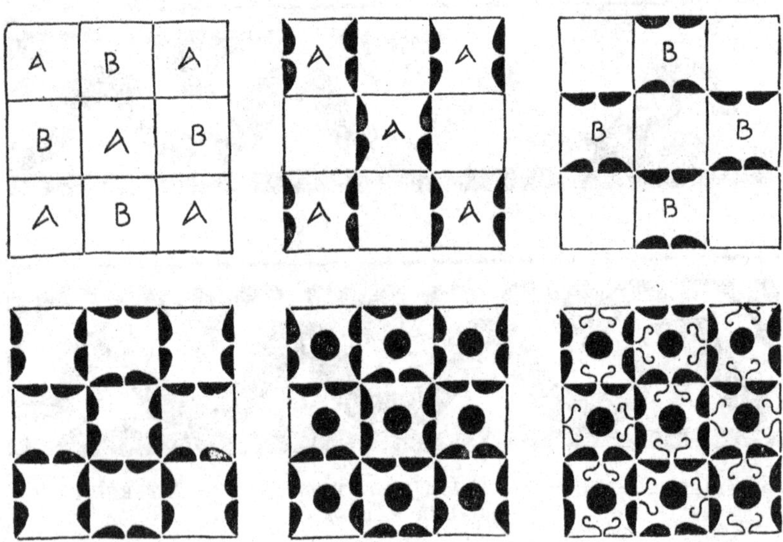

203. DIAGRAMS SHOWING STAGES IN THE DESIGN OF A GEOMETRIC DIAPER.

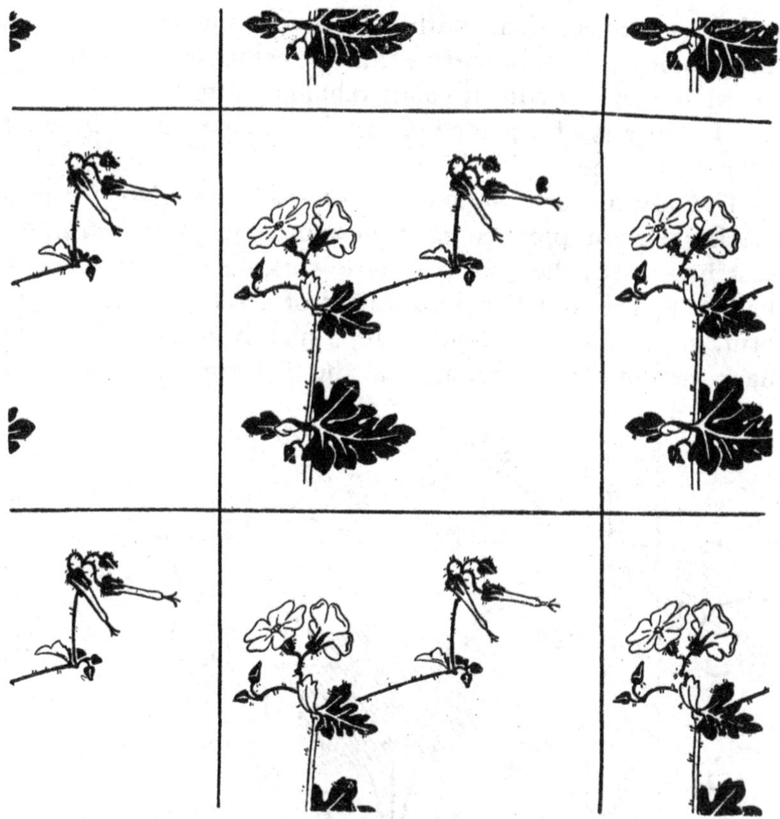

204. DIAGRAM SHOWING A FALSE START IN DESIGN.

has been explained, form any part of the pattern. But, if they do, it is easier to trace the steps by which it came to its effect.

Take the simplest of patterns, a border (201) in which the repetition is only in the horizontal direction, and begin with a wave line down its centre dividing it equally into two halves, the one white the other black (A). Following the lines of the wave on the one side, and of the margin on the other, we arrive in the simplest way at a sort of double wave giving a white enclosure in the black space and a black one in the white (B). To turn these into flowers (C) and to give them stalks to connect them with the waved line is an obvious thing to do; and so we arrive, almost before we know it, at a complete and consequent counterchange pattern.

The genesis of a geometric diaper (202) is scarcely more difficult to trace.

The initial idea worked out on page 180 (203) was a flooring pattern, planned upon the square therefore, or rather, as it happened, the double square working as a drop. The double square and the desirability of retaining the square form, suggest an equal-sided unit, merely turned about, to mark the double square, and (in the flooring) to prevent the

205. DIAGRAM SHOWING THE START OF A DESIGN.

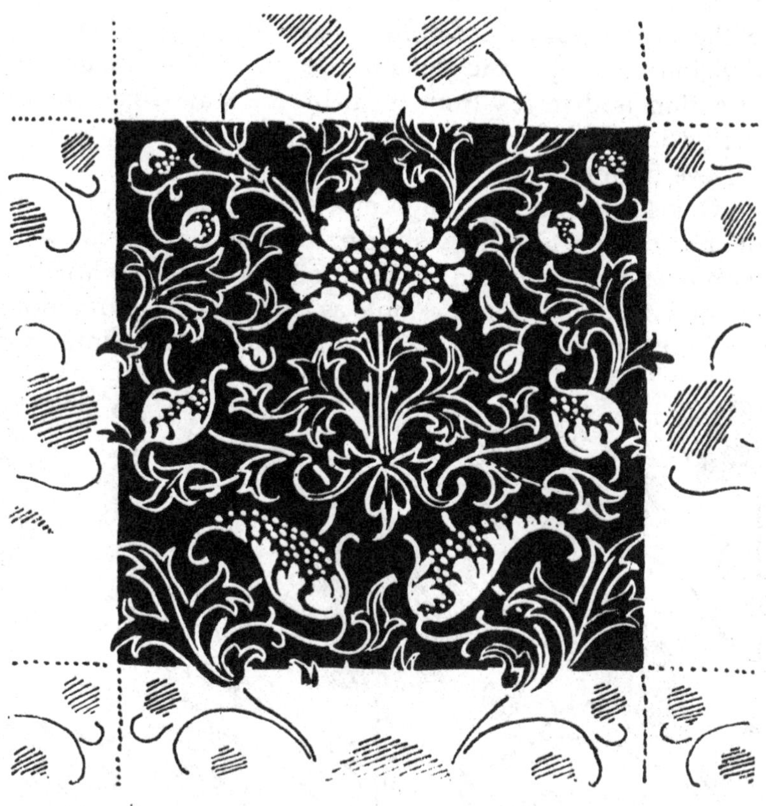

206. DIAGRAM SHOWING DEVELOPMENT OF 205.

effect of lines in one direction. But though it was advisable to retain the square form it was not desirable that it should assert itself too prominently. The pronounced additions to square A in the second of the smaller diagrams (203) effectually prevent any such danger; and, repeated in the cross direction in squares B, they give in the fourth diagram already a coherent pattern. But it is empty, and the proportion of light and dark is not what was wanted. A central disc of black upon the white puts that right, and the continuation of the curved lines in the direction of the disc does away with the disconnected look of the various parts. The completion of the design (202) is then only a matter of detail. The square divisions are kept, and remain a feature in the design; but attention is diverted from them by the wave-lines crossing the lattice, which give yet more emphatic features, and take the eye from them.

One sets about the design of a pattern of which the lines of construction form no visible part in much the same way—with a definite idea, and on definite lines, but *never* with any definite detail, such for example as a natural spray of flowers.

Painters unpractised in design assume sometimes that

207. DIAGRAM SHOWING START OF A DROP REPEAT.

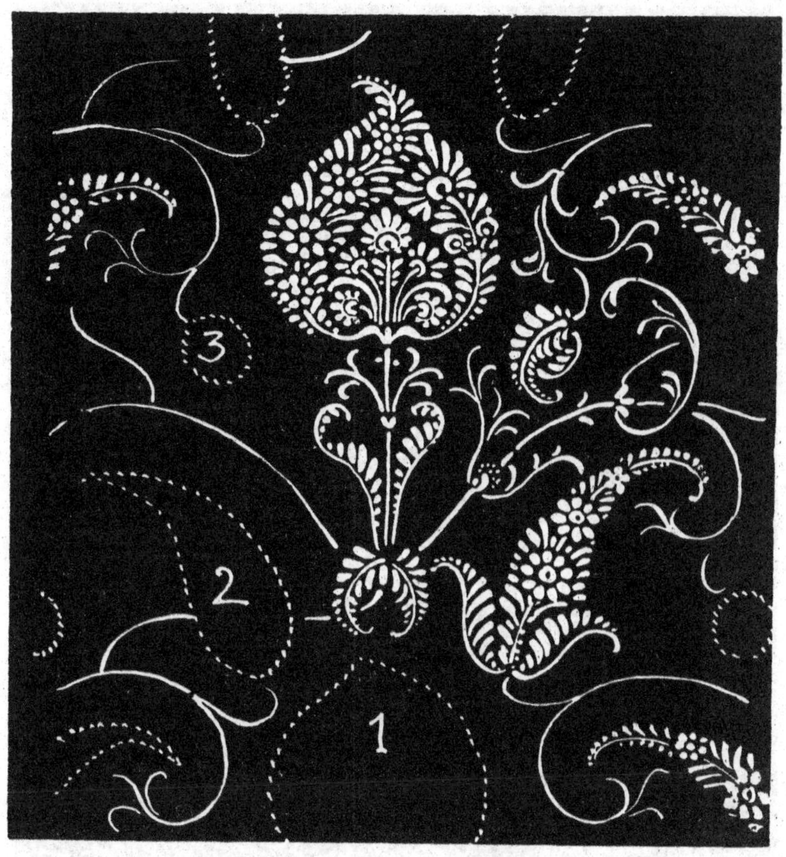

208. DIAGRAM SHOWING DEVELOPMENT OF 207.

they have only to repeat at given intervals no matter what study from nature, and make good the connection between the repetitions of it, and the trick is done. It is not quite so easy as that. Let any one try and connect the isolated details (204) on page 181.

The natural lines of a flower, determined by no thought of repetition, are scarcely likely to bear repetition very well, and the difficulty of working up to nature, and comprehending such naturalistic details in any satisfactory scheme of

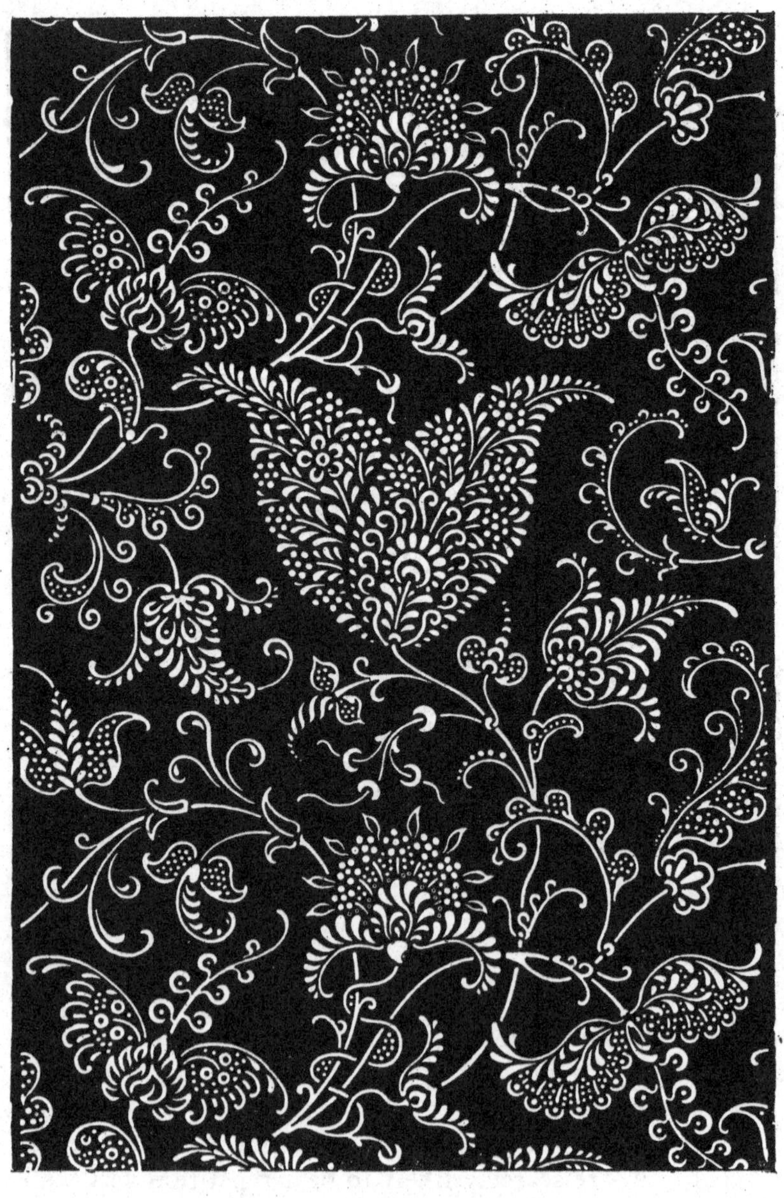

209. WALL-PAPER PATTERN

composition, is extreme. If anything results that way which goes for ornament, it is by accident and not design. Emphatically that is not the way to set about it. A designer makes his flowers grow his way.

He starts, never with detail but with one or other of the two important factors in design, line or mass—whichever, according to his aim, naturally takes precedence. In the case of a scroll, he will first get right the sweep of the lines, before beginning to clothe them; in the case of a floral pattern, he will more likely dispose his flower masses in the order in which they should come, leaving lines of growth and foliage for after-consideration.

It must not be supposed that defects of construction are to be made good by clothing or disguised by foliage. No one worth deceiving is deceived that way; and any one disposed to scamp preliminary work should know that in the end it does not even save labour. Starting with the idea of a symmetrical design in which the flowers and buds shall be the prominent features—the designer starts naturally with what he desires should first be seen—he begins by planting somewhere about the centre of the repeat, say, a heart-shaped mass (1) diagram 205. That perhaps suggests to him at either side a smaller bud-shape (2), near enough to the margin to group with its repeat, and so be useful in taking the eye from the joint, designed to balance the heart-shape, but not compete with it in mass. These forms repeated suggest, as a means of breaking the plain space below, features of intermediate size and different shape from either (3). A still remaining vacant space or belt of ground between these and the heart-shape below, determines the introduction of a pair of smaller buds (4), which in repetition give groups of four, valuable if only for variety's sake. A space of still too open ground suggests additional budlets (5), far enough apart to appear singly in contrast to the pairs about them. These points of interest determined indicate of themselves the lines to connect, correct and counteract them. The order in which they successively occurred is given by the letters A B C D.

The designer may or may not, in planting such features on the ground, have somewhere at the back of his mind an idea as to the way they shall eventually be connected; but the connecting lines must in the end be determined by the necessity of accounting for those masses as they stand. Supposing them to be flowers, they must grow in some coherent way. Lines and masses once determined, the next process is to give them more specific shape, and to modify them to some extent in so doing (206); to evolve perhaps out of the heart-shape a conventional flower, out of the smaller shapes husks with berries. The lines become connected stalks, clothed in the end with foliage, the scale of which is fixed by the spaces to be occupied, and the character by that of the flowers.

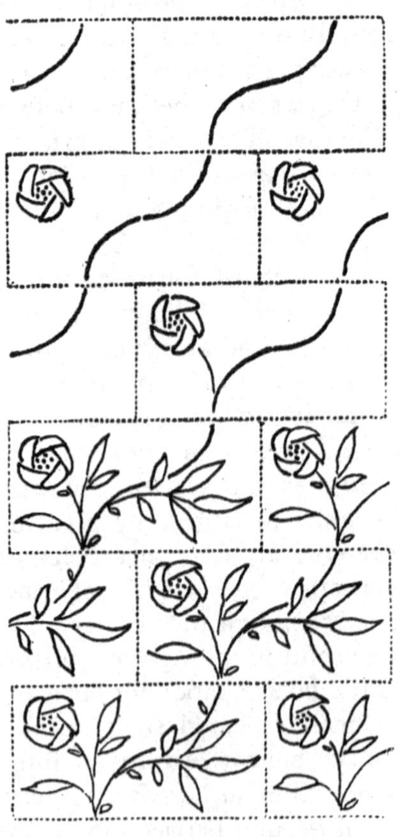

210. DIAGRAM SHOWING "BRICK-WORK" PLAN.

Invention, it will be seen, is here progressive. Each advance enables the designer to see further ahead, as when, in climbing, you reach another ridge of hill. To a man in the vein, one move suggests the next—he may not have known what he was going to do, but, one step made, he feels the next

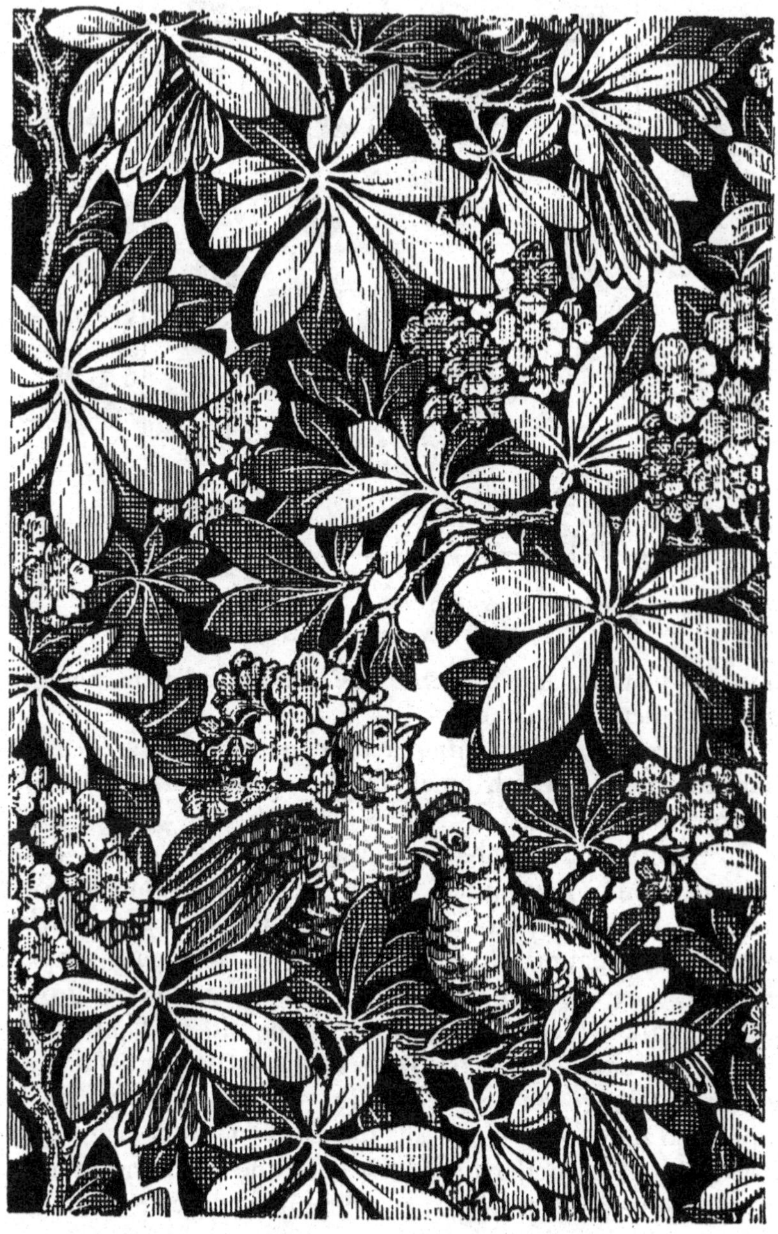

211. PATTERN IN WHICH THE DISTRIBUTION OF FLOWERS AND BIRDS WAS THE FIRST STEP OF THE DESIGN.

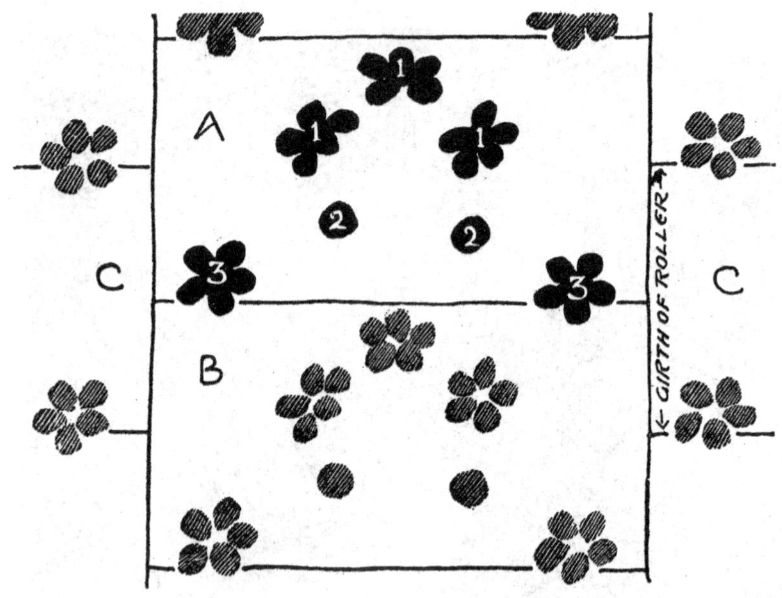

212. DIAGRAM SHOWING FIRST STAGE OF A DESIGN.

must be just so, and no otherwise. What is done pledges him to something further.

The process of designing a drop pattern is set forth in diagram 207, in which much the same forms as before are purposely employed.

In this case it is more than ever necessary to repeat each form, as soon as determined, in the outer spaces round about the central square (containing the unit of design, but not the parts of the pattern in their entirety). The cone-shaped feature (2), for instance, not only oversteps the line, but grows from a stalk which trails over from the side. That much settled, the balance and the lines to the artist's satisfaction, he can safely go on to the details—in this instance, as it happens (208), very different indeed from the last—from which it will be understood how little the planning or first roughing-out pledges one to any definite character of detail. Either of these two rough first suggestions might just as well have been carried out after the manner of the other. The completion of a pattern very similar in detail to 208 is shown on page 186 (209).

The main point to bear in mind is that there must be harmony between the detail and the way it is planned. Comparatively natural flowers must grow in a comparatively natural way (211). Forms more deliberately ornamental (209) demand correspondingly formal lines to accompany them. It is in the precise relation of the two that the taste of the artist is shown.

The evolution of a design beginning with line instead of mass, is shown in the diagram illustrating the brickwork plan (210) in which the consecutive steps were: the wave-line across the brick; the continuation of the line across the other bricks, to see how it would come; the placing of the flower spots to steady the effect; their connection with the main stem; and the final filling out with foliage.

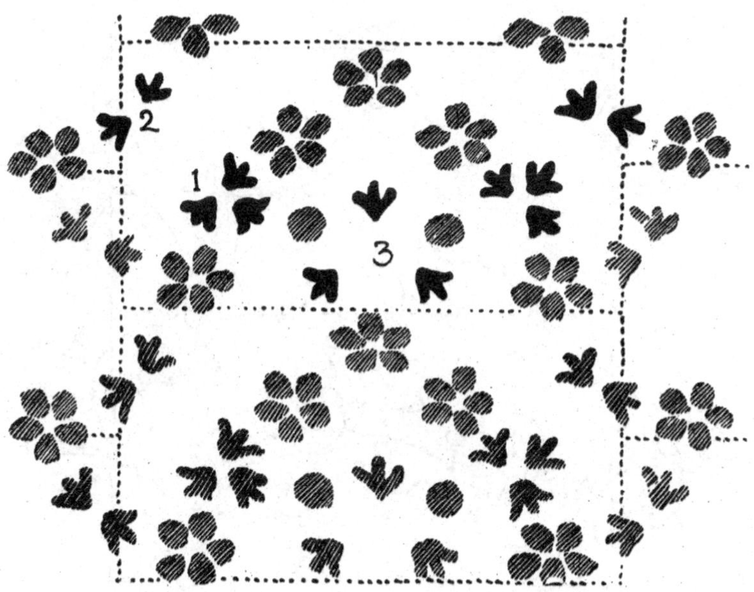

213. DIAGRAM SHOWING SECOND STAGE OF DESIGN (212).

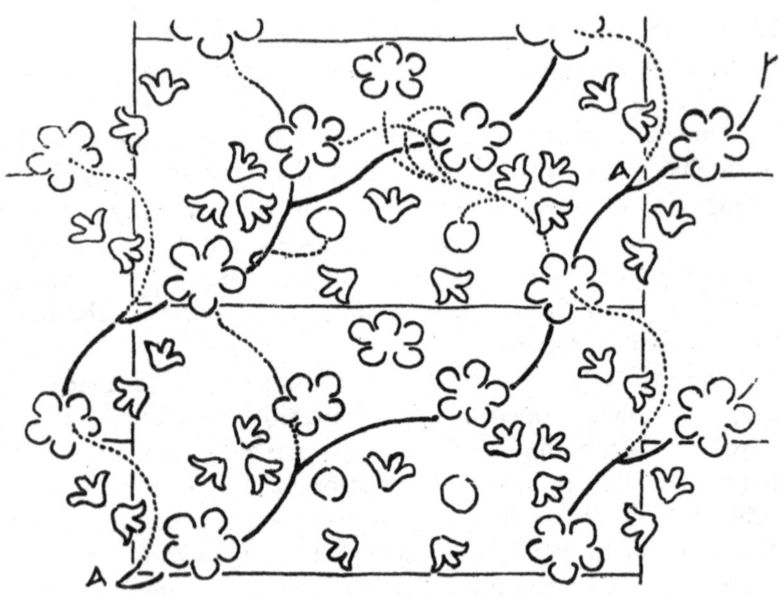

214. DIAGRAM SHOWING THIRD STAGE OF DESIGN (212).

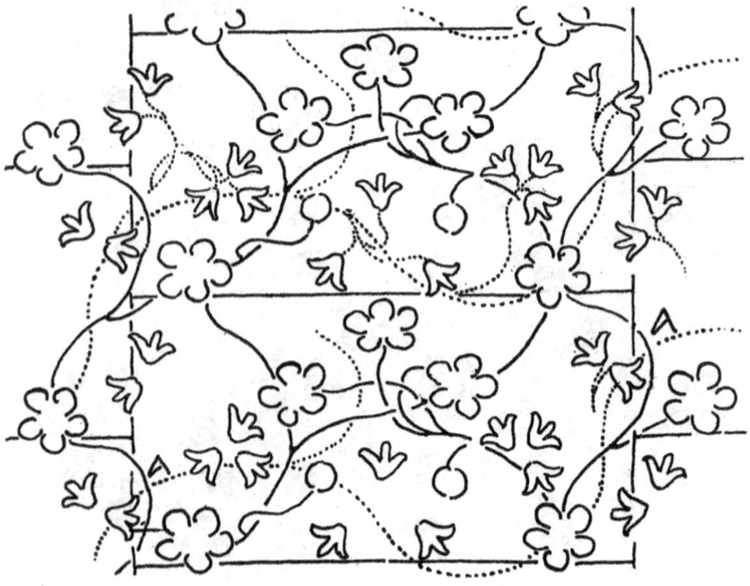

215. DIAGRAM SHOWING FOURTH STAGE OF DESIGN (212).

Whether it is better to start with line or mass depends upon what you want to do. It is as well to begin with what is most important. If you want grace of line, that must be your first thought. Line deserves prominence in design only on the condition of its being beautiful. That is where the designer comes in.

In the case of deliberately floral design (211), the more convenient plan is to begin by distributing the flowers (assuming they are to be at all prominent), settling where they shall occur, their size and shape, grouping them here into bunches, there breaking the ground with isolated blossoms or smaller buds, but considering them always as so many colour patches. The main stems from which they grow may then be thought of, and finally the foliage which is to occupy the space between the flowers, avoiding them it may be or backing them.

The stems of flowers (which must be natural in proportion to the naturalness of the flowers and leaves) are a standing

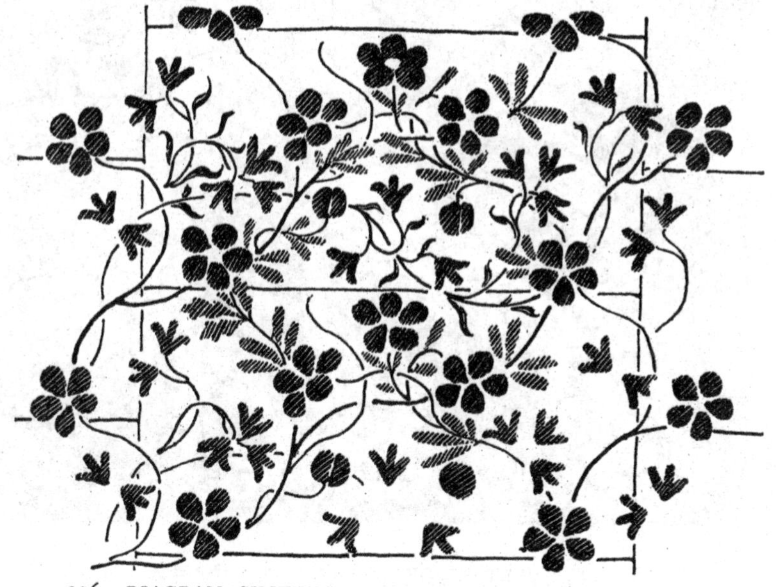

216. DIAGRAM SHOWING FIFTH STAGE OF DESIGN (212).

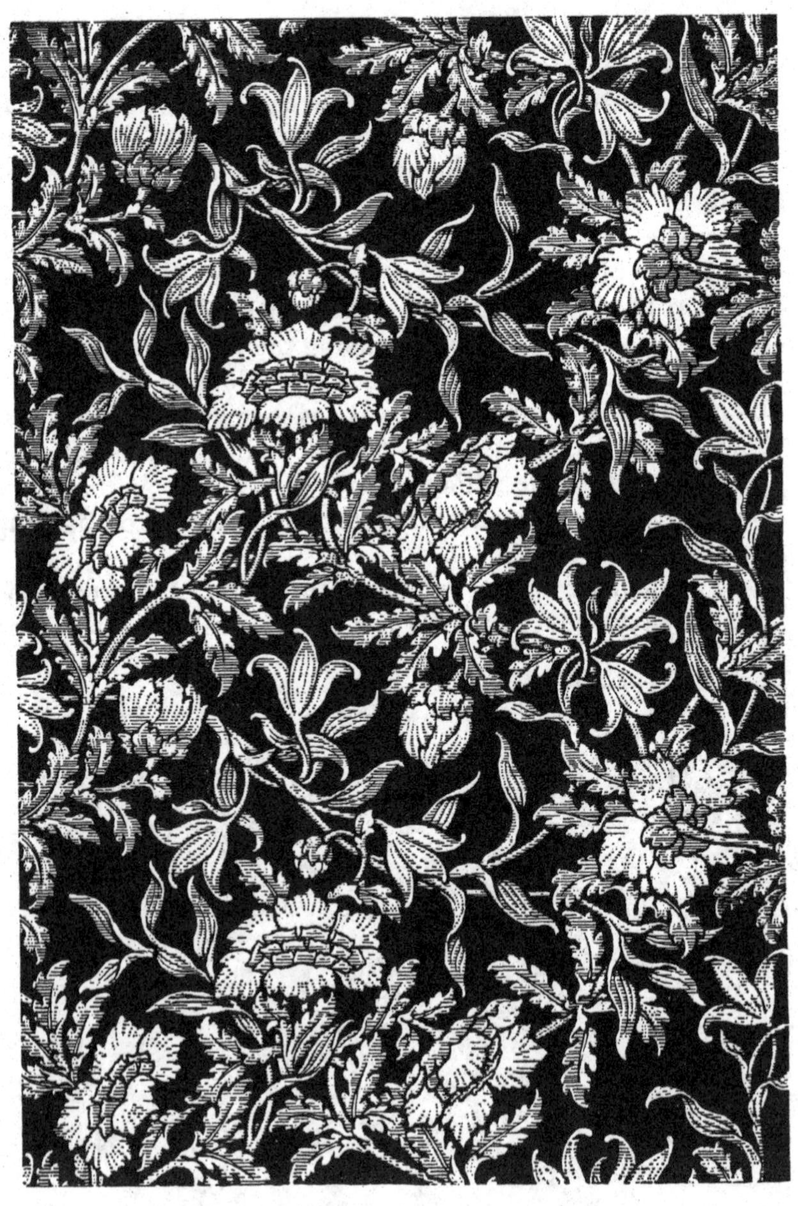

217. PORTION OF DESIGN 212 FINISHED.

difficulty in design. You must have them, but you do not, as a rule, want them to be marked; and they have a way of marking themselves very determinedly. The wary artist in planning his design bears in mind from the first the necessity of something like natural growth in a natural flower, but still he starts with the flower masses—unless, of course, the flowers form no important part in his scheme; in which case he begins with the foliage, if that is more important; but flowers insist as a rule upon being the first consideration. Absolutely natural growth is rarely possible in pattern, even were it to be desired. It takes beautiful lines but seldom quite the lines wanted in a given pattern. It is expedient in such case to disguise or lose the line of growth in foliage—much as it is lost in nature.

The development of a fairly complicated floral, but not too naturalistic, pattern, is traced in diagrams 212 to 217. The initial idea was a free-growing pattern in which flowers of relatively large size should be supported by smaller ones, of different colour for variety's sake—a double growth that is to say. That would give also an opportunity for variety in the colour of the leaves. Naturally one growth would be more prominent than the other.

The first thing to do, having settled that it should be a drop pattern (the dimensions of the printer's roller settled that it should be twice as wide as it was deep), was to plant the more important flowers in place, as at A (212). A central group of three large flowers (1) and two small buds (2), when repeated as at B, suggested the placing of further flowers (3) between, rather nearer to the side edges. These repeated as at C, there seemed to be sufficient of this sort, remembering there were others to come. The number and position of these others (naturally of a different shape) was determined (213) by the ground left bare. They are what the vacant spaces seemed to call for: a group of three (1), to stop the downward gap; a pair (2), to break the joining line; three separate flowers (3), to fill the vacant spaces in the centre.

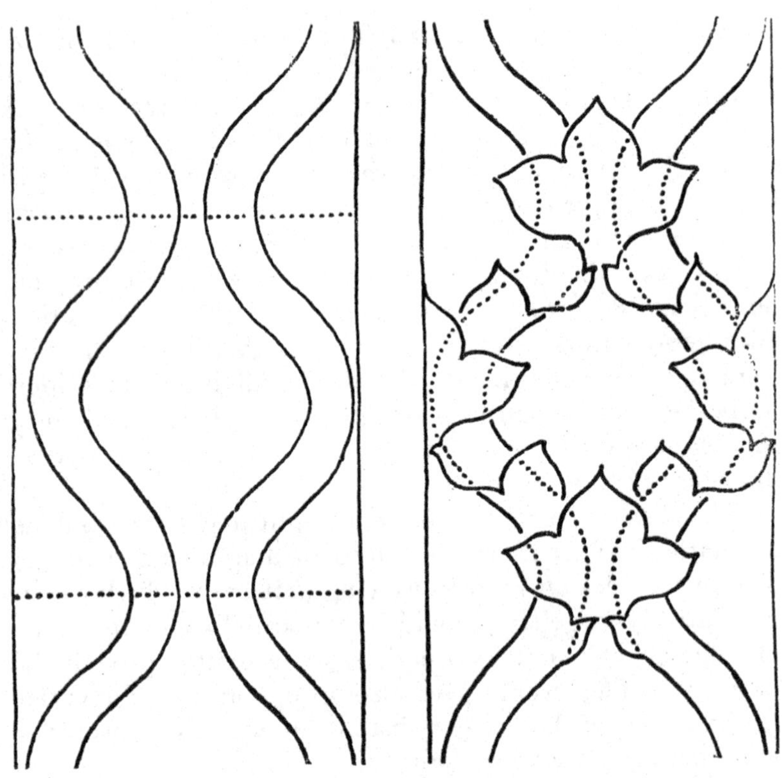

218. DIAGRAM SHOWING FIRST AND SECOND STAGES OF A VELVET PATTERN.

The next consideration was the order in which the flowers should grow, and first the larger ones. A solid line from A to A (diagram 214) shows a stem which runs through and joins on satisfactorily at the sides; it had only to be repeated in the upper part of the drawing to suggest the more or less contrasting (dotted) lines connecting the flowers with it.

The growth of the larger flowers accounted for, that of the smaller (given in dotted lines in diagram 215) had to be schemed, which left only the leafage to be blotted in (diagram 216) and the map of the pattern was there.

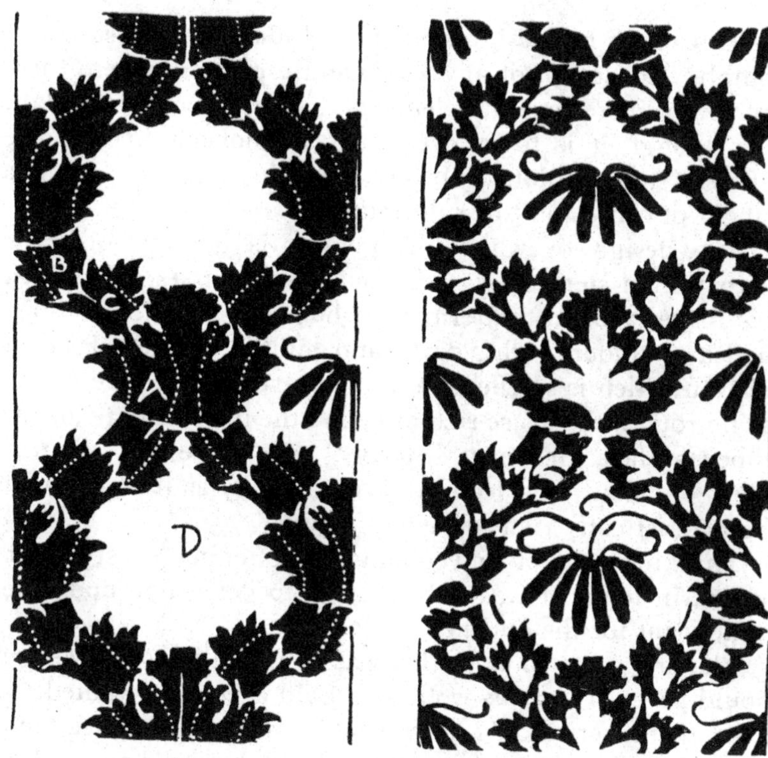

219. DIAGRAM SHOWING THIRD AND FOURTH STAGES OF A VELVET PATTERN.

In carrying such a sketch further (a portion only of the finished cretonne is given on page 194) the shapes of the forms might well want considerable modification, something would have to be erased or added, but the groundwork would be all there, the plotting done, and the designer free to follow the promptings of his artistic impulse. A design of this kind is easier to manage if the distinction between the separate growths is made clear by the use of very pronouncedly different colours, such as red and yellow for the flowers, blue and green for the leaves—even though there should be no intention of any such sharp contrast in the final effect. Some such guide is almost necessary, to enable the designer to keep the threads of his design separate. Indeed, in the case of a complicated design of any kind, and especially where there are two or more separate elements in it, it is not a bad plan, even though it is to be eventually in monochrome, to use different tints in plotting it out. It reduces the very serious danger of confusion to a minimum.

The design of which the genesis is next given starts neither from stem lines nor from flower masses. The idea was to get a broad pattern, bold but not too bold, in three shades of colour, light, dark, and middle tint, the kind of relation which is so effective in old velvets, where the glossy satin ground, the dense rich pile, and the intermediate uncut, ribbed surface known as "terry," give three very distinct stages of colour, and lead, almost naturally as it seems, to a characteristically rich sobriety of effect.

Thinking still of velvet and the softening effect of the outline in terry, it was only natural to determine upon the middle tint for the outline.

The first thing to be settled was the main lines the design should take. It was as well, as a bold effect was wanted, to make them very bold; they could always be refined and softened. That being so, there could be no better plan than waving bands which in opposition give the ever satisfactory ogee shape (218). But as it was not a geometric pattern that was desired, these broad bands had forthwith to be broken in some way; which was very simply done by treating them as bands of foliation, twisting about, and to some extent disguising the too plainly geometric planning. This was a means of getting, too, some life into the lines. It was high time by now to think of the pattern in mass as dark upon a light ground (diagram 219), and to sketch in not merely the turning over of the foliage but the serration of its outline. The broad bands began on this to disappear, but the lines were still stiff, and the masses of light and dark in too crude contrast. That was corrected by the introduction of dark foliage into the ground space D, which very distinctly

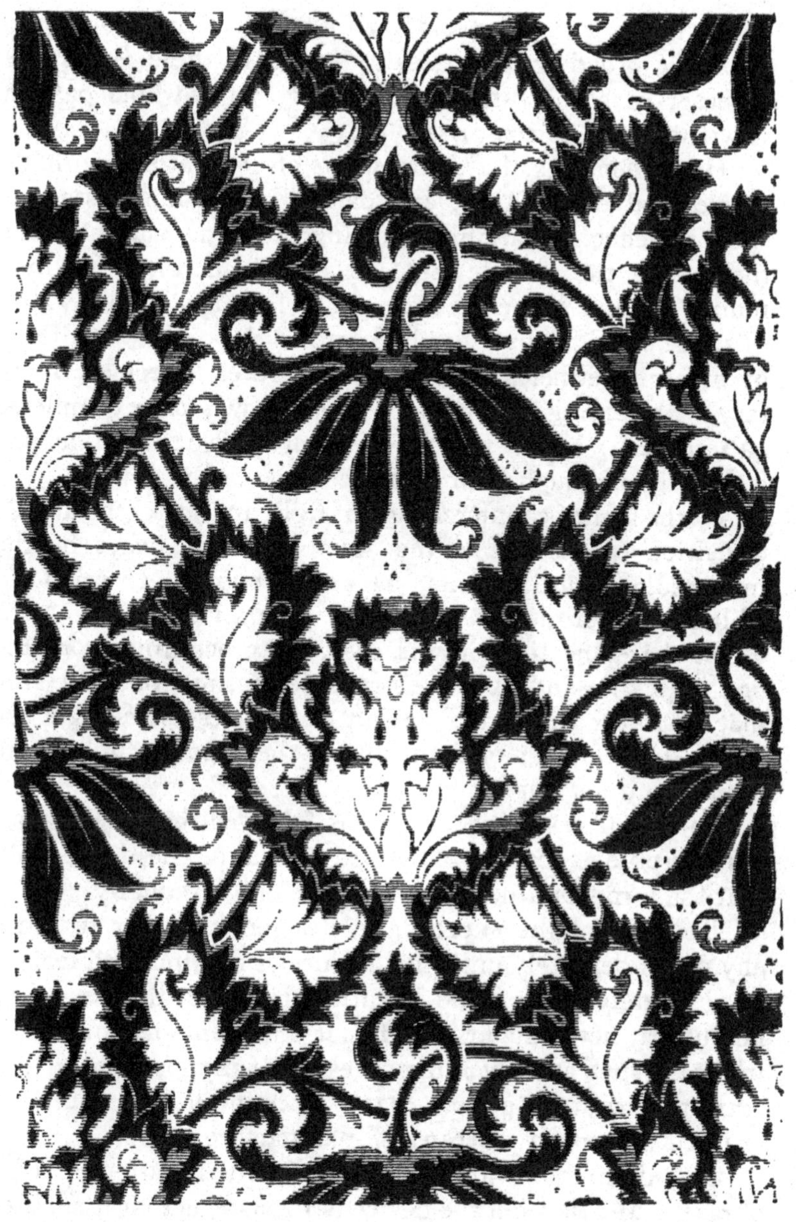

220. FINISHED DESIGN OF VELVET PATTERN.

asked for it, and of subsidiary foliation in the ground tint upon the broad scroll spaces A, B, C. In these four spaces together with the turnover of B and C, the whole pattern, it will be seen, is comprised.

Here then was the distribution of the pattern with the desired balance of light and dark. It is not necessary to show the effect of carefully drawing the forms and outlining them with the middle tint. A certain hardness of form remained, and the effect was generally rather bald. How this was set right by slightly foliating the outline itself and by breaking either light or dark, wherever it seemed necessary, with veining in the middle tint, is shown in the completed pattern (220), where the bands upon which it is set out are lost to sight though their influence is no doubt felt.

By the sort of counterchange of light and dark (the abrupt transition of the one to the other softened always by the intermediate outline tint), a certain mystery is produced which is one of the aims of surface decoration.

At the same time it was easy, by proceeding from the first logically, and upon well-considered lines, to make sure that whatever lines might assert themselves—some eyes are keener to detect them than others—they should at least be orderly and not ungraceful.

The intelligent reader who has followed the working out of the problems thus far explained will hardly need to be told that the forms of a design take shape only gradually.

The way of the experienced designer is never to settle any detail definitely until the balance of his lines and masses is completely to his mind. Outline is almost the last thing he puts in, never the first. After it there remains only to fill in details such as the veining of leaves, if any, or perhaps that extra pattern upon pattern (221) which meets the conditions implied by certain processes of manufacture.

One distinct advantage in "inhabited pattern" (the phrase is Morris's but the device is Persian) is that it enables one to conciliate those who look at a design with their nose

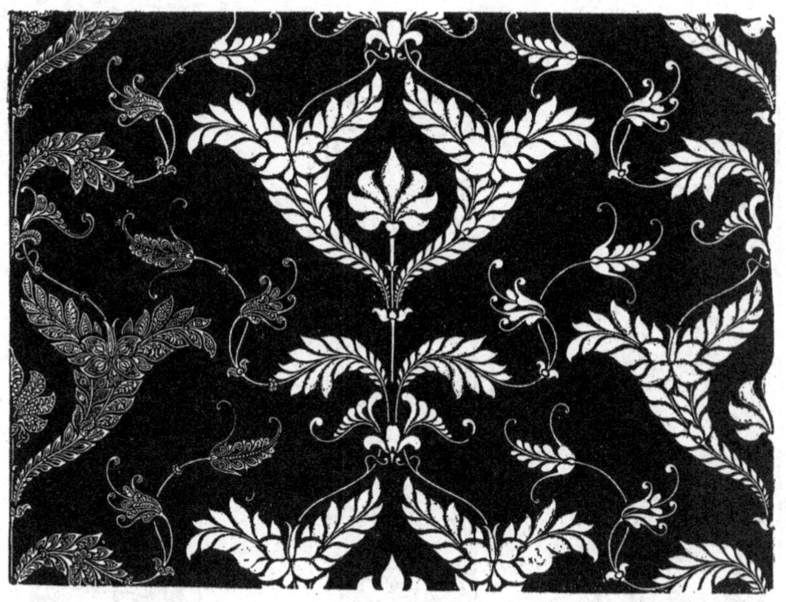

221. SIMPLE PATTERN AND ITS AFTER ELABORATION.

too near it, without sacrifice of breadth in the end. For, in its place the "pretty" detail goes only to qualify the colour, and the broader lines of the design reveal themselves.

The lines and masses first put down upon paper are, at the most, provisional. It will never do to begin with finish. The very mention of such a thing is a flat contradiction in terms. Every line mapped out in your rough scheme may have to be altered; and the advantage of, in the first place, only blotting it all in, and in fact the reason for doing so, is that you are not committed to anything, and that you have not yet carried any one part of it to such a degree of finish or satisfactoriness that you are loth to wipe it out. Your mind remains open to every suggestion which may arise out of the perhaps accidental coming together of the lines on your paper. Pledge yourself to a single bit of detail, and there is no knowing what trouble you may have in trying (after all vainly perhaps) to accommodate everything else to it.

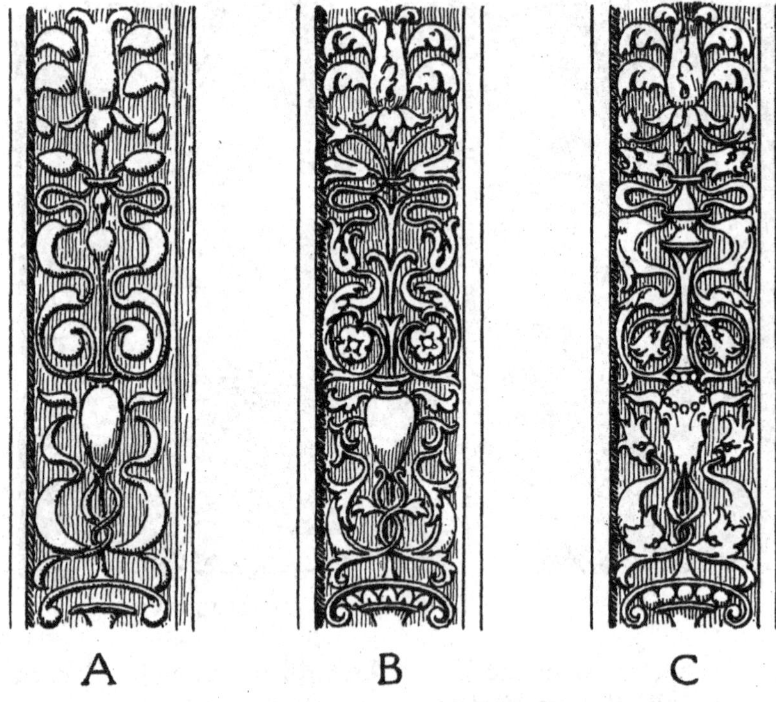

222. DIAGRAMS SHOWING DEVELOPMENT OF DESIGN.

The chances of design are illustrated in the diagram above, setting forth the possible evolution of a portion of a pilaster —not, for once, repeated. The sculptor had an upright space to fill. He began with vague forms (A, 222), thinking so far only of the way they occupied the space, their grace and balance, and the pleasant way they broke the upright band. The actual drawing of the shapes was still very much in the air. As likely as not, he had no idea how he would carry them further. That would depend upon what they suggested to him once he had roughed them in. They might have developed into foliation, buds, a central vase to steady the design, as indicated at B, the kind of thing familiar enough in Italian arabesque. As it happened they took another shape, the form of grotesque creatures more nearly animal than vegetable (C). What might have been buds became heads, and what might have been their stalks long necks or other impossible limbs, the vase-like feature the skull of an ox, and so forth, after the manner of grotesque ornament.

A designer can see quite plainly in the finished work (C) the lines on which the sculptor set out to design his pilaster; and it is the perception of the underlying lines which gives him satisfaction in the work: they show the ornamental purpose of the man.

I have chosen this example of grotesque ornament because it is with animal forms that designers oftenest go wrong. They make use of animals to fill up a space, or on the futile supposition that they enhance the value of ornament. They do so only on the condition of being first of all ornament.

A designer does not import animals into his pattern. He starts with certain vaguely ornamental forms. As the pattern grows, he feels the want of here and there a solid shape or patch of colour bigger than the rest, which develops it may be into animal or human form. It was the want of a greater weight of ornament as a termination to the spiral in the pattern overleaf (223) which suggested the scroll's growing into a creature; and that led naturally to its bursting out into life at other points too—a freak of invention, it seems to me, excusable only in proportion to the reticence of the design. Creatures thrusting themselves upon the attention would be unpardonable in ornament. As giving a certain point and piquancy to a tangle of scrollery, they justify themselves now and again.

Pattern, as I have insisted throughout, should be systematically planned—the particular plan adopted will depend, of course, upon the kind of pattern and its purpose. A designer naturally avoids the plan which has a tendency to encourage lines contrary to his scheme, and *vice versa*.

It is not meant to say that the designer should be hemmed in with arbitrary rules. Occasionally he may start very much

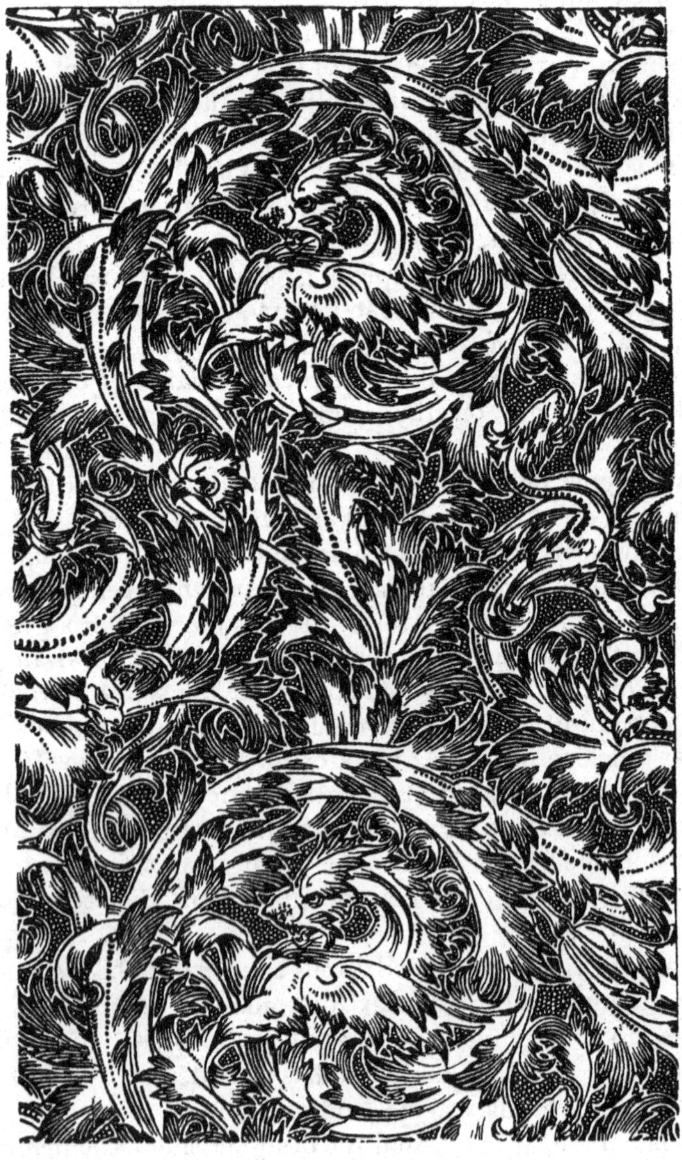

223. SCROLL PATTERN, BURSTING OUT INTO GROTESQUES.

at a venture, pledging himself (on the understanding that he is always free to retract) to something quite experimental, just to see what will come of it in repetition and what it will suggest. That is better at all events than hesitating on the brink of beginning. The plunge is salutary, and stimulates invention. The difficulty is to know when to give up an abortive attempt. Only the artist himself can say at what point his endeavour is hopeless. But he may be cautioned against persisting in it when it is past hope.

There comes a point (and it comes very soon sometimes) when, unless he is very firmly convinced that there is something in his idea, it is better to abandon it and start afresh. It costs a sharp pang to let go, but, the disappointment past, we realise the wisdom of such sacrifice. Any way which leads to satisfactory design is right; but as a rule it is waste of time to plunge recklessly into pattern. There is not often much use in putting hand to paper until you have a notion of what you are going to do. Do not scribble about. Wait until something comes to you. In so far design is inspiration. It comes to you. It happens. You have in your mind's eye a glimpse of coloured patches disposed in such and such a way, or of lines flowing sweetly into ornament; you have a vision of luxuriant growth bursting happily into bloom, or of barely clad branches austere against the sky. Your starting point may be a memory of something whispered by nature; it may be a provocation, a challenge from the lips of art. Possibly the decorative or technical problem may itself ask for solution and so set you on the track of design.

Without some sort of notion a designer does not make a promising start, and the clearer his idea both of the construction of his pattern and of its ultimate form, the better; but the longer he can keep his ideas in suspension, to use a term of chemistry, the more freely will he work.

A notion is manageable only so long as it remains in the fluid state. Once it has been allowed to crystallise into definite form, it is no longer possible to mould or modify it at will.

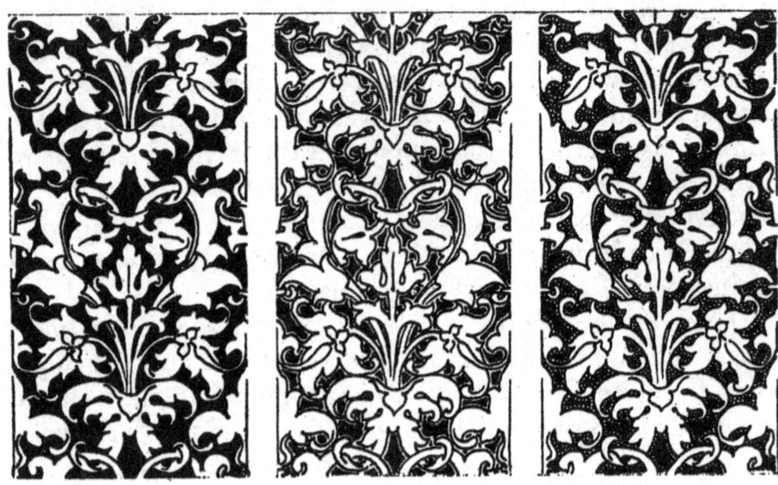

224. DIAGRAM SHOWING AFTER-THOUGHTS AS TO TREATMENT.

Every advantage should be taken of the possibilities which open out as a designer proceeds. Many a design works out in such a way as to compel departure from the initial idea. What was to have been an open pattern promises to be better as a full one; what was to have been full reaches a state when it is advisable to leave it open. The diagram (224) shows three states of the same design—the first as it was originally planned, the second with an extra outline filched as it were from the background, the third with a softer dotted outline belonging also to the ground. After-thoughts of this kind enable one to fatten a pattern which looks starved—and otherwise to save the situation. Expedients of the kind have been abused, it is true; but if we were bound in taste to abstain from every practical device which had been turned to vulgar account, the possibilities of design would be reduced to a minimum.

The available lines of design are by no means exhausted by the instances given in this chapter. Nor need design proceed upon any one of the plans set forth. Men of initiative will always find ways of their own to their own ends. All that has been attempted is to explain how some designs have grown, to indicate some ways in which an idea may develop and take shape. Designers with exceptionally retentive memory may be able to carry the stages of development further in their minds than others; but it seems natural to an artist to put them down on paper in the order of their progress.

XV. TO PROVE A PATTERN.

The unit of design a repeat—Repeat to be tested—One repeat not enough to show how design works—More must be indicated—Test of roughing out on one plan and working out on another—Accurate fit essential—Proving to be done at early stage of design—Test of cutting up drawing and rearranging the parts.

A DESIGN is contained within a single unit or repeat. That unit is all the artist has to design; but he must conceive it *as a repeat*, thinking always of its effect in repetition. And, unless he is repeating himself, and doing only what he has often done before, he has usually to test the repetition, before he can consider it done. Else he may have made a beautiful drawing, and yet turned out a very bad pattern.

The mistake is not to sketch out enough of the design to show how the lines will come—a common mistake of the inexperienced, of just those who can least trust their work to come right.

The safe plan is, not to be content with a single unit, but to indicate, however roughly, the equivalent to three or four repeats. One complete unit and four half-repeats, with perhaps four quarter-repeats (diagram 225), is no more than enough.

This roughing in of repeats is not the most exciting part of a designer's work; but neither is it a joy to find, when a design is finished, that it wants doing over again, or to see in executed work, too late to mend mistakes, the glaring evidence of your incompetence or carelessness.

Moreover, having thoroughly tested your repeat to begin

with, you have no occasion to draw more than the bare unit of a pattern. It is a common practice to draw more of the pattern than is necessary for working purposes, and yet not enough to show how it will come in repetition.

An alternative test is to rough out your design on one plan and then try it on another—to begin it, for example, on the diamond and to finish it on square lines, or *vice versa* (see diagrams 125, 127, 128, 129, 133, 134, 227). By that means you see it, as it were, from two points of view, and can form a fair idea at all events as to how it works at the joints. For this purpose, also, it is necessary to start on a sheet of paper large enough to contain more than one repeat.

The best of all possible tests is, to see it repeated. And the important thing in repetition is, that the repeats, roughly as they may be drawn, should be placed exactly in their right position; that they should not be freely sketched (freely in such a case means inaccurately) but traced, or, better still perhaps, stencilled. That is a test which any one can apply; and it is infallible.

The earlier the stage at which this testing is done the better. A designer is bound in the interests of his own reputation to make sure of the satisfactory repeat of a pattern before he lets it out of his hands. He may be working at a

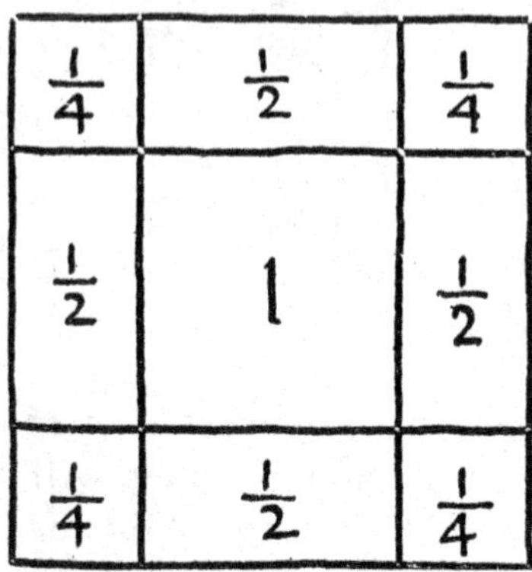

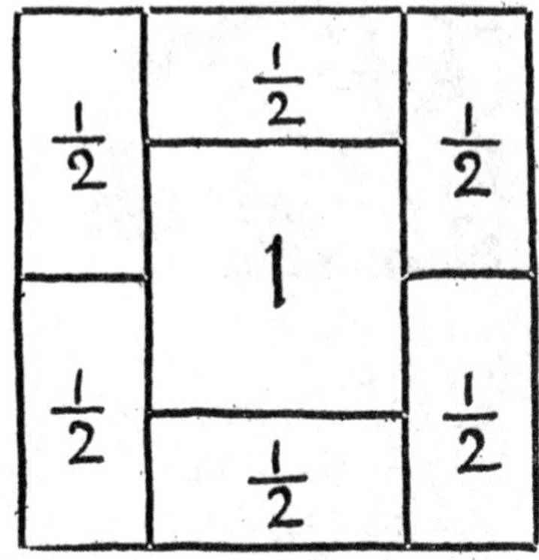

225. DIAGRAMS SHOWING HOW MUCH OF THE REPEAT MAY WITH ADVANTAGE BE ROUGHLY SET OUT TO BEGIN WITH.

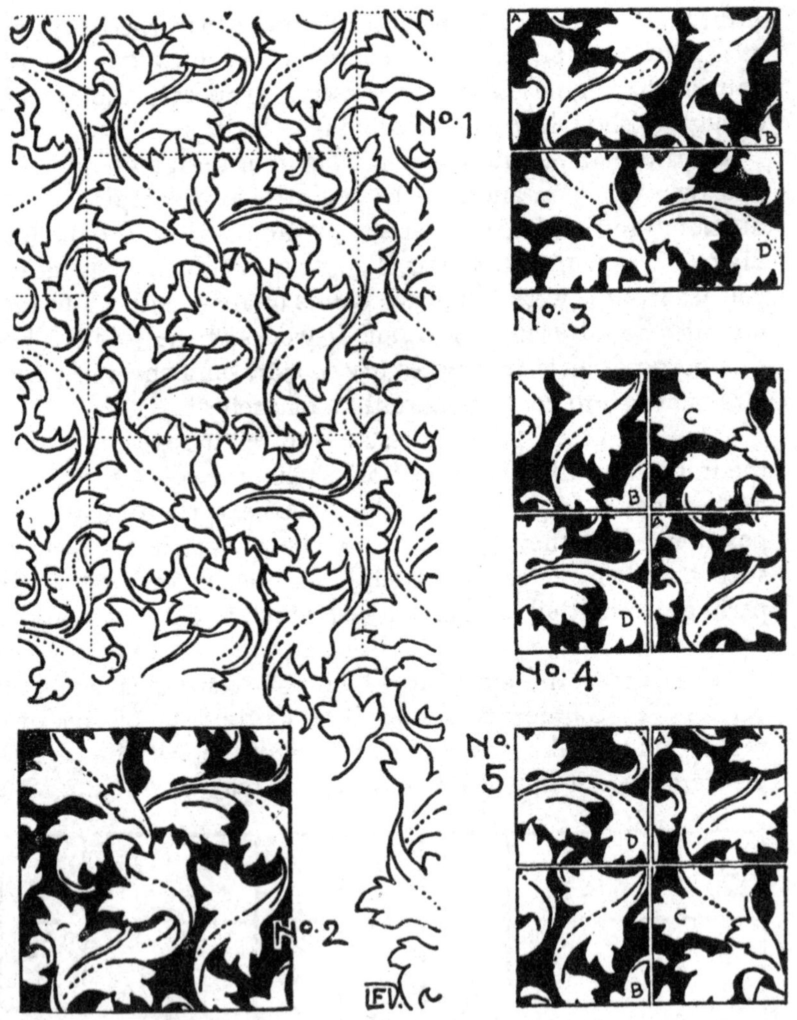

226. DIAGRAMS TO SHOW THE PROVING OF A PATTERN.

price at which he thinks that is not to be expected of him; but, if his design does not repeat satisfactorily, it will be reckoned against him, no matter what the price paid for it; and, on the other hand, work is likely to flow towards the artist whose designs work out all right. This much by way of warning and encouragement. But it is not merely on the grounds of policy that this much of honesty is recommended. There goes to all good work something for which we get neither pay nor credit, but which an artist must persist in doing if only for his own artistic satisfaction. The grudging workman who is careful to stop short at what is remunerative, is not unlikely to stop short of art.

A practical designer learns to attach no great value to the look of his drawing. He finds it expedient, often, to cut it up, and rearrange the pieces—in that way testing the repeat to some extent. What it enables him to do perfectly, is to test the joints of the design. This is illustrated in diagram 226. To the left (No. 1) is the pattern, as the designer might sketch it in, enough to show the lines it will take. The unit of repeat is shown below (2). In the next instance (3) this has been cut across into two equal parts A B and C D, and the two halves transposed, so that what were before the upper and lower edges are brought together. If at this stage the lines did not fit, it would be easy to set them right.

The joining of the side edges has then to be tested (4). Once more the drawing is cut in two, vertically this time, so that portions A and C can be transferred to the right of B and D. But, since this is a "drop" pattern, they have been transposed. In the remaining diagram (5) parts A and C have been left as they were (in 3), and parts B and D, duly transposed, transferred to the left of them. The four quarters of the design have thus been shuffled and dealt out in every practicable order, and each portion of it in turn promoted to the position most in view.

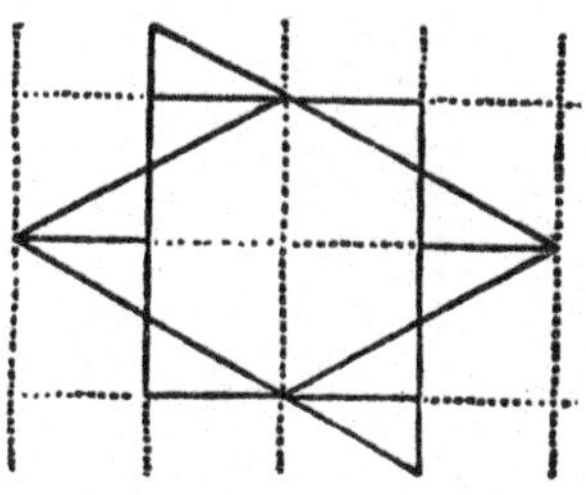

227. DIAGRAM TO SHOW HOW A PATTERN DESIGNED ON DIAMOND LINES MAY BE PROVED.

In the case of a pattern which did not drop, the proving would have been a yet simpler matter. The way in which a diamond may in like manner be cut up and the parts re-arranged to form a square or a slanting figure, is sufficiently indicated by the accompanying skeleton lines (227). To form the slanting figure the triangular portions on either side have only to be cut off and transposed. To form the square, they need to be bisected and the wedge-shaped pieces fitted on to the hexagon.

XVI. PATTERN PLANNING IN RELATION TO TECHNIQUE.

Dimensions of design determined by conditions of manufacture—Possibilities in block printing—Limitations in weaving—Narrow repeat a condition of the loom—The "turnover"—A space of "single"—Borders—Table damask—The lengthening piece—Difficulties resulting—Conditions affecting colour—Change of shuttle—Its use and danger—Carpet weaving—"Planted" colours—Chenille—Characteristics of style accounted for by technique.

It has been shown how the pattern designer is practically compelled to design, not precisely on square lines, but on the lines of a parallelogram. And not only that. The distance of the lines apart is almost certainly laid down for him. It is a parallelogram certainly of restricted size, and possibly of arbitrary proportions, with which he has to do. Without uniformity in the width of stuffs—silks, velvets, carpets, chintzes, or whatever they may be—it would be difficult to estimate off-hand their relative cost; and estimating is a matter of everyday necessity. Without stock sizes of tiles, the price by the yard, and the cost of fixing them, would not be easy to settle.

The width of stuffs is determined, if not by mechanism, by custom and convenience. The length of a woven pattern is restricted by considerations of economy, and that of a printed one by the girth of the roller, or the size of the block it is convenient to handle; so that in a vast number of cases a designer has to work within conditions which fix for him, not only the size, but the proportions, of his design. It resolves itself into his working within the lines, say, of a parallelogram 30 by 15 inches for printed cotton; or 21 by 21 inches (at most) for wall-paper; for tiles, within a square mesh of lines 6 or 8 inches apart. And he is free only within such limits. Theoretically, it is true that a design for wall-paper may be spread over an area involving any number of blocks; as a matter of fact, it is not. The designer is occasionally allowed in the case of sumptuous papers, and of certain single prints, a repeat of 42 inches long; but patterns spread over a larger area than that would cost more to produce than paper-hangings are usually worth. And, over and above the commercial consideration (which is in itself enough to prevent that kind of extravagance), it is a point of craftsmanship not to waste labour. It is the test of a designer's capacity that he should not ask for further facilities, but make the most of what the conditions offer him.

The mechanical conditions of block printing permit certain extensions of plan which roller printing does not. It is possible with a single block 21 by 21 inches to print either a radiating or a turning-round pattern which in the hanging shows a repeat measuring 42 inches each way.

Imagine the square lines in diagram 228 to be 21 inches apart. The unit contained in one of the divisions A stands for what the block will print. The printer has only after printing one impression (A) to give the block a twist round before printing the next (∢) to get the result shown at the bottom of the diagram, which represents also the width of the paper. As yet, however, we have only half a pattern. It remains with the paperhanger to set that right. He hangs every other strip as it were upside down (∀ ∢) and the complete pattern results on the wall.

The design given on a smaller scale on page 216, in which also the repeat is actually 42 inches across, is got out of a single (21-inch) block in the same way.

Further, it is possible by means of two 21-inch blocks to print a pattern of which the repeat works on a rectangular

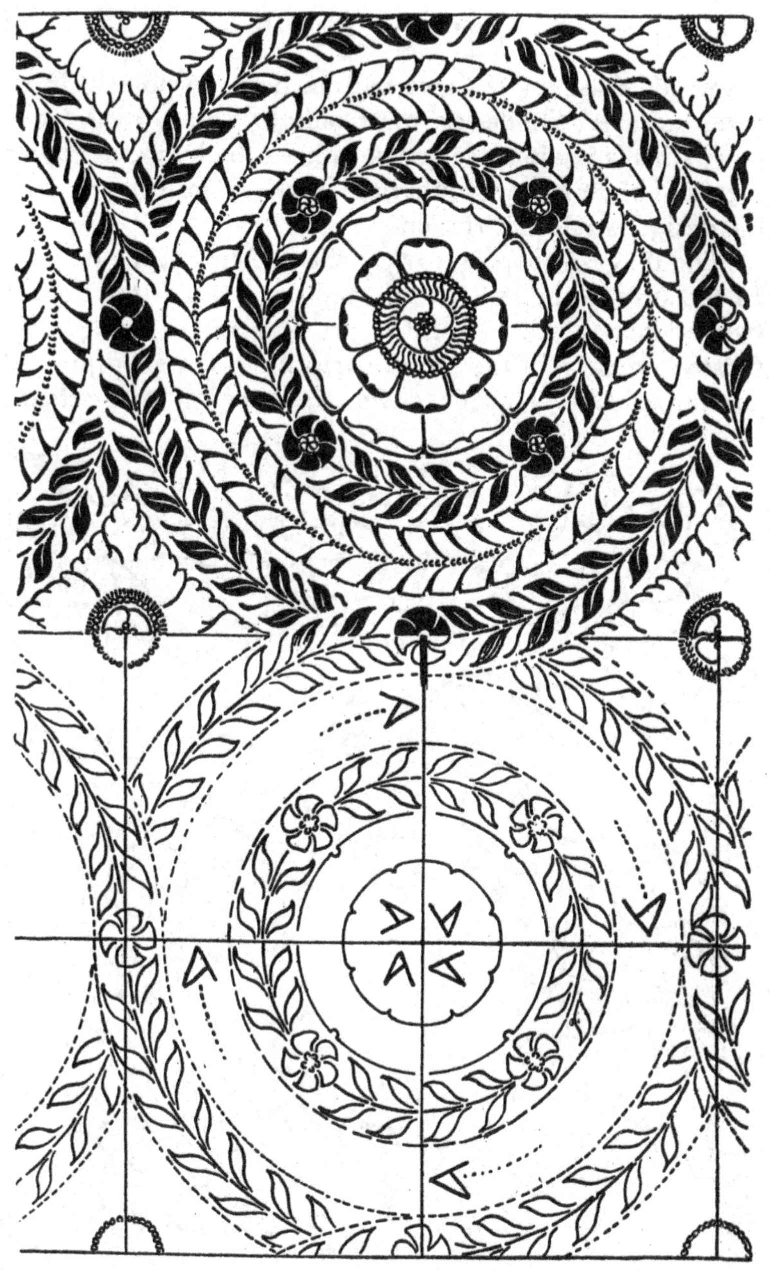

228. DIAGRAM TO SHOW A HALF-TURN OF THE BLOCK IN PRINTING A CEILING PAPER, AND THE REVERSAL OF ALTERNATE STRIPS IN THE HANGING.

diamond measuring 84 inches from point to point. In this case, however, the design must radiate, and not turn round —or, when the alternate strips came to be hung (as to complete the pattern they would need to be) opposite ways about, the design would not run on.

The diagram opposite (230) shows four widths of paper. In the strip to the left A and B represent the prints from the two 21-inch blocks, ꓭ and ⋖ prints from the same blocks twisted round. In the second strip BA A B a strip precisely similar to ꓭ∀ ⋗ ꓭ upside down, the hanging is so schemed

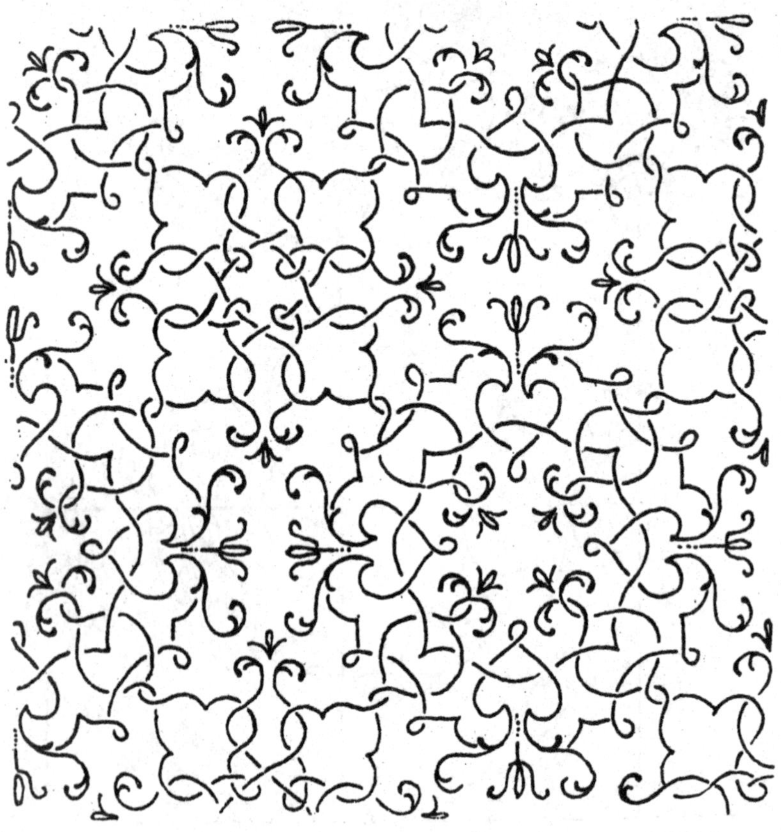

229. DIAGRAM OF CEILING PATTERN (IN EFFECT, 42 INCHES ACROSS) ON THE PRINCIPLE OF DIAGRAM 228.

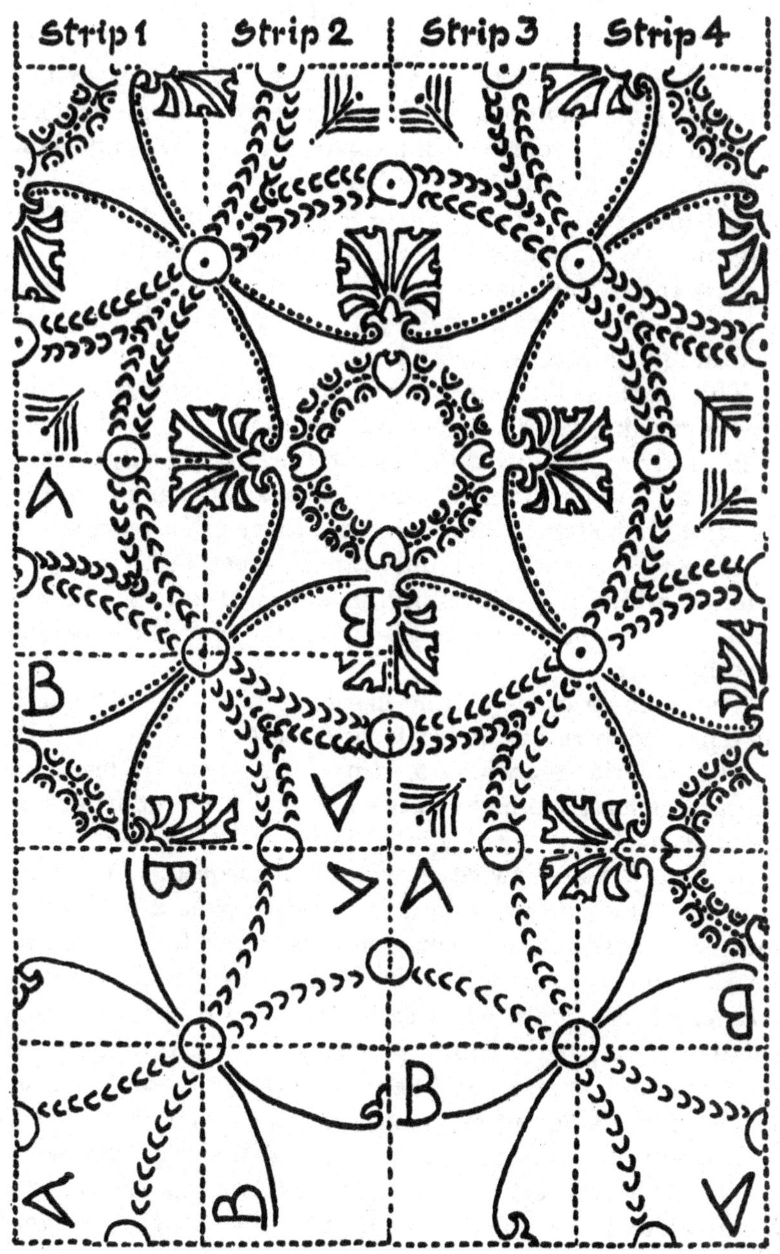

230. DIAGRAM SHOWING A PATTERN IN EFFECT 84 INCHES WIDE PRODUCED BY TWO BLOCKS EACH ONLY 21 INCHES BY 21 INCHES.

that ꓭ is on a level with A and ∀ with B. The third strip is hung the same way up as the first, but so as to drop 42 inches below that. The fourth strip is again the same way up as the second, but so as to drop 42 inches below that.

All this would be difficult to follow in print, but for the diagram. With that to refer to, it is easy enough.

Patterns of this character are not wanted in wall decoration; but for ceilings they give not only a sufficient scale, but just the lines which are most serviceable.

These devices by no means exhaust the possibilities in the way of cunning contrivance. But the block printer does not look kindly on designs which ask of him a little extra care—and as for the paperhanger, he is persuaded that the use of his brains is no part of his business. Indeed that scheme last explained is already too intricate to have been put into practice, which it might easily have been if only the paper-stainer could have depended upon the goodwill of the paperhanger.

The designer of wall tiling has every reason for scheming his repeat to work on the brick system (231).

The material for which a man is designing settles, in a measure at least, both the dimension and the proportions of his pattern. Thus, for a printed fabric the roller commonly allows him an area twice as wide as it is deep. For wall-paper the block allows him at the most a square of definite dimensions, except that he may on occasion be free to use two blocks. For a woven fabric the loom gives him a considerable length of pattern not greatly restricted by expense, but usually only a narrow width, precisely fixed according to the loom, and affords him very likely the opportunity of doubling the width of his design by turning it over. So uniformly are these conditions so, that an experienced designer can often tell, from the proportions and scale of a design, the kind of manufacture for which it was made. The copyist, on the other hand, who finds a pattern which has apparently been overlooked, and thinks to appropriate it to his own use,

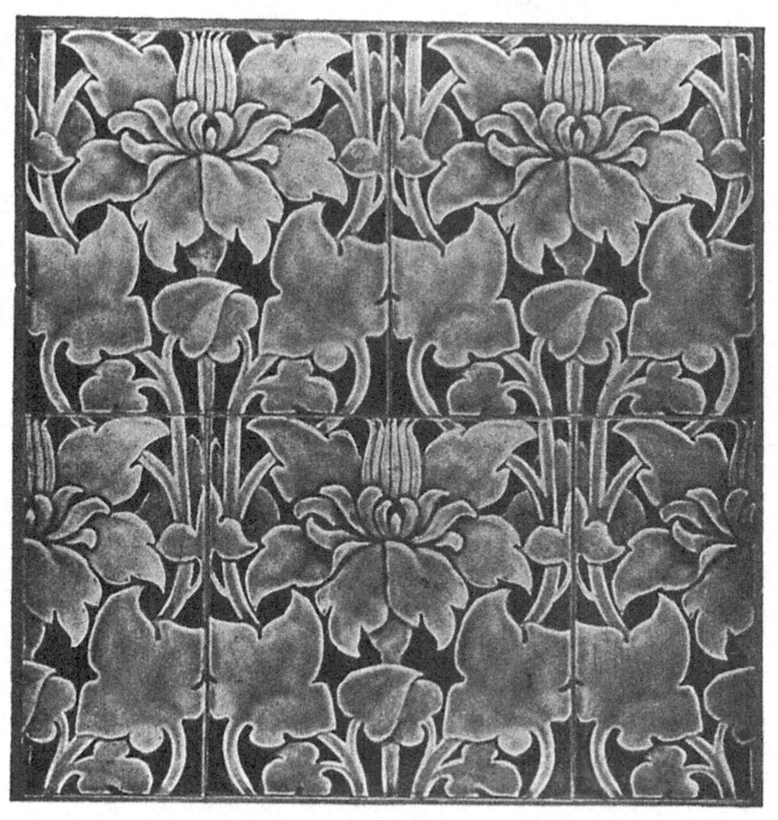

231. SIX-INCH TILE PATTERN DESIGNED TO BE FIXED BRICKWISE.

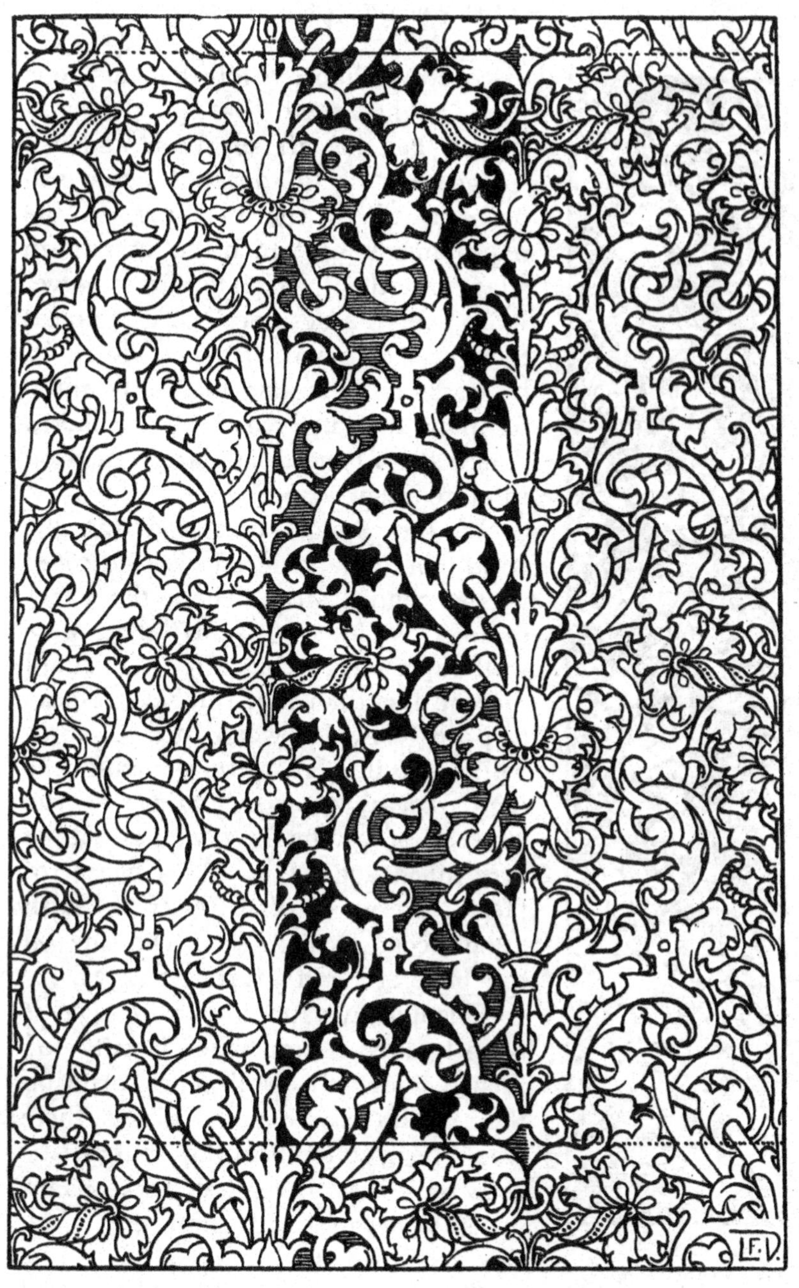

232. NARROW TURNOVER PATTERN ADAPTED TO WEAVING.

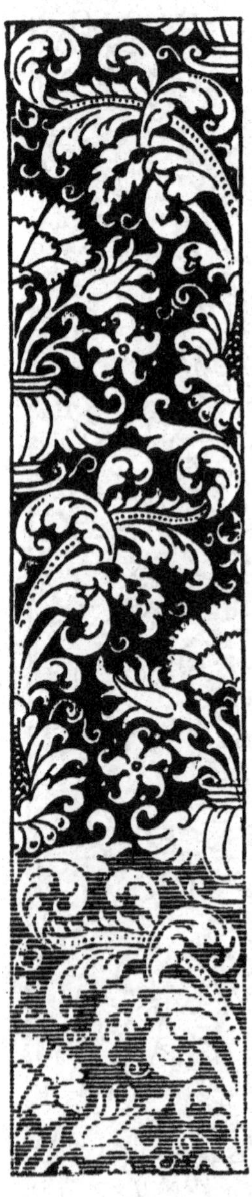

233. NARROW WOVEN DAMASK PATTERN.

discovers perhaps, before he has done with it, that there was good reason why it had not already been annexed—inasmuch as it depends upon proportions which the machine, to the requirements of which he desires to adapt it, will not permit him to preserve. Even among a designer's own happiest thoughts there will be some which (if he works only in one material) must, for much the same reason, be stillborn. A new set of conditions starts a man off in quite a new vein.

In the design on page 221 the width of the material is indicated in the central strip, where the background is filled in. If that were wall-paper, 21 inches wide, it would take no less than four full-sized blocks to print it—which would not be worth while. If it were a woven stuff, the long repeat, though adding to the expense of production, would not be very much against it. As a matter of fact, patterns of that relative length often occur in textiles. The one on this page is again a turnover (233).

The narrow pattern opposite (234) is a wall-paper design which is only 10½ inches wide. In wall-paper printing there is no economy in this as there would be in cotton printing—but artistically there may be very good reasons for using sometimes only half the width the block allows.

The weaver adopts the long and

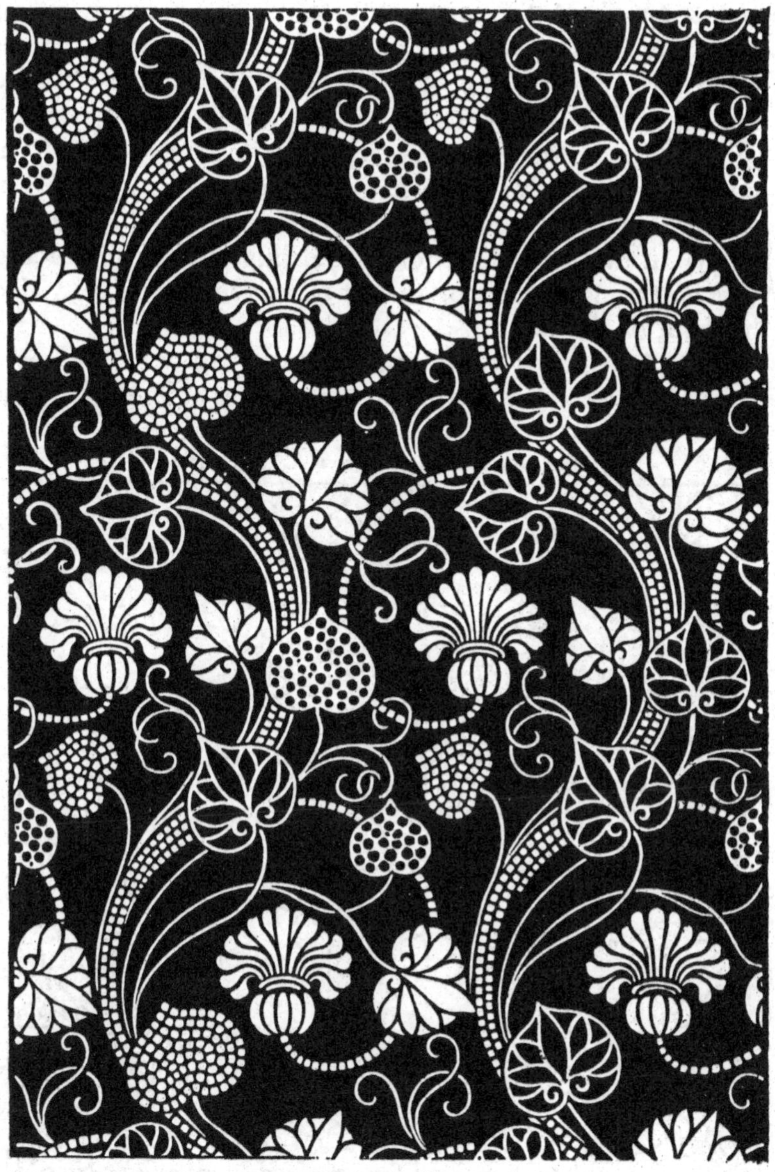

234. WALL-PAPER PATTERN 10½ INCHES WIDE BY WHICH NO ECONOMY IS EFFECTED.

narrow repeat all the more readily that he has a handy means of counteracting its too upright tendency. The cross stripes which form the pattern of an Indian dhurri or an African blanket represent the handloom weaver's simplest means of changing colour—that is, by changing his shuttle. In more elaborate pattern he has the same facility, and can always cross his upright strips by bands of colour carrying the eye in the other direction. And this scheme of banding extends through much of the early weaving, affecting also the form of the design.

A Byzantine or Sicilian weaver of old was the more inclined to make use of the horizontal lines suggested by the

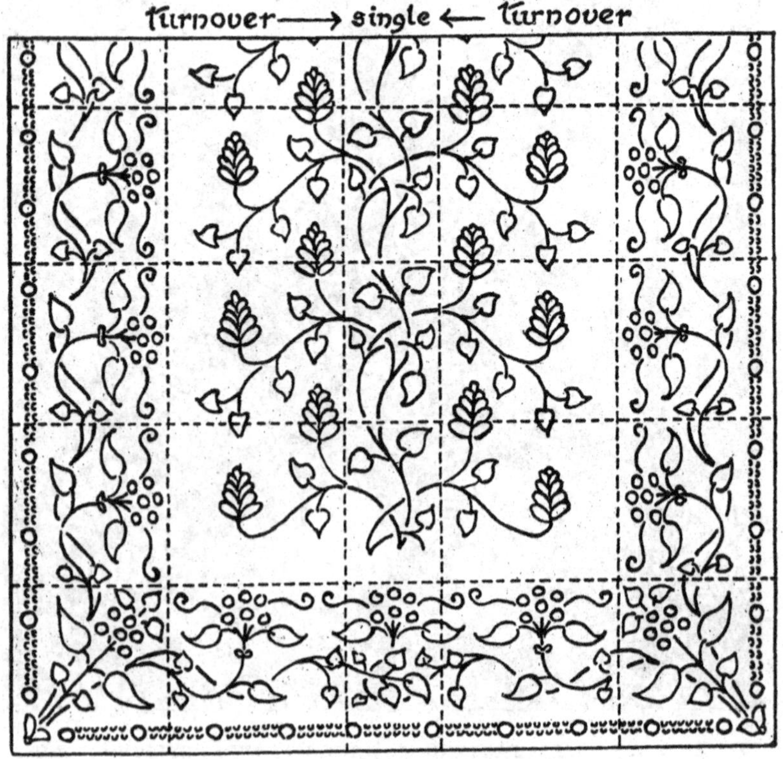

235. DIAGRAM OF WOVEN PATTERN, "TURNOVER" AND "SINGLE."

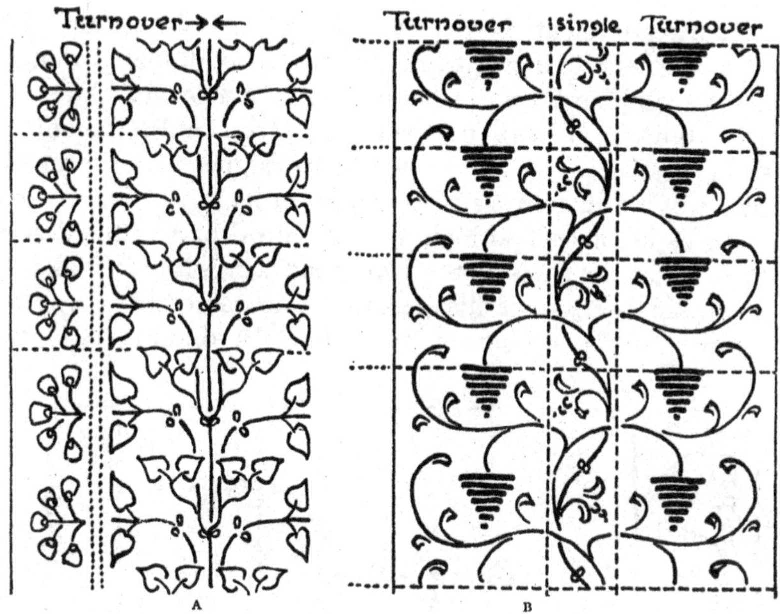

236. DIAGRAMS SHOWING CORRESPONDENCE IN DEPTH OF REPEAT BETWEEN THE PARTS OF A DESIGN.

shuttle, because he had no fear of their asserting themselves. In fact he was in the habit of insisting upon them, for he valued stripes as a means of marking the folds and showing the fullness of a hanging. They do that so effectually that a flat wall-design in horizontal stripes seems to want folds, and to suggest that it was borrowed from a textile. Many a pattern borrowed from an old stuff—by its stripes you shall know it—is far from satisfactory as a wall-paper.

The proportions allowed for the repeat naturally affect the character of the design. You cannot without considerable allowance in the way of length indulge in boldly flowing scrollwork; nor, where the width is narrow, avoid a certain upright tendency in the growth of pattern—counteract it as you may by cross bands.

The weaver's custom of reserving in the centre of a turnover pattern a space in which the design is not reversed has been already mentioned (page 93). By that means the stiffness of a definite upright line, the formality of mere reversal, and the obtrusiveness of what is after all a mechanical device, are avoided. A loom may be so harnessed, and commonly is so harnessed (235), as to allow the designer a space up the centre of his curtain (or of the repeat of it) in which he is free to do as he pleases so long as this central part of his design joins on at the sides to the two broad wings which make up the main portion of his design. The same thing applies equally to the design of a border. In diagram 235 the

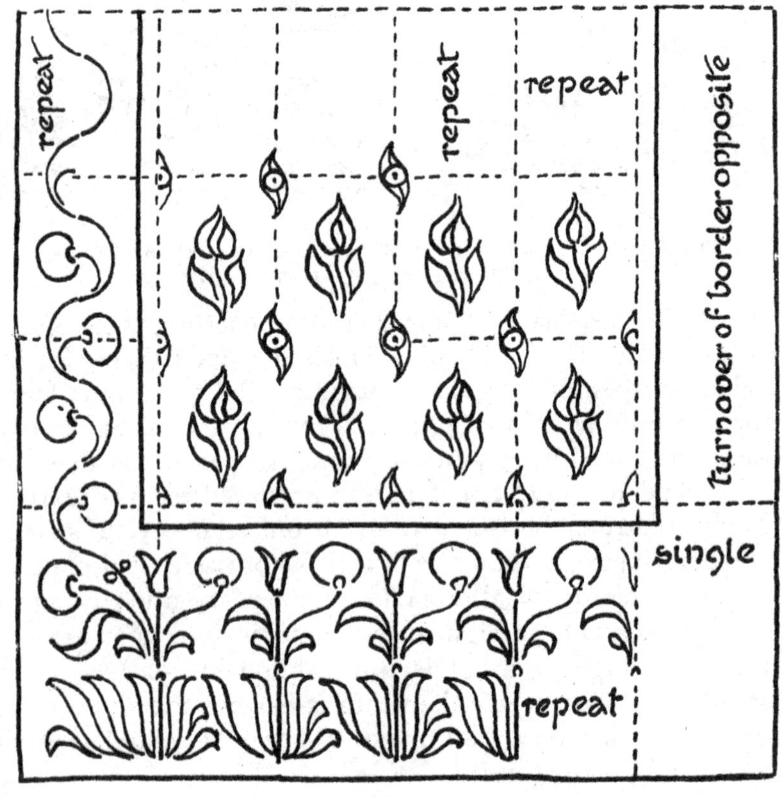

237. DIAGRAM SHOWING RELATION OF DIAPER REPEAT TO REPEAT OF SIDE AND BOTTOM BORDERS.

border on one side is a turnover of that on the other; but the turnover might equally well be within the border itself. Filling and border pattern, that is to say, may alike be turned over; and in each may be reserved a central strip of what is technically termed "single." The width of that portion of the design is a question of arrangement and partly of cost. An important consideration to be borne in mind is that the introduction of any proportion of single design is at the cost of possible increase in width.

The device of turning over gives one, for example, double the width otherwise allowed, say, for a border. Instead of a "free" pattern 9 inches wide it allows a bisymmetrical one of 18 inches. But it is only so much of the width as is turned over that is doubled. If, then, you reserve let us say 3 inches in the centre for "single," the extent of your border would not be 18 inches but 15—the sum that is to say of 3 inches (single) and twice 6 inches (turned over). The technique of weaving has here, it will be seen, considerable bearing not merely upon design but upon its plan.

Single and turnover portions of a design must naturally correspond in length. They need not of necessity be equal as at A 236, but it is practically convenient to make them so. The design B could, of course, be woven; but, if the repeat of the turnover measured 9 inches, a manufacturer would not allow 18 inches for the single. In the same way the repeat of a border must naturally correspond at the side of a curtain with the depth of a filling pattern, and at the bottom with its width (235, 237)—and if part of the filling is single, the corresponding portion of the border also may be.

In the case of a narrow and not very important border it may be shorter than the filling as long as its length is divisible into that—a 9-inch filling may have a border of 4½ inches, or 3 inches, or 1½. And so where the border is the main feature and the filling a mere diaper (237), that may measure only half or a third or a quarter of its length. And were it mechanically possible to weave border and filling the

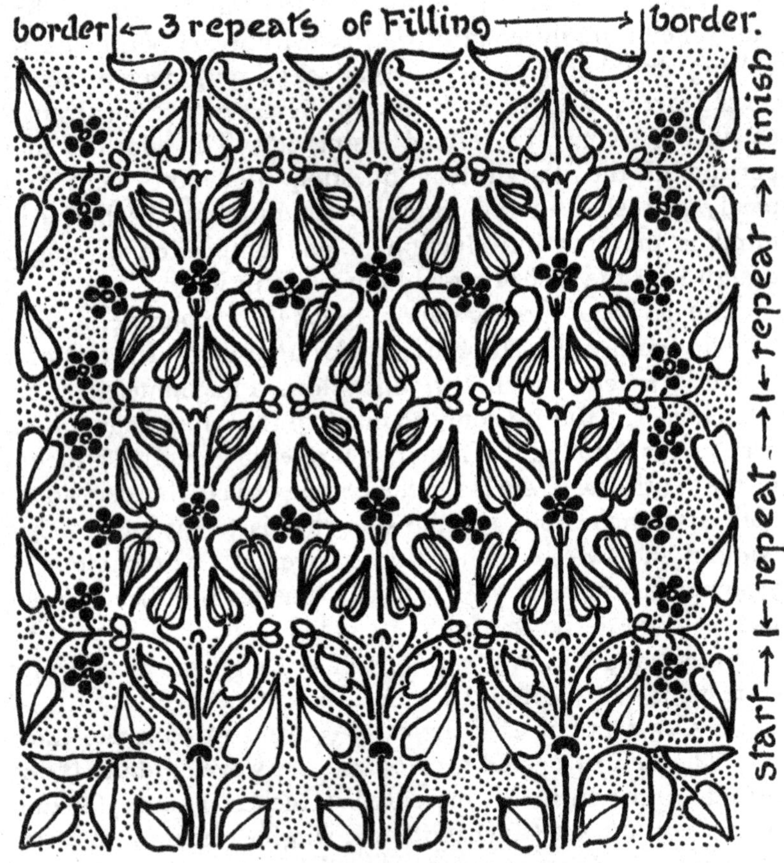

238. DIAGRAM SHOWING PORTIONS OF DESIGN ANSWERING PRACTICALLY TO BORDERS.

repeats of which measured respectively say 7 and 9 inches, it is doubtful if artistically it would be worth while: the simple thing to do is commonly the right one. It is sometimes desirable to make a curtain or other pattern complete in itself with start and finish (238). For working purposes these may be regarded as borders, and must conform to the conditions regulating border design.

Further complexities occur in the design of table linen.

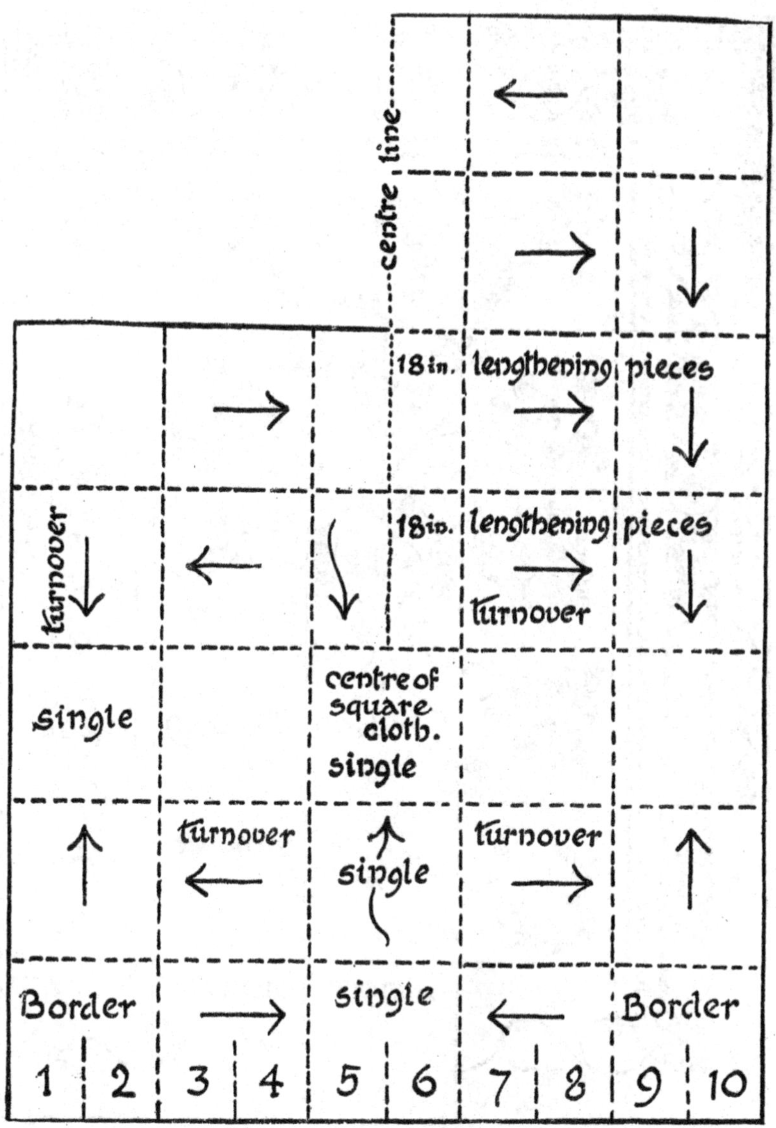

239. DIAGRAM SHOWING HOW A TABLE DAMASK DESIGN MAY BE PLANNED.

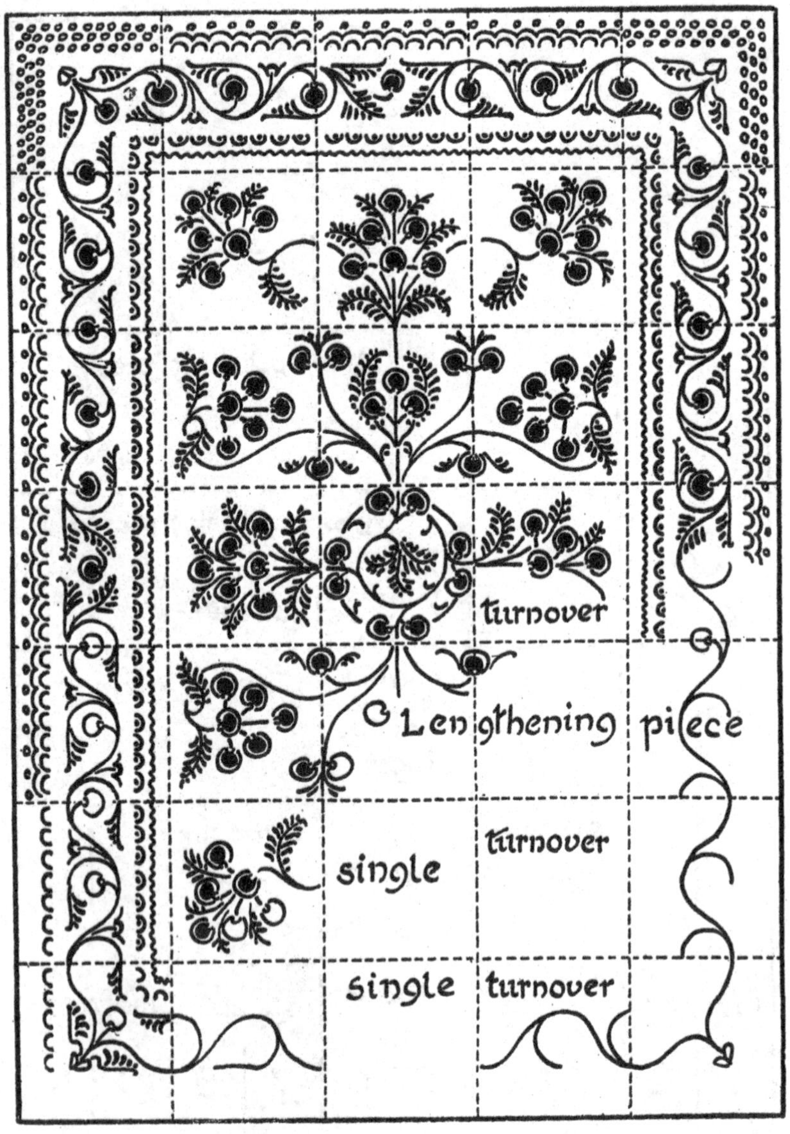

240. DIAGRAM OF TABLE DAMASK DESIGN PLANNED ON THE LINES OF DIAGRAM 239.

The conditions seem at first sight to allow great freedom to the artist. He has only to design a square or oblong cloth each quarter of which is a turnover of the other, and in the centre he may have a space where there is no repeat. That is charming in theory. In practice his task is not so simple. It is complicated by the necessity of arranging some means of lengthening the cloth to suit tables of various dimensions. And it resolves itself into his having to design a lengthening piece (usually of 9 or 18 inches) which must be so schemed that it can be inserted once, twice, thrice, or any number of times, to make a cloth of any length. The scope which the manufacturer gives with one hand he thus takes back with the other. To such an extent is his freedom restricted that the artist is inclined at first to think his possibilities are narrowed to little more than the extension and finishing off of the design for a lengthening piece.

Where it is not desired in any way to acknowledge the centre of the cloth the problem may be resolved into the design of an 18-inch repeat (reversed or not in the centre) merely finished off at the edges or cut short by the border.

Where it is desired to give importance to the centre of the cloth the loom can be arranged so that there is no turning over there; but if the end portions are turned over it is difficult to scheme a growing pattern in which the stems do not grow two ways. Again, if the artist is disposed to take advantage of the area allowed him to get good sweeping lines in his main design, his ardour is damped by the reflection that he must somehow combine them with the comparatively restrained lines which are all that is possible in the lengthening piece. This affects the border in particular very seriously. Try to introduce into a sweeping scroll design a yard long a lengthening piece of half a yard, and you will realise the impossibility of it.

Counsels of safety are: to confine oneself in the main design to lines such as can be repeated in the lengthening piece: to allot spaces at least in the design to sprigs, sprays, or disconnected diaper: to avoid, like the Arabs or their imitators of the Renaissance, growth so natural as to be hurt when it is suddenly doubled back or made to grow two ways. To take full advantage of the apparent opportunity of design afforded by the dimensions of an ample tablecloth, and at the same time to preserve something like logical growth, is what any but an experienced damask designer will find it difficult to do.

The accompanying diagrams (239, 240) may be of use to the beginner. The first of these is divided, it will be seen, into ten divisions each measuring 9 inches (tablecloths are always measured by quarter yards), two of which are given to the border and two to the single piece up the centre, which leaves two for the turnover piece between.

The plan shows three-quarters of a square "ten-quarter" cloth (a smaller size is "eight-quarter"), and, above, to the right, one-quarter of a cloth into which two lengthening pieces are introduced.

The corresponding diagram (240) shows the beginnings of a pattern planned on similar lines, but with the two lengthening pieces inserted, one above and one below the centre.

An 18-inch border practically represents that portion of the cloth which may be presumed to fall over, and the central six quarters the portion which will lie flat on the table. Any extra border within that space is reckoned as part of the filling; any part of the filling which extends beyond the six-quarter area is reckoned as border. The lengthening piece or pieces need not be introduced as shown in the diagrams above; they may come in the centre of the cloth.

The plan more usually adopted by damask designers is to halve the design, open it out, and let in the lengthening pieces. Diagram 241 (opposite) represents a square which might stand either for an eight-quarter cloth or the centre portion of a larger one. Below it (242) is the lengthening

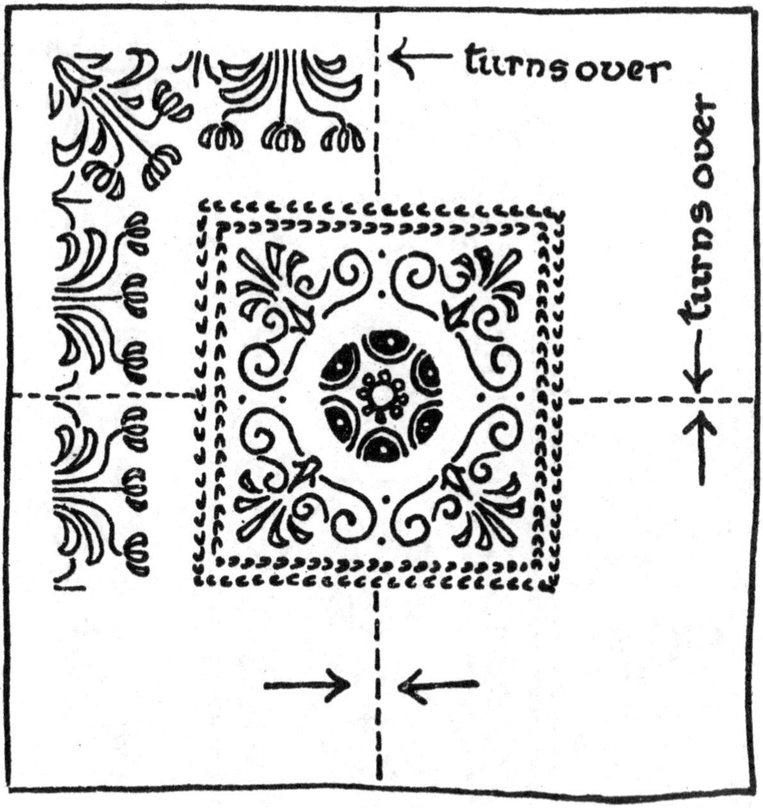

241. DIAGRAM OF CENTRE PART OF SQUARE TABLECLOTH.

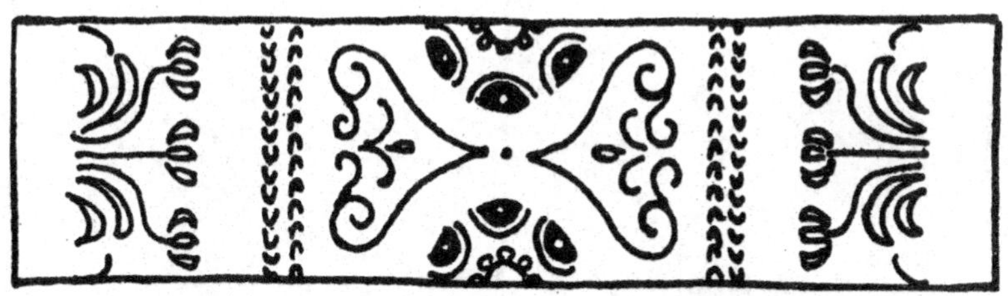

242. DIAGRAM OF LENGTHENING PIECE TO CORRESPOND WITH ABOVE.

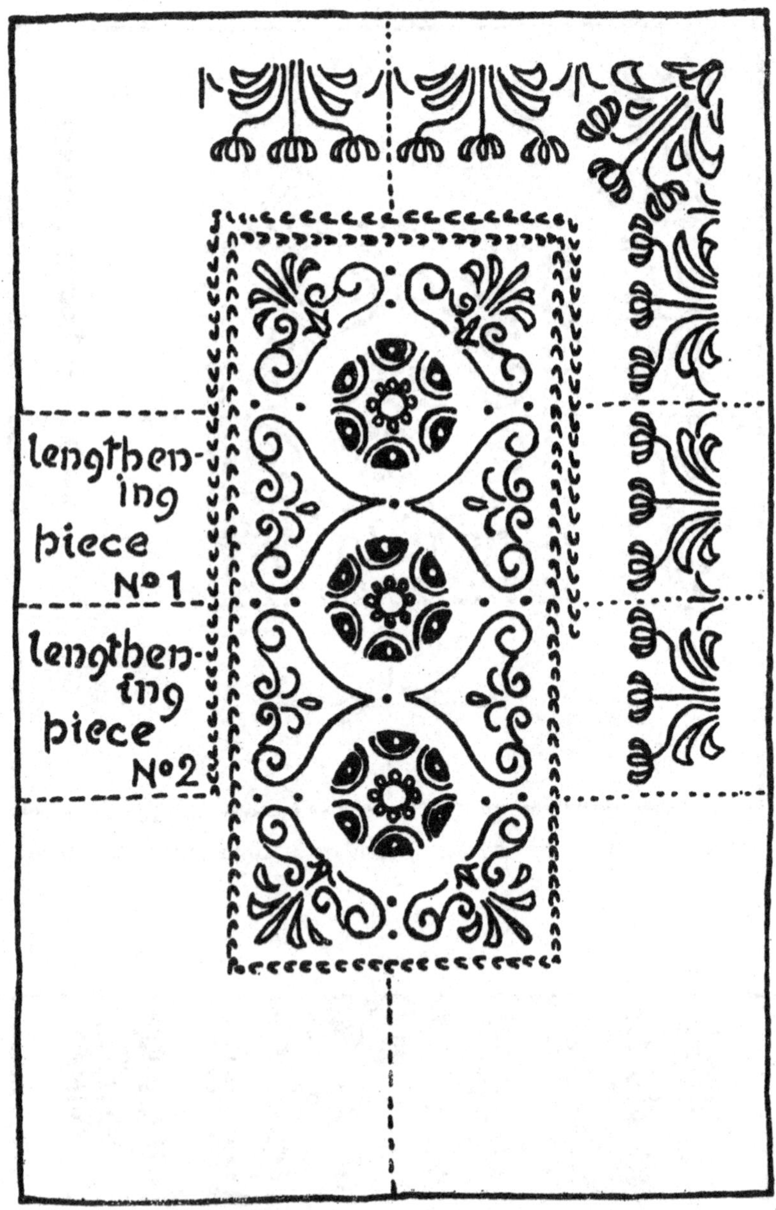

243. DIAGRAM OF CENTRE PART OF LONG TABLECLOTH SHOWING INTRODUCTION OF LENGTHENING PIECES.

piece, and opposite (243) the result of opening out the square and letting in two lengthening pieces.

The changing of the weaver's shuttle, responsible for the stripes in a dhurri, gives scope to the designer of more sumptuous and less simple fabrics. There can be no more colours in a stuff than there are threads of different colour in its make. But each group of threads may be brought to the surface at the option of the designer—and, if for any group or groups of threads he prefers to use instead of a single colour alternating bands of different colours, he can do so—and if these particular colours do not come often to the surface, he can get as it were jewels of extra colour without calling attention to its occurrence in bands—but it takes some ingenuity to do that. The stripes have a persistent way of asserting themselves. Successfully to divert attention from the mechanism underlying such a distribution of colour is within the scope only of an expert designer. His task is easier if he is free to gradate the various colours so that they die one into another or into the ground; but even with flat colours a man who knows his trade can effectively disguise the means employed to variety.

The kind of variation possible is illustrated in diagram 244, where the strawberry blossoms are successively of three different tints, indicated in black, in dots, and in diagonal lines, and the changes of the shuttle are very plainly shown in the bands at the side which may represent the selvedge.

What one weaver does with the weft another does with the warp. The carpet designer, working for a material of which the warp comes always to the surface, does by the arrangement of his warp threads in bands what another weaver does by changing the shuttle. In a "five-frame" carpet five series of warp threads are brought to the surface and give a design in five colours, but if in one of them (or it may be two or even three "frames") the threads instead of being all of one colour are arranged, as it were, in ribbons of different colours, these various colours can just as easily be brought to the surface as threads all of one colour.

According to the number of stripes in which the threads of a " frame " are arranged is the number of the colours to be got out of it. But, as in the case of the changing shuttle only the colour of that one shuttle could possibly occur in the line across which it was shot, so in the case of the warp

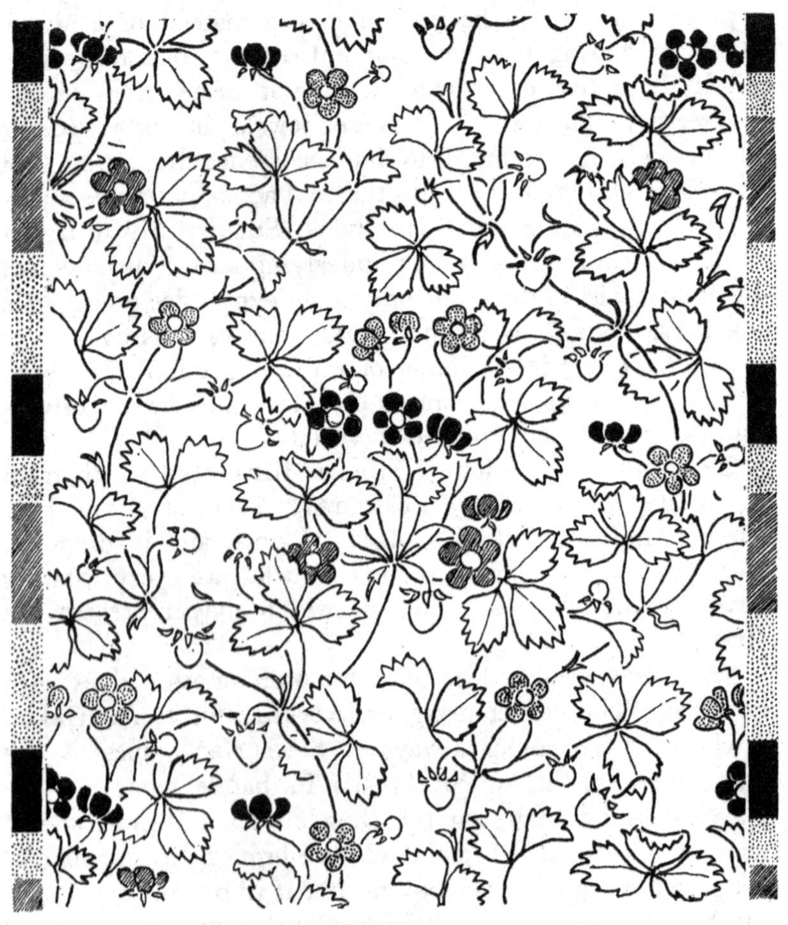

244. DIAGRAM SHOWING CHANGE OF COLOUR IN THE WEFT THREADS.

245. DIAGRAM SHOWING CHANGE OF COLOUR IN WARP THREADS.

threads no one colour in a given frame can cross the path of another—it occurs only in the line of the underlying stripe.

Diagram 245 shows one frame of the warp divided into six stripes which give only three colours. They might just as easily have been six, and they might each of them have been gradated from light to dark or from warm to cold. That would have made with the other four frames ten colours in all —as it is we have seven, only four of which the artist is free to use as he will.

There is no real difficulty in scheming a pattern to meet such conditions as these. And even in the more complicated case where two frames or more are thus divided into stripes all that the designer has to do is to make sure that his "planted" colours, to use the trade term, do not exceed their bounds. This he can easily do either by ruling guide lines on his drawing, or by the use of a strip of paper painted with each colour in its order and proportion which he can move

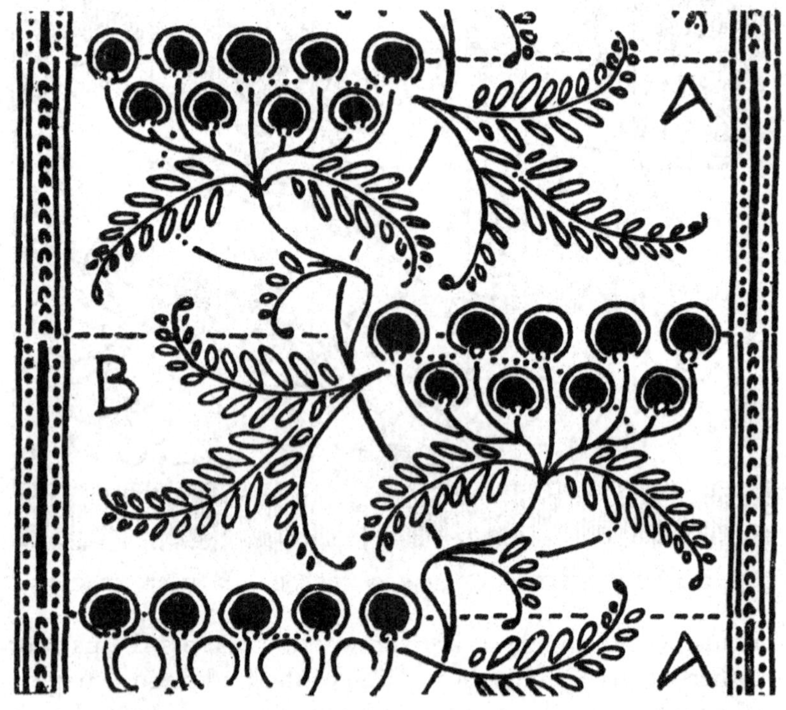

246. DIAGRAM SHOWING REVERSAL OF DESIGN IN CHENILLE WEAVING.

about as a gauge. With a clear head he should have no great difficulty in keeping one colour out of the way of another.

He is not always careful to make his details correspond precisely with the colour stripe, and by the occasional overlapping of the form by a colour not apparently belonging to it, or *vice versa*, the appearance of abrupt transition is avoided. It looks as if mistakes in gauging had resulted occasionally in happy effects of confusion, and that the device had since been employed deliberately.

It will be seen (245) that it is mainly in the flower centres that the planted colours are used—the mass of the flower itself carries the eye far beyond the spots of colour, which might otherwise run into stripes. The idea is, of course, that in the confusion of flower, leaf, ground, and outline colours the order of these jewels of bright colour shall not be too apparent. In the diagram they are purposely insisted upon, and the foliage is barely indicated. In the woven fabric the form of the pronounced foliage would help very much to give that mystery of effect which is at times so valuable. The complicated mechanism necessary to the frequent changing of the shuttle in powerloom weaving leads in many modern fabrics to the use of a number of warps, any one of which can be brought to the surface wherever the colour of it enters into the design. If yet more colours are wanted, they may as already explained (page 236) be "planted." Each additional warp adds naturally to the heaviness of the stuff.

A very exceptional facility is afforded by the process of chenille weaving. The design may extend right across the curtain—and the repeats need not follow one above the other in the usual way. Each alternate one may, if it is desired, be reversed. The repeat of the design (246) on page 238 would in the ordinary way include two groups of flowers (A, B), and there would be no economy in making one the reverse of the other; but in chenille weaving there would; and the repeat is comprised in the unit A, of which B is the reverse.

In the Persian carpet (frontispiece) an effective scheme is evolved by the use of two contrasting grounds of dark blue and lighter red, broken and diversified by a large amount of small detail. In the modern Viennese designs (258) the two contrasting shades in the fish design, No. 3, serve to emphasise the form, but in the flying cranes, No. 1, have a tendency rather to disguise. The centre shows how similar forms in three different tones can combine pleasingly with a well-tinted diaper background.

The characteristic lines of time-honoured patterns are for the most part the direct result of the restrictions under which the designer was working. Fashion has had her say in the matter no doubt—it is a wicked way she has—but, though certain lines of design may have become associated in our minds with a particular period or country, it will be found, I think, that there was always some technical or practical reason why in the first instance they were adopted. Appropriate pattern lines do not come of themselves—growth and fitness go together.

Pattern design has always been and will always be considerably affected by considerations which never occur to the uninitiated.

XVII. PATTERN NOT STRICTLY REPEATING.

Balance of design—The decoration of a space or panel—Mechanical subdivision not the way an artist sets to work—Measurement by the eye—Panelling—Composition—The border—Attacking a panel from the outside and from inwards—Borders inseparable from the filling—Diaper conforming to the conditions of a panel—Rules of composition not to be laid down—Delights of daring—Charm of order—Systematic construction of pattern—Artistic anarchy.

Of pattern not strictly repeating there is less to be said, and would be practically nothing to say were it not that there is often repetition in it. That is where the geometric element comes in—and the occasion to discourse of order. The balance of ornament not subject to repetition is so entirely a question to be determined by the eye that, even were it possible, it would serve no purpose to lay down rules and regulations to be observed in its composition. However, in so far as there is repetition in it, it needs to be discussed.

Given, then, a surface to decorate, not with repeated pattern, but with ornament in which there is repetition—how to set about it?

Let us take for our surface a rectangular space or panel. The shape and proportions of this typical space are either satisfactory or they are not. In the one case the artist should be careful not to disturb the satisfactory condition of things. In the other it is his business to amend or correct. This is precisely the province of ornament.

There is a simple way of covering a surface with pattern which has too readily been accepted as sufficient. To divide it into quarters, and these again into quarters, and so again, and perhaps again, until you arrive mechanically at subdivisions small enough to form the ground lines of a harmless diaper, is not so much to plan a design as to shirk the responsibility of invention. The ground plan that "happens" is not greatly to the credit of the artist. And that is not, in fact, the way an artist sets to work.

Geometrically planned pattern may be the very thing; but the designer will find it expedient to consider, before he begins, the proportions of the space with which he has to deal; and will subdivide it into divisions which are not necessarily quarters, or quarters of quarters, or quarters of quarters of quarters. The given area will itself suggest to him its subdivision into twelfths, or thirtieths, or parts of subtler proportion, determined, in the first instance, not by measurement but by the eye. Afterwards he will find it a saving of time to measure them and set them true. A diaper should naturally have reference to the space it is to occupy. It should not be casually designed and recklessly cut short, but neither should it be *mechanically* proportioned to it.

Such subdivisions are commonly but the ground plan of design, only to be traced by those conversant with pattern construction; but they may be, and often are, conspicuous parts of the pattern. It is convenient thus to divide an area of considerable extent into sections, each of which becomes in turn the subject of consideration—to be decorated or not, as in the case, for example, of panelling, where the panels (for the most part bordered with mouldings) are some of them left plain, some enriched with ornament. This may either run through them and connect them, or it may be confined within the limits of each separate panel into which it enters.

When we speak of the "pattern" of a panel it is very much as a painter sometimes speaks of the pattern of a picture, to express what amounts practically to *composition*—a matter by no means of rule but of artistic instinct. We

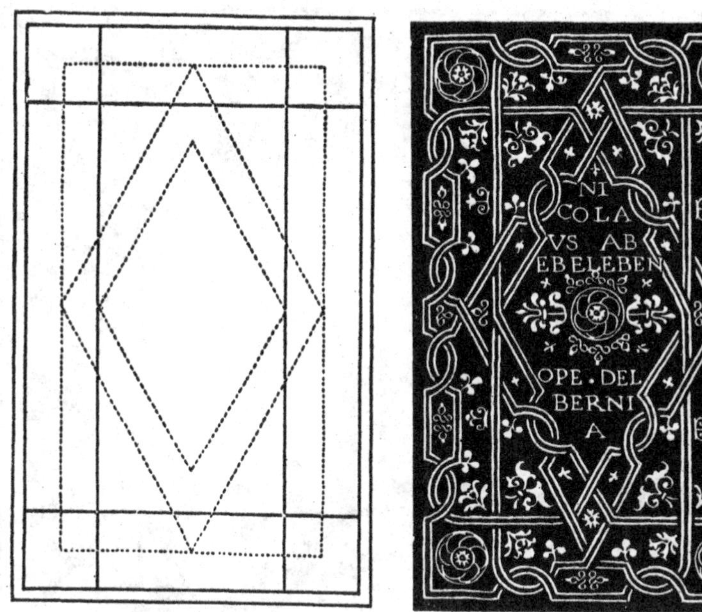

247. BOOK COVER IN WHICH BORDER AND FILLING DESIGN ARE INSEPARABLE.

look at a panel and find it too long or too short. Instinctively we lessen its apparent length by lines in the horizontal direction, or add to it by upright lines in our composition. Or by a judiciously measured border we call attention to the more satisfactory proportions of the inner space.

A border may be all the pattern that is wanted. For by the introduction of it we do not merely lessen the area to be filled, we fill it perhaps sufficiently. It is wonderful what a mere border will do. But the due proportioning of it is not to be prescribed—it must be felt by the artist. And it need not be all of one width, nor yet confined within rigid marginal lines.

There are roughly speaking two opposite ways of attacking a panel—from the outside or from inwards. You may begin,

248. CENTRAL ORNAMENT GROWING OUT INTO BORDER.

that is to say, with the border and creep cautiously inwards, or you may boldly plant your first blow in the centre space and let the design spread outwards to the margin. How far the border itself extends inwards or the central ornament outwards, it is again for the feeling of the artist to determine. A strong border may call for an emphatic feature in the centre of the field to keep it in countenance; a heavy central feature may insist upon support.

The border may flow over from, or flow into, the space it surrounds. It may be so mixed up with the filling pattern as to be inseparable from it. It may exist, that is to say, only

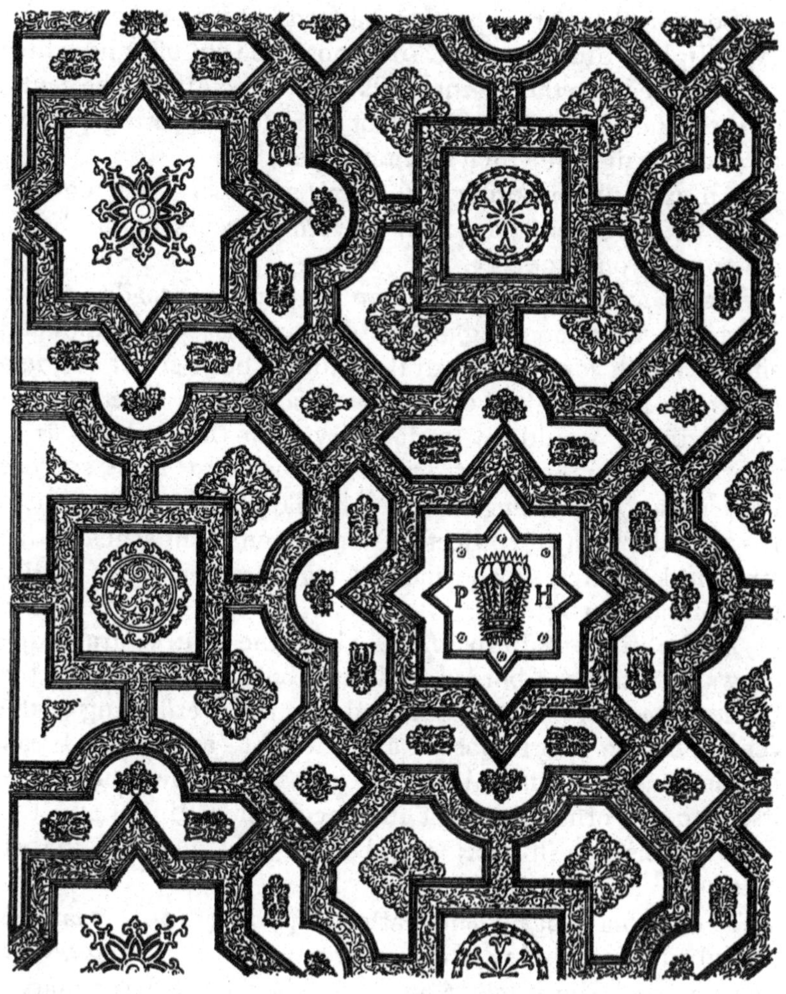

249. JACOBEAN PLASTER CEILING FROM PRINCE HENRY'S ROOM, 17 FLEET STREET, LONDON.

as part of the filling. There are patterns in which it is difficult to say where the border begins, still less whether the designer began or ended with it. All that is certain is that he did mean to frame in his panel or whatever it might be.

So, too, there are repeating patterns which at the margins take slightly different form, so as not to be cut off, and which are gathered together at intervals, and especially in the centre of the panel, so as to become not so much repeating pattern as panel design in which there is repetition.

An example of border and filling so closely knit together as to be dependent one upon the other occurs in the book-cover (247) on page 243.

There are indications of two borders, a broader and a narrower, corresponding to the dimensions of the diamond shapes which form the central feature; but neither of them is perfect in itself—the strapwork is so twisted together that to unwind it would be to do away with the design. It is tolerably clear how the designer must first have set out border lines and lozenges (which he happened to begin with, it would be rash to conjecture) and upon them schemed his strapwork, content in the end to suggest rather than actually to define bordering.

In the niello pattern (248), where the central arabesque grows out into the border, it would be safe to say that the border lines were first set out, and that the overflowing of the central device into it was an afterthought—as was the break in the inner marginal line, and the way it accommodates itself to the ornament. In the Jacobean ceiling (249) the design consists, in fact, of what is practically a diaper pattern.

The Roman pavement pattern opposite (250) may be described as consisting of a very broad border framing a very small panel. But it may equally well be regarded as a diaper pattern gathered together in places, and finished off at the edges so as to result, more by accident than of set purpose, in a central panel with a broad border, enclosing within it smaller spaces again.

The relation of these "patterns in which there is repetition" to "repeated pattern," discussed in earlier chapters, is apparent enough.

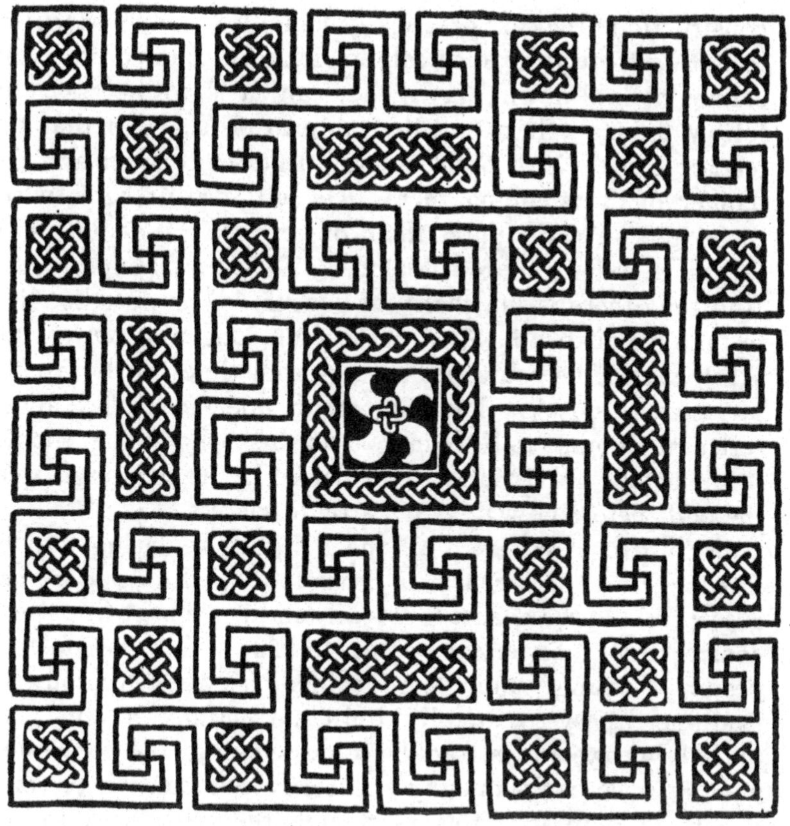

250. ROMAN PAVEMENT—MORE OR LESS GEOMETRIC DIAPER, RESOLVING ITSELF INTO A BORDER.

A point to be observed is, that in none of these last designs would the results arrived at have been reached, but for the planning of the pattern in the first place upon the geometric lines insisted upon in the case of repeated ornament. The rules, therefore, which govern repeated pattern, though no longer applying to pattern in which repetition merely happens to occur, have still a bearing upon it.

In discussing repeated pattern it was possible, and even necessary, to be somewhat dogmatic as to the lines of construction—they are practically compulsory. In pattern not repeating there is no such compulsion: rules of composition cannot be laid down; or, if they can, it is not necessary to follow them, perhaps not desirable to do so. All that the teacher can do is to point out safe lines of conduct and the danger of overstepping them. He will not, if he is wise, insist too strongly upon their observance. We must risk falling if ever we are to run alone. We learn by experiment. And then there is the charm of danger. Who does not like to take his chance? Art would be no congenial pursuit for a live man if he could not indulge sometimes in the luxury of running a risk. The sum of all one has to say about restraint amounts to little more than this: that a man should think before he ventures, look before he leaps, weigh well the odds before he wagers his artistic success.

Admitting, however, all the delights of daring and of freedom, there is a charm in order too; and a designer not susceptible to the charm is scarcely in his element in pattern construction. Experience goes to show that satisfactory design, seemingly quite unrestrained, is, when we come to examine it, systematically built up. Many a time the underlying system is frankly confessed—and the confession wins at once our sympathy and ready condonation of some departure from it. It is as though the artist said in the lines of his design: I claim my freedom, but I have due respect for law and order. And we like him the better for it.

But, though it is refreshing to find an artist not afraid of disturbing order upon occasion, the occasion should be something more than just impatience of restraint. We live in days when it is as well to be on our guard against a spirit of anarchy, which takes at times possession of us, inciting us to repudiate not merely outworn laws—the best of laws wear out in time—but the very need of any law at all. The old ideas of art may need reform, revolution perhaps—though in the last quarter of a century we have made, for good or ill, great strides towards freedom; but the artistic anarchist, whatever his good intentions, is not working to that end. The reign of anarchy would surely bring with it the ruin of design—the very existence of which is bound up with order.

XVIII. EXPEDIENTS IN PRACTICAL DESIGN.

Full-size drawings—Small scale drawings and their use—Methods of drawing—Charcoal—Chalk—Roughing out—Use of blackboard—Designing in colour—in masses—Pencil drawing—Sponging down—Colour designs in colour from the first—Colour as a help in complicated design—Form and colour—Design only a map of form and colour—Precaution against self-deception—The evolution of a design—Tracing paper—Accident — Mechanical helps — Hardness — Precision essential — Body colour—Water colour—Systematic use of mixed tints—Working drawing only a means to an end.

PATTERNS are best designed full-size. The designer, it is true, must learn to work to a reduced scale. It is necessary in order to secure the commission; and if he is in the habit of working always to the same scale, there is not much fear of his misreckoning; but the small scale drawing is useful mainly to save time and labour in setting out the lines, proportions, and repeat of a pattern, before it is determined to take it seriously in hand. It is as well not to carry it too far, nor yet to pledge oneself in it to anything very definite in the way of detail.

A man's method of drawing, and to some extent the medium he employs, will depend upon the kind of thing he is doing.

Charcoal is not a good medium in which to finish working drawings of patterns. It is not merely that it makes a dull and sodden-looking drawing, but that the lines are not precise and sharp enough for practical purposes. To work in charcoal is not fair to the workman into whose hands the drawing is put. How is it to be expected of the engraver to render in hard wood or yet harder metal what the superior artist found it expedient to leave vague in soft charcoal ?

Neither is chalk a very good medium, if, as is mostly the case, it is outline and not modelling it is necessary to express.

But chalk and charcoal answer admirably for the first rough sketch of a design, especially in monochrome. Working in charcoal the designer is not tempted to put in detail prematurely or to niggle over "finish." He can rough in his masses so as to see plainly their weight and balance, and, what is equally to the purpose, he can easily wipe them out again. The knowledge that he can dust it off easily gives him freedom in the use of charcoal ; there is nothing more paralysing than to know yourself definitely committed to the line you have put upon paper. A delightful way of starting a design is upon the blackboard. Drawing paper gets ingrained with charcoal, or chalk, or pencil. Even were erasure easier than it is, one is apt to pause before rubbing out what it has taken some pains to put upon paper. Many a design has fallen short of its promise because it went to the heart of the designer to undo his doing. He has no misplaced tenderness for chalk lines on a blackboard. He never hesitates to wipe them out ; but does it gaily and without regret. It is a pleasure rather. And he goes on wiping out until he has the design absolutely as it should be, or as he would have it. The medium gives him a sense of greater freedom than charcoal, and his work is proportionately more spontaneous.

It is a simple matter to trace the white chalk drawing on to paper, and either finish it on that, or transfer it to drawing paper. (Failing a blackboard, a piece of common American cloth answers the purpose almost as well.)

For designs in colour the preliminary drawing may just as well be in coloured chalks or pastels. Working on paper, it is a good plan to splash in almost immediately the colour masses, in thin washes, foreshadowing as it were their distribution. One chooses, naturally, colours which can be washed down to a mere stain on the paper. The main lines and masses settled, you may proceed to sketch in pencil or charcoal the details of the design. If, as is very probable, these have to be rubbed out in part, there is always the stain of colour left to guide you in starting afresh; or out of a number of tentative lines you define the chosen ones in colour. Something of the freshness of the first sketch may be preserved in a drawing begun and finished on the same piece of paper—if only you can keep the drawing clean and sharp enough for working purposes; but that is not always possible. A design in which the masses count for anything is better drawn in mass, not merely in line. It should be designed, that is to say, in colour or in solid black and white—even though it may be necessary afterwards to make an outline drawing (on tracing paper perhaps) for the guidance of the workman.

You may rough out something in pencil, and carry it to a point at which the lines indicate fairly what you mean. But it takes all your concentrated attention to follow them, if they are at all involved (as in a sketch they are very likely to be); and if you have to lay the design aside for awhile, it is not easy, when you come back to it, to take up the thread of the pattern; you may easily have lost meanwhile the very clue to the intention once so definite to your mind. The roughest daubings of colour are relatively easy to follow; they explain much more to you—little as they might convey to others. And if there is a point at which they are vague, it is the simplest thing to put in the lines necessary to show, for example, the overlapping of one shape by another.

In a design blotted in however roughly in colour, you see at once where it is empty or too full, where wiry stalks want thickening or luxuriant details thinning, and can form a fair idea as to the way the notion will work out. It is to be remembered that the masses shown in it will be, as a matter of fact, what on the wall or in the finished fabric will first strike the eye. You have only to get them right, and you foresee your effect.

A point is often reached in design at which the lines and masses are all right, but the details will not do. It is a good plan in such a case to sponge it down, until only a trace of it remains. The vaguer the forms the more freely you can go to work in defining them, sketching them perhaps first in pencil or charcoal, and then filling them in in colour emphatic enough to make the superfluous stains upon the ground (left from the original sketching) of little or no consequence.

Designs, then, for colour should be thought out, and are best worked out from the beginning in colour. It is never advisable to finish a drawing and then first consider the colours of it. They should by rights play their part (and it is a most important one) in the very plan of the design.

Even in design for monochrome, colour may be helpful—more especially if the scheme is at all involved. It is quite a common experience to get so many more or less experimental lines on your paper that it is almost impossible to see clearly what you are doing. In the case, for instance, of two separate but intertwining growths of ornament, it is not always easy to keep in mind which is which; but if they are drawn in two different colours, there is no confounding them. So also a main stem, to be disguised in the finished design by flowers and foliage breaking across it, is kept for the time being sufficiently in mind by a distinguishing tint. By colour, again, flower masses or other prominent features are defined in such a way that you can't help keeping their prominence in view, and realising the patch they make, and the effect of their recurrence. In complicated design some such device is almost necessary to enable the designer to keep the various strands of the pattern distinct—which he must do from first to last, even though he should mean them eventually to be lost in the general woof of the pattern. There must be no confusion in his mind. The one thing needful in design is to "know what you mean to do, and do it"—and whatever keeps you to the point is helpful. You may with great advantage sketch in the mass you want in one colour and the detail within it in another. The essential forms once for all committed to paper in a colour which may be trusted to leave an indelible stain upon it, you are free to experiment in detail with another which can easily be sponged out.

There is a temptation, against which the artist is not always proof, to get over harshness of line or form by the use of conveniently subdued colour. In dealing with forms already fixed that is often the only thing to do. (See Chapter XIX.) But where the forms are not fixed but remain, equally with the colour, to be determined by the designer, it is an evasion of the difficulty of design. It must not be supposed that when you have designed a pattern which looks well in the colours of your drawing, you have done all that a manufacturer requires of you. On the contrary, what he wants is a design which will work out satisfactorily in half a dozen different schemes of colour. The problem is, not so much to design a colour-scheme, as to plan a pattern which will lend itself to being worked out in a variety of ways. To do this you must have clearly in mind the value and function of each particular colour, rather than its hue. You must know, and should be able to explain, which colours are to assert themselves and which to retire, which (if any) are of equal importance, and what is the relative value of each—all this irrespectively of the charms of some one seductive colour-scheme which might easily lead a designer astray from practicality; for from the manufacturer's point of view a pattern depending entirely upon one colouring is not, as a rule, worth producing.

A word here as to the way designs should be presented to the manufacturer.

A sketch should indicate either the design of the thing that is to be or its effect in execution. The artist's aim should be to show what he is going to do, and he should confine himself to that. Whatever he puts down on paper should go to make clear his meaning. A sketch is a promise, and it should be made in all frankness. Nothing should be done with the mere purpose of making the drawing look pretty. As to the expedient of giving to it charms of colour or effect which the executed work will not have, it is about on a par with showing a sample of goods to which the bulk does not come up. A quite conscientious control of his imagination may possibly cost the artist his pains and lose him a commission. But, what then? Honesty is not a matter of policy, whatever the proverb may say. And, if it were, the only possible policy for an honest man is to go straight. The object of a sketch is to give an idea of something that is to be done. It should give a fair one. A certain vagueness is permissible, on the supposition that the idea has not yet reached a point at which it is possible to be definite, or on the understanding that the working drawing will make all clear.

A working drawing is no longer a mere promise but an undertaking, and a very definite one. It is pledged to tell the workman what he has to do. All that goes to his information is to the good. Whatever does not do that is superfluous—or worse; it may serve to mystify or to mislead him.

A practical designer will therefore not pay much heed to the prettiness of his drawing. As an artist he will naturally present his drawing in such a form as to appeal to the eye. He will draw in firm and expressive lines, will choose his tints with taste, and float them on with dexterity; but that is only by the way; he will not hesitate to disturb the effect of his drawing if by so doing he can amend or improve the design. On the contrary, he will ruthlessly destroy its pleasing appearance, soil his even wash with corrections in body colour, erase, mend, patch his drawing, score it over with written notes of explanation, if only by so doing he can make more sure that there shall be no possibility of mistaking what he meant. Indeed a very *sweet* production is almost open to the suspicion that it is not a perfect drawing to work from; for to the ideal working drawing there goes a precision which is apt to be rather hard in effect. The outlines are firmer than they will appear in, for example, the woven fabric, and the tints (to be blended together perhaps in the general effect of the material) are pronounced with a deliberation which in the executed work would be annoying.

And, then, design is design—that is to say experiment—a seeking for something not always found at the first go off, found perhaps only after many failures, each of which leaves behind it traces not conducive to prettiness.

The designer intent upon design cares too much for its effect in execution to be careful of its appearance upon paper—and will sacrifice all immediate satisfaction to its satisfactory working out. He looks to the end in view and knows his drawing to be only a means to that.

I prefer myself, in designing, let us say, a damask pattern, which in execution will be in two not very distinct shades of one colour, to make the drawing in colour upon white paper—it might even be black on white. The stronger the contrast, the more flagrantly the faults in the design stand out: you see your work at its worst. Make it satisfactory in that pronounced form, and you may be sure it will be more than satisfactory in the not too obviously different shades of a colour—supposing of course (what may be taken for granted when the designer knows his business) that you have all the while in view the relation of the two shades naturally resulting from the process of figured damask weaving. A design, on the other hand, worked out in very tender tints may blind not only the manufacturer (whom perhaps it is meant to deceive) but the artist himself to the defects of his design; and if, as may happen, it should eventually be woven in contrasting colours, great may be the disappointment.

It may not be politic to submit to the manufacturer a drawing in which the design is seen at a disadvantage; but it is sometimes worth an artist's while to rough out his design in colour contrasting frankly and even brutally with the ground, and only when it has passed muster in that form to proceed to present it in guise attractive enough to please the purchaser. The use of colour (not essential to the purpose of the design) as a bait to catch the incautious customer, is a trick of the artistic trade, the resort to which, it is not unfair to say, implies some doubt of the designer's confidence in the resources of his own invention.

There is no one way of preparing working drawings. Design being what it is, a process of evolution, one never quite knows how it will work out. Mistakes have to be made good, and the making them good may lead to wide departure from the method originally proposed.

Supposing, for example, a design to be unsatisfactory in detail. The natural thing to do is to sponge it down, and work over it again ; but if it happens not to come out--it may be convenient to wash over it a deeper colour, just allowing the original lines to show through, and start afresh in body colour, this time, light upon dark—the very reverse of your original intention. If, by the way, a pattern is meant to be printed light upon dark, it is better to draw it at once in body colour upon a deeper ground. There are, it is true, certain kinds of design (full, as a rule) the background to which it is as well to fill in last. But if spontaneity and freedom count, it is false tactics to work from the outline inwards, and especially to outline lines : a line drawn with two strokes instead of one is likely to be relatively stiff. Further, it is not so easy to be sure of forms which you do not see in mass until the background is filled in round them. The surest and subtlest lines are drawn with one sweep of the brush.

It often happens that in a first sketch, done at white heat, there is something you do not want to lose. In carrying the design to a finish there is every likelihood of losing it. And yet it is essential that in a working drawing every detail should be precisely defined. The sketchiness which is charming in a sketch has no charm for the man who has to carry it out, to whom in fact you leave the thankless task of doing what you dared not do yourself. A satisfactory compromise is to leave the sketch as a sketch, and to make a finished drawing on tracing paper over it.

In so working there is no fear of undoing what was done. If the drawing does not come right at once, you have only to make another tracing, and another of that, if necessary, refining upon refinement until you have done your utmost. And all the while the original in its pristine suggestiveness is there to inspire you. The full use of tracing paper is known only to the experienced. Students are sometimes taught at school not to use it. That is all very well in drawing lessons; but in practical design it is contrary to reason. Certain lines have to be repeated or turned over, and the readiest and simplest way is to trace them. The quality of accidental difference obtained by freehand drawing, charming as it is, happens here not to be to the purpose. It is in fact a drawback. Repeats must fit, recurring lines must be level. To draw them without mechanical assistance is to take the greater trouble to do the thing less well—which is absurd. Any hardness which results from mechanical accuracy can easily be corrected when once the necessary exactness has been ensured.

Moreover, in a working drawing a certain degree of hardness is by no means the evil that it would be in a picture. The drawing is here of no account in itself—it is merely a means to an end—absolute precision is essential to its proper interpretation. A vague draughtsman is the kind of genius for whom the manufacturer has no use.

It is impossible to insist too strongly upon the necessity of what I may call plain speaking in practical design. It is the business of a working drawing to explain, not merely to suggest, the designer's meaning. The design which is not fit to put straight away into the hands of the workman is not so much a design as the promise of one.

The suggestiveness which is charming in a sketch is

unpardonable in a working drawing. It is the first duty of the designer to leave nothing vague or undetermined. If his habit is to feel his way towards what he wants, it may be necessary for him to make a new drawing to work from, or to supplement the first by an outline drawing which there is no mistaking. In a working drawing every necessary information must be given, and given clearly. The limits of a tint, for example (which perhaps in the result will merge into another), must be defined so that there is no doubt as to where it begins and ends.

The theory, true or false, that there are no outlines in nature does not concern the designer. He will find that the man who is to work out his design must have them. You may leave, of course, a good deal to the workman you have educated and can trust; but you cannot otherwise rely upon intelligent interpretation on the part of the man who comes after you; and you have no right to expect him to define (as he must if you do not) the lines you yourself hesitated to make clear. If you give any one occasion to spoil your design, it is your fault, not his. Balance against the charm of sketchy drawing the disappointment of seeing it mangled in execution and you will not hesitate to harden your drawing—to brutalise it somewhat, if need be, rather than that some one not in sympathy with you should perhaps vulgarise it.

So essential to the serviceableness of working drawings is precision that some manufacturers insist upon their execution in distemper or body colour. The solid medium does make it fairly certain that the boundary of each separate colour or shade of colour shall be definitely marked enough to prevent any doubt as to what is meant. That much secured, there is no valid reason why the designer should not work in whatever medium is most sympathetic to him—the one over which he has most control, or which best expresses the quality of colour peculiar to the material for which the design is to be made. Distemper gives the effect of wall-paper printing, water-colour gives more the quality of printing in dyes, silk weaving or tile painting; and a design for either of these last in body colour would give a false impression, which might be misleading. There is not the least necessity for showing in a working design the effect of the finished thing, but neither is there any occasion to suggest a quality alien to it. It is not as if distemper were the only means of definition. A wash of colour, it should be remembered, has only to be laid on wet enough, and it dries to a crisp outline—so clearly marked indeed that the designer has to bear in mind that no such line will occur in the printed tint, which may therefore possibly need strengthening. So, too, pencil lines left in the drawing may be misleading, and should be carefully erased.

The danger, however, of an artist's misleading himself is slight compared with his leaving to those who come after him any excuse for going wrong. A designer must not proceed as a painter would, mixing his tints, as he goes along, on the palette, or manipulating them on the paper—he must prepare them before he begins, must keep them separate, and lay them as flat as need be. It does not matter much if they are not quite even, so long as there is no possibility of confounding them. His business is to furnish a definite, intelligible, and even unmistakable drawing. Any possible doubt should be cleared up by written notes even though they deface the drawing. Naturally a good workman likes to turn out a clean crisp drawing; but that is not the point in a design. It is no part of the purpose of a working drawing to look pretty. Rightly considered, it is after all only a means to an end. Neatness itself is dearly bought at the expense of revision which would have done good to the design. A designer intent upon design should not be afraid to wipe out what he has done, or to spoil in order to perfect. The man who hesitates to sacrifice the prettiness of his drawing to its efficiency is lost. As to finish, a working drawing is finished when it tells the workman just what he has to do.

To that end, the only end of a working drawing, the designer must know precisely what he means, and say it plainly—with emphasis even, that there may be no doubt about it. Any medium which allows him to do that will suffice.

XIX. COLOUR.

Close connection between form and colour—Effect of colour upon design —Drawing should show not merely effect of colour but its plan—A map of colour value and relation—Differences that colour makes—Casual colour —Colour and material—Geometric form softened by colour, accidental or cunningly planned—Confusion of form by colour—Emphasis of form by colour—Change of colour in ground.

COLOUR and construction are more closely connected than is commonly supposed. The colour scheme is part of the construction.

It is sometimes thought that a design may be schemed independently, and the colour left for after consideration. So, in a sense, it may, but the colouring will in that case possibly be very difficult to scheme.

Left to the last, it may make or mar the effect. It should be planned from the first. You may safely rely upon it then to make good what would otherwise be a defect or a deficiency in the form, to enliven what would be dull, to loosen what would be too tight, to steady what would be too busy, to emphasise what might else be tame, to give an air of mystery to the otherwise obvious. You cannot rely upon it to do that when the drawing is once made, though even then an ingenious designer may do much to make amends for shortcomings, if not always to rectify mistakes.

It is astonishing what havoc may be made with a design by colouring it amiss. Secondary or unimportant forms have only to be coloured insistently, and the design is at once pulled hopelessly out of shape. And this sort of thing

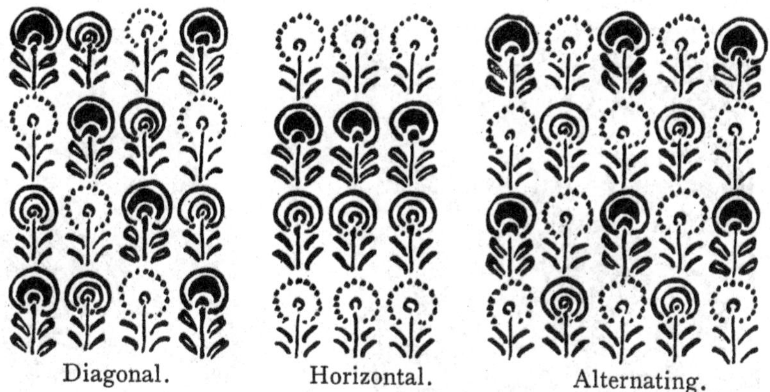

251. DIAGRAM SHOWING EFFECT OF DIFFERENT COLOUR SCHEMES UPON THE SAME DESIGN.

happens continually where an artist's designs are coloured by some one who does not see (he would have perhaps to be himself a designer, and one in sympathy with the artist whose work he is tampering with, in order fully to see that) what he was aiming at.

This may be sometimes, or to some extent, the fault of the artist who colours his design without regard to the condition (implied by commerce) that a design will be published in a variety of colourings—for which he is in duty bound to provide. The fact is a design should be coloured, not so much to show its effect in certain colours (an effect perhaps impossible to be got in any others) as to give a map of the relations of a certain number of tints, to be employed in weaving, printing, or otherwise producing it.

An artist should have clearly in his mind, and show clearly in his drawing too, which are the prominent and which the retiring tints, and what the order of their prominence or retiring—as well as which of them (if any) are designed to balance one another; for it is all a matter of design.

It concerns the designer again to know, and to show, precisely the part each tint is to play in a design. An outline

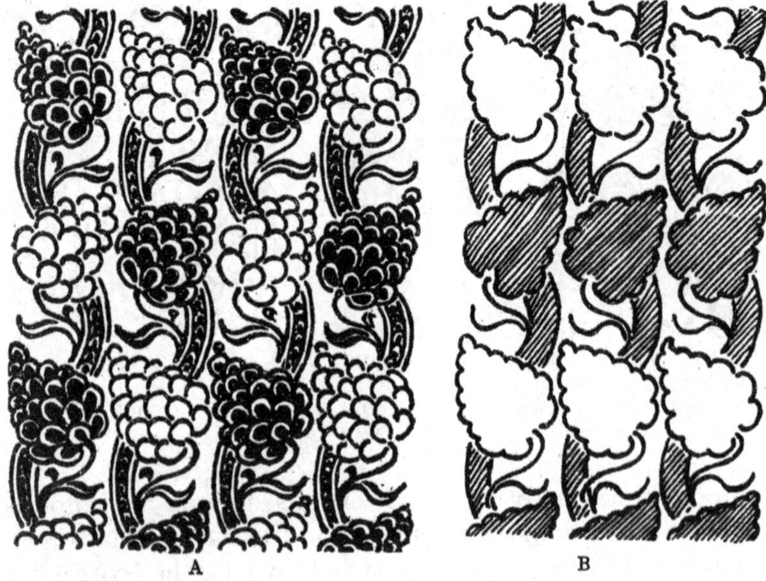

252. DIAGRAM SHOWING EFFECT OF DIFFERENT COLOUR SCHEMES.

colour may be introduced for example in the form of a patch also; but, then, it must not be too dark, or it would emphasise itself too strongly; and, with a view to its use for the double purpose, it may be necessary to draw a much broader line than would have been desirable if the colour could have been stronger. To tamper with the strength in the drawing is dishonest.

The colour is, in short, part of the design, and should be so considered from the beginning. You may, of course, translate a design in one colour into a design in many; but the happiest effects are not translations but spontaneous inventions.

The lines of a pattern may be deliberately counteracted by the colour of it. A pattern planned on the chequer may be made, according to its colouring, to show perpendicular or horizontal, diagonal or cross stripes (251), the stripes of course asserting themselves in the direction of the continuity

253. WALL-PAPER DESIGN IN WHICH THE SMALLER DETAIL, EVENLY DISTRIBUTED, GIVES AT A DISTANCE SOMETHING OF THE EFFECT OF A TINT.

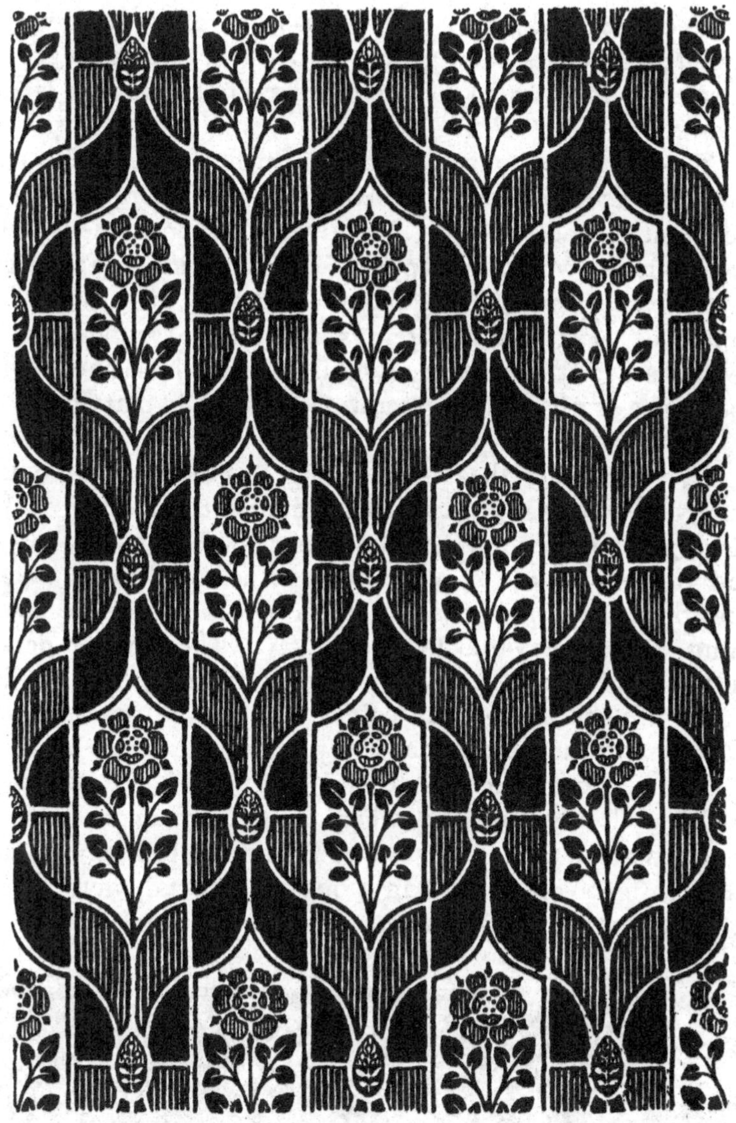

254. NET PATTERN IN WHICH FORM IS TO SOME EXTENT MODIFIED BY COUNTERCHANGE IN COLOUR.

of the colour. All this is so obvious as hardly to seem worth saying; but the bearing of it upon rather more complicated pattern, is so commonly lost sight of that it wants saying.

The change of colour in a design such as that (252, A) on page 264 does not merely enliven it by variation, and as it were enlarge the scale of it, but gives a diagonal line which, except for it, would not appear. In monochrome the horizontal bands (emphasised in light and dark at B) are what would be most prominent; as it is they are practically neutralised. It is clear how easily the vertical line might equally be emphasised by alteration of colour in that direction (254).

The mere fact that in the diagrams here given (252) change of colour is indicated by a different rendering of the form, goes to show the interdependence of form and colour—how one may take the place of the other and do its work, how there are sometimes two ways of expressing the same thing, the same value that is to say. The smaller detail in the wall-paper (253) is designed to merge at a distance with the background colour and give an intermediate tint defining the cusped shapes—which are a feature in it.

Instances occur in the interlacing strapwork, for example, in Celtic illuminated MSS. where the colour changes without other reason than that the painter thought fit to interrupt the too even tenor of the tints in a quasi-accidental way. Even in more flowing ornament the artist is at times tempted to

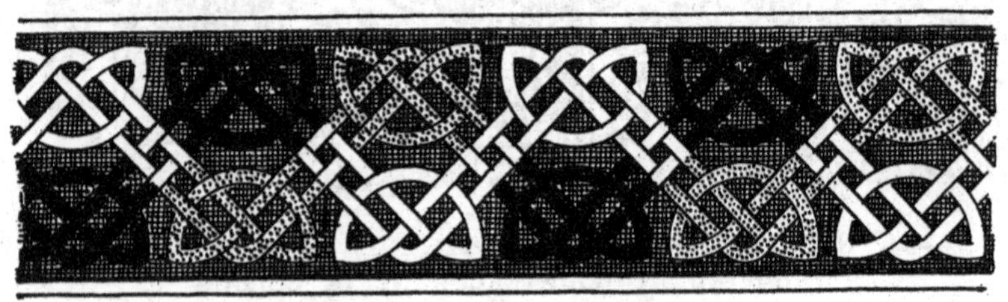

255. CELTIC BORDER. ARBITRARY CHANGE IN COLOUR.

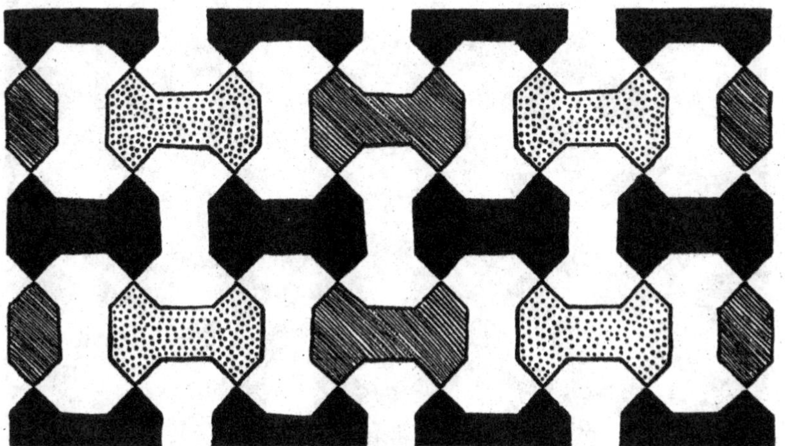

256. DIAGRAM SHOWING SYSTEMATIC DEPARTURE FROM THE SYSTEM OF COUNTERCHANGED COLOUR.

diversify the effect by colouring it in patches quite irrespective of the form.

The severity as well as the monotony of pattern may be mitigated by colour; and the designer may therefore often be severer and simpler in his drawing than he could dare to be but for his reliance upon its help. This is very apparent in the case of absolutely geometric ornament in which the form is tempered by colour.

There is no doubt the use of geometric forms was encouraged, say in Opus Alexandrinum, by the use of marble, in itself always unequal enough in colour to neutralise harsh form, or in Cosmati mosaic, where the little facets of glass catch the light at all manner of angles, and give a glitter of colour defying the utmost severity of form. But it is not merely the accident of colour which is used to counterbalance too great certainty of form. The Arabs, for example, were adepts in contradicting the ground-lines of geometric ornament and bringing into prominence forms which, but for it, one would never have suspected to be there. The colour in many of the tile mosaics in the Alhambra appears at first

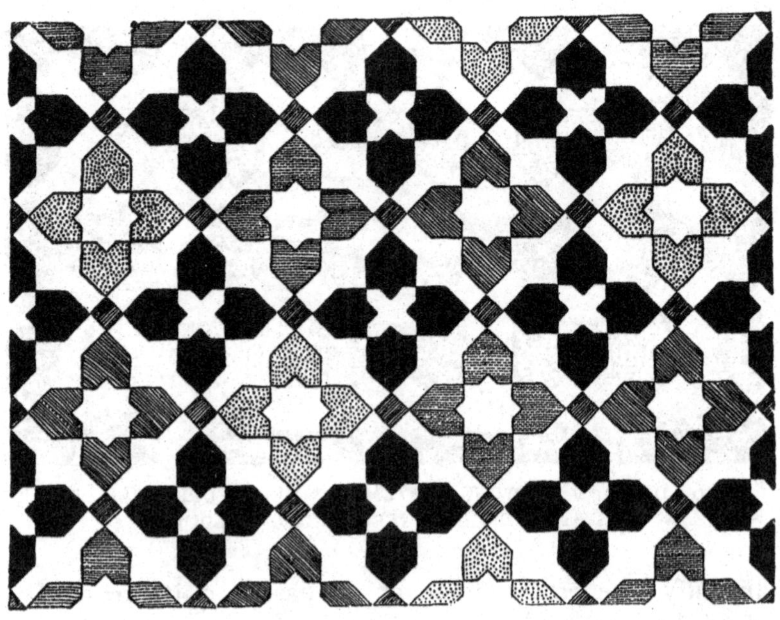

257. DIAGRAM SHOWING SYSTEMATIC DISTURBANCE OF THE UNIFORMITY OF GEOMETRIC DIAPER.

sight to be quite casual. It proves upon examination to be most thoughtfully planned. Sometimes it is focussed into points which successfully break the monotony of intersecting lines. Sometimes it is disposed in rings and rays so effectually disguising the lattice lines on which the pattern is built that it is only at a distance that they pronounce themselves.

A simple and most effective plan of theirs is to devise what would be a counterchange, but, as on page 269, whilst keeping the light units white, to vary the dark ones (256).

A further subtlety is to make, say, half the dark units black and the remaining half alternately green and yellow.

In the design (257) above, the main forms of the pattern are as it were framed in white; half the pointed cross shapes are in one colour, the others are alternately in three different colours. But the diagonal line they would give is almost neutralised by the steadying effect of the darker forms.

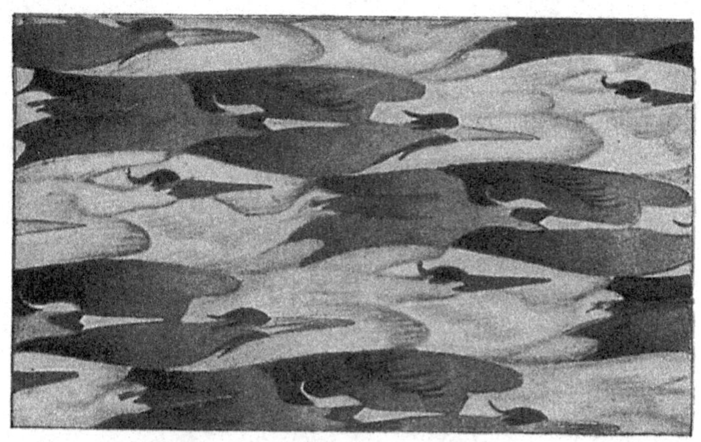

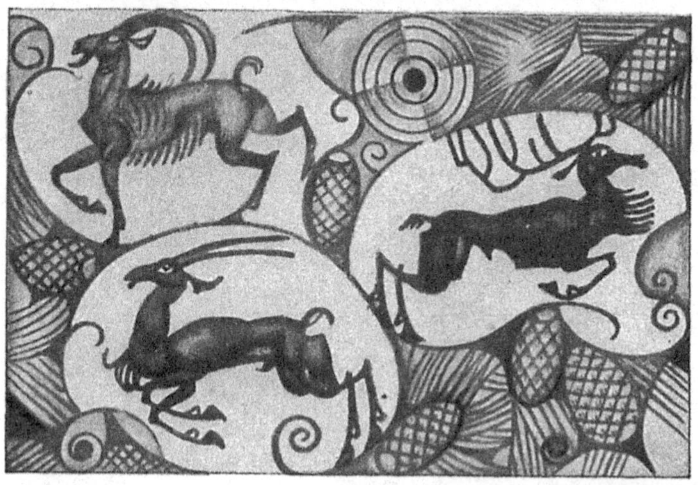

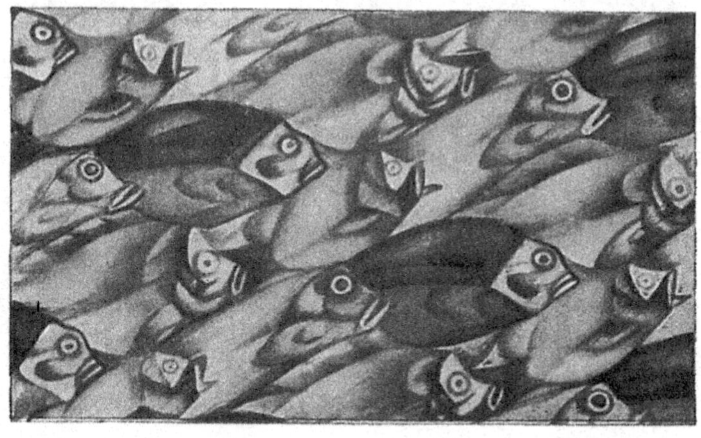

258. ANIMAL DESIGNS FOR FLAT ORNAMENT.

BY ERWIN PUCHINGER, VIENNA.

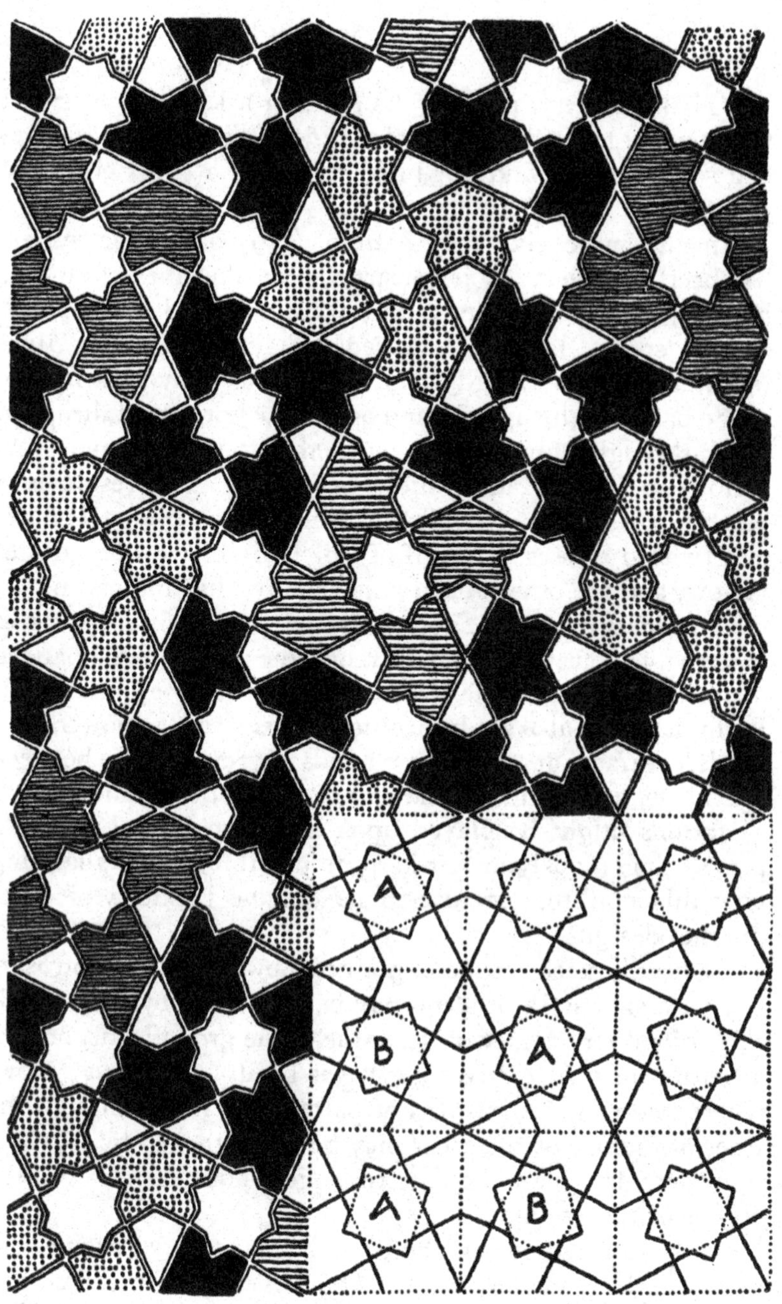

259. ALHAMBRESQUE TILE MOSAIC SHOWING SYSTEMATIC DISTURBANCE OF GEOMETRIC FORM BY VARIATION IN COLOUR.

All this is very much to the good in a kind of pattern, I will not say too orderly, but too evidently in order. It gives you something to find out in it—which is a great charm in pattern.

In the more elaborate pattern (259) a similar system has been observed. It is constructed on the lines of zig-zag bands (opposed to one another, so as to give diamond-shaped spaces between) crossed by similar zig-zag lines (similarly opposed). Mystery is given to it by making one of the bands in the upright and one in the horizontal direction black throughout, and breaking up the others alternately into yellow and green and yellow and blue. The result is a pattern in which the conspicuous features are strange, square-cut, twisted crosses, one-half of which are black, one-quarter yellow, and the other quarter alternately blue and green.

The effect of colour upon design of a less formal character is shown in four very different renderings of the same pattern opposite (260). At A the flowing line of the conventional scroll is emphasised, at B the horizontal tendency of the flowers and smaller leafage, at C the waved bands of ground space between the stems, at D bands in the opposite direction: and further variations might be played upon the same tune. Devise a pattern ingeniously and it is quite possible, by emphasising now this now that feature in it, to give the idea of quite distinct designs.

It hardly needs to be explained how easily an obtrusive but necessary stalk or stem may be kept back by reducing it to a colour very nearly of the value of the ground tint, or how attention may be called to a flower by its brightness; how, where two or more growths of pattern are intermingled, the lines of the one or the other may be strengthened by it; how point may be given to a pattern by judicious variation in the colour of the ground.

Change of colour in the ground wants very careful, not to say skilful, management. The difficulty of contriving it judiciously is in proportion to the extent of the change. The

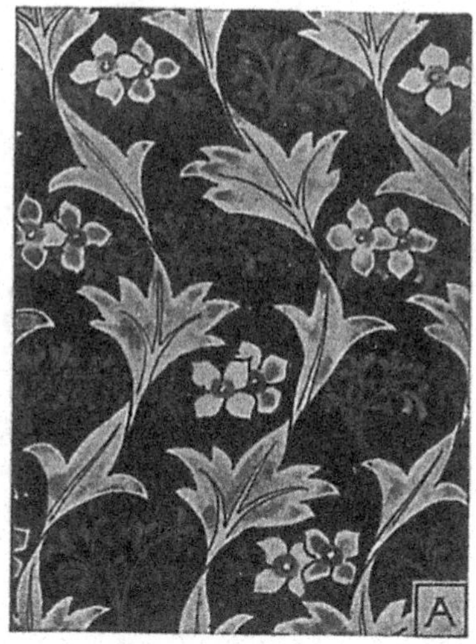

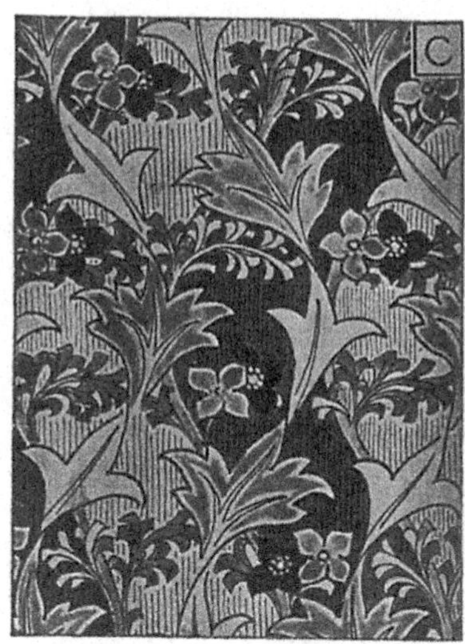

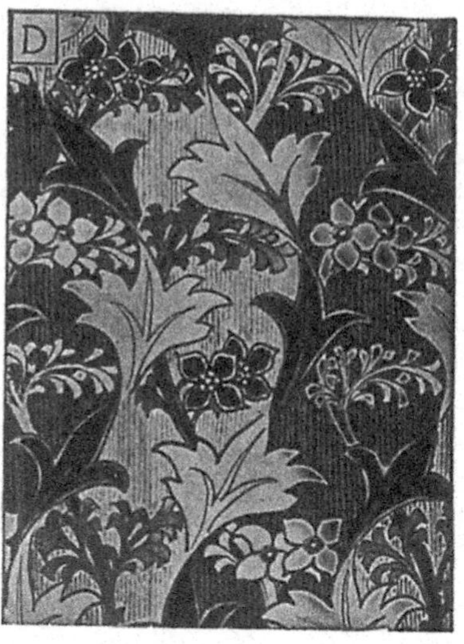

260. DIAGRAM SHOWING EFFECT OF DIFFERENT COLOUR TREATMENTS OF IDENTICALLY THE SAME FORMS.

danger is, lest the patch of differently coloured ground should attract too much attention, not so much to itself as to the shape enclosing it. It is part of the game to enclose it, and, what is more, with circumscribing lines which really play a not quite unimportant part in the composition of the pattern —not, for instance, with the casual outline of leaves converging towards it.

The notion of varying the ground colour may be to some extent an afterthought, occurring only as the design progresses; but the shape as well as the position of the colour patch is best determined at an early stage of its development.

Colour is equally of use in emphasising or in confusing form, either of which it may be expedient to do.

XX. THE INVENTION OF PATTERN.

Imitation and translation—Memory and imagination—Old-time content with tradition—Modern self-consciousness—Originality—Conditions of to-day—Inspiration—How far nature helps—The use of old work—The designer and his trade—The artist and his personality.

A PATTERN, says the dictionary, is "something to be copied." Perhaps that is why design is so commonly confounded with appropriation, or at the most with adaptation. Translation is a trade of which no one need be ashamed, unless he calls it all his own; but it is not design.

And yet the literal interpretation of the word invention is the true one—something not all ours, which we find, and make our own.

What we think we imagine we more than half remember. Our wildest imagination is only a reflection of something which existed outside of us, in some sort a distorted image of it; and the personal accent, which comes of the mind's mirror not having a flat surface, counts, according to the quality of the individual mind, for or against the version (or perversion) of the fact which we call imagination.

Time was when designers less sophisticated than we are would accept or take for granted familiar lines to work on, and were free to devote all their energies to the *perfection* of pattern—theirs only in so far as, by bettering it, they made it their own. Byzantine mosaic workers were content to play infinite variations upon familiar combinations of triangular cubes; Sicilian silk weavers designed upon the lines of the stripe, and the later Italians upon the principle of the turnover. Gothic textiles took the continual form of what is called the pine or cone pattern. There was a period when the diagonal stripe prevailed. In later stuffs the plan was for a century or more almost invariably on the lines of the ogee. And so they arrived at mastery. We are for our part too self-conscious, too anxious about the novelty of what we do. The dishing up of stale patterns is not of course design. But neither does originality mean novelty. An artist of initiative will show marked originality in the treatment of the oldest theme. He need not think about originality. If he has it in him his work will be original: he cannot help it. And it is that originality in spite of himself which alone gives charm to a man's work.

Designers of the present day do not live under conditions the most favourable to their art. It is their misfortune that they are not left to work out the vein of design natural to them, but are continually called off in some other direction. What matter whether there is gold or silver in the neglected working, if it is brass or pewter which happens to be the fashion? We are free neither to follow tradition nor to perfect a style, be it ever so distinctly our own. It is the glitter of newness that attracts.

But in the very variety of the demands made upon us, there is some compensation for their unreasonableness. They excite our ingenuity. The difficulties put in our way provoke solution. To the making of a practical designer there goes an element of pugnacity—he enjoys attacking a tough problem. An artist of feeble capacity may under favourable circumstances arrive at beautiful results. It is in reaching them in spite of adverse circumstances that he proves himself a strong one.

Inspiration comes to a man from without as well as from within: every competent designer, you may be sure, has made an infinite number of studies, both from nature and old work. But he does not work from them, nor often refer to them, except perhaps to refresh his memory by way of preliminary to design. The sight of them before his eyes would hamper him.

Spontaneity of design is only then possible when the idea, whencesoever derived, is, so to speak, fluid in a man's mind—so that what his eyes took in as fact flows out at his finger-tips in the form of fancy.

Neither is it possible to design straight-away from nature. A designer acquaints himself with natural form, natural colour, natural growth and so forth, and especially with everything suggestive to him of ornament. But in designing he uses not so much these as memories of them. Just so much of nature as comes to him at the moment, and just that in nature which comes unbidden is to the purpose. The rest is overmuch. Ornament can digest no more.

And as with natural motives, so with suggestions from old work. Tradition has become so much a part of a man that he is no longer conscious whence he had it; does not realise that it is not entirely his own to make use of as he likes. Moreover it is dangerous consciously to borrow if he would keep alive within him the faculty of design.

Towards practical design the first step is to realise how much is involved in working for even the simplest handicraft or manufacture. Amateurs turn with not altogether unwarranted disgust from trade pattern sheets, with the comfortable conviction that they could do better than that at any rate. And so perhaps a person of taste might do, had he the requisite knowledge of technical conditions. Not having it, he cannot.

All trades want learning. In the path of beginners and pretenders difficulties spring up one after another to hinder their advance. The inexperienced have no doubt they could design patterns, if only manufacturers would give them a chance. But it is not so easy as all that. Or rather, it is easy only to those who have been doing it all their lives. A designer, whatever his natural gift, is of no practical use until he is at home with the conditions of manufacture. It is only when he knows full well the difficulties of the case that he is in a position to avoid or meet them—according to his courage.

Over and above the mechanical construction of design, the designer must needs know all about the materials in which, and the means by which, his designs are to be carried out. He must learn to work to given proportions and with the palette given him, restricting himself moreover to a very limited number of its colours. He has to take into consideration that his design will be judged from two opposite points of view, as seen in the pattern book, and in its place in a scheme of decoration; and, withal, he has to face the hurrying fashions which foolish or interested persons are continually trying to foist upon him.

And then, when he has learned his trade, and when he has developed, let us hope, to the full the sense of beauty and the faculty of expression that may be his, he has further to be an artist. Unless he has something to say there is no great advantage in his being able to say it perfectly. The best in design is that which there is no discussing. It is there, or it is not. You feel and appreciate it, or you do not. To the expression of that indeterminate something—joy in nature, purpose, thought, human sympathy, feeling, poetry, whatever it may be—there goes, it is true, the training of the workman; it is in workmanship that the artist finds expression; without it he is inarticulate; but, say what we may about design and its mechanism, it is not simply the workman that interests us, nor the artist even, but the man at the back of it all. It is his personality which gives to art its real and lasting value; not the conscious self he thrusts upon us, but the individual revealed, perhaps without his knowing it, not only in his work and in the high ideal inspiring it, but in the very way he goes about the quest of beauty.

XXI. DEVELOPMENT OF PATTERN DESIGN.

AN ADDITIONAL CHAPTER BY AMOR FENN.

Sources of nineteenth-century design—Augustus Welby Pugin and the Gothic revival—Designs for the Houses of Parliament—Mid-Victorian vogue—Owen Jones and ancient Western and Oriental art—Bruce J. Talbert—Edwin William Godwin—William Morris—The Art Workers' Guild—Walter Crane—Lewis F. Day—C. F. A. Voysey—Arts and Crafts Society—E. W. Gimson—*L'art nouveau*—Continental designs—W. Lovatelli-Colombo, Paris—Josef Hoffmann, Vienna—Futuristic influence—Maurice Dufrène—Burkhalter—Geometric motifs—Stépanova—Modernistic art—Georges Valmier—Strong colour effects—Hermann Huffert.

THE following plates illustrate pattern designs from the mid-Victorian period to the present time, as far as possible in chronological order.

In mechanically produced fabrics, particularly wall-papers, cretonnes and tapestry, the repetition of a unit is a technical necessity, and they have been modelled in the main on early Sicilian tapestries, though painted Chinese wall-hangings, which were imported into England in the seventeenth century, have also influenced design.

An outstanding personality of the early nineteenth century was Augustus Welby Pugin, architect, designer, and writer on art. He was intimately associated with the Gothic revival, and was responsible for much of the decorative detail of the Houses of Parliament at Westminster, in conjunction with the architect, Sir Charles Barry. Two of

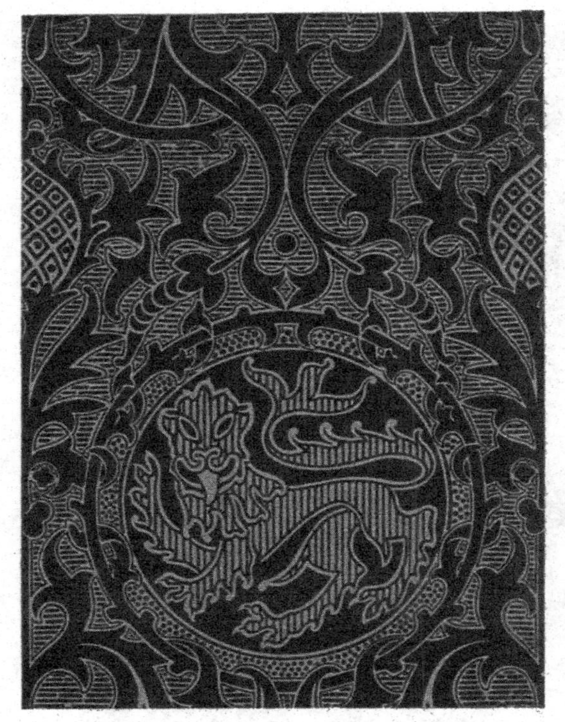

a

261. BLOCK PAPER DESIGNED BY A. W. PUGIN FOR THE HOUSES OF PARLIAMENT, 1848.

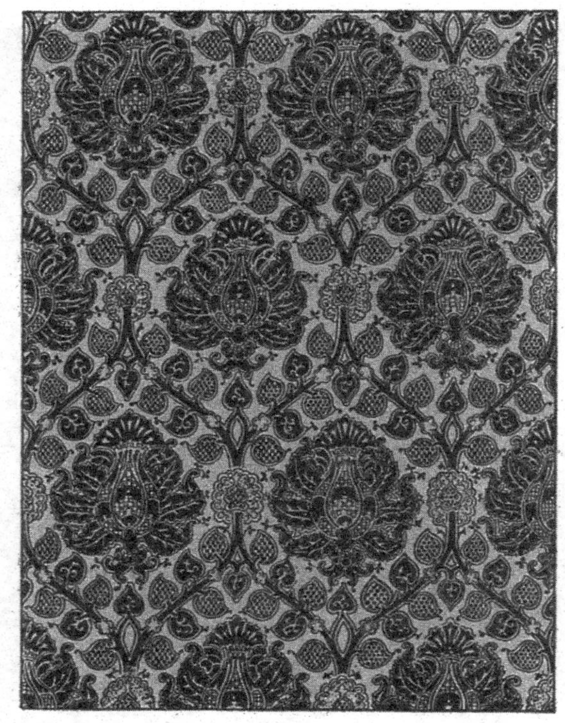

b

DESIGN FOR TAPESTRY.

A. W. PUGIN.

262. PANELLED TREATMENT BY OWEN JONES.

his designs are illustrated (261, a), a flock wall-paper for the Houses of Parliament, and (261, b) a design for tapestry.

Prevailing style or fashion has generally been a factor in design. The mid-Victorian vogue was to divide the wall-surface into panels: wall-papers were designed as fillings, with borders for the framing of these. About the beginning of the present century this fashion was revived.

An example is shown (262) which was designed by Owen Jones, who was regarded as the greatest authority of his time on ancient Western and Oriental art. This design was exhibited by Messrs Jeffrey & Allen at the Industrial Exhibition held in Paris in 1867. Owen Jones' "Grammar of Ornament," a unique work of great value to students and all concerned with stylistic decorative design, was published in 1856.

Another prominent name of this period is that of Bruce J. Talbert, whose personality was a dominating influence in the design of furniture and decoration. Though a follower of Pugin, he treated Gothic in a manner quite his own, which, though true to the style in principle, was comparatively free from formalism, and was rather a development suited to the domestic conditions of the period in which he practised. Later in life he exploited the Jacobean style, in which, however, personality is evident in the decorative details which display undoubted Japanese influence. Talbert's "Gothic Forms Applied to Furniture, Metal Work, and Decoration for Domestic Purposes" was published in 1868, and was followed in 1876 by "Examples of Ancient and Modern Furniture, Tapestries, Metal Work, Decoration, &c." This latter work illustrated several of Talbert's designs which were exhibited at the Royal Academy. His "Sunflower" wall-paper design (263), produced by Messrs Jeffrey & Co., was awarded a gold medal at the Paris Exhibition of 1878. This was extremely popular, and the sunflower became the dominant motif in the decorative phase known as æsthetic.

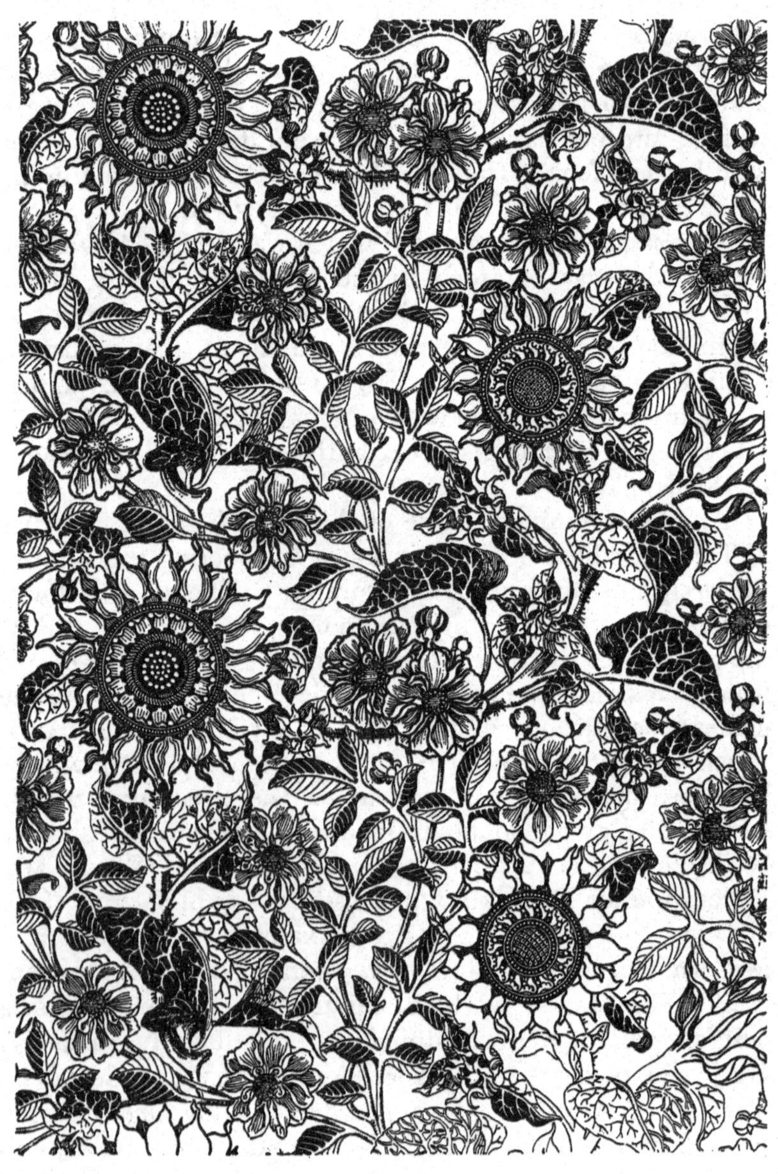

263. "SUNFLOWER" WALL-PAPER BY B. J. TALBERT.

Contemporary with Talbert, Edwin William Godwin, though trained as an architect, was more conspicuous as designer, lecturer, and writer on applied art. The prevailing interest in Japanese art is apparent in his wall-paper design (264, b), which was produced by Messrs Jeffrey & Co. in 1873.

The greatest name in modern times associated with craft work and decorative art is that of William Morris. As early as 1861 he helped to establish the firm of Messrs Marshall Faulkner & Co. in Queen Square, and in 1877 opened offices and show-rooms in Oxford Street. The studios and workshops at Merton Abbey were established in 1881. According to Lewis F. Day ("Monograph on William Morris," *Art Journal*, 1897), "The earlier work of the firm was, of course, pronouncedly Gothic in style; so much so that the medals awarded to them at the Exhibition of 1862 were given 'for exactness of imitation' of mediæval work. The wording of the award may express more nearly the point of view of the judges than the aim of the exhibitors; but it was inevitable that the new firm, starting when it did, and as it did, should begin by working very much in the old way. However, Morris soon made Gothic his own, and used it to express himself."

The "Trellis" (265, a) was the first wall-paper designed by Morris, and was produced in 1862. The "Trenton" printed linen (265, b) is a typical Morris design in which Gothic tradition is evident.

William Morris was one of the founders of the Art Workers' Guild, in company with Walter Crane, Lewis F. Day, and others. He was also prominent in the formation of the Arts and Crafts Society, which held exhibitions of members' work, of which the prevailing features were utility and simplicity, particularly in furniture, in which the proper use of material and good construction were the main considerations, as opposed to unnecessary ornamentation. The Society ruled that the names of designers and craftsmen must be published—a tardy act of justice to a class of workers who were previously unknown outside trade circles.

Walter Crane, painter, illustrator, and designer, achieved an early reputation in the illustration of children's books. His first wall-paper, produced by Messrs Jeffrey & Co. in 1875, was designed as a nursery decoration, the theme being "Sing a Song of Sixpence." Though reminiscent of Crane's illustrations, it is certainly decorative in treatment: the frank divisions and alternation of subjects exonerate it from criticism rightly bestowed on undesirably pictorial renderings. A gold medal for "great excellence and chastity of design" was awarded to his "Margarete" wall-paper, which was exhibited in Philadelphia in 1876. From 1870 to about 1890 it was customary to divide the wall into frieze, filling and dado; in more recent times the dado went out of fashion, but the frieze, either plain or decorated, has been retained. The "Margarete" could be used by itself, or as a filling, between Crane's "Alcestis" and the "Lilies and Dove" dado. These are illustrated on Fig. 129 of Sugden & Edmondson's "History of English Wall-paper" (Batsford, 1925). Another design, "Peacocks and Amorini" (266, a), was equally successful at the Paris Exhibition of 1878. The "Macaw" (266, b) was designed in 1908.

Lewis F. Day was contemporary with Crane, but had a much wider range in the sphere of applied art, in which his technical knowledge was extensive and supreme. Though his work was intensely personal, with a convention entirely his own, yet his attitude was catholic, and he was always ready to appreciate the work of others—whether old or new. He was lecturer on Historical Ornament at the National Art Training School, which later became the Royal College of Art; and for many years was examiner in several branches of design to the Board of Education, and Assessor in the National Competitions which were open to Art students throughout the British Isles. He was also for some time

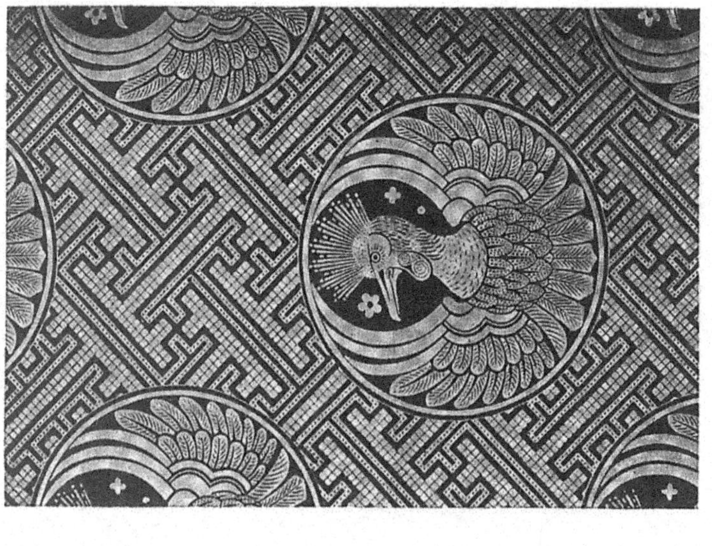

b

WALL-PAPER.

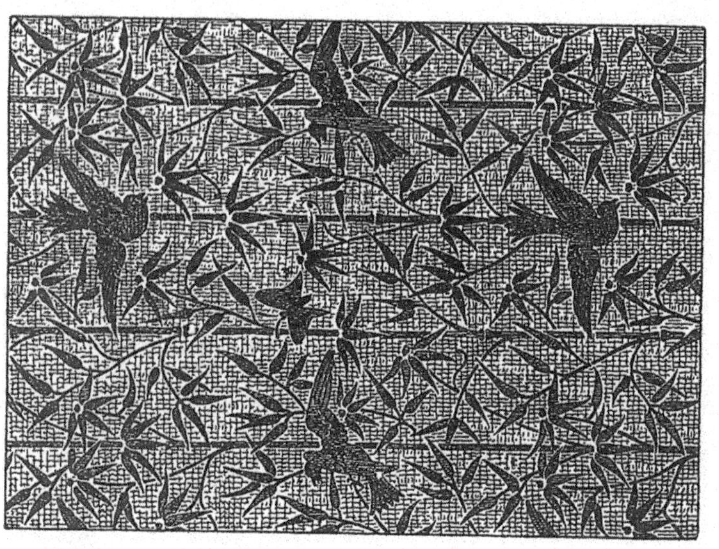

a

TEXTILE.

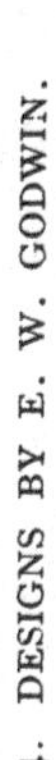
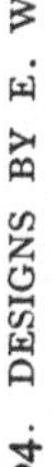

264. DESIGNS BY E. W. GODWIN.

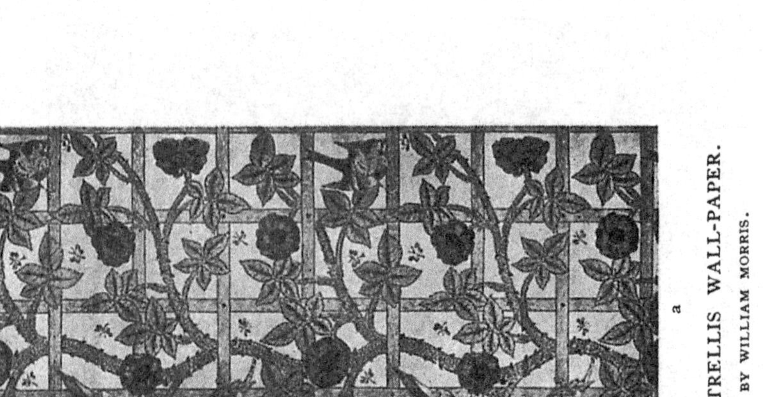

265. a

TRELLIS WALL-PAPER.

BY WILLIAM MORRIS.

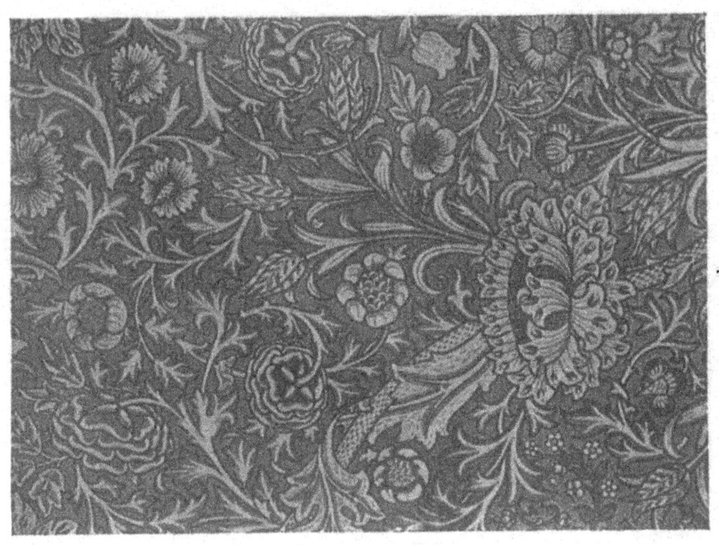

b

"TRENTON" PRINTED LINEN.

BY WILLIAM MORRIS.

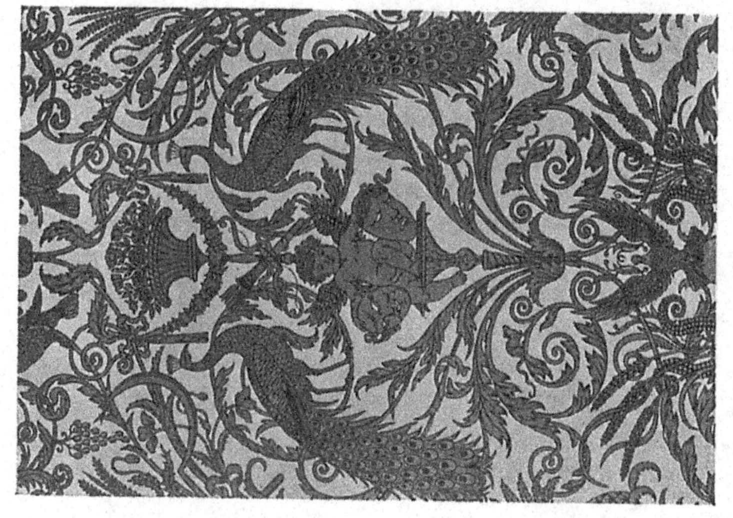

a

266. "PEACOCKS AND AMORINI" WALL-PAPER.

WALTER CRANE.

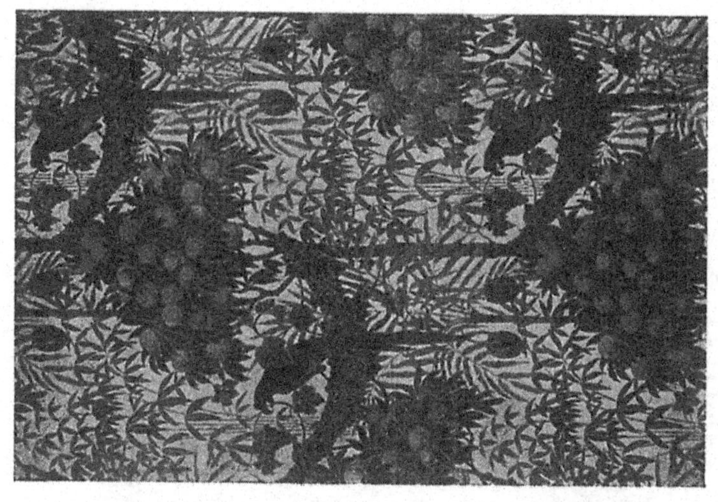

b

"MACAW" WALL-PAPER.

WALTER CRANE.

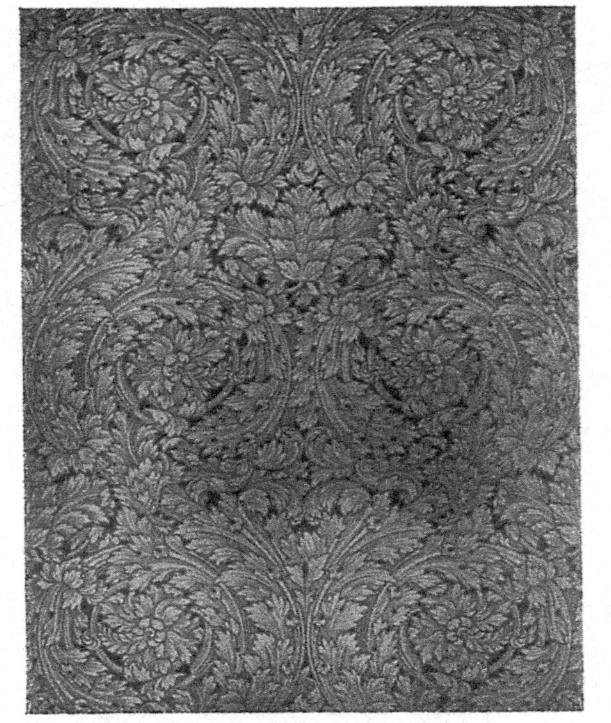

a

267. THE "ROMAN" WALL-PAPER.

L. F. DAY.

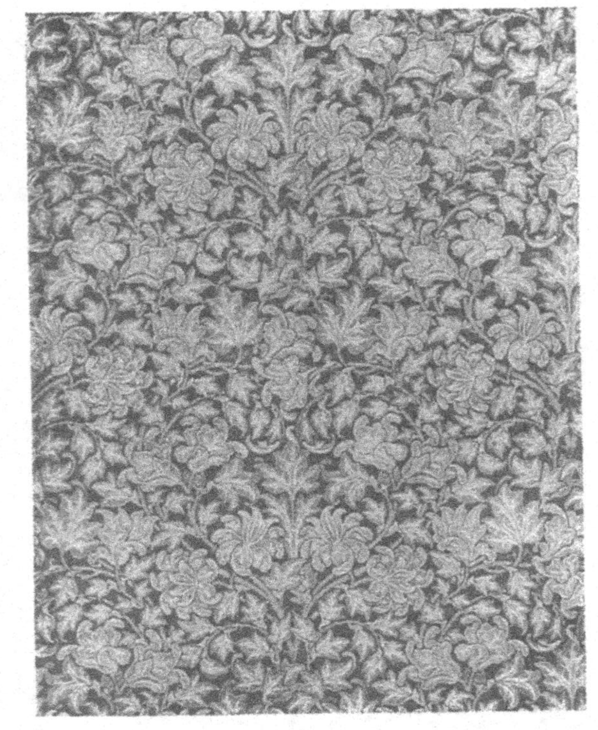

b

THE "COMO" WALL-PAPER.

L. F. DAY.

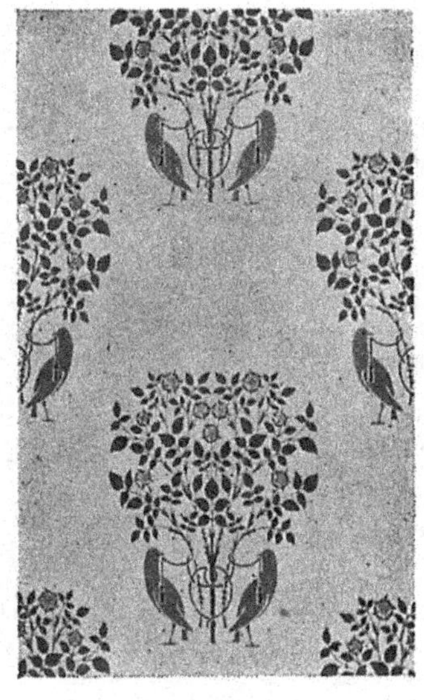

a

C. F. A. VOYSEY.

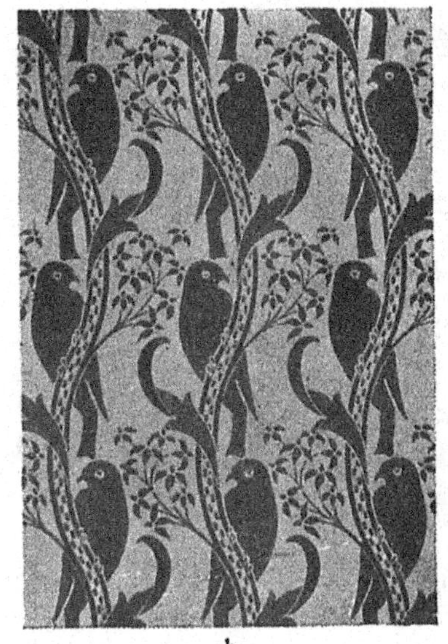

b

C. F. A. VOYSEY.

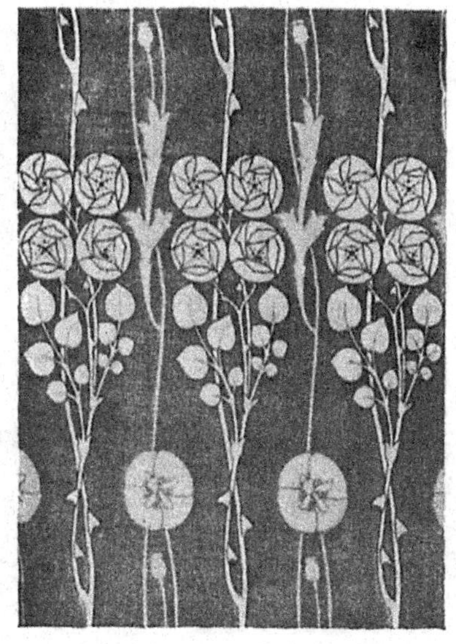

c

LIBERTY & CO., LONDON.

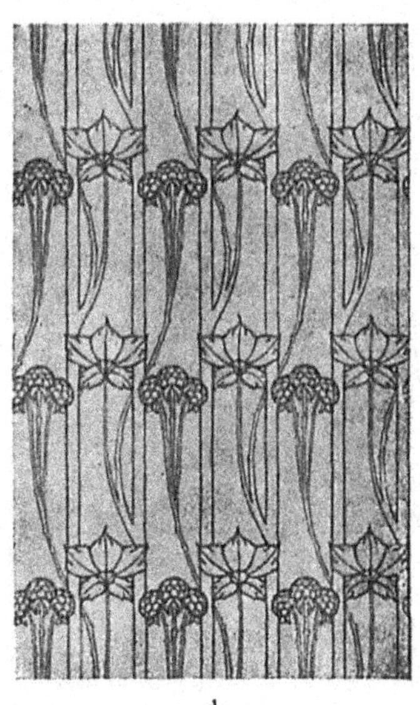

d

ROTTMANN & CO., LONDON.

268. ENGLISH DESIGNS OF ABOUT 1900.

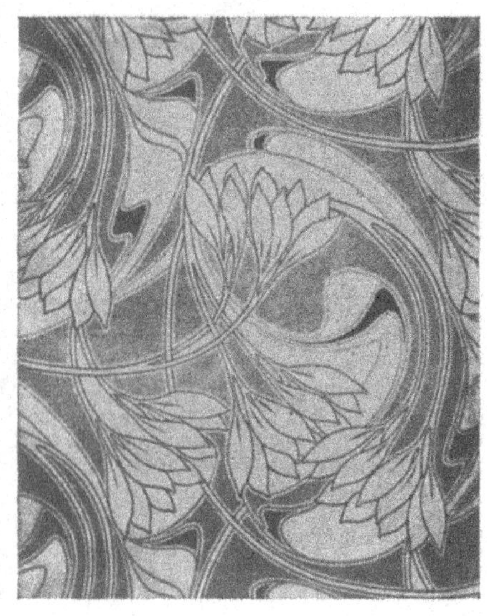

a

LOVATELLI-COLOMBO, PARIS.

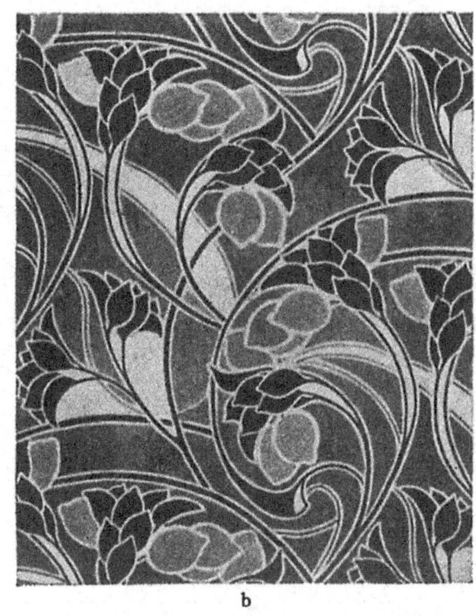

b

LOVATELLI-COLOMBO, PARIS.

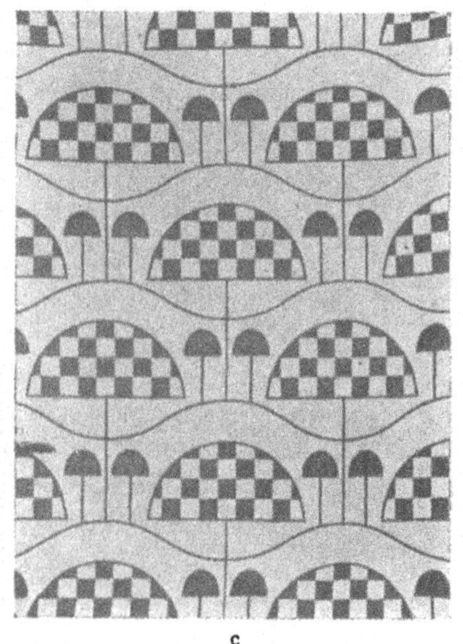

c

PROF. JOSEF HOFFMANN.

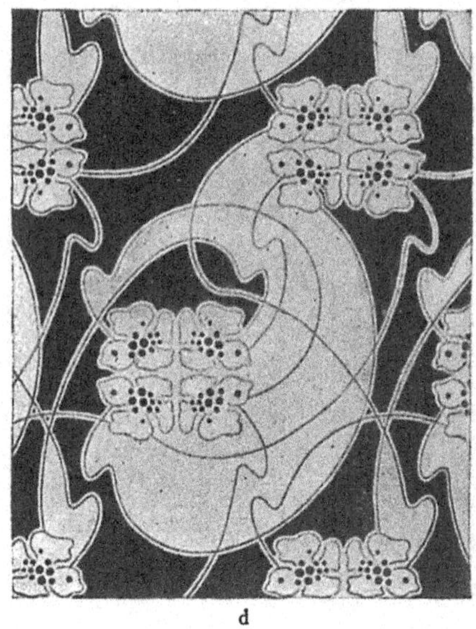

d

LOVATELLI-COLOMBO, PARIS.

269. TYPICAL FRENCH AND GERMAN PATTERN OF ABOUT 1900.

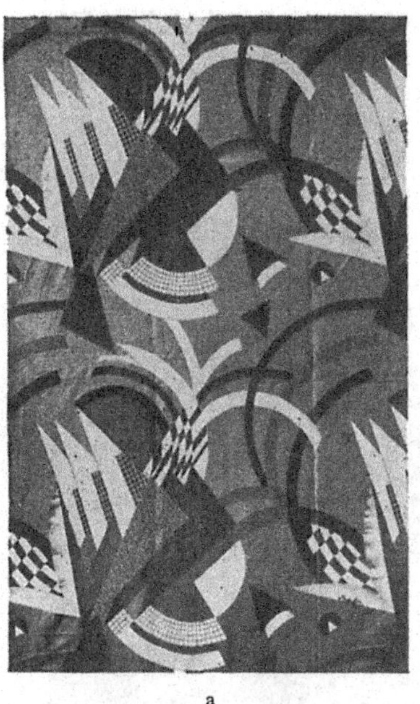

a

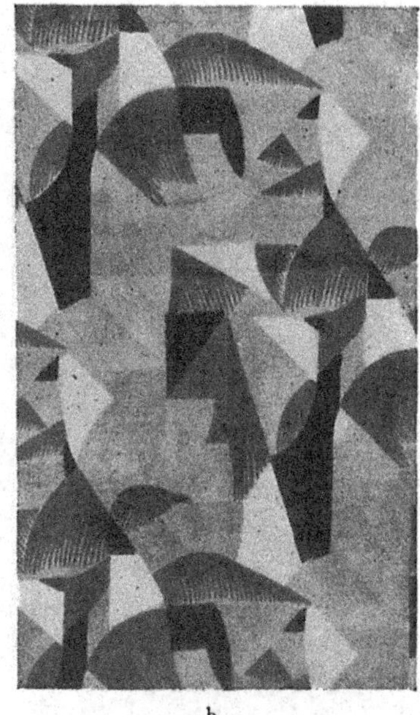

b

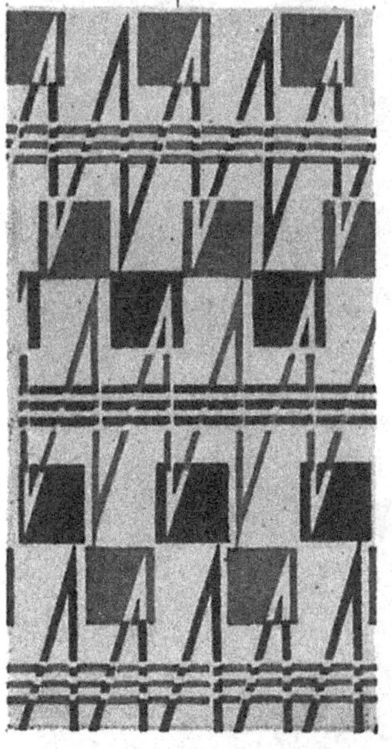

c

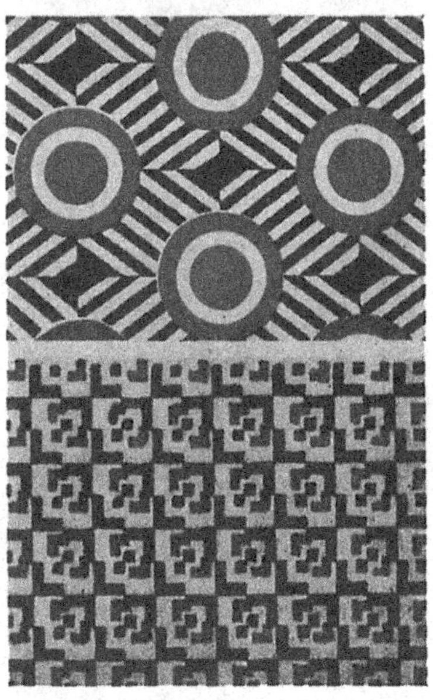

d

e

270. MODERNISTIC CONTINENTAL PATTERN.

a, MAURICE DUFRÈNE. b, BURKHALTER.

c AND e, STÉPANOVA. d, POPOVA.

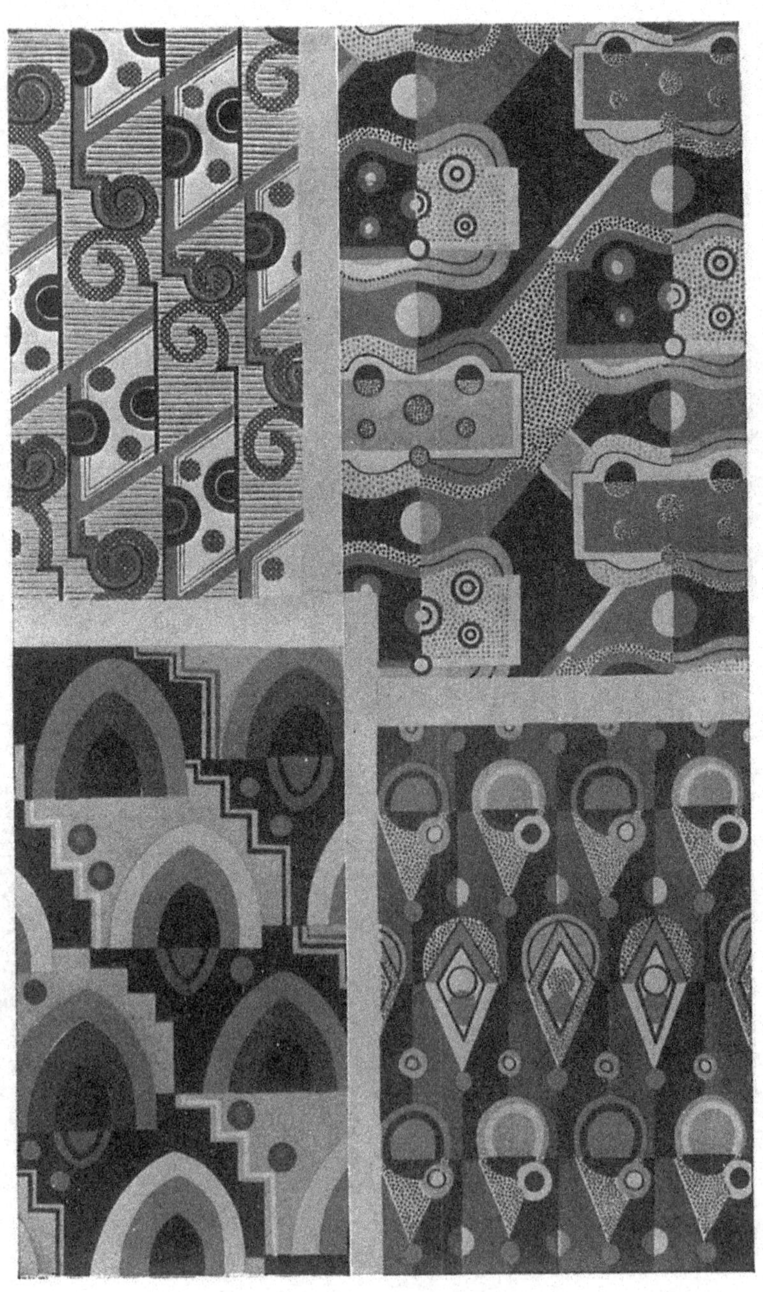

271. GEOMETRICAL PATTERN.

BY GEORGES VALMIER, PARIS.

Editor of the *Art Journal*. Day's interest in art was universal, and it was at his residence in Mecklenburgh Square, in 1884, that the formation of the Art Workers' Guild was discussed, and four years later the Arts and Crafts Society. An indefatigable worker, he yet found time to write a series of books on pattern and applied art that are possibly the best ever written, and are invaluable to students, for whom they were intended. The earliest of these was "Every Day Art," 1882, followed by "Nature in Ornament." Then came the trio of "The Anatomy of Pattern," "The Planning of Ornament," and "The Application of Ornament." The first two of these were enlarged and united in the present volume, "Pattern Design," first issued in 1903; the third was re-issued in a greatly extended form under the title of "Ornament and its Application" in 1904.

Two of Lewis F. Day's designs for wall-paper are shown in this volume. The "Roman" (267, a) and the "Como" (267, b) were both produced by Messrs Jeffrey & Co. in 1894.

Design is regarded by many as a specialised form of art —particularly applied art. This is a misconception. Design is necessarily incidental to any creative work, whether in painting, sculpture, or architecture. It would also appear to have an attraction for art workers who have not been specially trained as designers. Walter Crane, for instance, was a painter and illustrator; Pugin, Owen Jones, Talbert, and Godwin were originally trained as architects. So was Charles Francis Annesley Voysey, who, notwithstanding his reputation for domestic architecture, is probably better known as a designer. He embarked on this phase of work owing to the difficulty of obtaining such furniture and accessories as would satisfy him and would be in harmony with his buildings. Voysey's range in design embraces furniture, wall-papers, fabrics for hanging, carpets, fittings for lighting, and even table-ware and cutlery. In all his designs simplicity is the keynote, effect being obtained by choice of material, good form, proportion, and strict regard to craft conditions, without any adornment that is not incidental to direct construction. His pattern designs form admirable settings, though extremely conventional and restrained, and are conspicuous for his use of bird forms. Two typical wall-paper designs are shown (268, a and b).

Prominent members of the Arts and Crafts Society as designers of furniture were Voysey and E. W. Gimson. Undoubtedly this Society had a profound influence on furniture-design, and helped to develop the phase known as "New Art." The design of wall-papers, textiles, and decoration generally was also affected. Detail became more rigid in arrangement and flatter in rendering. Two examples typical of this style, about the beginning of the present century, are illustrated: a brocade by Messrs Liberty & Co. (268, c) and a wall-paper produced by Messrs Rottmann & Co. (268, d). Comparison between these English examples and contemporaneous French designs brought out by W. Lovatelli-Colombo, Paris (269, a, b, and d), will show the flamboyant tendency that culminated in the succeeding phase *l'art nouveau*.

A design by Josef Hoffmann, of Vienna (269, c), an extremely simple arrangement, anticipates the more recent exploitation of purely geometric forms.

The years 1914-1918 were naturally unfavourable to all forms of applied art, and it was not till after the latter year that activity in this direction was resumed. Even before the war there was some indication of change in taste, particularly on the Continent, where a revulsion from *l'art nouveau* had already set in. Satiety demands change to the opposite extreme, and the new tendency was towards severity, as opposed to flamboyant licence.

In some directions the futuristic movement in fine art became an influence, as is apparent in the designs shown by Maurice Dufrène (270, a) and Burkhalter (270, b). There is something distinctly courageous in the employment of

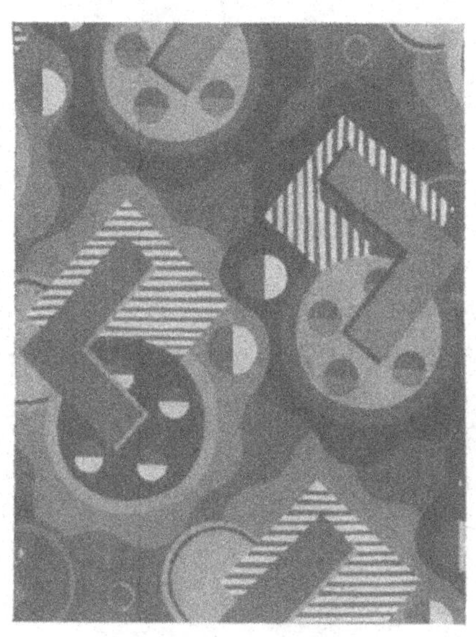

a

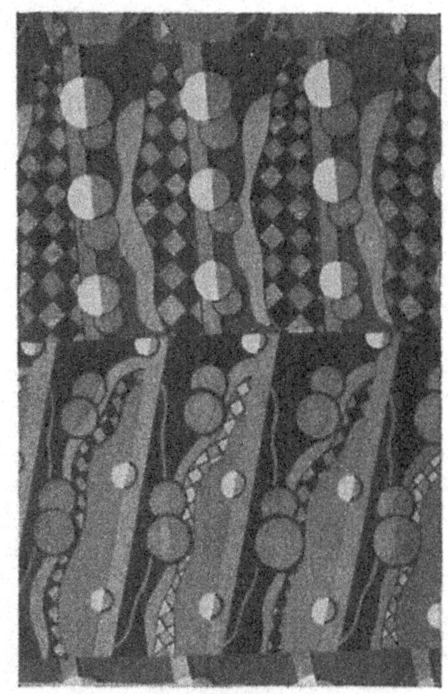

b

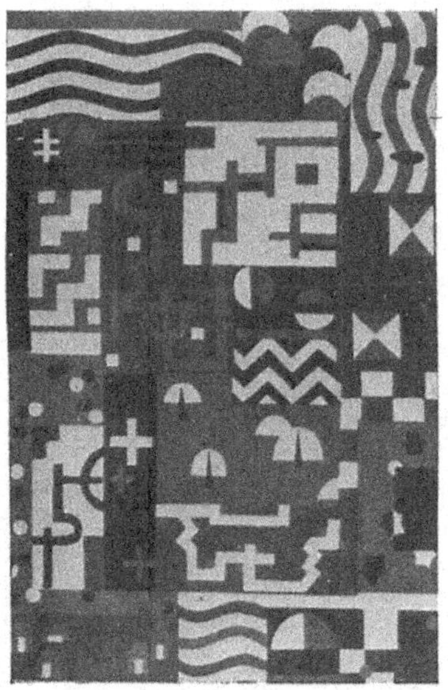

c

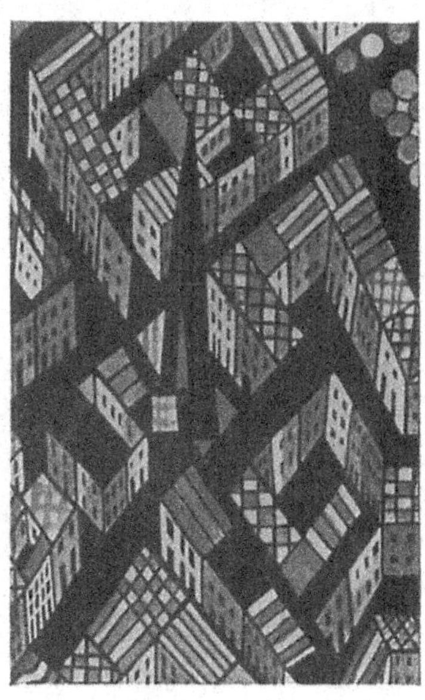

d

272. PRESENT-DAY CONTINENTAL PATTERN DESIGN.

a AND b, TEXTILE DESIGNS BY GEORGES VALMIER, PARIS.
c, TEXTILE DESIGNS BY HERMANN HUFFERT, VIENNA.
d, TEXTILE DESIGNS BY JOSEF HOFFMANN'S CLASS, SCHOOL OF APPLIED ART, VIENNA.

simple geometric motifs in the design by Stépanova (270, c); but the two other designs (270, d and e), one by Popova and the other by Stépanova, are simply suggestive of primitive weaving.

Change in taste is more marked since 1918, particularly in France, in the phase termed "Modernistic Art." This, however, is reminiscent—unavoidably so, perhaps. It is a truism that there is nothing new under the sun, and it is generally possible to detect some stylistic influence in what is claimed to be new. Newness may merely consist of the manner of rendering. Certainly in modernistic design the influence of the Louis Seize and Empire styles can be detected.

The designs of Georges Valmier which are shown on Plates 271-272 are interesting as departures from the exploitation of traditional conventional ornament. The details are frankly geometric, and the interest is mainly that of colour.

The tendency for some years for bright and even crude colour, not always harmoniously juxtaposed, is presumably due to post-war reaction.

Geometric elements are less noticeable in the textile design by Hermann Huffert, of Vienna (272, c). The colour scheme is restrained but extremely effective and well disposed, consisting merely of black, white, and red.

A variant of the "Landscape" pattern is shown in d on the same plate. This type has often been exploited but in many instances with doubtful success, generally erring by being too realistic; the inevitable repetition of a unit incidental to mechanical production involves extremely conventional treatment in order to ensure a satisfactory pattern.

The example illustrated is a product of Josef Hoffmann's class at the School of Applied Art, Vienna, and is an excellent treatment of a bird's-eye view of a city; there is no attempt at actual representation—the details are purely symbolic and well arranged as an all-over pattern.

The modern tendency may not meet with universal approval, but, when sincere, it must be regarded as healthy and stimulating, and its exponents should be credited with courage in attempting to depart from formalised and hitherto accepted conventions.

The development of art through the centuries has been a process of evolution. Through all the changing styles, out of the welter of influences and cross-influences, art is constantly reborn—the same impulse, yet ever new—the result of accumulated experience guiding, stimulating, and concentrating the effort of innumerable workers. Constantly changing, overcoming apparently irreconcilable differences, art is seen to be the work of many minds, pursuing steadily the same ideals.

INDEX

(*The numerals printed in heavy type indicate the figure references of the illustrations.*)